ADULTERY
At
MIDLIFE

FIRST AID FOR
BETRAYED WIVES

ADULTERY
At
MIDLIFE

FIRST AID FOR
BETRAYED WIVES

Pat Gaudette

Founder, The Midlife Club

HOME & LEISURE
PUBLISHING, INC

Home & Leisure Publishing, Inc.

Adultery At Midlife
First Aid For Betrayed Wives

Published by
Home & Leisure Publishing, Inc.
P O Box 968
Lecanto, Florida 34460
www.halpi.com

Copyright 2013 Pat Gaudette

ISBN 978-0-9847852-9-2 (paperback)
ISBN 978-0-9847852-5-4 (e-book)

Library of Congress Control Number: 2013901377

First Edition: February 2013

While the publisher and author have used their best efforts in preparing this book, they make no representations or warranties with respect to the accuracy or completeness of the contents of this book. The advice and strategies contained herein may not be suitable for your situation. This book is not intended as a substitute for advice from a qualified counselor or legal professional. The intent of this book is to provide accurate general information in regard to the subject matter covered. If legal advice or other expert help is needed, the services of an appropriate professional should be sought.

The conversations in this book are based on forum posts by current and prior members of the midlifeclub.com forum. The conversations have been edited to protect the confidentiality of members and their families. Any resemblance to actual persons, living or dead, or to events or locales is entirely coincidental.

Cover image © 2013 Jupiterimages Corporation

Printed in the United States of America

To the women of The Midlife Club who learned how to survive their husbands' betrayal and now pass that knowledge on and to those women who now desperately need it.

When a man of 40 falls in love with a girl of 20, it isn't her youth he is seeking but his own. -- Lenore Coffee

I couldn't stand that my husband was being unfaithful. I am Raquel Welch - understand? -- Raquel Welch

For every stunning, smart, well-coiffed hot woman of 40+, there is a balding, paunchy relic in yellow pants making a fool of himself with some 22-year-old waitress. -- Andy Rooney

If you marry a man who cheats on his wife, you'll be married to a man who cheats on his wife. -- Ann Landers

CNN found that Hillary Clinton is the most admired woman in America. Women admire her because she's strong and successful. Men admire her because she allows her husband to cheat and get away with it. -- Jay Leno

I have to accept that he cheated on me, that he broke my heart, that life goes on, and I have to keep living in it. -- Vanessa Mojica

Husbands are chiefly good lovers when they are betraying their wives. -- Marilyn Monroe

I love working out but I really have more enjoyment cheating on my husband with other married men. -- Amy Fessler

Contents

Introduction

There's very little that can decimate a marriage as much as a spouse who cheats. Even if the cheater wants to reconcile and repair the damage caused by adultery, the betrayed spouse may decide divorce is the better option. The loss of trust is often impossible to overcome.

Adultery can occur at any age and men are not any more prone to adultery than women although the reasons that people cheat seem to vary by gender. Because this book focuses on support for betrayed wives, future references will be on "his" cheating and "husbands" who cheat.

Men can cheat at any age and some do. Some otherwise faithful husbands will look outside their marriages at midlife prompting many betrayed wives to blame adultery on their husbands having "a midlife crisis." Indeed, for many wives, an adulterous husband is the crisis at midlife.

So, does a midlife crisis cause a man to cheat? Or does a middle-aged man cheat for other reasons? In my opinion, it's a combination of both.

When I first established The Midlife Club online forum in 1998, it was named "The Midlife Wives Club" because almost all members were women who were dealing with their husbands' erratic and hurtful actions at midlife. A rough estimate of eighty-five to ninety percent were dealing with adultery. It seemed that the wives could deal with almost any type of bad behavior except adultery.

Adultery adds a third person, the dreaded "other woman," into a marriage meant for two. Too often the other woman becomes the "next wife," forcing the long-term wife out of her safe home and environment and into struggles she never imagined she would ever have to face.

Instead of spending "the rest of her life" with the man she has spent the last twenty, thirty, or more years with, she now faces a future without him.

Have all women been cheated on? I haven't met one who hasn't although that doesn't mean there aren't women who have never known betrayal at some point in their lives. Again, I have never met one.

I am not a psychologist, psychiatrist, trained counselor, or other type of relationship professional. I have a strong personal interest in relationships, and have written books primarily about "relationships gone wrong." I have also established websites that provide support for the same.

This book is written to provide support to wives facing the betrayal of the man they expected to honor their marriage vows, the man they expected to grow old with, the man they trusted intimately and unconditionally. It shares the knowledge and experiences of women who have dealt with, or are still dealing with, adultery.

It was suggested some years ago that I write a book on how to survive adultery but there are many good books already available on the topic. However, as I read the conversations of women on The Midlife Club forum who were dealing with adultery, and the responses of women who have survived their husband's adultery and come out much stronger persons because of it, I decided that it was time for this particular book to be written.

I asked members of the forum if they would participate in this book by answering some questions that I posted as well as sharing their stories for the book. I promised anonymity which is why I have not included names or even forum IDs in this book.

I have edited posts for ease of reading, removed the abbreviations common to online forums, and edited details that might compromise a member's identity.

I have chosen not to edit the anger or rage that many women express in these conversations. Raw language is a part of the survival process. Rage is normal; anger is natural.

If you are uncertain whether your husband or significant other is cheating or you know for sure he is, this book will give you insight into how other women in your situation have dealt with him, her, the kids, friends, and family.

You'll find legal tips should you decide on divorce or if he wants a divorce. You'll see how some couples have fared with marriage counseling and reconciliation.

This is not a book of absolutes, it is a book of what worked and what didn't work for these women. They are not trained professionals. They are not legal experts. They are women who have struggled, and are struggling, with issues they had no prior training for.

The first section of this book is one woman's early steps through the adultery minefield. I include this since her story is not unlike countless others and her attempts to put a name to why her husband is cheating, as well as blaming herself, are common threads throughout forum posts. Both adultery survivors and new members offer support and advice in the lengthy conversation.

The rest of this book is a compilation of questions I posed as well as questions from women relating to situations they are dealing with. Many of the stories are eerily similar which can be somewhat comforting to women seeking the understanding of "someone who knows how I feel."

There is no right or wrong way to read through this book. Find the particular discussion(s) that are of most interest to you and read them first. Some discussions are lengthy while others are brief. Some will hit "hot buttons," while others will not.

You are cautioned to "take what you need and discard the rest." What works for one woman does not automatically work for another. But, what works for one might inspire you to modify her actions to use in your own situation.

I am grateful to the women who have shared their stories to make this book possible.

I am truly sorry that you have need of this book and I wish you good luck during this painful journey.

~ Pat Gaudette

A warning for men

The affair is over, for whatever reason, and you want your life back to "normal." Juggling two lives, one with your lover and one with your wife, has been extremely stressful and even more so as the affair with your lover has been coming to an end.

You're tired of arguments. You're tired of shouting. You're tired of walking on eggshells. You're tired of trying to make everyone happy. You're tired of the crying and the tears. You're just plain tired!

Maybe you've been searching for a quick fix so your life can get back to the way it was before you screwed up. Maybe you picked up this book thinking it could give you some tips for fast marriage repair.

Sorry to disappoint, but your wife is probably not about to "forgive and forget" so easily. An affair isn't a slap on the wrist and a "better not do that again" offense like running a red light or accidentally backing over the neighbor's dog. Those are mistakes that people make.

Your affair was an on-going, coldly calculating, series of events that you set in motion and kept going. You cheated, you lied, and you knew what you were doing was wrong. But it didn't matter because the pleasure *you* were getting from the affair was worth every penny of the cost.

It's time to pay the price for the damage your affair caused and will continue to cause. Unfortunately for you, and more particularly for your wife, there is no quick recovery from betrayal. The steps to recovery are slow, plodding, difficult steps.

Before you can think about asking for a second (or third or fourth) chance, you need to know the depth of the pain she has felt as a result of your betrayal. You also need to understand why she may not want to give you another chance.

What follows are the conversations of women who have been betrayed. They aren't sugar-coated or edited to spare your feelings or to give you false hope that repairing your marriage will be easy to do.

You need to know the scope of the anger she may be dealing with that you'll have to overcome.

If you can't handle the heat of her anger, or don't want to put in the necessary work, you may want to just walk away now.

Have you completely cut contact with your affair partner? Do you still have feelings for her? Is she trying to reestablish a relationship with you? Are you trying to remain friends with her? Do the two of you have a child or children as a result of your affair? Do you want everyone to "just get along"?

Continuing any type of contact with the other woman will only deepen the loathing your wife probably has for the woman. Understand that any loving emotion or kind feelings you direct toward this woman will be emotions and feelings that belong to your wife.

How much does she dislike the "other woman"? What does she think of you? Could she ever forgive and forget?

Give a listen…

What did I do to deserve this?

My thoughts WILL NOT STOP! I am thinking consistently, they change consistently. This is all I think about day and night. I feel I am choking with what I think is anxiety. The lump in my throat, and the burning feeling in my stomach, IT ALL HURTS SO MUCH.

I don't know what to do, we all have similar stories, but different situations in our own homes, and trying to piece together all that I have read here, books, internet stuff I have read and downloaded — to try to make the right decision for me is just very, very hard. One minute I am strong and decisive, and in that SAME minute I am not. I am at a loss and would appreciate anything you may advice or just plain point out to me. Frankly I can't seem to be able to make a decision long enough to follow through with it.

Please bear with me I will be long; I have kept it all inside for so long I feel my heart will burst at any moment. I just want and need to talk to someone. It is comforting to know you understand what I am going through. Please help me sort out my insane story.

I had been married for 29 years when I got "the speech." Since then I have not been able to eat or sleep, or think of anything else. I have lost a lot of weight — which is the only positive thing to happen, I feel so devastated and hopeless.

In early days I decided to confront him and finally get some answers about what was going on with him. I asked him yet again if there was someone else and he once again said there was not. He said I was only "competing with his mind" he was quiet for a while, then tells me "I think I have fallen out of love with you" followed by more words but I cannot remember what they were. I go numb, a rush of something goes through my body, I hug him and I began to cry for what seemed forever. He tells me he is sorry. I want to die.

The next day I cannot think straight and decide to call a counseling place through my job. I only know I want him to love me again and I will do whatever it takes. Since there is no one else there is still hope. The counselor tries to tell me that there is a big possibility there is someone else, but I tell her he said there was not and I believe him (did I mention what an IDIOT I AM?).

I made another appointment with the counselor in hopes that my husband would go with me even after he had told me "he did not counsel," but to my surprise he agrees to go with me which makes me very happy. Whatever is going on we will get help.

Then we are at the counselor's office and after a little background she asks him if there is another woman. His answer: YES. Is it sexual? YES. The numbness and rush of something through my body returns. I am speechless. I had asked him so many times before and he had denied it, and now this. I turn to him stunned and lost at his answer, and without emotion he looks at me and says "you knew that." I DID NOT KNOW THAT!! BUT I KNEW NOW.

I had apparently dropped the paper with the phone number and e-mail address I had found previously — my husband found it and assumed I knew about her, and he just let it out. If not for this I don't know how much longer he would have continued to lie.

He proceeds to say this has NOTHING TO DO WITH SEX — this IS AN EMOTIONAL CONNECTION — She is his best friend and he can talk to her about anything, something he can't do with me. She makes him feel Special. She makes him feel like a King.

For the next two weeks or so I plead, beg, cry and ask over and over WHY? How could you do this to me? Telling him over and over "I love you," "I will change." He says he is "unhappy," he has been like this for a long time.

He tells me I will never change because we cannot change our personality which is my problem. I am an angry person who has never been happy and he has given me a million chances. It is too late; he no longer cares, he has found someone else and he is "finally happy." I have squandered my happiness away with him. This is all my fault. Now I must find my own happiness.

I have never denied that there were times when I did push him away because I did not want to have sex, but there were also many times when I looked forward to it. Of course our perceptions are different. He tells me he no longer needs the sex part; guess the fact that he gets it from the other woman is a bonus. Confusing that if he doesn't need it why get it? Guess he is still a man and this makes him feel even more wanted.

He says he repeatedly throughout the years told me that I was taking him for granted, I was pushing him away, I was rejecting him, I assumed he would always be there, and that I did not appreciate him. Unfortunately for me he did say these things in his times of anger, but I always thought it was just a couple disagreement thing. He NEVER sat down with me and told me how "unhappy" he was or these things or if I did not change that he would have to look elsewhere. IF ONLY I HAD LISTENED!!

I believe I AM to blame for having lost him. I still don't understand how I took him for granted or why it was wrong to assume he would always be there, but I am to blame. I may not have made him have an affair, but I did push him to it. How can I keep holding on to something I on my own destroyed? He is (or was) the loving, caring, thoughtful man every woman wishes to have, and I had him. Now because of my own selfishness someone else will. What a difficult pill to swallow.

Nothing is the same now, I don't know what to do, how to act, and things are so awkward at home. My husband is a very quiet, not very social, very intelligent man. Communication was nonexistent in our marriage because the man will not talk to me.

In any disagreement he will always walk away from me. It is very frustrating. I have always tried to get him to talk to me about his problems or anything, but he always turns away because he says it was the best thing to do with me.

My husband HATES, HATES, HATES CONFLICT, so him not talking to me or telling me about the other woman was because he "knew this would hurt me" and he did not want "conflict." So this is the better solution? He doesn't even care that I hurt now — in fact he contributes more and more to it.

This is really where my big confusion in this mess comes in: We continue to live together, he only offered to leave the day I found out about the other woman but my adult kids knew nothing about this, and in my shock of it all I told him not to leave. He has not said another word about it again. We sleep in the same bed but we have not been intimate — he is "faithful" to her as he wears his clothes to bed and stays on his side for the most part, although at times he comes over a bit and we touch (something I think he knows somehow).

I honestly don't know why he is still at home. My theory is that he is just buying time till summer when he is off. He has been saving up vacation time so we can take an extended European vacation. He stopped talking about vacation plans months ago but is the trip still on with the other woman instead of me?

He works seven days a week so we don't see each other much as it is. How can he live with himself by putting me through this on a daily basis? There is probably also that she has other obligations right now and he cannot be there even if he wanted to. I have had contact with the other woman. Not lately but I have had and know a little about her.

What happened to the lovely man who claimed to love me for so long? The letters, cards and flowers I have that told me so. He won't read any of it now.

He has stayed out all night only two times, but he always comes home very late. He is basically using his home like a hotel. He showers, sleeps and has dinner here two to four times a week. We don't speak except small talk about something on TV, or maybe about the kids, otherwise non-important things. NEVER about us or what he plans on doing about this situation. I sometimes feel they are just laughing at me for putting up with this.

He does bizarre things like greet me with a "Hi sweetie" and bringing me a soft drink. It's just weird when he doesn't even want to look at me or talk to me that he does this. He has just come in from being with the other woman and acts like it is a normal thing. I am grasping at straws and I know it. This is disgusting, what the hell is wrong with me.

My question to all of you, if you are still with me is: Do I keep holding on to this so called marriage which I know is nothing. We are living as roommates and nothing more.

He has shown no indication of reconciliation and in fact he has taken off his wedding ring which I questioned and got "I am just not comfortable wearing it." The blows just go on and on.

After almost four months of constant pain I thought all week to tell him to leave, even though I don't want to. The wedding ring has really hurt and is there really anything more to hold on to?

Books, e-books and other information on midlife crisis all say it is easier to work on the marriage if they are around. They are going through a difficult time and holding out for the affair to fade may just happen. Everything I read and from here as well says I have to detach and think of me which my mind agrees, but my heart refuses to accept.

I just want to know that I am doing the right thing. I still love him. I am so very afraid of the future without him; I don't want to believe that it can happen even if all indications show he is already emotionally gone. I still 'see' him and I guess that still means a lot to me.

For over half my life I have known nothing more than my life with this man, and all of a sudden I am to detach and accept. I can't. I am trying but I just can't. I know you all cannot help me with this, but I would still appreciate anything you can tell me about the decision to ask him to leave, or let him stay until HE decides to leave.

I think maybe in this I can show a little self-respect and some pride (something I sorely lack), but then again will I have compromised or thrown away any — and I mean any — hope of him staying with me. I never knew any person could feel this much pain.

◆◆◆◆

I firmly believe you can't "work on a marriage" by yourself. If he's immersed in an affair, has an "emotional connection" he's expressing physically with her, and openly admitting to you in front of the marriage counselor, and has taken off his wedding ring, then he is NOT interested in "working on the marriage" at this point.

So, your choices at this point are to end your marriage yourself (you cannot FORCE him to leave), or put the concept of "marriage" in cold storage for now, continue to live as roommates, and hope that in time and with no further damage being done, your marriage might be something he wants to restore with you.

And those remain your choices every second of every day — unless HE chooses to end the marriage.

Nobody has a perfect marriage or is a perfect spouse. That's why the vows say "for better or WORSE," to give us the opportunity to mess up and then make amends. Beating yourself up doesn't do any good and blaming yourself for HIS choice to cheat is unfair. He could have opted to end the marriage before he went outside of it.

It's not a matter of what we "deserve." Life gives people all sorts of things, good and bad, that they didn't deserve or earn. So, try to put that concept out of your mind, too. We just need to always do our best, and learn to cope with what happens.

♦♦♦♦

So, so sorry for your pain. I never thought that heartbreak was physical.

Who is this other woman? Is she single? Does she live by herself?

Now is the time for thinking about YOU. Not you as an extension of him, but the real YOU. Underneath your shock, and discounting your fear of "what would happen if" — what would you like to do? And that doesn't mean "for him to come to his senses" because that is wishing.

I mean your two courses: to kick his ungrateful sorry ass out or to carry on as you are — what would you deep down like to do?

Are you working? What are the finances like at the moment?

Your husband hating conflict fits my husband to a "t." It's very typical for men in midlife crisis whose coping skills just aren't up to the job of midlife change. That is the crisis. An affair is a VERY aggressive "I am so pissed off with you" act.

ALL you can do is work on yourself, those deficits which contributed to this. Your husband is showing connection, even while he is completely disconnected. You are on the roller coaster from hell.

♦♦♦♦

You really can't do much about your marriage right now. He has already left it sexually and emotionally. I remember those days of when it was all I could think about. It leads to the midlife crisis diet and new sleep habits. I'm so sorry, but you are NOT alone.

◆◆◆◆

You are NOT responsible for your husband's moral choices. Adultery is WRONG. Period. It's wrong. I don't care if you NEVER had sex with him. It doesn't make adultery RIGHT! He had a moral obligation to communicate his concerns CLEARLY with you and to be lovingly open to working on the problems WITH you. He chose NOT to do that. He tore up his "good guy" card when he decided that having an extramarital affair was an ENTITLEMENT.

Please stop blaming yourself. He'll try to convince you that you're to blame. Don't buy it!

◆◆◆◆

You don't want him to leave; then you don't have to. But you can request he sleeps in another room. Sleeping in the same bed with his clothes on, why does he even bother?

At the moment he has all the benefits re using your home as a hotel because you let him do that. How long you do this is up to you.

I don't think you can work on your marriage while there is a third person in it.

Personally I couldn't do what you are doing. It would hurt so much to have the man I loved coming and going to the other woman whenever he pleased while you are still doing everything else for him, cooking, cleaning, etc.

You are NOT to blame for him choosing to have an affair that was his choice. You are NOT to blame because he didn't talk to you about how he was feeling. This is NOT your fault at all. You will know when you have had enough.

◆◆◆◆

I cannot force him out, but I do know that if I ask he will do so. This would be as far as I go with the relationship. I agree with you — I cannot work on this alone. If he wishes to end it completely it will be on him.

Right now I feel that he has lost all respect for me, his children, and his home and of course his marriage. And at this very *moment* as much as it is hurting I think I do need to ask him to leave. Maybe this is the moment when I know I have had enough.

Confusion, confusion. My mind changes consistently, it is absolutely insane.

The other woman is a co-worker who is either separated or divorced, I don't know. She has a child but I don't know if she has her full time, plus she supposedly takes care of her mother.

When I first found her number I texted her asking her to back off. She called one weekend and this is when she told me (about her mom). I know the rest is true.

We have also e-mailed, although I have not heard from her in a long time, but then why should she? She has the upper hand right now and she knows it.

This leads me to think that perhaps her obligations at home keep her from moving my husband in. To me they are buying time until this can happen, or maybe in the summer if he takes time off as had been planned, and then he will be gone. I have resisted contacting her again actually, I wonder if she would answer me now.

I am working but don't make much. As far as the finances go it is a totally different subject. I have been completely dependent on my husband. He takes care of everything financially. He pays the mortgage, bills, insurance, college, EV-ERYTHING. I only take care of groceries and other small expenses.

I am truly afraid of what I am going to find out. Other than knowing we owe a lot of money for college, the house, I don't know how much else is out there.

Thanks to my finding this site, and reading things here, I realized I had to know about my finances before things went any farther. I have no access to passwords so this is difficult, but I have access to files and I have been working on those. I'm not sure just how much to do.

I talked to a lawyer, and it sounds like until he actually files for divorce there is not much to do, or at least I don't know how to go about it. I am preparing myself as much as I know how.

I never thought I would have to guard myself against the man I love so much. He has become so secretive, so deceptive, so cruel and uncaring. He is another man completely.

I know I could ask him to sleep somewhere else, but there is no other room and I know he will not go to the couch. Besides I don't want my kids to see that, they are adults and they know most of what is going on but I just don't want that right now. I rather he leaves all together. So once again it's just something else I will deal with.

Another sad thing is that up until last week I was washing and ironing his clothes. He did indeed have the best of both worlds. Until I realized that roommates do not do laundry for one another, and what's funny is that as I write this he is loading the washer. I am learning — slowly, but I am learning.

♦♦♦♦

Have him leave. You are in no condition right now to deal with his comings and goings and oh, the resentment of doing his laundry, etc.

Yes, he is paying the bills and such — it's his job. You're doing your job. You can't continue to do your job until he's out because he's changed the dynamics here. The awkwardness on top of this fresh hell of pain will be too much, especially if you're constantly reminded in "little ways" that he's not interested in the marriage.

I know you feel alone. I know you feel hurt and that there's no other man for you, but because you are in the first stage — shock and disbelief — you'll do anything to ease the pain, including blaming yourself for why the marriage fell apart.

Wait until you get into the "anger stage" — stage two. Your tune will change dramatically and that's when it will dawn on you that only he can make himself happy, all the other bullshit he's saying you did is, well, bullshit.

Only you can make yourself happy. Reminiscing about the past and how good it was between you is normal but torturous, because the answer isn't there either. It's just making things now seem worse because you're trying to find a justification and there isn't one.

Sometimes, some people's lives come with major changes. You happen to be going through one right now. It's like a 20-year-old tree having all its branches chopped off all at once. Those branches are going to have to grow back slowly. But they'll be stronger branches.

This will be a hell of a growth process for you but YOU WILL GET THROUGH IT. But you don't have to endure the awkwardness HE is creating waltzing in and out of the house.

Tell him not to come back unless he wants to repair the marriage or to get the rest of his things. You can't waiver in between this one because you'll get the brunt of the pain.

You need to sort things out in your heart and your head. You need to continue counseling until you've said everything over and over until you're sick of saying it.

Your self-esteem is so low — you're blaming the breakup of a 29 year marriage on yourself. That's a very human way of trying to obtain some sort of control over this when in reality, you have no control except over yourself.

The odds of a relationship based on an affair (lying, selfishness) has a five percent chance of surviving. Trust me. If he moves out it's his problem (and always was) to end up with her because the fantasy will diminish. He shows up at her place, everything's bliss, he goes home.

She doesn't have to do his laundry or cook. If she's after his money in any way (and boy are there some other women out there that are) and you get a divorce with a good lawyer on your side, her little idea of their "happy faux family" will take a nose dive. He won't be so "wonderful" to her anymore either. If that happens, by that time, you'll have grown and will be ready to move on.

But I'm jumping ahead of myself, because I can see the big picture. So can so many of us who have gone through this and have felt, said the same words and have cried so much so long. Been there, done that.

Take it one day at a time. That's how we get through it.

◆◆◆

You all really do know what those of us coming in are going through. It is extremely difficult to see hope and some sort of happiness for the future. It all seems so far away and hopeless.

Just seeing the five percent chance of surviving this puts some things in perspective. I need to accept this and I need to do so now (easy to write; doing it not so much).

However, my decision to ask him to leave is still strong. If I can hold on to this strength, and my mind and heart hold up I will talk with him tomorrow. I have been practicing trying to get the right words and hope that I can pull it off. I need to keep composure and hold my words at a neutral tone, so I have some work to do. I don't want to break down.

I am still thinking that when I ask him to leave that he will not fight it, but I don't know who my husband is anymore, so his reaction may not be what I am expecting at all. I need to be prepared.

Will see where I am tomorrow evening. Pray for me that I can go through with this and the outcome goes my way.

◆◆◆

The other woman is a SYMBOL — of pure, true exciting passion, of freedom, of being young, of no responsibilities. So let him live his fantasy. Throw him into "her open, understanding arms and open, loving legs." Remove his hateful, stifling, mean, etc. self, if that is what he represents right now.

This all hurts so much. Focus on you, work on the faults you know you have, use your courage and your faith to take on this new challenge of being betrayed, abandoned, and GROW into a better, stronger more competent and independent person.

Do you know what? My husband ADMIRED me for doing that, and it gave him the impetus to stop blaming me and look at himself. Have faith in God, and in the inner strength He has given you, which you have temporarily lost being a wife and a dependent.

♦♦♦♦

I do have one caveat regarding asking your husband to leave. Sometimes when you do that, they are then in the position of saying forevermore, "you threw me out" thus becoming the "victim" in all of this. I know it sounds crazy, but there you have it. Then you get to deal with your children having their father say that to them, as in "poor me" look what your mother did.

Don't do anything precipitously. Think about what you will say to your children. Do you think it is in your best interests to tell them their father has admitted to having an affair, and you cannot live in the same house knowing that? Or, ask their father to move out and not tell them why? It can get complicated.

Once that ball starts rolling, you may lose the opportunity to find more information regarding finances. I am not trying to confuse you more, just suggesting giving it all some thought, and some planning.

Think it all through carefully; which is a hard task when your brain is so frazzled. As for the finances, get busy on the fact finding. Think of it as your part-time job. Try and separate it from your emotions. You don't have to tell your husband what you are doing; you are now putting yourself on the front burner, because you have to. Information is power.

And, finally, unbelievable as it may seem, your husband has been way down the track ahead of you and you are playing catch-up. Not fair, but that's the truth.

Don't be afraid. We have all been where you are. You will survive, one day at a time. And, you will surprise yourself in the process. My mantra, which I posted on my refrigerator the day after my ex moved out after a 35 year marriage: Dignity and a Sense of Humor at All Times.

♦♦♦♦

I kept my wayward spouse in the house for six weeks after he asked for a divorce and began to openly date the other woman. I begged and pleaded and even tried to guilt him into working on our marriage for the sake of the kids. I thought that if he was still there he would change his mind and that we had a chance.

I finally realized that I had to respect myself enough to ask him to leave. He obviously didn't respect me and I wanted my kids to know their mom as someone worthy of respect and to do that I had to respect me first.

I told him that if he couldn't respect me enough not to date while under the same roof as me he had to leave. If he was willing to pause his relationship with the other woman for long enough to sort things out he could stay in the same house as the kids and see them all the time, if not...

He left the next day. Painful, yes, but I felt good about myself for standing up for myself. It was a start, it's still a long hard road, but I respect me and am trying like hell to hold onto that.

He and the other woman will do what they do; having him stay would not have changed that.

♦♦♦♦

Follow your heart, your gut and your soul. You will do what is right for you when it is right for you to do so.

♦♦♦♦

We are all in this together and you have gotten some good advice. Remember... it is not your fault. Your story sounds very similar to mine, married for 27 years and together for five years before marriage.

My husband avoids conflict and never really says what is wrong until he has packed all his stuff in his car and speeds away. We are not mind readers. Ask yourself, what did your husband ever do to repair the marriage? Nothing. You have nothing to feel guilty about.

Concerning finances, my suggestion is to photocopy every single piece of paper (bank statements, insurance, 401Ks, or anything else with numbers on it) and file it away. Don't let him know that you are doing this. While he is still at home, at least you can accomplish this. Also, open your own checking account at a different bank and start socking away some money, however little.

Here is the most important: FOLLOW YOUR HEART AND ACT ACCORDINGLY. You will receive so much advice from well-meaning people here and in your life and everyone has their own two cents. You need to filter it out through YOUR OWN EYES. You have been living with him. You know him like no other does. So trust yourself. Be strong.

◆◆◆◆

When my husband was threatening to move out, I invited our adult kids over to talk about it and to tell them together. It infuriated him but for me it was the right thing to do. He waited about a week or so before actually moving out, still claiming no other woman.

In your case since he admits to the other woman so you can ask him to explain that he needs to go to her. At this point I also invited the kids to see a counselor with me.

I never asked him to move out; he did it when I was out of town, the day after he said he was staying. I waited for him to file for divorce.

My message is: for my adult kids it was better to have them see part of what was happening and for them to see that I was trying to make a go of it. It was my oldest kid that finally said "Mom, this is abusive to you!"

You need to go no contact with him. It made a huge difference to them that I was willing to work on the marriage but he filed.

Each story is different in some ways. Today I reflect on the amazing change in him... I see him and think about him as an insect on a stick; interesting (behavior) and as a business deal (financially). I really wish you some peace, but peace comes at a cost.

♦♦♦♦

Well here I sit at 9 p.m. and he is not home. Strange because he always came in around 8 before, so with this it will not be done today.

Maybe he decides to stay out all night, and that will be the fuel I need to keep my anger going.

I have already made copies of every single paper that was important in those files. He does not have a clue. I think I have discovered a lot of things that he does not realize I know. I may not be that smart, but I am certainly learning.

Need to go to bed, have to be at work early and I need to try and sleep. Even the darn sleeping pills are not working.

At least I think I was planning on doing it. I can be proud of me even though I did not get the chance to test myself.

♦♦♦♦

Good job on copying things, remember to do credit card statements, bank statements, etc. as well, also all household accounts, so if things don't work out and you are looking for support then you have copies of gas, heating, power, phone, food, etc. at your fingertips.

One thing my lawyer did tell me when I had to do that was to take the higher amount bills (winter) so I wouldn't be caught short.

If your kids are all adults they will understand when told. Hard having only one bedroom in the house, but I do wonder why he will sleep there fully clothed, that is so pathetic of him.

As for the rest, one day at a time.

◆◆◆

Well the jerk did not come home last night. I am more resolved now to follow through with my decision.

I have always had low self-esteem (I cannot afford therapy or I would be there), but I have always known that about myself.

I have always allowed people to walk all over me. I have always felt fear of "life," people not liking me, worrying about what they think of me etc.

There have been many times in my life and certainly within my marriage where I have regretted not having defended myself, not sticking up for what I believed, not said something so he would not be upset.

I was always afraid I was not worthy of such a wonderful man, afraid he would leave me. I felt so blessed that he loved me, and now it appears I was at least halfway right. I will not let this be another regret in my life! I feel so disrespected, angry, hurt, and any other emotion out there. It's hard to say where I'm at; I am so confused all the time.

His sleeping with his clothes on should have been an indication to me about where he was starting to be in our relationship. Not to mention the cherry on the top with the ring.

Thanks to everyone again for the advice I have learned so much in such a short time, and hope to continue learning. I know I am in for a painful ride.

I am petrified of the unknown future without him in my life. I just never thought I would have to do so; he is definitely the crutch I have leaned on for so long, perhaps this will help me grow up.

♦♦♦♦

Well I thought I would have to wait another day to talk to my husband about leaving since he did not come home. Then the next night he got home really late, in fact I was getting ready for bed thinking he once again would not be home which was making me really angry.

He comes in, and as if nothing has happened gives me my usual "hi sweetie" greeting. Are you kidding? I told him we had to talk — which usually means I will talk and he will respond at times (it's like pulling teeth to talk to him). He says... ok what do you want to talk about?

Unbelievable! You just got home after almost two days of being gone and you don't know what I want to talk about? I guess he thought I had put up with it two times before so it should be nothing new to me. This is how it went:

Me: I can't do this with you anymore; you are showing no respect for me, the kids, and your home. I will not be treated like this any longer.

Him: What do you want to do? Do you want me to leave?

He has always tried to put things on me. Like asking me what I want to do. And I just want to scream "I want to make you love me again!" "I want to hold you!" "I want you to give us another chance!" What do you mean what do I want to do?!

Giving me another chance was never something he was willing to offer. It was too little too late — he had already given me thousands of chances (I didn't even know I was working on my first chance let alone all those thousands of chances).

Well this should have been my out, but when he said that… he looked at me as though he was daring me to tell him to leave. I told him that was HIS choice and proceeded with my speech which I had practiced over and over.

Me: You said we always have choices, and it would appear you have made yours but nonetheless I will give you mine which are:

A. Stay and work on resolving this relationship which I told you then and I am telling you now. I am willing to take the time and effort it takes to make any improvements, there is always room for improvement. Obviously our marriage is not perfect, we have made mistakes, but we learn from them and we try not to make them again. I prefer you were there to work this with me, but I will work on it without you.

B. You, go be where you "think" your happiness is. All this is about you and YOUR "happiness." Whatever direction you wish to take is YOUR DECISION. I am just asking that you make this decision quickly. The sooner the better.

I was supposed to add a time limit but frankly I got scared (I don't know what of, but I did) so I did not give him a date which was a mistake I think. He continued staring at the computer and said nothing... just typical of him.

I needed to emphasize to him this was all about him and make him think about his actions, and after the way he asked me if I wanted him to leave all I could think of at that moment was No! You are NOT going to put this on me. If you want to leave then it will be because YOU chose to do so. He will not have the "well she told me to get out" excuse.

I walked into the bathroom (we were in the bedroom), and when I came out he had gone to the living room. I thought he might leave, but he did not. In fact I woke up at 2 a.m. and there he was in our bed... REALLY?

After what I just told you, you turn around and get back in bed with me. I admit he is still in jammies and shirt as he has been, but why come back into a bed you no longer wish to share with me. This makes no sense to me at all.

I now wait to see what happens.

♦♦♦♦

This is a time when you have to be crystal clear in what you said. I'm not shocked he climbed back into bed. You never mentioned the word "bed" at all. One of the things my counselor told me was that if I wanted him to know something, I had to say exactly what it was. I could not trust that he could read ANYTHING between the lines. Looking back on things, it is so true.

If you don't want him in your bed, you have to tell him exactly that.

♦♦♦♦

This man needs for you to make the decision and you desperately want him to make a decision. I've been there and done that. It sucks because you are too damn scared to make a decision. I understand this, I really, really do. Mine put it back on me too and really if they do not say anything, then nothing happens.

You will follow these dance steps until one of you gets too uncomfortable. Took a long time to understand that one, but wow is it true.

Just remember in all of the madness, try, and try really hard to stay true to you and your values. For a while there I did not. Two years later it is really hard to say which was the worst, him doing what he did or me tacitly going along with it to try to save my marriage.

My only advice to you is to try very hard to start living your life as if he is not a part of it. Superficial talk only and that is only if you want to. At this point, there are no answers and I am willing to bet that it is going to be a very, very long time before there are.

Last thing, remember do not ask any questions if you cannot handle the answers.

Start looking after only you and make choices and decisions based only on you.

◆◆◆◆

I think at the beginning I did not think about the bed thing until I saw him there. Sad thing is I like him being there. Sick I know.

In fact last night I had gone to the gym and got home later than usual, I was very surprised to see he was home. It was much earlier than he has been coming in, and after the conversation I figured he would definitely stay out later. It did please me that he saw I wasn't here for once just waiting for him. Not that he even cares!

Deep down though I was so glad to see his car... just knowing he was here instead of "there," which is also stupid because we spent the rest of the evening in separate rooms.

I hardly see him at all even under the same roof, so why do I insist on holding on to this misery?

I know I am causing my own pain, but I just don't know how to stop it.

Today was a very difficult day at work; a co-worker even asked me if there was something wrong because I have not been looking good.

I am so alone and I have been crying so much lately my eyes hurt, but my co-workers cannot know anything yet. I am not ready. I'm not ready to admit to myself let alone anyone else.

My son caught me crying this morning, he is very angry at his father, and he has been so supportive of me really stepping up (he lives at home) doing the yard and other things without being asked. I told him it's ok if he is angry, but he must remember that he was still a very good father to him all these years.

Not sure about my daughters as they seem to be angrier at Ashton cheating on Demi than their father on me. Little confused about that, maybe I'm just really selfish and wish they were at least a little angry at him, or maybe they are I just have not seen it.

I can't get my act together these days. I am feeling the same hurt as day one. After asking him to make decision to leave and have not gotten answer, I am so confused about what my next step should be. Confusion and hurt are ruling right now.

◆◆◆◆

I can so relate to your situation as I was married for 23 years and also have three kids. I went through my ex-husband's affairs twice, both long affairs with co-workers.

I put up with the first one for about eight months until he finally filed for divorce then changed his mind and we reconciled for six more years.

Then when I found out about his second affair (he was bragging about it and refused to move out) I had to file for divorce before he did.

I wanted to use the joint credit card so I filed first because when he filed for divorce six years earlier the legal paperwork forbid me to use any joint credit cards or money which I would have needed to hire my own attorney.

My woman attorney filed a "vacate the marital home order forthwith" to make him move out since he was completely disrespecting me and using our home as a convenient hotel.

He was so angry and swore he had nowhere to go and that I threw him out! But I then found out that he and his married other woman had rented a condo together near our house months prior to my finding out.

◆◆◆◆

It is much easier to be angry at someone you don't know than to be angry at someone who supplied half your DNA. Don't take this personally. It sounds like your daughters are working this out the best way they know how.

◆◆◆◆

I know my daughters are very confused. They love their father as they should and they love me. It was just my selfish thought of the moment. I am so caught up in this incredible life of hurt right now.

It is really crazy how we read so many stories and relate to them in so many, many ways. It was one of the first things I noticed because I thought I had a one-of-a-kind man (you know the thoughtful, caring, loving kind). Boy was I WRONG. He is just another man now, one I don't know anymore. It's very scary.

Makes me wonder on a daily basis why I want to hold on to him. Perhaps it is all fear in me to be alone, to be responsible. I have let him have control of everything for most of my adult life. It's hard to think of having to do so in such circumstances. Bam!! There it is... learn it... live it. VERY SCARY FOR ME.

As for the finances, we have both joint and separate accounts, and I have found out that both his and mine are maxed out. We have been paying for college which is where this has come from. I have to say it really scares me to hear from different people here and realize that he might actually turn into an ugly person with our financial situation. We don't have much at all, and I have even less. I have to pray that this will end in a good way.

◆◆◆◆

I am so crushed at this moment. I am losing my mind Last night I found a note in my husband's wallet from the other woman in which she said "I can't wait for you to come home" blah, blah, blah. Ending with "your bff and future roomie."

I had asked him to make a choice to stay or leave. I expected he would leave but he has said nothing and made no changes at home to indicate anything. This note should not surprise me. IT JUST HURTS LIKE HELL!

I don't know what to do. I want to throw him out today, because I want it to be me who says it first. Do I mention the note or just let it go and throw him out by saying something else? I want to say the right things, but what are they?

♦♦♦♦

This is why it's not a good idea to leave decision-making up to the person having a midlife crisis. It puts YOU in the position of waiting on whatever they decide to tell you, IF they decide to tell you.

It's also why I strongly discourage snooping. For one thing, you can never tell if he PLANTED that note in his wallet to catch you snooping! I mean, why would he need to save something like that in his wallet?

He may be trying to provoke YOU into "throwing him out," so he doesn't have to make the decision (and take responsibility for it and its consequences) himself. Plus, he can look like the injured party.

Now, maybe she DID write the note. It certainly sounds juvenile, though, doesn't it? "Future roomie" and "bff"? So that doesn't mean he's decided a thing, actually — she's swooning like a schoolgirl doodling her crush's name on her notebook. BUT — he saved it, so maybe he's swooning, too.

In either case, I don't think it helps you to fly off the handle right now. Finish your preparations for separation. You are making them, right? Getting documents copied and safely stored, setting your budget, consulting with lawyers? Then, when you are fully prepared, inform him that you no longer wish to cohabit.

But as far as "throwing him out," what will you do if he says "NO"? Do you have plans for that possibility?

Bottom line is, you don't need a sappy love note from a potential girlfriend to decide your current living situation isn't tolerable.

And finding the note doesn't really change your situation from how it was yesterday. If he hadn't told you of a decision to recommit to the marriage by yesterday, then the answer was "not yet" anyway. And if it's "not yet," that leaves YOU with the decision of "What now, in the meantime."

So, as much as the letter hurts, don't REACT to it. Just add it to the long list of inputs into YOUR decision.

♦♦♦♦

You are right I should not have let that stupid note cloud my better judgment. I have calmed down from this morning. Juvenile behavior is an understatement... the things they text each other he did not even say when he was 20. They are acting like a couple of horny teenagers; it's unreal.

This much I know. She did write that note because I found others in his car, and my instinct tells me it was not done on purpose, he has no clue about the things I know.

Tonight's development: About a month ago I found an application to a condo development, an expensive place that I assure you he cannot afford. Then last night for the first time EVER he asked me for help to make my car payment.

It is my car but he has ALWAYS paid for it. I had made other payments and this was going to wipe me out but I helped him anyway. I asked him why he did not ask me sooner and he said he did not know he would not have enough money.

He was in the shower and I just came in from checking the trunk of his car (where he keeps a lot of info that has helped me), and the application is gone. I don't want to let my imagination run away with me, but it just seems to fit. I truly think the bastard must have put a down payment on this expensive condo, which is why he did not have any money left.

So far everything I think is happening... is happening. I just want to exit this freaking mess under my terms not his. I need to make sure he leaves this house because I asked HIM to, and not because he is telling me he is.

It is so important for me to do that because I feel it will give me some sort of self-respect and dignity after putting up with so much crap.

As for him saying NO to leaving, I don't think that will happen as he has asked before if I want him to, but I have not said YES simply because I want HIM to make the decision. This is not going to fall on me.

My head is spinning again with what my next step should be, do or not do. I don't think I have ever thought this much in my life.

◆◆◆◆

My head is spinning, too! You WANT him to leave, but you want HIM to make that decision and not "force" you to make it "for" him. But, he's a "bastard" for making alternate living arrangements? For making the "wrong" decision?

And you won't tell him "yes" you want him to move out, because it's supposed to be his decision, yet you think you'll regain some dignity and self-respect because you asked him to leave, he didn't decide it on his own? HUH?

You can't make him want to stay. And, honestly, you can't MAKE him leave.

If he leaves, whether you asked first or he decided privately, HE is still the one taking the step out the door. And your dignity and self-respect are not something you lose or regain based on HIS actions, only on your own.

You're both playing a bit of a passive-aggressive game here. Well, until he actually takes the initiative to move out — unless he then spins it as your fault somehow.

I know, most of us probably know, that our own feelings don't have to be any more logical or sensible than theirs are. It does suck that he's choosing to move out, get his own place, rather than renouncing the other woman and extra marital affair and "new life."

But, the sooner you can see your own conflicting emotions and behaviors, the sooner you'll untangle them and find peace.

◆◆◆◆

First — the guy is a bastard no matter what. Second, I made it more complicated than intended.

RIGHT NOW, Do I want him to leave? YES (well no, not really, but, no choice for me).

RIGHT NOW, Will I ASK him to leave? YES (and I'm sure he will leave, I won't have to MAKE him do anything, which is actually very depressing to say).

Thank you for the clarification. ABSOLUTELTY CORRECT... HE is still the one walking out the door— with or without my choices or decisions. DAMN IT!

Two weeks ago I gave him two choices: a). stay and try to resolve our situation, OR, b). leave and be where he thinks his happiness is. But… two weeks later I have not seen ANYTHING different in his comings and goings, he has not spoken to me about ANY decision to stay or go.

Therefore, I can now tell him that because he has shown me that he is not interested in our marriage, that the obvious conclusion is that he has CHOSEN to be with someone else. It then became HIS decision NOT mine. The only thing I am responsible for is the date I am giving him to leave. This may all sound crazy, but for some reason or another, this is important to me.

Respect and dignity is my own, but I have always had low self-esteem and he knows it. I just want to SHOW him if only this one time, that I do indeed have some.

I don't kid myself — I KNOW that when all is said and done I am still the one that will hurt, and the one who will cry and be miserable. I will be the one left ALONE.

I am praying that I can get control of my emotions, and find that peace you speak of and I so badly need and want, but right now I feel so alone and lost, I just don't care about anything.

♦♦♦♦

You gave him choices two weeks ago but by when? And, or else, what? I mean, he had those choices every day of your marriage so far. Plus, c). Stay and do nothing about the marriage, while continuing whatever extracurricular activities he's chosen

He's choosing C. So, now what? What is truly in your power to enforce? He might leave because you "threw him out," but he doesn't HAVE to go. And, what's to keep him from just turning up on your doorstep again, in a day, a month, a year?

I'm not being argumentative; I'm just sharing loopholes you don't seem to have planned for. Loopholes that have bitten many a left behind spouse in the butt when she wasn't looking.

♦♦♦♦

I do have a lot to learn still. Just when I think I have made a good decision, you open my eyes to other things I frankly did not think of, or maybe didn't want to.

No, I did not give him a date to get out, I have always thought he would just leave when I asked, on the basis he had offered to do so before. I should think more with my brain instead of my heart, it might help... or not, who knows.

Thank you for pointing things out. That is why I am here. I need people like you to slap me around a bit. Perhaps I'll EVENTUALLY get it.

In the meantime I'm back to square one: WHAT DO I DO?

I am trying to move on with my life without him, but he IS still here and it hurts like hell to be near him while he acts like I'm not even here. Why are they so cruel?

♦♦♦♦

I'm sorry if the information feels like being slapped — or splashed with ice water. The thing is it's better to hear it from an impartial third party than it is to get it directly from someone you loved and trusted!

And just because bad stuff is POSSIBLE doesn't mean it WILL happen. It's just better to be aware that it COULD happen, and have a fallback plan. Don't let it make you miserable, paranoid, or paralyzed.

The hard part for many betrayed spouses is learning to stop thinking within the old framework, the loving/trusting one that couldn't even consider operating on such a "ME" mode.

We were used to, and happy with, thinking as part of a cooperative couple! It feels bad, wrong, and unnatural to shift into the same "as if single" mode that our wayward spouses have already adapted to.

And, we aren't "just like them" when we shift our perspective away from "couple" and over to "individual" mode. We're not out to hurt anyone, and we're not oblivious when we do. There is a BIG difference!

And we usually don't have a little "muse" whispering self-serving suggestions in our ear, while stroking our ego and feeding our Id.

◆◆◆◆

One thing to remember is (and a lot of betrayed spouses don't realize this) he is NOT the same man you married. He's different now because of the affair. Affairs do change people.

He is not going to snap back to the husband you once knew. If there was a shred of initiative in him to save this marriage, he would drop the other woman, go to counseling with you, help pick up the pieces, move on with you while working on himself.

The hard question to ask yourself is: does this sound like what he wants to do? All the evidence is pointing to the opposite.

He's made other plans with his life right now and what you say, want and do is secondary to anything and everything he wants.

You know he wants to move in with the other woman, you looked at the emails, he asked you for money, and he comes home sporadically, treating your home like a hotel.

It takes two to save a marriage not just one person who wants to so badly. His actions right now are the complete opposite of what you want out of him.

If you two work it out after the other woman in the future, fine. But right now, you're just torturing yourself with snooping and finding out more and more evidence that YES — he's moving in with the other woman. I don't know how much more proof you need.

I'd rather you have him leave and not know what he's up to and doing because he's out, rather than again, letting him come in and out of the house as he pleases and give you not even the courtesy of explaining the truth and how he feels. He just doesn't respect you right now.

Like I said before — you're still in the "shock" and "denial" mode which explains your actions. When you get to the anger stage, I hope he's out of there by then.

Expect things to continue as they are right now for you — torture. Until you finally put your foot down and tell him to leave. You will not lose any dignity in doing so and who cares who says it first.

◆◆◆◆

As I read the last of your words I sit here waiting for him to come home. AGAIN. But, I realize that this is not what I want to do anymore. I just can't and won't do this anymore. This is my ENOUGH moment!!

I have been feeling that anger, and have thought it was finally the stage I was waiting for, but NOPE, it seems this comes and goes on a daily basis, or from hour to hour. I feel like I can handle anything when I'm in that angry moment, it is a good feeling. Too bad it disappears as fast as it comes.

I will WAIT and when he decides to show up, he will know how I feel, and he will be ASKED to leave. God willing I will be strong enough to keep it together while I do this and that in fact he does leave without a struggle.

Thankfully the longer he stays out the longer my anger holds out. So far so good

◆◆◆◆

Well I was REALLY WRONG!! I asked my husband to leave... BUT I can ASK but it does not mean he will do it. HE did/has not left.

I waited that night and talked to him briefly. I told him how much he was hurting me and the kids, and asked him to please leave. I was so strong, I spoke calmly, firmly, and I did not shed a single tear, I was so proud of myself.

I was looking at him the whole time and noticed his eyes tear up, if only briefly not that it mattered one bit. He never did look at me and he NEVER spoke a single word! I waited for a few moments to see what he would say or do, but NOTHING.

I heard him go about in the kitchen, so I went to bed think-ing he was waiting for me to be out of the way. I had taken my sleeping pill and for once it worked all night. When I got up in the morning there he was! Unbelievable!! I just asked him to leave, he does not want to be with me, but he contin-ues to be next to me in our bed?

I cannot understand a single thing going on here. He had offered to leave before, I told him it was his choice, he did not make it, so I made it for him, but now, he is still here? The very sad thing is... that I don't know why, only that it's not for me.

I went to the gym in the evening, I come home and he is there. I got so nervous, thinking he was probably packing or something. NOPE... he was with our daughter watching TV. He had his home clothes on so I knew he was not planning on going anywhere then either. I also had no opportunity to ask him why he had not left.

So here we are and no action has been taken, all his things are still here, so I'm guessing he will be back today. I am so very tired of hurting this way. My days are so depressing, and seeing him has become unbearable.

I am back to square one again. What do I do now? Do I have an option on what to do? Do I leave it alone? I am really struggling with life right now. I don't know what or how to hold on anymore. I can't even get rid of him.

I am trying to move on with my life but I am just about out of rope.

◆◆◆◆

The next step is to start scheduling free consultations with Family Law attorneys in your area. These are usually free sessions, so go to as many as you can — at least three or four.

You can get a good idea of what the law is, what local legal precedent is, what your various options might be, and what it might cost to pursue any of them. You don't have to do a THING with this information, but just knowing what's what is calming and empowering.

Plus, any lawyer you consult with can't represent your husband, should it come down to it. So, a good tactic is to ask each lawyer who they dislike facing in court, then consult with that one, too!

If you do have to continue to cohabit, consider what adjustments you can make physically to give yourself some space. Is there a room you can make your own, where you can escape to read or sew or exercise or talk on the phone or sleep when you need to?

A mental adjustment you can make is to start looking at him as if he's just a boarder, a tenant in the building. Don't interact with him on any more personal level than you would a boarder, and don't expect anything more in return.

If you stop thinking of him as a husband while he's not acting like one, it really does get easier even if you hate every minute of it!

◆◆◆◆

Thanks for the advice; I would never think to do any of that.

So do I ask him again to leave, or do I ask him why he hasn't yet?

As far as adjustments to cohabit, they are fairly simple as he is hardly ever at home anyway. He works every day and then I'm sure he is spending every other minute with her, so he returns home late every night.

It's just me and my loneliness as I don't have any friends either thanks to him and my stupidity. Thankfully, I am enjoying my time at the gym for at least an hour every day. I am losing weight like crazy but it feels good, and I think I look better also. Too bad he doesn't notice or care.

He IS just a boarder here... that's what hurts. He is using his home for a hotel, we rarely speak, and the kids see this as well. It is so painful for all of us. I'm really looking forward to the "easier" part.

◆◆◆◆

I wouldn't bring it up again, at least not until after chatting with a few lawyers and exploring your legal options. His lack of response is all the answer you're likely to get and you're just proving that he can get away with this, until you find out what you CAN do about it.

And, you *may* find out that you can't make HIM leave, but YOU could. It's not ideal, but it *is* possible; lots of women have done that when life at home became too unbearable. But a lawyer can guide you through how that must happen; you can't just walk out and THEN expect to sort out the finances and legalities.

Of course, you could schedule a lot of overnight visits to every relative you can track down... just make sure you announce far and wide that you're just VACATIONING a lot.

◆◆◆◆

My going is definitely out of the question. I will not leave my kids. I rather put up with his crap, but I can't understand why this is getting harder and not any easier, I feel such an incredible emptiness.

I can't stop myself from looking at the clock waiting to see when he is coming home, and then when he does I am a total basket case thinking about where he has been.

It is totally obsessive and ridiculous I KNOW and I just hate it. I hate him for what he is doing!

I went through some bills today, and found he is late on payments. He got home just a little bit ago and I asked him about them. He said he ran out of money because he was paying the school loans. Which I understand, but it's not like the loans are new.

He has always budgeted those in before (at least I assume that because I had not seen late notices before), and then I fell into the stupid comment trap again and said that it does become hard not to have money when he is having to pay for hotels and such. He had NO comment. That took me by surprise!

All I can do is hope and pray that my time to be in HELL expires soon.

Thanks for all your help. It means a great deal to have someone helping me out in these matters so alien to me. I will really have to look into all this scary stuff.

◆◆◆◆

Leaving the marriage, or leaving the home, *doesn't* mean leaving your kids. They could go with you. It might be crowded for a while, but there are options.

And maybe if those options are so much worse than living as roommates, it will make the roommate situation more tolerable.

But it might not have to come to that.

TALK TO A LAWYER. OR SIX.

◆◆◆◆

I was exactly the same and it nearly killed me. I completely understand not leaving your children, or ripping them from their home.

But to survive you have to take a step back and stop looking for things.

If you find them it makes you unhappy, but it won't stop your husband doing what he is doing.

Can you survive financially without him? If you can't, go to a lawyer and get some protection in place for you and your children. But please STEP BACK from the cauldron. Stirring it won't help, let it bubble away until it eventually boils dry

♦♦♦♦

My kids are all adults. One away at college; the other two are at home with one going to college locally. They are very close to me and IF and WHEN I should go they would go with me although my son is planning on moving in with friends.

I am financially incapable of being on my own, and I have no family around. I at least have a job that I can count on a paycheck (small as it is) and benefits.

So until my husband decides that he wants a divorce and tells me what he plans on doing, I will have to live this horrendous nightmare.

I don't think he will file soon as I don't know where he would get the money for it. I still think he is waiting for the summer to move out, but we will see. It is apparent something will happen as the other woman calls him her "bff" and her "future roomie."

♦♦♦♦

WHEN you go for those legal consults, ask them about "constructive abandonment." It's applied differently in different jurisdictions, but in many places, if a spouse is making life insufferable at home, such as blatantly cheating, and won't leave, let alone file, you can use constructive abandonment as grounds for separation and/or divorce, and YOU can leave the home, AND receive support.

♦♦♦♦

Great advice and something I will look into and ask about, yet it sounds so definitive, why does that bother me?

I hate that I still love him, and that this hurts, hurts, so very much. I know it's over... I do. Eventually I hope my heart catches up with reality. Truly thought I was making progress at one point. So much for that. Dust off and try again.

♦♦♦♦

Well, it's "definitive" in that you will be defining your options, and eventually your boundaries, based on the information you gather. But none of it is obligatory, and none of it is necessarily permanent, including divorce.

There are plenty of examples of people who were separated and on the verge of finalizing the divorce when they changed course.

Consider this just one more means of "damage control," for your own psyche, for the remains of your relationship with him, for your finances, etc.

♦♦♦♦

Boundaries, options... I know I need to get answers and prepare myself for what may come my way, and thanks to you I have a starting point. My emotions were all over the place today with the crying, the anger, the feeling of humiliation and disrespect.

If I knew I could make it on my own right now financially I would just pack up and leave, I want to SO BADLY this very minute, but I KNOW I CAN'T, I JUST CAN'T. DAMN HIM!

I apologized to my daughter again for not being able to stop crying in front of her. I know she feels bad and prefers to just look away. It was just one of those days when anything/everything made me so depressed that the tears just came. I almost did it in front of my husband, and that is something I have not done in a very long time.

Believe me this is EXTREMELY hard because tears come very easily for me, I don't have to try very hard at all. Guess my anger is balancing the hurt when I'm around him, just so I don't show him I've been crying. It's the last thing I want him to see from me right now.

Life is not about fairness, I understand, but it sure does feel so "unfair" that he has it all... lover, happiness... A LIFE... while I get to watch it all disappear for me in front of my eyes. It all seems so hopeless; maybe it is.

Went to go see a lawyer today; did not get great info. It appears I have three options.

My husband has been living at home since I found out about the affair; he offered to leave that day but, never offered again. After so many months of this nonsense I asked him to leave. He never responded, has never told me what he plans on doing, when he plans on doing it or anything for that matter. The man says absolutely nothing to me. He is still here, and I cannot do anything about it says the "law."

I have a doctor's appointment in a couple days and hope to get some meds to see if this helps. I took some about two months ago, but guess I did not take it long enough because I thought they didn't work very well. I needed IMMEDIATE results and just did not wait so I gave them up. I will try them again.

So back to my options which are I either live with my husband and put up with his shit for however long he wants or I leave which is financially impossible or I would have done so already or I file for divorce which honestly I do not see myself doing because I cannot afford it and because right now I am not ready for it (crazy but true).

For now I pray that I can hold on for now to whatever is in store for me. Of course what would be best would be if he chose to leave (but better not hold my breath). My mind is so distorted right now. I want... I don't want? I think I am just as sick as he is; it is so depressing.

♦♦♦♦

I can feel your pain because I lived it just a short while ago. My husband would never admit to the affair though. But I knew about it because I snooped and found some things and even took secret photos of them going into the hotel and strongly hinted to him that I knew.

He made life a living hell from then onward. He treated me hatefully and mean. For a while I was in denial that this could really be happening. I tried EVERYTHING I could to become the perfect wife he wanted. He was already done with our marriage and all I was doing was becoming a lovely little doormat.

He started threatening to divorce me "after Christmas, so the kids can have a good holiday." Yeah, it was a great holiday with Dad treating Mom like garbage and refusing to be anywhere near me. He was also taking the kids to his parents' house every time they were free just to punish me and if I said anything, it turned into an episode of him yelling at me which greatly upset the kids who are young teenagers.

I began to do my preparation work. Found a lawyer I liked. Opened a new bank account to use in case he cleaned ours out (which he eventually did). I copied every single piece of paper I could find which was good since he's taken many of them now.

Money was not an issue because he had a great job, so while I had access to the joint funds I stocked up on household goods and stashed away a little bit of cash for emergencies — NOT like hotels and gifts of perfume that HE was spending OUR money on.

I got confirmation of the affair that's been going on for seven months or more. I did my sleuthing and uncovered lots of proof.

He was still living here and blatantly going about his life in such an arrogant and mean manner. Three months later, through support I got here and from my friends, I finally filed. I never thought I could.

I truly believe marriage vows are forever. But I just couldn't live like that anymore and he refused to move out. I wasn't ready to file for a long time. I just couldn't do it. I waited and waited for him to file as he was threatening to do. But then I read a post here.

Someone commented about the Serenity Prayer and I realized that I was only praying for the serenity to accept the things I could not change (his affair, his treatment of me, his disinterest in saving our marriage). I had overlooked the second part of the prayer: "the COURAGE to change the things I can."

I finally had the strength to change MY life and my kids' life. I just couldn't live that way anymore. It took three weeks after I filed to finalize the temporary orders and force him to move out. He now has to pay me child support and spousal support to pay the bills.

I have been on your emotional roller coaster. I hate that ride. I lived in the ANGER mode for months and now I'm entering the depression part. But my emotions fluctuate by the second. I'm right there with you in the low self-esteem and this mess may be more than I can recover from.

I do want to tell you that my nightmares stopped when I filed. I was having nightly dreams where we were pretending to co-exist and then he'd turn on me and yell at me. When I finally took that power and filed, the dreams stopped. I'm still a basket case emotionally, but it did feel good to take a little of MY power back.

Hang in there. I'll scream with you on the scary parts of the roller coaster ride.

♦♦♦♦

See at least THREE lawyers before you decide anything or even believe what they tell you. Think about it. Lawyers are human beings, often males, often middle-aged males. They, too, have biases and prejudices. Also, HALF of them graduated in the bottom half of their class. That's true for any profession! How do you know how experienced and energetic and "good" at his job this particular lawyer was?

I interviewed SEVEN lawyers. One of them turned out to be completely off the mark; gave me bad information that the other lawyers and a little internet research debunked. Two others weren't very enthusiastic or energetic but at least their advice was accurate.

The first lawyer I actually hired sounded good but didn't perform very well. The SEVENTH one I interviewed, and hired to replace the first one I hired and ended up firing, was the charm.

♦♦♦♦

I do intend to see another lawyer or two. Through work it looks like I may get a discount of some sort, so will check into this sometime this week. I am just hoping to find another that will give me the free consult as it seems most of the ones I called wanted some sort of retainer.

I decided to talk to my boss who was very understanding (she is a good boss), and if she can come up with something that may help me, I know she will do so. She was surprised that I did not "show" more anger.

I guess she is right. I am still so afraid of what is in the future for me that I have not truly been as angry as maybe I should be. The shock and mostly hurt of it all overrules the anger (at least for now), but in my mind and through advice posted on this forum, I believe I am doing some right things for now that may help me later.

Thank you for bringing up the Serenity Prayer. I guess I too overlooked the "the COURAGE to change the things I can" part even though I have read it so many times. I DO lack courage! I can't see myself filing just yet, but I am going to TRY one more time and ask him to leave.

The situation is taking such a toll on me. I truly don't know how much more "prepared" I can get, so whatever happens... happens. I know I must be patient and think things through; I cannot hurry things, and wind up screwing it all after having put up with so much crap from him already.

I certainly hope that he leaves and that I have sufficient information to help me. Gosh how this hurts. It seems I can't say that enough.

Thank you so much for the advice once again and for the encouragement that I so desperately need. I love coming here as this is the only place where I am reminded that I am not as ALONE as I feel.

♦♦♦♦

Just remember that divorce changes your legal status, but YOU still have to change your mindset about all of this. Divorce may provide financial protections, but you still have to protect your heart and mental and physical health.

And divorce isn't necessarily a sign of courage, nor is taking your time an indication of fearfulness.

So, "The wisdom to know the difference" is at least as important as courage and serenity!

Some lawyers will charge you their hourly rate for that initial consult. Can you blame them, when so many of us take advantage of the free consults and don't end up giving them any paying business?

It's well worth the hundred bucks or so (that's what they charged in my hour, anyway) for the consults, if you can possibly scrape that together.

Divorce can be expensive, depending on your situation and location, but not getting the right advice and the right representation can be DEVASTATING, both financially and emotionally. Don't cut corners here!

♦♦♦♦

You're right. It all costs money and the lawyers need to get theirs, I understand. It is very difficult for me to come up with money of any sort right now, but I will keep trying especially now.

I decided to ask my husband last night why he was still coming home, why he was still here. His response... he will be moving soon. I asked when and he said about two weeks.

I was thankful to have an exit date (that is what I wanted right?), and at the same time another stab to the heart.

Now I know when he is leaving me forever to make a life with someone else. Is there a worse word than devastated, because I feel it?

I asked how he plans on taking care of two households. He said I will be responsible for payment of my car and the utilities of the house, he will continue to pay the mortgage. I kind of agreed but there was really no discussion. He will be giving me the information I need before he leaves.

At the beginning of the conversation I asked what was happening with US, and he once again asked what I wanted. I told him he was the one walking out of this relationship what did he want.

I guess I kept thinking he would eventually tell me to be expecting divorce papers or something. BUT, nothing about divorce was ever brought up.

Maybe he knows he cannot afford it right now, perhaps down the road (especially if asked by the other woman I'm sure). Don't really know where he stands on this and I really don't know what to do either.

Do I wait for a while and see what happens or just think that it will be my call and file? The uncontrollable crying began early this morning. I'm on my way to work. I need to pull myself together. I have to somehow.

◆◆◆◆

I ended up taking out a personal loan to pay my lawyer's retainer. Even though I did not have a lot of credit in my name and only a part-time job, at the time I had an excellent credit score, due to my name being on the mortgage. It is worth exploring, at the very least. Sometimes, you have to bite the bullet and invest in your future.

♦♦♦♦

In my case, I wanted to remain married. I wanted to keep my marriage on life support even after he was gone. That was the emotional need part of the decision. I wanted to remain married despite the hurt and confusion and abandonment I felt.

The separation agreement we had made that possible, along with the fact that he wasn't out to hurt me and was quite responsible financially, as far as that goes with a wayward spouse. Legally and financially I was also better off remaining married as long as possible.

After four years of separation, he finally filed for divorce. He decided that he'd tried "everything" short of that, and that he "needed' a divorce. Well, turns out that divorce wasn't the solution, either, but there you have it. We're divorced.

Actually, it's not nearly as bad as I thought or as good as he'd hoped! Basically, he says it "changed nothing." I beg to differ, but it didn't change what he THOUGHT it would!

The general advice is, file if YOU want or need to be divorced. Don't file for any other reason, ESPECIALLY if you're just doing it "for" him or to prove something to him.

♦♦♦♦

That is what my husband said when he was deepest up the other woman. What do you want? Total projection. He also didn't want to talk about divorce.

I had two years of the hell and pain you describe. We are now in reconciliation, and he sent me a text today: I am so lucky to be married to you, xxx

Work on you, and just follow your gut. IF he continues to pay the mortgage and utilities, and does what he says he is going to do, that takes the pressure off.

♦♦♦♦

To keep my marriage is all I have wanted. The thought of a divorce just was not something I wish to do, and is still not something I am comfortable even looking into, even though I know that I should, and I am.

I know it's over and he has shown nothing to indicate anything can or will change. Since he has not brought it up, then I think for now I will hold on as well.

IF in the future I start to see he is not keeping with his promises, or he decides that he wants to file, then we will proceed from there.

Perhaps it is wrong of me to believe that if he says he will continue to make the payments he says he is, then at least for now from a financial point it seems there is no real reason to take that step.

I have a feeling that if it's not going to work out with him trying to take care of two households that I will find out soon enough. For now I will hope and pray that I am making the right decision.

The sadness, emptiness and loneliness that I feel, and that I know all of you here have felt is such an indescribable feeling. I am so grateful to have found this place, where I can let this out and know that I am understood. If only HE could understand the same way... IF ONLY.

♦♦♦♦

Divorce is definitely not what I wanted but unfortunately I had to follow up after he filed two years ago. He has done nothing from that point on but he is sinking deeper and deeper into financial ruin and I need to protect myself.

Like someone said, it's a business deal. He's already ruined my once great credit; I have to start digging myself out of the hole. I hated to do it but have no choice. My house is now on the market and I made a deal with my lawyer that I would put a retainer down and she will get paid the rest when the house sells.

♦♦♦♦

I had no more reason than anyone else to trust that my husband would keep his word about his financial promises. I mean, if he broke the BIG promises (in my book, anyway), how much easier would it be to break the others?

He never did. NEVER.

And when he got in financial straits after our separation, he still honored his obligations to me FIRST. I think, after the other betrayals, this became important to him, one final line not to cross. Whatever...

So, it is possible to just watch carefully, and not take definitive action until you see something that requires it. The key is, you have to watch carefully, and be willing to take the chance and be able to afford to take a loss if you miss the first signs of a problem.

♦♦♦♦

I don't know how I'm going to make it through this. I am hurting SO BAD right now. My husband got home two hours ago and went straight to the bedroom and I have not seen him since. And I hardly saw him this weekend. He is getting ready to leave within the next week or so, and this is just killing me. I just want to die.

My daughter living at home is very angry because she wants to move into an apartment with friends for college and I just don't know how we can do that. She wants to get out of this house. If she leaves it will be just me. There is no need for me to have this house by myself.

Other daughter's birthday is in two weeks; what a surprise I have for her. She is away at college. We (kids and I) are driving up next week and I will let them all know together. They do not know as of now that he is leaving. As much as this is hurting me they need to know what's about to hit them. I hate this so much!!

My days are just absolute nightmares, I am getting nowhere in trying to not think about him, all I want is to have him love me again. I know its WISHFUL, UNREASONABLE thinking and it is just hurting me like nothing I have ever experienced in my life.

I am almost 50 years old, I have never been alone and the thought of this frightens me. My children are grown and will start their own lives. I have no family nearby and even if they were I am close to no one. I have no friends as I never did anything without him.

It is so hard to think of starting over at this point in my life. I try doing stuff, but nothing helps me. NOTHING HELPS ME TO STOP THINKING ABOUT HIM. I AM SO ALONE AND SO AFRAID OF BEING ALONE.

◆◆◆◆

The only child I had living at home moved out when the going got tough because of the shit he was pulling. When he left, I too was alone in the house. At first it was annoying and scary and although my spouse had traveled a lot for the past several years, my kids were always coming and going, so this was pretty final.

I had to do something so I redecorated a bit and began listening to music I like. I would listen to music, drink wine, cry and write in my journal. I also spent WAY too many hours reading online looking for the "magic bullet" to fix things.

As time passed, I did what my physician friend told me to do. I began to read and try to meditate... a good book is by Jon Kabat-Zinn called *Wherever You Go, There You Are*. It is short articles and stories about meditation. But they really helped me understand that I had to rely on ME and I had to let go of my dreams of a future with him.

I still cry, and I am still not divorced, but I will be so glad to be divorced.

This year of self-discovery, pain and gained strength, has been so hard, but in no way would I say it is the worst year of my life. In fact, in spite of the pain, I reflect that in some ways it has been one of the best.

My kids, family and friends rallied around me to help me, I have had hugs from complete strangers and I have experienced complete support from some of my coworkers. All in all it has be an amazing year, for all its pain.

Here are some tips that I did when I was alone in the house....

I began to put the house to "bed" with a certain pattern walking clockwise through the house, so I didn't miss a light or candle etc.

I put chairs under the door knobs for the first few weeks, then realized that was a little silly... however I do have bells on my doors (big ones that my dogs ring to ask to be let out),

If they started ringing in the night the dogs would probably bark.

I go to happy hour at a quiet local bar about once a week, to eat; I eat while writing in my journal.

I light a fire almost every night, it is comforting.

I almost always have long lasting fresh flowers or an orchid blooming somewhere.

I have a phone near my bed and alarm clocks in places that force me to get OUT of bed.

I would go out with a magazine like *People* and sit in espresso bars to see people (I prefer books, and other magazines, but when I am upset, I have the attention span of a mosquito.

Sadly, or gladly, I actually have found it a relief to be on my own. My soon-to-be-ex was very passive-aggressive so my life is actually in most ways better.

Now when I am away for very long, I really wish to be home with my fire, glass of wine and music.

Take care of yourself; find small things to celebrate... a hummingbird, a flower, a smile. You are not alone on this journey.

♦♦♦♦

Thank you for the tips... it is awful of me to think they all sound good (I especially like the wine part). BUT I still can't help thinking in spite of all those things that he will be gone soon, and that at the end of that day and the rest of my days... he won't be sleeping next to me ever again.

I just can't seem to find a positive to anything, I am truly tired of myself and the pathetic way I feel. Does at least knowing and admitting that I know this about myself help me at all?

I am going to see if I can afford counseling soon.

◆◆◆◆

I think we all use that one (the wine part), at least for a while. But be careful with that, and I don't mean "you'll become a drunk."

What I mean is alcohol of any sort messes with your sleep cycles, which are probably already out of sync. So even when you aren't drinking, you may not be fully recuperating and resting at night.

Stress often causes us to wake up, wide-eyed, around 3 a.m. Alcohol also causes this (it's called rebound; you fall asleep because the alcohol makes you sleepy, but then it wakes you up just when you need your deepest sleep!)

This in turn feeds depression and confusion and poor judgment.

All of this originated with ex's counselor and is explained further in the book she recommended to him, *The Mood Cure*.

Of course, there's also "drunk dialing" to consider. Many a betrayed spouse has regretted the texts or calls she made while "under the influence." So, you might want to give someone custody of your cell phone if you're going to have a few drinks!

◆◆◆◆

No worries about the alcohol. I just liked the way it sounded to relax, but I rarely drink, and it has not been in my thoughts to do so.

However, that 3 a.m. wide awake thing was perfect. That is the witching hour. I had already started to sleep somewhat better, now I'm going back to the beginning.

◆◆◆◆

The 3 a.m. thing is a direct result of the stress we're under messing with our brain's supply of serotonin and melatonin, the hormones that enable us to fall asleep, remain asleep, go through the full sleep cycle, and awake refreshed.

Lots of stuff we eat or drink affects those hormones, for good or ill. That's what ex's counselor harped on as the basis of fixing what's off-kilter, before you add medications to the mix.

Lots of us are prescribed SSRI's — Selective Serotonin Reuptake Inhibitors — such as Prozac. Basically, they cause your body to re-use serotonin over and over, since your supply isn't being replenished properly. It can lessen the immediate symptoms, but doesn't solve the *cause* of your serotonin shortage.

Anyway, probably a lot more than you wanted to know about wine and sleep!

♦♦♦♦

Right now my main problems are the feelings of depression, or anxiety. I'm not sure what I'm feeling. There is this nervousness. I can't stop crying (anywhere). I feel this tightness in my throat to my chest. I just don't know what is happening to me. Again I just feel so hopeless, devastated, and mostly very alone.

♦♦♦♦

If you have a doctor you need to go see him or her now. I resisted that for a while, but finally went. I am feeling much better, not so anxious anymore. I rarely slept all night at first as well, so I know your pain. I hated waking up in the middle of the night. I took over the counter sleep aids for a short time and they worked.

My doctor prescribed anti-depressants for me, but I'm such a lightweight with meds that I couldn't take them during the week and function at work. He adjusted them and I only take them when I'm having a really bad day... it just takes time.

I never thought I'd start to feel better, but I started doing things I wanted to, seeing my friends, keeping busy and it is helping.

All my friends in real life that have been through this, as well as those on this forum kept telling me it will get better. I was skeptical at best, but lo and behold they were all right.

♦♦♦♦

I'm so sorry. Believe me I know how much it hurts. You are right I am very fortunate to have family and lots of friends who are supporting me.

At first I did not want to reach out to them, but I made myself. My oldest son gave me a book to read called *Who Moved My Cheese?* by Spencer Johnson. You should look it up; it helped me make myself move.

I get the want to see him not want to see him thing as well. It is hell. I'm finally beginning to realize that the man I loved is not the same as the man he is now.

Last evening he tried to rehash the why our marriage went south again. I simply said, I can't change the past, I can only work on the future. It was hard, but the more you say that the better you feel.

Believe me. My oldest son's wedding is tomorrow and my husband will be there because I asked my son and he finally decided it was the right thing.

My husband will not be at the reception, he is not invited. That will most likely be a challenge, but choices have consequences. I'm finally letting him own them.

It will get better. Don't beat yourself up too much when you mess up, another thing I'm learning.

◆◆◆◆

Well last night was the first night my husband slept in my daughter's room (she is the one off to college).

The room has been empty but he had not left our bed this whole time.

Even after I had chosen to sleep in that bedroom over the weekend instead of my own, it felt a little weird knowing he had done the same.

I had been crying all weekend and did not want him to see me. He on the other hand has other reasons for not wanting to be with me, so it hurts me, but I guess its more detachment for him. Just a look at the future without him.

Why are we unable to detach from them as easily as they have from us?

I still don't have a date on when he is leaving, but I have the feeling it is soon, and I am feeling the anxiety of it all.

I look around the house and it feels so lonely already, hard to imagine what it will be like when he is gone physically not just emotionally and has taken his things. IT SUCKS BIG TIME!

◆◆◆◆

He had a head start at detaching. He probably had already left the marriage before you had a clue. Sorry — this SUCKS big time!

◆◆◆◆

My daughter told me last night that she wants to leave the house which she says is not HOME anymore. She wants to move in with some college friends.

I told her we could not do that. She was angry over it. I asked her why she wants to leave me and she said it's more of a NEED than a WANT. I asked why, and she sincerely told me it's because I make her sad.

My heart broke to hear her, and I completely understand why she wants to leave. Hell, I WANT TO LEAVE. This does NOT feel like my home either, and I told her that, but it is financially impossible to move her out.

She also does not know yet her dad is moving out soon. That I will be responsible to pay things I have not had to pay before, and he is getting to where he is paying things late, something he has never done before.

I am sure that trying to settle into paying for two homes is getting pretty hard. I wonder just how long that can go on.

The kids and I will be together this weekend and I intend to tell them all together.

As of today my husband has not even spoken to my son about what he is doing (he only told my daughters). He knows because I told him.

My husband has been such a coward. I don't know when he plans on telling them about his leaving... maybe when he has his bags packed. But I intend to be honest with them as I have been.

I have been going through some very difficult days, it will be nice to spend Mother's Day with my children. I am looking forward to that.

♦♦♦♦

I can understand why your daughter wants to leave. Mine are about fed up with my obsessing over him. I'm fed up with my obsessing over him. I'm in counseling and trying so hard to work through it.

◆◆◆◆

Had a wonderful breakfast with my children, we had a good time. I am blessed to have such great, thoughtful kids. It makes me feel I did something right.

I had decided to talk to all of them together about their father leaving the house soon. It was truly gut wrenching as they just sat there and heard me out.

My daughter who has not yet gone through what the others have at home started to cry... she is very close to her dad and I know this is hurting her deeply.

I was as honest with them as I could be especially after my son and daughter who are here with me told me they were angry and disappointed that I had not confided in them when all this started. They knew something was wrong and they are ashamed that they carried on being 'normal' around their dad while the whole time I was hurting.

I apologized telling them that I felt that it should have been him to first bring up what he had done, and to somehow protect them from the hurt and pain this would cause for as long as I could.

I now must have faith in knowing that they are smart adults, and that they will make their own decisions about how they handle this... as I told them they should. Kids at home are very angry with their dad right now and want nothing to do with him once he walks out the door. Will see what the future holds.

◆◆◆◆

Letting the kids know was so hard, especially as their dad fed them a pack of lies that took almost five months to catch up with him. We are trying to rebuild our family, now, without their dad.

I hope your kids continue to support you. It is so hard for them, to see their parent choose this path, so destructive to their identity, emotions and lives.

♦♦♦♦

It was a wonderful feeling in a mom selfish sort of way to know my kids were with me for now... things may change later but for now their support is everything to me.

My husband and I still live under same roof but rarely speak and/or even see each other. There is no contact of any kind (texts, calls). The man avoids all eye contact. It is an extremely difficult situation living like total strangers. So bizarre.

Yesterday afternoon he comes home with flowers (not my normal roses he used to get for me but flowers none the less), handed them to me and said "Happy Mother's Day." I got up from my seat said "thank you that was so thoughtful," walked over to the garbage can and threw them out, then went back to my chair. He walked away to the bedroom, and I did not see him again.

It took every ounce of courage to do that because deep down I loved that he did that even though a bunch of flowers won't change the situation and I know this too.

I may be over analyzing this perhaps it's just that I cannot help but wonder... is it just to keep the peace? He is so very unusual, especially as I compare him to what others seem to say about their husbands here. Just trying to figure things out that I know really have no answers. Sorry for going on and on, my head just goes crazy.

◆◆◆◆

Mine had the audacity to call me from the other woman's house yesterday on the phone SHE gave him to wish me a Happy Mother's Day. Jerk!

◆◆◆◆

No you did not deserve this! This has nothing to do with you! I've been dealing with this for six months and it took me a couple of months to realize all of this is him and what he is going through. I've heard all the stories about how he connected with the other woman and how they are meant to be together. How he wasn't sure he still loved me and this one I really liked "How the affair was MY fault because I didn't love him enough to stop him."

What? I didn't even know it was going on. I have been through all the emotions of love, hate, and bewilderment and will probably keep going through them for a while.

Stay in counseling it does help and isn't it amazing that the husband is in counseling with you? Mine is too and he scheduled individual counseling too.

I think that we may pull through after 35 years of marriage. I hope so, we are talking a lot more and he has finally stopped blaming me for everything. Hang in there!

◆◆◆◆

Actually neither of us is in counseling right now, although I certainly need it. I know I have not been dealing with this very well, in fact it's been so very hard lately. Maybe because I know he is leaving. He only chose to do three sessions and then he decided I was the one that needed it most.

He is done with me completely. He continues to see the other woman and makes no attempt to make me think otherwise.

All this hurts so much on a very daily basis because he is there for me to see every day and every day remind me that he is no longer the man I loved, but more importantly the man that LOVED me.

Everyone talks about detachment, and thinking of you, and it's all true, but after five months I have not figured out how to do that. I just cannot let go of my feelings. I HATE IT!! Just when I think I have a grip, it all falls apart again. He was MY everything, how can he "forget," or "not care" I was HIS?

◆◆◆◆

The sort of detachment we recommend does NOT require letting go of your feelings. It requires letting go of trying to manipulate, change, or control HIS feelings!

Think of it as "disentangling" your emotions from his, rather than detaching, if that makes more sense to you.

◆◆◆◆

Detach yourself from HIS emotions. Don't let his actions control your emotions! Keep going to counseling if only for yourself. It will help, it just takes a while. One of these days you'll realize that you finally don't hurt as much and it slowly gets better.

There are still times when I wonder how much more of this crap can I handle, I get so tired. I started keeping a journal to help clear my head. I'm not sure it would help everyone but I feel better when I get all my tangled emotions and thoughts down on paper.

My husband moved out a few months ago. It's hard being in the house by myself but I'm getting used to it. The kids are calling more often which is nice.

He and I are meeting in two weeks to discuss his moving back home. I will consider it because he is in counseling and has been doing much better. But any decision will be in my best interest.

Do something good for yourself don't wait for him because you could be waiting for a long time!

◆◆◆◆

I guess I am confused on the detachment thing. I don't ask things, I don't tell things, I just don't talk to him at all. I do try not to have his actions affect me, but they do. It all does.

I brought my daughter home from college today, and she got to see firsthand when her father gets home. She was actually happy to be coming "home" but as soon as dad got home she decided she would go out to see a friend. She unfortunately is about to see that the "home" she left just a few months ago is no longer the "home" she is coming back to.

Amazing how things have changed in such a short amount of time. She did not want to talk to me about this awful situation, but I told her I am still here if and when she ever does feel like talking to me.

Now that we are all together again (at least under the same roof) we will see how he handles it. He has got to sense that they are angry and disappointed in him. Not that that will matter in his decision-making, but this cannot be easy.

I'm sure he is counting his days. How sad it is to see him give it all up for this other woman. How sad for all of us.

◆◆◆◆

I know it seems hard to believe, but I think you will start to heal faster with him gone. With him there, in your face, it is hard to get past the hurt. Every time he ignores you, it hurts.

The best thing my husband did was leave the day he gave the speech. The distance allowed me space to grieve and begin to heal.

◆◆◆◆

It seems hard to believe that not seeing the man you love, hearing his voice, just being in his presence can somehow be easier when he is gone. I hope it is true for me as it has for all of you.

He left last night, since my daughter is back in her room, I guess it was better for him to leave... the couch or our bed were his only other options.

Can't help but think if this will help him make his leaving decision earlier than he may have wanted. This is why I can't see things being easier.

My goodness I miss him already, and feel the loneliness setting in my heart. Even harder to accept he is not looking back at all.

◆◆◆◆

I can feel your pain in your post. I'm sorry, but now you can stop wondering when THAT shoe is going to fall.

Maybe the sleeping situation finally gave him an EXCUSE to leave. He didn't have the courage to just go; he needed to shroud it in something else.

Scream, rant, curl up in a ball and sob under the covers. It hurts! Let all that out. Let yourself feel all of it. Then tomorrow, take your daughter and go and celebrate the two of you.

Maybe you want to go to dinner, go to a flower shop and buy a pretty plant for inside, find something special to put in your house that is all about you.

It does hurt; it feels like it will hurt like this forever. I know how it feels, most of us do. It will get better.

◆◆◆◆

It does hurt like nothing I have ever felt before, I love him still so much and just want to understand how all this happened so quickly.

I had a terrible time at work today... everyone around me seemed so happy, laughing, talking about nothing, the way I used to. I just want to be happy again... I want him back (his old self back).

My life just feels like it's over, I don't want to be here. I felt so loved just a few months back and now it's all gone, yes I have my kids I know that, but they are young adults and have their own life to live.

I just don't think I will have anyone love me like that again or ever. It's just not in it for me.

Day to day is getting hard to live with. I am coming back to reading things on this forum over and over just to get me by. It helps while I read everyone else's story to know I'm not alone in what I am going through, but I AM ALONE.

◆◆◆◆

You are not much more alone than you have been, truly not. He was sleeping in the bed hugging the edge so he wouldn't touch you, then he moved to your daughter's bed.

He has been gone... his ghost has been hanging at your house when it was convenient. He has been gone. Now he took his clothes with him.

For now, your job is to get through one minute, one hour, and one day at a time. Try really hard not to let your head worry about "forever," your focus needs to be on the now.

Is there any help available through your job for situations like this?

♦♦♦♦

I am brand new to this forum, but your story reads almost word for word like my life. I too am struggling on deciding what to do.

My husband is my total financial support as I have been out of the work force for a LONG time. We are basically roommates. I have known him for over 30 years. I know he has another woman because he has basically told me so.

I have adult kids too, but they are busy trying to go their own way and I haven't told them anything. I don't have any extended family to call upon. We are friendly for the most part, but there's always the elephant in the room. As I said, I need to decide the course.

I am sad most of the time and have stomachaches/headaches/sleep problems but still I "live" in Being Undecidedville. Since we are on a semi-cordial "roomie" basis I am planning on waiting a while longer (it's been about four months), but feel it won't ever change really.

Thank you for sharing your story. It helps you and it helps the rest of us spouses who, after 30+ years, never thought it would happen to them.

♦♦♦♦

I am so sorry for your pain; this is a very painful journey to go through. I am living on a minute to minute basis; I have not been dealing with this very well. I come here often sometimes just to read, but it is amazing how our stories are so similar.

So many times one person just stands out because you think that is your own life. It's like a written script. The years together... the actions... the words said to you... most times cruel and insensitive... the way they used to be loving and now who knows who they are... the way they used to treat you and tell you they love you and now... BAM... just like that after so many years together they are no longer happy and find it so easy to give it all up, to throw us and their families away for the other woman. To treat us as though we no longer exist. It is just a sick feeling.

I lived in hell for four months living with him and living as roommates... it hurt that he looked so comfortable living this way while I was dying inside, trying to do what everyone suggested... to leave him alone, to let him be... go no contact was best... the thing was is that he did the whole detachment and no contact from me very well and I just had to follow along. It was super hard on me.

He has now been gone for eight days and the only contact we have had is an email giving me my password to make my car payment. Then Monday he texted and asked me what I had in mind for our daughter's birthday. I thought he was interested in sharing the day with us so I told him the plans. I never did hear from him again.

He did take one of the girls out to dinner the day before, the other chose not to go, I guess he thought that was enough.

I am still crying every day and hoping not to wake up the next. I love him still, but I know that he will never be back. I feel so lonely all the time. I feel comfortable here and I can let it out, plus everyone have literally kept me from doing something stupid.

I continue to think of my kids and daily convince myself I will make it through another day without him... and I have. As they all say, keep coming back and post, there are great people with great advice.

◆◆◆◆

Thanks for your words. I do read some of the posts to get a sense of direction. At times I think "maybe it's just a phase" and if I'm patient, it will be ok. Perhaps the other woman will get demanding and trivial and he will get tired of it and see that the grass is not always greener.

I do not know or have seen the other woman; she is out of town. My husband travels on business a lot, so it is not unusual for him to be gone. In fact, I would probably still be clueless if I hadn't accidently come upon something a few months ago. I have never told him what I found.

I do not know passwords and he keeps his phone with him like it's an extra arm. We have talked a couple of times cordially but seriously so I know where I stand. I was not surprised by our conversation, but saddened when I actually heard the words.

I am like you. He hasn't even physically left and I feel lonely, but honestly, I've felt that way for longer than I'd like to. I am at a loss as to what to do. I don't really have anywhere else to go either. I am trying to get my ducks lined up so I'm not caught by surprise.

I haven't told anyone except a good friend and now this forum. I do know no one can make the decision for you and as for me, right now, as idiotic as it may sound I have to be absolutely sure of my next steps. I know it will never be the same.

I will keep you in my thoughts and I know you will be fine and thank you for helping me.

◆◆◆◆

It is this extreme loneliness and emptiness that is so very hard to feel minute to minute, hour to hour, and day to day. If only I knew... if just a thought of me crosses his mind... does he miss me just a little?

Does he think about coming back? Since he is not here guess I did know after all.

I am glad I could help you somehow as there have been many who have helped me. It seems you and I are similar in our dependence on them, and that we know so little about what is actually going on in our own homes (passwords to financial situations, phones they don't let go of. I found out he had a second phone just for her calls, and who knows what else).

I always trusted him to take care of all of it, the few times I asked about such things I should have pushed until I got answers, but I never did, guess because I just knew he was there and it never bothered me enough.

Nnow it may come back to haunt me... if only I knew then what I know now. I feel so stupid to have trusted to that level, but I did.

◆◆◆◆

I felt stupid too, but then I was living up to my idea of what marriage was about. I assumed he was living the same way.

◆◆◆◆

I'm curious — I've never seen the other woman; he is being discreet and "respectful." Has anyone else peeked at things, or followed their husband to see who the other woman is? Discreetly, of course.

I'm SO in the same boat as y'all, but somehow today I feel empowered. I have a new mantra: "It's not me, it's you." Then again, tomorrow is another day.

◆◆◆◆

I know who she is. When I first found out about her I did several things to find out who she was. He has two jobs and so I did not know where to start, but I had no problem finding out. To this day THEY don't know that I KNOW who she is.

I had contact with her through email and I have spoken to her... she asked me if I knew who she was and what she did for a living... I told her what I thought she should hear... it's a long story.

My husband was never one to care much about looks. I don't know whether to be jealous or insulted after seeing her. I am not that attractive but I think I am much better looking than her, especially now that I am down almost 40 pounds thanks to them.

Then again it's not always about looks is it because I was told it was an emotional connection.

If I think about it now though I wonder if it is better not to know because images appear in my head that otherwise would not be there. It was a catch-22 thing for me. I wanted to know but I did not want to know. The shock, anger, disbelief, disappointment, and rejection of it all pushed me to do it I think. It's too late now.

♦♦♦♦

I confess at the beginning I searched for her online and found her home address and phone number but no picture anywhere. So all I really know is that she's about 15 years younger than my husband, and I know the names of her kids.

Note to all: if you don't want just anyone knowing the names of your children DON'T include them on your greeting on your phone answering machine!

I believe that it started out as an emotional affair, but who knows where it is now a year and a half later? And I can honestly say I barely care anymore, except as it relates to my daughters.

At first, I really, REALLY, REALLY wanted to know what she looked like, more about her, etc. But as time went on I truly realized that it wasn't about me versus her, but about his crisis. He is nearly incapable of functioning if he lacks a relationship, so she was his "soft place to fall."

He's settled down and has been decent to me in regards to our daughters (the only contact I have anymore). In turn, I have little, but cordial, contact when necessary. Though he's no longer the person that was my husband at least he's being financially responsible for our daughters as they finish/enter college.

Here's hoping you eventually can get past the pain and knife-in-the-heart of knowing there's another woman. I assure you it is possible (mostly...).

♦♦♦♦

The other woman my husband sees is in another town. He usually only goes to see her once a week. I'm trying to decide if his wanting to stay here the majority of the time is a having your cake and eating it too moment or, as I've read other places, a small victory for me. And no, there is no "sharing," if you understand my drift.

That being said, I know it will never be the same. And, I am preparing myself in case there is that moving out moment. He'd only be going in body; right now, the spirit has already left the building.

My anniversary is coming up soon. Who knew I'd be in this boat? I can blame him for the other woman, and I would not have done that, but there are some things I wish I had done different that I know added to the problem. Hindsight is always 20/20.

Today I am not such an empowered person. My husband just left for the rendezvous. He simply packed his overnighter and left without a word. I asked him if he was leaving and then he said yes, I will be back tomorrow. So, I will get to eat alone and go home alone while he and the other woman are eating out, shopping, whatever. He always hated shopping the whole entire time we've been married.

Since she lives out of town, so I won't run into them. He thinks that is being respectful of me. I think he likes that the other woman is younger, and he can be the caring, older gentlemen that has a young girlfriend and can buy her things. And he does.

She must hang on his every word and it doesn't bother her that she sleeps with a married man because he takes her out to eat, buys stuff, etc. etc. I suppose she fills a need for my husband and it is a small price to pay for the benefits.

There are many reasons why I haven't had a complete meltdown and kicked him to the curb. It is a strange ride. Thanks for listening.

◆◆◆◆

Have you tried some anti-depressants? I avoided them at first too but then had a panic attack one day after soon-to-be-ex called me at work and yelled at me for some stupid thing. The anti-depressant has helped along with getting counseling.

Your spouses are not worth the pain they are causing you. Please just try to take one day at a time, or even one hour if that's easier. And if you are a believer in something, pray.

♦♦♦♦

I started taking anti-depressants about two weeks ago and they just now seem to be working. I actually went through a day at work without crying.

I still have this "strange" feeling in my chest and throat, it just feels weird. I guess its stress... hopefully even that will go away.

Am trying really hard not to think about him, but it is Friday night and I am alone. My kids are out doing their thing and I was supposed to be enjoying my evening with my husband.

I used to look forward to the weekends with him. Thoughts of him being happy with someone else during weekends or any day are very very hard. I was rejected and abandoned... this is what stands out

♦♦♦♦

Being home alone at night is the saddest part of all, at least for me. I hate watching the commercials even that show a family.

I don't know if I specifically miss him or just the thought of once what was, having a partner to be with, to do things with.

My kids aren't here either. I don't have any extended family. I have a true friend that I confide in, but I'm probably wearing her out. You have to be careful who you tell. Only my friend, my husband and y'all know the story.

I am a believer in what goes around, comes around and it is sad to see the person I think he has become (I'm sure he feels justified).

♦♦♦♦

I'm at home alone now too. My teenaged son was here for a while with his girlfriend watching a movie. Weekends are hard and I try to find something to do. Most of the time now I don't think about him and the other woman and what they are doing. Life is too short to worry about them.

No, it doesn't seem like it now but it does get easier as time goes by. You are both still unsettled as far as your marriages and you feel like you are in limbo, don't you? It's tough when things are out of your control.

♦♦♦♦

I guess I have also wondered if it was him I am missing or just the way things were. It would be nice to know for sure... that would definitely change things would it not.

Then again I still love him... DAMN IT! I still miss him, his touch, his laughter, his beautiful eyes, his love (the love I know he had for me).

♦♦♦♦

I love the line I found on this board that said, "I miss the misconception I had of you."

You miss the old relationship, the old him. He has changed himself and his brain. When you make choices that rock your foundation of being, you have to live with those choices and you have to change your brain to accept yourself for what you have done. He has changed. Cognitive dissonance has changed his brain.

◆◆◆◆

Yes he has changed. The most surprising part to me is that after all these years, how easy it is for him to lie even when I already know the truth. He didn't do that before a few months ago. I think he prefers not to say anything about where he's going so it really won't be a lie, just a non-answer.

One of the things that really chaps me is I know he must be spending money on the other woman and part of that money is mine. So, I'm spending money on the other woman. Hate to sound materialistic, but there you go. I think it is the fact that I know about it now; ignorance is sometimes bliss.

◆◆◆◆

Well here is another day I have spent crying for a man who could care less about me. He has been gone for eleven days now and it feels like day one.

It's a great thing to hear from those of you who have picked yourselves up and allowed your grief to somewhat come to an end. To realize that life goes on and you are what is important.

I am watching a show with country music and all the songs make me cry... the words to some of these songs are so sad. I find something depressing in everything because somehow/somewhere/something reminds me of him. I miss him terribly.

One of my daughters told me that her dad texted them today just to ask how they were doing. The one daughter, who told me, does not want to speak to him, so she did not answer. The other one I have to say has changed a lot since she has been home from college. She will not even tell me if she hears from him.

I think that because she was not around to see what my other kids have seen all along from their father... the coming home late... the inattentiveness... that it has made it easier for her to not feel as angry at her dad as her sister and brother do.

My son has yet to hear a word from his dad, not that he wants his dad to contact him (or at least that's what he says) but it makes me so angry and sad that my husband is doing that to him.

My daughter said something very hurtful the day I took them out for breakfast for their birthday. She said she feels sorry for me but her dad cheated on ME not on HER. He had left the house but had not abandoned them.

I could not say anything to that... she was right... it still hurt to hear it from her that way.

As I said before... my husband and I always knew she would not leave him even after what he did ... I repeat... we were right… she will always be there. I do understand. It's her dad and always will be, I just hoped it would have taken a little longer for her to forgive him, especially when it seems to have affected the close relationship that her and I also shared. Just another pile of hurt to the enormous mountain of hurt I feel already.

Truly I cannot see an end to this torture that I may be creating for myself. Sorry once again for the pity talk. It helps me to let it out. This is exhausting

◆◆◆◆

I hate to read you are struggling so, but it is good that you are posting your feelings on here. I've not been on this forum for long, but there are a lot of helpful people. Everyone still has their moments, I suspect, even if they have moved on.

I don't know you personally, but as we've stated in our earlier posts, we seem to have a lot of similarities. My husband hasn't moved out, but sometimes I think I have more conversation with the check-out lady at the grocery store. It is always playing round and round in your thoughts.

◆◆◆◆

Is my husband cheating or is he about to?

First let me say that when I found this site the penny finally dropped after suffering in silence and wondering where I had gone wrong in making my husband so miserable. NOW I KNOW IT IS NOT ME. I have read a lot of posts and I see a lot of things I can relate to.

MY situation: last year my husband completely withdrew from me and he lost his temper with me over the smallest things, criticized me for everything. Then I found messages on his iPhone from an ex-girlfriend in another country telling her how much he loved her.

I left for four days which is as long as I could stay away from my beautiful kids. We decided to work on our relationship -- me stupidly thinking he would stop calling her and a month later we got a $1000 phone bill. After that things turned ugly, me stealing his phone to check calls, him tackling me to the ground to get the phone from me.

He denies being in love with her and maintains "if his dick doesn't smell he is doing nothing wrong." He blames me for not loving him the way I should (god like). It is all my fault, he doesn't want to be with me. He hasn't actually said he doesn't love me but talks about being done, there is no relationship, I hate the person you are, and lots and lots of other hurtful things.

I have done the stupid thing and taken the bait and argued and yelled back at him.

He has struck up friendships with lots of women some I know about and some I don't. He has bought a secret phone and he sleeps with his iPhone in his hand so I can't look at it.

His porn usage has gone up I don't know how much is normal?

I have become completely paranoid and I am currently trying to find out if he is sleeping with one suspect ex-friend of mine; he has opportunity because he works away a lot.

He also has talked about being dead soon, life's too short, trying to impress every lady he meets, dissatisfied with our sex life, wants to buy a sports car, regretful of all the things he has not done, delusions of grandeur. So I find myself alone; family aware but can't/won't help.

I have a few questions. 1. Do all men in midlife crisis cheat? 2. If I suspect he is cheating is it happening? 3. If he hasn't cheated yet how do I stop him? 4. How can I get someone's address without raising suspicion (tried phone book, electoral roll)?

Believe it or not I can actually handle all the other stuff but if he is unfaithful then I am done!

◆◆◆◆

1. It would appear that most men in midlife crisis DO cheat OR (more likely as I see it) the bad behavior that accompanies cheating gets called "midlife crisis."

2. Never discount your gut feelings... they are usually correct.

3. You can't actually stop him from cheating; you CAN, however, (with some thought and planning) arrange things so that the cheating is very, very difficult for him.

4. Addresses can be gotten online. There are sites which for a small fee can provide that information... if you have the names.

Good luck. Sounds like he is sex addicted what with the porn and all.

You do realize don't you that only immediate and painful consequences have the best shot at getting his attention. Not much else is going to help... addicts are particularly devoted to getting their fix.

Take care of you... ESPECIALLY FINANCIALLY... that 1K phone bill would probably have seen me ballistic. And I would not be paying for such.

Have you consulted an attorney? Sounds like it might be time to do some homework about how to put the skids under Mr. Irresponsible.

◆◆◆◆

1. Depends on how you define "cheating." Do all men in midlife crisis have sexual intercourse with a person other than their spouse? NO. Do they take energy and affection and attention away from the marriage and invest it in any number of other people or places? ABSOLUTELY. There are a million shades of grey in between.

2. Your gut is an "early warning system" that SOMETHING is not right. That much is 100% reliable. The hard part is figuring out exactly what is wrong, "and who is responsible for fixing it." Nine times out of ten, around here, there's not much the betrayed spouse is truly responsible for or able to fix; it's up to the wayward spouse.

3. You can't stop him from doing anything, any more than you can make him do anything. His behavior is entirely his choice. What you can do is influence his decision-making process, by making sure you have clear boundaries with clear consequences established "If you do THIS, then I will do THAT," and then demonstrate that you will follow through on them.

4. Why do you need to secretly identify an address? If you are planning to divorce him using adultery as grounds, hire a lawyer and maybe a private investigator to obtain the evidence you need, legally.

If you're not planning to divorce him on grounds of adultery, the information is useless to you. You have much better ways to invest your time, energy, and money, because you already know more than enough to know there's a big problem with him.

♦♦♦♦

Nothing you can do will make him cheat. Nothing you can do will make him not cheat.

Sorry, but the decision whether he goes outside the marriage or not is his alone! He is going to do it if he wants to do it and there isn't anything you can do to stop it.

The only thing you can do is make decisions for yourself. If he DOES cheat, what will you do? Where are your boundaries? What will the consequences be from your side if he crosses them?

You can indicate very clearly up front where your boundaries are but whether or not he chooses to respect them is his choice, not yours.

Good luck. Sounds like you are in for a roller coaster ride like many of us are/have been on!

♦♦♦♦

I would like the address on someone in another country as I believe it might show he is cheating and if he is I will file for divorce.

Other than that all I can do is work on him regarding his ex-girlfriend. Any ideas of what sort of threat to make?

I can't leave. I have nowhere to go and he won't leave. We have already had all those discussions. I am, at the moment, being super nice to him and not reacting when he is three hours late or talks about how everybody loves him except me.

◆◆◆◆

I think you missed the point we've all tried to make:

YOU CANNOT THREATEN, SEDUCE, BEG, REASON, COERCE, CONVINCE, LURE, MANIPULATE, OR IN ANY WAY CONTROL WHAT HE DOES.

You can only decide what YOU will do, given what HE is already doing, or indicating he is likely to do.

◆◆◆◆

You're on a hamster wheel, so obsessed with finding out "who" he may be cheating with that you're not really dealing with the fact that he IS cheating.

You have a couple of options.

1. Stay with him despite his cheating. Continue chasing your own tail, expending all your energy on playing detective.

2. Leave or ask him to leave. This will create a lot of practical issues, but none of them are insurmountable if you put your mind to it.

Finding the home wrecking ho and plastering her picture on the front page of the daily news won't change a single thing. Except maybe it will make him even madder and more disrespectful of you.

◆◆◆◆

I do get what you are telling me. My husband at the moment as far as I know it is talking to lots of women. This is bad and unacceptable but it will help me move on if he has cheated. I don't want to make other woman pay I just want to confirm my suspicions so I can leave. I suppose I need justification.

The kids worry me a lot that they won't understand what the big deal is and why I am leaving and taking them away from their home.

I am in denial that all this is happening to me! Are all my dreams and hopes for a family life gone forever? I just can't believe it. I am so sad, hurt, confused.

♦♦♦♦

I will never understand why infidelity is the ONLY thing some people will consider a valid reason to end a marriage.

There are many ways to break your vows! In my ceremony, we promised to Love, Honor, Cherish, "and" forsake all others.

If he's not demonstrating the first three, why isn't that enough reason?

♦♦♦♦

Is this a religious thing... you can only divorce him in the justifiable case of adultery?

He has already "betrayed" the marriage. You need to do what is best for you, beginning with seeing to your future financial needs.

We have all let the other woman have too much rent-free space in our heads. Stop doing that. If it weren't her... he'd have another "excuse" for his lack of commitment and integrity. His character is piss poor whether he is doing someone else or not.

Find what it takes to make you content. And, it isn't going to be saving the marriage because the marriage has already suffered a mortal wound administered by him.

♦♦♦♦

I come here for continued healing six years after my husband's emotional affair and as far as I know, his private parts never met hers. An emotional affair (where his brain, heart and loyalty went) was fully transferred over to her and he treated me thusly... just as your husband treats you.

If you are certain that you would divorce for infidelity, then go ahead and do it... what you describe is a husband who is GONE. But many of us here came to realize that how we chose to respond is not exactly what we thought we would do in that situation.

You can wait or you can divorce him, but if you are waiting for more proof of infidelity to justify divorce, wait no more. Some people recover and some don't and there is no telling which your husband is.

♦♦♦♦

If you want proof of something, what is getting someone's address going to do for you?

It sounds as if he is cheating in some way — he is ringing up phone bills talking love-talk with someone who is across the world. Is that not enough that he promised he would stop, but continues to do this?

Is it not enough that he has a secret phone and his regular phone? You smell plenty of smoke. Do you have to see the house in flames before you believe there is a big problem?

If you really feel you need proof if he is cheating or not, hire a lawyer and private investigator that your lawyer recommends. But, you must think about what you'll do if they cannot find concrete proof that he is having an affair.

Think about what your needs are in a relationship — besides monogamous fidelity.

How do you need to be treated in a relationship? Do you require honesty? Do you require to be treated with respect?

Come up with a list of four or five things that are absolute, bottom-line REQUIREMENTS for you to be in a happy marriage.

Then, sit back and think about whether he has been meeting those requirements. You may need help (such as a private investigator to prove infidelity), or you may see the answers with your own eyes very clearly.

◆◆◆◆

My advice: do not go on a search for more proof. Depend on your gut feeling. You may get more than you long for.

My "husband" (not married, but living together long term so I just call him my husband) gave me "the speech" about three weeks ago. He was confused about everything, his life, his love for me, not sure if he ever really loved me. That entire BS.

I tried my best not to "nag" him with my worries. He was already very "cold" for the past year (looking back everything falls into place). So I gave him the space to work things out himself, like he asked me to. What can you do?

A week ago I had to use the laptop he was using every second of the day to be on Facebook, sitting next to me banging on the keys while I was watching TV. He "forgot" (?) to close the page he last visited, and up pops the last chat between him and the other woman.

There it was: she said she's ready to tell her husband she was going to leave him. My husband returned that with a "You're the one I want, I will do anything for you, I choose you, F*CK THE REST." He ended the conversation by saying he's ready for the night now.

I remember that same night we made "love" or at least I thought it was love. But he needed the other woman to get him ready for me, I guess.

The other woman is still married, with three children. She's a childhood friend of his family. We saw them at birthdays and stuff. I always did think of her as a nice, very social woman.

Well, I was right about the "social" part. For the last few months alarm bells went off: something was wrong and she wasn't just a good friend. But how can anyone that nice do such things? And she knows who I am!

I confronted him. He wasn't angry I read the conversation, but was disturbed by the fact I found out so soon. He wanted to tell me not just yet. But after me confronting him and after him crying and getting angry for a few days, he felt the urge to share some more. After all, I love him and want to know what makes him happy.

He's been at her place a few times as a friend but later on they started to meet somewhere else. He took the other woman places where we've not been in a long time, the beach, restaurants, and nice places. She sat on my seat in our car.

They could talk for hours, and when things started to get more intense, they tried to not talk every day. It had nothing to do with sex, they never had sex. But she understands him and he can't talk to me about anything, because I wouldn't understand anyway.

She may be the one he's been waiting on all his life. She's the one; she's the best thing that ever happened to him. And the other woman is having difficulties in her marriage, so he wants to protect her and is feeling sorry for her and her kids.

And how a while ago they already talked about how life would be if they got together.

STOP!! I get the picture; I already was exposed to your very clear conversation on MY laptop.

The only thing that terrifies him is me telling it to other people. He is scared to death that when his family or her husband finds out, everything backfires on him. And that will disturb his secret romance with the love of his life.

No holding back, no shame or sensitivity at all. For me, he's the love of my life. And I have to convince myself a lot that it's not by my doing he's leaving me for the other woman.

I'm looking for a new place to live and enough money to leave while he's upstairs on "Facebook" right now. And sometimes he goes out for some "fresh air." When he can't see, I'm still crying my eyes out.

In my mind I keep seeing the chat they had on Facebook which made it all too clear, and that's an image you don't want to pop up every other minute in your head or in your dreams. You know something is wrong, you don't need more proof because it will hurt much more than "just" knowing.

Listen to the alarm bells ringing, that's all you need to know to take the next step, whatever that may be.

◆◆◆◆

My husband said the same, didn't know how many sunrises he had left, deserved to be happy, had to be more than this to life, and didn't want to miss out on anything because he maybe had ten years left, more but you know the drill.

He was never ready or brave enough to tell me about his married other woman. I found evidence way before I found out for sure and he freaked.

Told me it was a schoolboy crush, he never said anything to her. Now he and the schoolboy crush are living together; not sure what the future holds.

♦♦♦♦

I feel for you. I just cried when I got to the bit where he wanted to protect her while leaving a trail of carnage behind him. When the reality of the split hits home their love bubble will crash.

Walk tall out of this mess. At this stage there is nothing you can do but look after yourself and your children. Whatever energy you have, spend it on looking after yourself, the kids and getting legal and emotional support.

♦♦♦♦

Before you move out please talk to a lawyer. Mine told me that I shouldn't move out under any circumstance.

♦♦♦♦

I know you are sick to your stomach right now, as I was when my husband had his affair. He denied too — I saw the texts. He denied, denied, denied. And do you know what he told me many years ago? That even if he were caught in the act he would deny it.

If you have a gut feeling something is wrong, it probably is. But a life of constantly checking up on him is not a life I would want to lead. When I did it years ago, it consumed me. It took me away from my kids. I can never let that happen again.

Long story short, go with your gut.

♦♦♦♦

My husband practically kicked me in the gut when he told me he was attracted to other women and would like to start "dating" not f***ing around mind you but actually dating someone he felt something for. He thinks one night stands are disgusting. He swears he hasn't acted on it but described in detail the women he was attracted to.

He also told me that I should have an affair to recharge myself. That we should both date other people for a year. That sometimes things happen when you don't want them to and you meet someone and it's God's Will. What church does he go to?

Anyway, now he doesn't want to have sex with me but says he'll service me if it will make me feel better. I'm still struggling with wondering if there is another woman or whether he's just saying these things to hurt me or if he's contemplating it. He goes out with friends he won't introduce me to and has business meetings he can't remember the name of the restaurant he went to.

Am I still hanging onto a dream that he's not seeing someone or what does anyone else think. Can this be depression or midlife crisis talking?

♦♦♦♦

How do I handle finding out there really is another woman?

A month and a half ago, my husband came home and said he didn't love me anymore and probably never did. It was a punch in the gut as I never expected this, although he said I should have seen it coming.

I don't believe that he never loved me. I don't believe that it's gone completely. I told him this from the beginning and also told him if he wants a divorce then he'll have to file.

I have always had a gut feeling this was because of someone else although he swore it wasn't. Well I recently found out there IS and she's 23 (he's almost 45). How do you go about dealing with this??

Up until I confirmed who it was and when it started I thought that we could get through this. Now I don't know if there is a remote possibility of us reconciling if I could ever get past this. I feel so lost and so helpless.

◆◆◆◆

Couples can and do get through this experience and reconcile, pretty frequently. That's why the 40-something guy dating a 20-something gal is such a cliché, and is so scorned.

But couples can and do end their marriage over this same situation. Some of those 40/20 relationships can last quite a while — and the fallout if they don't, can last quite a while, too.

Which way will your story turn out? There's no telling. There's even no telling how you will WANT it to turn out, because that may change from day to day.

Finding out there is a "someone" and not just a fantasy is gut-wrenching. It adds an entire new layer of complications and potential consequences to the problem of a spouse who is no longer mentally committed to the marriage, when they get emotionally or physically involved with someone else.

But that still doesn't mean you know what the outcome will be.

So how do you deal with "it"? The same way we all learn to deal with anything Life dishes out: one day at a time, the best way we know (or can learn) how. With as much flexibility, humor, companionship, support, information, and professional assistance as we can gather.

Keep reading all over the forum and you'll see the millions of stories and tips and warnings and examples of people who are struggling with the same situation, or sometimes even worse! At the very least you won't feel so alone, and perhaps you'll make some good friends and have a lot more information to base your own choices upon.

◆◆◆◆

I am in this boat with you. My husband has been having an emotional affair for three months. We've been married 25 years and everything has always been great, or so I thought.

I know it hurts so badly. This is a good place to be. People here will help you.

◆◆◆◆

My heart goes out to you. Most of us have been in your situation and share your pain. I'm two years down the road now and divorced. I can only describe the journey as a rocky roller coaster ride.

However your story turns out you'll have good days and bad days. Take whatever you need in support from those that love you, try not to look too far into the future and take each day as it comes. On the good days rejoice in your strength. On the bad ones recognize them for what they are: Bad days!!

I've come through the worst now and can see light at the end of the tunnel and one day so will you.

♦♦♦♦

It is quite a shock to find out your spouse is supposedly unhappy and no longer loves you, when all along you thought things were great.

I had the same thing happen to me and was completely blindsided and DID NOT see it coming. Then when he told me he met someone else (that "someone else" was a hooker) and thought we should separate, I was absolutely in shock. I remember needing to sit down because I thought I'd fall over. It was horrid.

I held onto hope for a long time that he would "come to his senses" but he never did. He ended things with the hooker and then put an ad on eHarmony and started dating a number of women, one of whom is now his current girlfriend, who conveniently knows nothing of his whore mongering.

I'm still struggling, though not as bad as those first few days/weeks. It's a horrible thing to go through, one of the most painful things I've ever had to face, and I've been through a LOT of difficult situations.

How I deal with it is trying to keep busy, connect with supportive people, have a good counselor, and sometimes all I can do is just cry.

It sucks, it's not what I want, and I'm not sure I'll ever fully recover from it, but there isn't much I can do about it. It is what it is.

♦♦♦♦

Try to fight the helpless feeling. You are not alone in this, we are here to listen to you, to share our stories, to tell you that only time and patience can heal (to a certain extent) the wound, but also that there is light at the end of the tunnel, even if you don't see any right now.

If you felt loved for the years together, listen to your memories, not to his. He is driven by his dick right now and he is likely to blame you for everything and re-write all history together.

Do you have children together? If so, please do concentrate on how to get the best custodial agreement and how to do what is best for the children and for you (e.g., regarding housing, finances, etc.). It doesn't mean that you give up any hope of reconciliation; it only means that you prepare for the worst. And hopefully better days than imagined are ahead.

From experience I can tell you that you cannot speak reason with a man in heat. And your husband right now is a man in heat, and his hormones will not be assuaged enough in the next one-four years to come.

I would say to really start thinking about a life without him, instead of waiting for him to wake up. If he does wake up (which may be questionable), he will appreciate you more for having taken care of yourself, for your finances and for your children together.

♦♦♦♦

So sorry to hear your story; mine is very similar. I found out my husband has been having an affair for over a year. His story now is he hasn't been happy since my daughter was born (she's almost 12). I know we were happy and I know he is making no sense.

I have done a ton of reading here and other places and it's so incredibly sad how many stories there are and these are just the ones people tell; you wonder how many people are suffering in silence.

Just wanted to let you know I'm with you and please hang in there.

♦♦♦♦

You are in for a rough ride I'm afraid. There is no quick fix to this. You cannot reason with them, they are out of their minds and it can last a long time.

You absolutely need to prepare for life without him even if it doesn't come to that. Be prepared to hear him blame you for all this, but know that you are not responsible. It's nothing you did.

At first you will be in denial and think your situation is going to be different, but unfortunately it is not.

Eventually after the shock you will be able to redefine your priorities in life and it will get better even though it doesn't feel like it and you probably don't want to hear that just now.

♦♦♦♦

I'm new to all this too and don't know how to deal with it. My husband refuses to tell me he loves me anymore. I say it and he just stands there quietly. I wish I had words of wisdom other than I know how you feel.

♦♦♦♦

So often we get women whose forty-something husbands have been with twenty-something other women. It's like a plague. The other woman either doesn't know he's married or she doesn't care.

The husbands don't care, period, because of the way they FEEL in this circumstance. Therefore, it has nothing to do with you except you are the "all too familiar" party in this situation.

You did not start this so you cannot really DO anything about it. BUT, telling him if he wants out he should file for a divorce, is good and makes him really think. He can put his money and lust where his mouth is.

Also get a good lawyer at counsel stage right now just to keep at hand, in case. And make sure he/she has sharp fangs.

Hopefully the latter won't happen when "something happens" with the other woman. But you can't get in between anyhow, that automatically brings your dignity down and focuses them on you instead of themselves when this all blows one day.

Time will tell... so wait and pay attention to what he does, not what he says...

♦♦♦♦

I feel your pain. My husband is 41 and the other woman is 22. They worked together. The pain is immense. Even when he says their relationship is far from perfect and he knows she isn't the solution. However the words don't mean a whole lot when they are still living together.

You will make it through this and become stronger than you ever thought you were.

♦♦♦♦

Am I an idiot to hold on to this little bit of hope?

My husband and I are both in our early 50s. I have been the main family breadwinner for the past 15 years (he works part time) but this is by agreement and for reasons that suited us as a couple, and not because he is lazy or unable.

I discovered when he returned from a trip away that he hadn't been alone and that he was having an affair with a work colleague some 20 years younger. Up to that point we'd shared almost 30 very happy years together and his affair came as a total surprise. I knew he was friends with her but he's had many female friends throughout our marriage and so nothing unusual.

I was aware she'd had marital problems and had confided in him a lot but I know he's a good listener and the type of person that people choose to confide in, so no alarm bells, and he never did/said anything to set off any concerns.

He said it happened as he was curious what it would be like to have sex with someone else (I had been his only sex partner). Since then he's gone on to betray me countless times with her, including bringing her into our home when I was at work, despite having assured me he'd ended the relationship etc.

They also used the internet and texting to enjoy sex when they couldn't physically be together, and they made films of themselves for each other to enjoy.

He did all the usual things like set up secret email accounts etc., and they even had a joint secret email account where they left messages for each other.

He has told me in the recent past (before moving out) that he's in love with this other woman, although in the early days he described her as a mistake and said he felt trapped and was afraid I'd find out if he ended it.

Up until that revelation we were still sharing a bed and having sex but after he told me that I didn't feel right having sex with him and he moved to the spare room before moving out.

The other woman seems to know how to manipulate him and press all his buttons, even convincing him she miscarried their child. We tried for children but were never successful and I'm now just beginning menopause so that chance is past. He hadn't ever used the lack of children as an issue and had always seemed very happy to have independence.

The other woman has a husband and two children. She's told him in the past that she'd leave them in a heartbeat if he'd have her, although he tells me that she's now "moved on" and doesn't "feel the need for him anymore" but I understand they're still very close friends and in daily contact; not sure if in "physical" contact.

Luckily for me, to date my husband hasn't turned into a monster or anything; he's still loving and attentive when we meet (we're trying no contact at the moment) and I know I could phone him and ask for anything and he would help me. I've never had any reason to suspect that he's used our money to fund his relationship.

Throughout the past two and a half years I've gone through the whole spectrum of emotions but sadly for me despite everything I'm still in love with him. From what I've read it looks like we're only part way through this. If only I could be sure that at the end of it I'd get my old husband back I'd endure anything but I know from what I've read that even if he does come back to me eventually he won't be "my old husband" and in my more sane moments I do know that I'd be better off without him, building a new life for myself.

He's repeatedly told me that he doesn't want to throw our marriage away, that he loves me but is very confused, and that he doesn't want to come back to me until/unless he's 100% certain it's for good this time.

He says he knows how much he's hurt me and that he's been very cruel to me and he doesn't want to hurt me anymore. He says he hasn't given up hope on our marriage but that at the moment he's struggling to give up his friend, but he knows he must do this if he is to come back to me.

I've been trying to figure out what I can best do to make things as simple as possible for both of us. I don't want to just give up right now, sell everything, split it and move on as the property market is bad and we'd end up losing a lot of what we've worked so hard to achieve these past three decades and I don't want to enter old age dirt poor having worked for so long.

I can't see there's any point in trying to force him into a decision about reconciliation or otherwise, as he's not ready to make one, and I know I'm going to find it hard when he moves back here because I just look at him and feel so sad over what I've lost.

I feel I've gone from having the world's best husband who I felt was totally reliable and dependable and I truly believed he loved me unconditionally, to the situation I now find myself in.

When I don't see him although I miss him terribly and cry myself to sleep most nights, I do feel more settled overall and I know that in time I would adjust and adapt.

It will be difficult to tell people that we're separated, that somehow makes it more real; very few people know of our difficulties at the moment.

I know it would've been easier if I'd just thrown him out a long time ago (hindsight is a great thing), but I didn't and I still love him and find myself clinging to that little bit of hope.

♦♦♦♦

We all hold on to that same level of hope. It sounds like you really understand all the possibilities that could happen. Unfortunately, speaking for myself, the hardest thing is just stepping aside and giving them the time and space that they need to heal.

I too just want to hug him, hold him and make it all better. But they are broken, and we cannot heal them. They need to figure it out themselves.

I'm in a similar situation to you. I know I love my husband 100%. We are currently separated and in the next two weeks or so, had planned to start seeing each other again. However, I can tell you, after listening to everyone here, and just what my gut tells me, it is not worthwhile for either of us while the other woman is in the picture at all.

It is tough, and only you can know when you hit key times for decisions. This board helps to tell you about similar experiences, and responses that can happen. Use this to help think about decisions outside of the emotion.

Listen to other stories, and what advice would you give them? That helped me a lot to realize that sometimes we are too close as well. Our hearts play such a big part of our decisions. But try to step outside of what is happening.

♦♦♦♦

Your reply has helped me to focus on what I CAN do which is important since there's so little I can do, most of it is up to him.

♦♦♦♦

This is just my view and usual forum rules apply -- take it or leave it as you wish.

Your husband's other woman is married with kids. It doesn't sound as though she's really interested in him. Hard to believe it may be, but there does seem to be a whole section of women out there who get off on breaking up other couples without the slightest intention of breaking up their own "happy home." My guess is that they're just testing their own power of attraction: "I don't want that married guy but I wonder if I can get him away from his wife."

In your situation, I'd tell him that you want him to go No Contact with you and to test out whether the grass is really greener outside the marriage.

Tell him to throw all his efforts into romancing the other woman. Tell him to explore the sincerity of her feelings and the reality of their affair.

Wish him well and tell him you're going to get on with building your own life and that if he decides to rebuild your marriage at some point, you're open to discussion. (Not ready and waiting -- just open to discussion.)

Then go strictly No Contact. Focus on you and your life and your interests and leave him to figure out his own chaos.

♦♦♦♦

I like what you say. It makes sound sense. I do think she probably thought it would be a great coup to get him away from me, as we really were close and, I thought, impenetrable.

The few friends that are aware of the situation have been similarly stunned. Let's hope this karma thing I keep reading about is real and that she gets hers in bucket loads and real soon, and all the others like her.

There would be some practical issues in terms of total no contact for a prolonged period because our financial affairs are totally interlinked and cannot at the moment be un-linked, but I will continue to think about ways and means to address that without significant financial loss.

♦♦♦♦

You are living in limbo. It works for him, but obviously not for you. It would be helpful to you if you could take back some control for yourself.

You sound like a very grounded person. You will feel better if you take your "stuff" to a lawyer and find out the best options for you going forward. You don't have to do anything with the info, but knowledge is power.

I always think it is amazing that these wayward spouses can state they "love" their spouses or significant others, yet continue with the most incredibly hurtful behavior one human can do to another.

I have always contended that there are three in a marriage; the couple and the "marriage" itself. Many don't like to "kill" the marriage and so will just carry on.

I get that; I believe my own ex grieved the death of our marriage. But in the end, staying in a marriage that is so unhealthy is just soul killing.

I wish you the best as you move forward in making tough decisions. Just keep yourself in the forefront, and not your husband.

♦♦♦♦

I have had a preliminary chat with a lawyer (free half hour when they just explain processes to you) but probably do need to take it further and pay to see someone armed with the myriad paperwork they seem to need before being able to give you any advice at all.

I'll struggle to afford it which is why I've not done it yet, but I think I'll just have to bite the bullet as it is fundamental to any next steps for me.

♦♦♦♦

My husband admitted to not only be in love but actually loving another woman I had caught him texting with six months ago but he had convinced me he'd stopped it then and there. He obviously had not done that at all.

I have been living in a daze since he told me this. I did not recognize this man who has loved me dearly for the past ten years. He's been cold, careless and cruelly left our house four times to stay with her for a couple of days, promising to be back and make a decision.

Three times he chose me but then changed his mind after a couple of days and went back to her.

It's been like a really bad nightmare, like being in the wrong movie. Very unreal. He has decided to stay with her but keeps in touch with me. He even wants to have lunch with me next week. I have no clue why. It feels like he wants to keep me "just in case."

He says he feels sorry about what he did to me but I don't think he realizes what he has destroyed. When I investigated midlife crisis I could check all the boxes for him. He has gone completely mad. Going back and forth not being able to make up his mind.

♦♦♦♦

No, you are not an idiot. Thank God someone else feels like I do. All of my friends and family keep telling me to move on, but I hold on to that little spark of hope that he will come to his senses, tell me he doesn't love the skank that he's with, ask my forgiveness and want to come home and work on it.

He left our beautiful home for a woman he had known for six weeks. Through conversations and texts he has told me that she is far from perfect but likes the same things he does so he stays with her.

I don't get it. I have been separated for six months and keep waiting for it to get easier. I find myself lying in bed at night asking God to send him home to me.

I actually did get my wish early last month. He showed up at my door, crying, shaking, begging me to take him home. He told me he couldn't stand the whore anymore. He loved me, missed me, wanted to work it out. Never wanted to leave again. Couldn't wait to start fresh. He texted me all day long professing his love, telling me he missed me. Six days later he was gone again, back to the whore.

No, you're not crazy. I'm right there with you, missing my companion, my best friend in the world, my amazing husband. I feel for you, I really do.

♦♦♦♦

Although we hold on to the little bit of hope I agree with the many posters here who say that at the same time we have to make sure we begin to make our own lives without our partner, sad though that is to contemplate, and I hope you are able to make a start on doing this; it will take time.

I still pray every night that, if it is right, then God will send him home to me. I always say "if it is right" because sometimes what we want isn't good for us, it's just that we can't see it at the time.

So we have to trust in God to know what's best, and if it is best then we'll get our husbands back. If not, then there's a whole new wonderful life out there for us just waiting to unfold but we just haven't realized that yet, but it will come.

◆◆◆

I can't stop looking for evidence of the other woman.

I think this rollercoaster is going to make me crazy. Each time I detach he says he thought he wanted something else but he wants me and loves me and when I let my guard down he turns into a teenager again.

I've found evidence of several different women on his "private" phone but the one that he started a relationship with from the beginning is talking with him on a daily basis.

I found a text a couple of months ago that he sent her saying "I love you" so I confronted him and he was furious at me? Things have been better and he hasn't been out of town but still talks to her every day.

He sent a text this morning saying "I love you with all of my heart." I thought I would be sick. He tells me he loves me every day? He's been out of work for several months and depressed through all of this but where do you draw the line?

♦♦♦♦

You are the one in charge of where the line is in your world.

♦♦♦♦

I know. It's just discouraging. So many stressful months of having to do everything myself is exhausting but I'm doing it. I actually managed to pay all of our bills after he informed me he hadn't paid the mortgage in two months. I'm still holding on to the hope that we can have a marriage again someday.

I read the forums a lot and that's what has helped me through this. That and faith. I get up early every morning and my business is growing. I do things with the kids and have family and friends that are very supportive. I feel pretty good most of the time and have a blessed life. I do miss him being a part of it.

♦♦♦♦

I know the feeling. All the plans that we made are such a joke now. I'm sorry that you are in this place like so many of us. Just know that we understand. We really do. The emotions you are feeling are the same as mine. What a crock! How dare they do this to us! Jerks!!

♦♦♦♦

You have plenty of evidence. No need for any more. Spend your time and effort on figuring out what is best for YOU and your children (if you have any).

Unless you want to keep living with the pain of knowing your husband is involved with other women, you need to begin to make plans on your own.

Start taking control of the finances — now that you're caught up on bills, protect yourself. See a lawyer to determine what the laws are in your state.

♦♦♦♦

You need to lawyer up and get a plan SECRETLY that you can bowl him over with on a moment's notice. Then tell him that the other woman has to go permanently and with NO CONTACT, if you are to even entertain the notion of working on any kind of reconciliation.

An other woman is an addiction and he will not leave his fix unless his balls are in a vice and he has to. The only way to put him in a position that he has to stop being a teenager and start acting responsibly is to put HIS problem back on HIS shoulders and tell him gently (but mean it): You will solve this or you will lose me and your family. I do not share my husband with anybody... physical relationship... emotional relationship... nothing can be restored between us until other women are gone for good. This is marriage not the "nookie supermarket."

Take care of you. This man is not your friend right now.

♦♦♦♦

Pay attention not to what he says but what he does.

He says "I love you" then you find a text to another woman saying the same thing. Mr. Duplicity is having a ball because he's not working, his self-worth must be down but infidelity is not the answer. He's being a teenager right now.

Instant gratification with her instead of patient, honest love with you will lead to a dead end. That's the lesson he needs to learn. But he won't learn it if you hang around. And it won't change if you hang around. For you and the sake of your sanity, get out of this poisonous situation and start to heal yourself.

♦♦♦♦

He needs to get a job. Even if it is flipping burgers. He has too much time on his hands to feel sorry for himself and we all know the old saying about an *idle* mind. I'd stop enabling him and tell him to find work or get out.

The advice to "lawyer up" and explore your options is the best you have gotten on here. Once they start this shit only IMMEDIATE AND PAINFUL consequences will get his attention. And, the consequences have to be so painful that the other women become something that has to go to get rid of the pain.

♦♦♦♦

Can my marriage be saved?

So is there any hope to salvage this marriage at all or is it just wishful thinking? I'm more confused than ever.

♦♦♦♦

It is very difficult to accept that the person you love isn't who you thought they were. Take your time figuring out your own feelings. His may be impossible to know or understand!

♦♦♦♦

At your stage, everyone hates that term "time" but, time really is your friend in this. It is not time wasted, it is time for painful issues to be worked out and resolved in your mind, to do what is best for you and your family.

Hold on for now. Take care of you. Proper sleep, nutrition and exercise are important to your functioning well.

Get legal advice to know what to expect no matter what you decide. Get your ducks in a row for all possibilities.

Counseling can help you with working out the issues. Also, a counselor may offer ideas on what boundaries to set, and how you can establish them for whichever decisions you end up making.

He is in chaos now also. Watch actions, not words.

♦♦♦♦

As my therapist said "now is the time for 'show me' and not just mere words." I am so past just his words.

With that being said, he sold the car and got a different one. The bitch mobile is no more! I know that he took a loss on the deal but what matters to me is that he showed me through action that he is maybe more serious about reconciliation. Notice I said "maybe." I don't trust anything at this point.

It is a start though. Considering that this man is so cheap! For him to take a loss on a deal is a big deal for him. He likes to come ahead on everything. So I will chalk one up on his side for now but I will remain skeptical.

◆◆◆◆

We had been married for four years and I was pregnant with our second child when my husband left me for someone else. It was devastating.

I confronted my husband and he then let me know what he was up to, he did not want the relationship anymore and wanted to come home.

I was in such a tough spot, with a baby due any day, I chose to forgive and work on trust and move on with our life. It was very hard but I felt God helping me through it all.

I don't think I was ever the same. We did make a new marriage and it was good for many years to follow. Now after almost 25 years of marriage, my husband informs me he loves someone else; he is not sure he wants to be married anymore.

Here I go again, our children are just about grown, and we were preparing for a wonderful life together just the two of us again, and now I am almost 50 and will more than likely be on my own soon. I really don't know how this will all play out.

That pain I thought I was long over from years ago has come flooding back. I love my husband dearly. I just want to feel happy again.

Follow your instincts you cannot go wrong.

◆◆◆◆

I know that things can go either way so the only thing I can do is to work on me and get myself together. I will never feel safe and secure in my marriage as this whole fiasco has forever changed me. I don't see my husband with the same eyes and probably never will again.

I have a new reality that I struggle with every day. Truth is, things will never be the same between us. Something died in our relationship that we won't get back.

I'm sounding pretty negative but it's how I see things now. With all that being said, I just take one day at a time and continue to learn and grow.

My husband says he's willing to work on us and so far he's doing good things. Is it enough? Will it ever be enough? Don't know. Maybe we can work it out, maybe not.

I cannot look into the future with any kind of certainty. I can only work on me and prepare myself for whichever way this goes. I think that I'm more at peace now than before.

◆◆◆◆

How do I get him to stop lying about the other woman?

The other woman is not a secret anymore. He goes to her every night then comes back in the middle of the night to sleep on the couch since the other woman still lives with her soon-to-be-ex-husband.

The good news: today I went to look at a condo, and if everything works out, I will buy it. Get out of here as soon as possible. If I decide to buy, it will take a few weeks. Until that day I will be living in the same house as him. We don't talk; weird situation.

I asked him if the other woman will move in with him as soon as I leave. He tells me that he doesn't know. But I don't have to buy a washing machine, because "We have one extra." First time he talked about him and the other woman as "We." OK... she's not moving in but her washing machine is?

Today I received a message from him saying this weekend he has to work. I think he's going to take the other woman to a hotel to spend the night. But that's just my gut feeling.

Anyway... the thing that really bothers me is that he lies about everything like most of them do. I hate that. I don't want to know everything, really, but if you don't want me to know just say so. I want to tell him to stop lying about things that I already know/expect.

Will I make things worse by doing so?

◆◆◆◆

You are free to say whatever you want to him. And he is free to ignore you.

Stop asking him questions, since you know you can't trust his answers. And don't count on the information he volunteers to be accurate, either.

It's just the way this stuff goes, unfortunately.

♦♦♦♦

I've found that pointing out his lies, or catching him in a lie, only makes him lie more to get out of it. Otherwise I get the stupid "what, me?" look I just absolutely hate. Or my very favorite "you don't know what you're talking about."

I've also read on some posts here that they don't always realize they are lying because they have created some fantasy world and they can't separate it from reality. Self-delusion.

Don't waste your breath! And don't waste your energy thinking about what his truth is. Just live yours and be happy.

♦♦♦♦

He can't tell you the truth. This whole thing is founded and based on lies. Lies are the foundation, the brick and mortar of midlife crisis. He can't stand to hear himself say "I'm an asshole for treating you like shit, you deserve better." Saying that and meaning it would result in him having to make amends and he's not there yet.

Move out. Have your space because being together in such a situation is toxic. You might want to consider the legal implications of buying a house before your divorce is finalized.

I think it makes it so much easier if you don't expect ANYTHING AT ALL from your husband. By anything, I mean anything, including truth and honesty. If you don't expect anything, you won't be disappointed. It works like a charm.

♦♦♦♦

My ex used to get his kicks from lying to me. He'd lie about ANYTHING... getting a haircut when he said he was off to get an oil change, stupid shit like that. In the end, I didn't call him out on the lies (and he was a terrible, hopelessly transparent liar), but I'd just kind of roll my eyes and say, "OK." Because I knew he was lying, and that the harder I pushed him to tell the truth, the more he'd lie.

That would make him defensive and he'd stomp off muttering, "It doesn't matter what I say, you believe what you want." Yep, because I knew the truth and it DIDN'T matter what he said. And he knew that, too.

◆◆◆◆

I got the same BS from my ex: "We can never get back together because YOU would never BELIEVE me about anything!" Well, duh, that's right. Because he was a pathological liar and did not know how to be either honest or transparent.

The thing is he was not like this just in midlife crisis (unless he was in midlife crisis for the entire duration of our marriage). He lied from the get-go.

Because his lies were so petty, and mostly over things that didn't matter to me, I made the mistake of thinking this was not a HUGE issue. He, of course, would always blame his lying on his ex-wife. "She would freak out about every little thing so I was afraid to tell you because I thought you'd react the same way."

It was really and truly messed up, and it bothered me very much that he would do this, but I never thought it would culminate in a major crisis of epic proportions the way it did. In retrospect, I feel I should have known better.

You can tell him all you want about his lying, but it won't make a bit of difference. He will still lie. It's all he knows how to do right now.

Of course, it would be easier (you'd think) to say "I'd rather not answer that" or "I don't want you to know what I'm up to right now," but they won't because they are so afraid of conflict and think we will follow that up with more questions. So they lie.

My ex couldn't even tell the truth to his hookers, for Christ's sake! And again, over stupid, insignificant shit that they would not have even cared about.

He would be with one whore, and tell the other that he spent the weekend with his friends and go into elaborate detail about what they supposedly did all weekend long.

Why on earth do you need to lie and explain things that are totally fabricated to a whore? I'm telling you, these guys are just plain nuts.

So, you can tell your husband the lying bothers you, or request him to be truthful, but it won't make any difference. They are like rebellious teenagers and if it's something that WE want, they are going to rebel and not do it, plain and simple.

◆◆◆◆

It's fascinating, I told him this past weekend that I know he lies. He said, "about what?" I said "if I told you, you'd lie about it..."

It's so ridiculous and amazing that I have come to expect anything and everything. The rollercoaster continues and I think I am facing backwards!

There's no point in asking for THE truth. They will only give you THEIR truth.

♦♦♦♦

Some of them will only give you as much truth as they want you to have. It was a form of control and power for my ex. He FELT powerless, so if he knew something I didn't, that was a big "fuck-you" to me and proved what an independent guy he was.

No woman was going to tell HIM what to do (even if that woman wasn't particularly interested in telling him what to do), because he'd just lie about his plans and do what he wanted.

My ex's mantra his whole life is that it's better to beg for forgiveness than ask for permission. What he didn't count on was being denied forgiveness — once I found out he had no intention of not repeating the same behavior.

♦♦♦♦

I spoke to a friend yesterday; she got a call from him. She told me he sounded as if he really needed someone to talk to, to tell his side of the story. Because she knows everything, she just let him talk.

It was a 45 minute "speech," defending himself and feeling sorry for himself and the other woman. All his friends dropped him (not true), he knows how I feel but I didn't give him the chance to work things out with me (not true). In the last three years (after having a burnout) he realized he wasn't happy. He tried to talk about it with me (not true) but I didn't understand. Now that he found the other woman he has never felt this happy.

When you listen to him talk and don't know everything, it all sounds very rational. But people who really know him, know that it doesn't make any sense. It's kind of comforting that he doesn't only lie to me, but to everyone. I wonder what he tells the other woman.

You are right: it's his truth. And every time someone tells him different he thinks its all lies.

♦♦♦♦

Lies. They lie to everyone, and of course, to themselves.

My ex started out his "new and improved" relationship on a foundation of lies. He was presenting himself as single on eHarmony even though I was still living at home and he was seeing hookers.

He described himself on his profile as "loyal and trustworthy" which was just laughable. He lied by omission for several months with his new girlfriend, by not telling her I was still living at the house. He finally had to come clean as I'm sure she was wondering after dating several months why she was never invited over to his place.

He HAD to have spun a bunch of lies to make himself look good, otherwise, why would she accept this? I'm sure it came out like "oh, things just didn't work out for us and even though she was controlling and unstable, I let her stay there as long as she needed because I just couldn't throw her out."

He surely didn't say "oh, I feel guilty pressuring her to leave because I was seeing whores and betrayed my life partner and now I'm moving on to you because you don't know my history and I can pretend to be the perfect boyfriend."

These men in midlife crisis lie. My ex's relationship with his new girlfriend is built on a foundation of lies. I believe his whole life is built on lie upon lie upon lie. No wonder he is so afraid to look at himself. His whole life is a fraud and a facade.

♦♦♦♦

Can a man ever resist the temptation of a much younger woman?

My husband had an affair with his best friend's wife. He's 46 she's 40. I don't think age has anything to do with it. It is the emotional/physical attraction rather than age.

♦♦♦♦

Unless he has damage to the area of his brain that controls impulses, YES, a man CAN control his actions, about women, food, money, you name it.

We *all* have choices about all sorts of things. At midlife, we just start questioning the values that led us to make the choices we've made in the past, and some of us start experimenting with different choices.

♦♦♦♦

All humans COULD (as in those who want to, can find someone willing); there is no one who is so universally unattractive that they cannot find someone.

Those who want to often do. Not all do. Some THINK.

♦♦♦♦

Of course men can resist temptations and control themselves! So can women!

Each of us are tempted by countless things every day and manage to resist. Depends on our character, integrity, and value system.

Whether it's being on a diet and reaching for that brownie or having an affair, it doesn't matter. WE EACH MAKE CHOICES. We do what WE WANT TO DO.

Nothing too mysterious about it and no other reason beyond that.

♦♦♦♦

Ex-husband did for many years. He was able to resist until he chose not to.

♦♦♦♦

Physical attractiveness is totally in the eye of the beholder. Temptation is always there for all. The cheat shows weakness, where the non-cheaters don't. It has nothing to do with sex or looks. It's character.

♦♦♦♦

Of course a man can resist. Many of them do on a daily basis. They pack it on up; they turn it around; they take it on home. Why? Because integrity, commitment, character, and family mean more to them than acting on whims.

♦♦♦♦

Replace "man" with "woman." If a woman can a man can.

♦♦♦♦

I am a woman who resisted cheating. For 20 years I never once cheated. I never even had the urge to. A couple of times over those 20 years I have been propositioned but didn't think twice about it cause I deeply loved him and would NEVER do damage to our children. It's ALL a matter of self-control and the values you hold dear in this life.

♦♦♦♦

I agree, we do have a choice. It is nice and flattering if other guys think you are attractive and I always thought a little flirt was not wrong. And I mean a little one. But at the end we have the choice.

I am not so sure any more if people in midlife crisis should be excused. In the case of my ex I would say there was lack of impulse control and FEAR. I have fear, too. I am not walking out and going to bed with any guy who promises me

great sex and listens to me because I am afraid or unsatis-
fied. I don't do this within my relationship. To be honest, I
don't do it when I am single either.

Midlife crisis or personality disorder which has been ag-
gravated by midlife crisis, I don't care anymore. It is shabby;
it is hurtful and cruel. It is callous and has the philosophy: I
don't give a damn about anybody else other than me.

No thank you.

♦♦♦♦

LIFE is not excusing them, so a left behind spouse who
makes allowances isn't really helping. Being held accountable is the ONLY way they're going to figure out how to get
OUT of crisis.

Midlife crisis induced behavior and muddled thinking
can be explained or understood, but not excused.

♦♦♦♦

I think that being held accountable does not do a lot for
many either. They are off in their world and would happily
nuke it as long as they can have their adolescent dreams/
new realities with other women and other lives.

♦♦♦♦

Precisely. If we simply look the other way, cover for them,
make excuses, etc., then they CAN have their "adolescent
dreams" at no cost.

Now, they may still choose those "adolescent dreams"
even if we (as a society, not just as individual left behind
spouses) hold them accountable. But, there IS a price to pay,
and paying it for them is NOT holding them accountable.

Now, I'm NOT advocating directly trying to punish them.
I'm just saying, don't enable the midlife crisis behavior and

then expect it to change! Let them deal with whatever natu-rally comes their way.

♦♦♦♦

To not be tempted is not resisting anything. It is when they ARE tempted that resisting or not counts.

♦♦♦♦

I'm not sure I see this the same way. I do think it "counts" when someone makes sure they avoid situations where they might be tempted. For example, to make it a policy not to go out and have drinks with someone of the opposite sex would "count" in my book.

Or refusing to go into bars if you're an alcoholic, so you won't be "tempted."

I think both those actions are aware and responsible and "count."

♦♦♦♦

Tempted to go to the bar, but resisted is resisting. Not going into compromising situations is resisting.

To not be tempted, is to not have or feel any pull in that direction. Not having an interest, is not the same as resisting temptation. Resisting is when self-will is USED. If I don't eat something that holds no appeal, that's not resisting. Resist-ing is walking away from that donut, not walking away from Brussels sprouts.

Resisting temptation takes effort or at the very least con-scious choice.

♦♦♦♦

But if you consciously decide to not participate in some social events aren't you then also consciously deciding to re-sist being tempted? I don't think a person has to put them-selves in a situation to actively resist anything. Wouldn't the wiser thing be to simply resist participating in the social situation and thereby not putting oneself in the position to compromise oneself?

I'm not quite certain I understand the whole concept of being "tempted to stray" when you love someone and are "happily" married to them. Just never dawned on me, nor did I have any desire, to go out socializing with anyone without my husband... guess I'm too old-fashioned.

Even pre-marriage, I'd do lunch with co-workers, but never dinner or out for drinks. First, never wanted to be *friends* with people I worked with -- friendly, but not friends -- just led to too many problems in the workplace, but, second, people go home to their families after work. Either I'm absolutely dense or I'm lost in a time warp and not able to *get with the times*!

♦♦♦♦

First paragraph yes, is conscious choice, and so resisting temptation. Second paragraph most honest people with good marital intensions fall into this category. That is living a good life, and being free of temptation. but not actively resisting. Just free of.

Actual RESISTING of temptation is when an urge or chemistry or TEMPTATION is PRESENT and resisted.

♦♦♦♦

I worked in corporate America in the 80's when women in management were few and far between. I had to travel frequently with all men. I made it a point NEVER to be alone with one man — either at dinner or for drinks — when traveling. It's not that I "felt" tempted, it's just that I had the good sense not to put myself in a situation like that.

Anyway, I think we're splitting hairs. I think the point may just be that there is a level of consciousness and awareness that needs to be present for temptation to both be avoided and resisted.

◆◆◆◆

When my husband said he never took up other offers it was because they did not tempt. This one worked at making the approach acceptable sounding. He succumbed, to me, at the first ACTUAL temptation. The rest were just day to day existence. The invitation to wrong, that actually does tempt, is where the character or lack truly shows.

To use the example of the bar. They are all over. Most walk by without feeling a pull. That's not resisting temptation because there is no temptation. The one who does feel that pull, and does not go in, is resisting temptation because that person is tempted.

Honesty and morals go a long way to avoid temptation, and for many that is all that is needed. But when something gets through to the point of FEELING temptation that is where resistance shines through to being a virtue. That is the point at which too many fall.

◆◆◆◆

We live in a consumer society and there are articles about the increasing narcissism in our times. I would subscribe to this. People have become exchangeable, younger versions are in demand, etc.

Ethics and morals might hold accountable. They have changed, too. Life holds accountable. You are right. I like reading about karma. It somehow soothes me.

◆◆◆◆

WE can choose to hold them accountable, or at least, not excuse them or try to protect them from the consequences of their choices.

No, we can't control "society" or what it "condones" (or appears to tolerate).

♦♦♦♦

Everybody faces temptation. Everybody can find it if they go looking, and anybody can put it out there. Whether you're at home, visiting someone's home, in an office full of "potential," at church, in a club or bar, or at 35,000 feet, there are always opportunities.

But, you can resist. Didn't we learn that lesson in high school?

It's only at midlife that we seem to lose our ability to deal with it.

♦♦♦♦

Many with integrity and a backbone do every day of their lives.

"A man without integrity is NOT a man."

♦♦♦♦

Exactly. A REAL man can. A pitiful imitation of a male of the species? Not so much.

♦♦♦♦

We all have choices about all sorts of things. At midlife, we just start questioning the values that led us to make the choices we've made in the past, and some of us start experimenting with different choices.

I really think this bears repeating as sometimes the midlife crisis thing gets carried away as if people have lost their sanity. Of course, to the left behind spouse, sometimes the wayward spouse's actions seem to prove that would be true.

But it all comes down to choices, whether we think they're logical or not. By keeping this in mind, I can realistically view my husband less as a victim of something that he can't "help."

♦♦♦♦

I think what catches a lot of people up is, one bad choice snowballs into a series of them, and THAT is what causes the "crisis" part of the experience.

That bad choice may or may NOT be the infidelity one; it could be a job change or some other catalyst. It can be tough to see the whole picture, and where things actually started going off the rails, until the whole train wrecks.

♦♦♦♦

Yes, a man or woman can resist temptation if they want too, some do and others don't.

Some want the best of both worlds. My ex said he never intended to leave, so I took that as he was going to have an affair on the side and I would never know but I caught him.

At the end of the day I have some satisfaction in knowing I got the best years of his life, the 28-year old is married to a 50-year old man, why she would even want someone that old I can't even fathom, but those declining years of his should be interesting. Wonder if she will be there to look after him as the years go by?

♦♦♦♦

My ex said, everybody is fending for themselves. If he needs to be looked after, he does not expect anybody to do so. He says this now, of course, with the arrogance of a relatively healthy guy who has found his second youth, or so he thinks.

We should not care about their aging and future frailty. We really should not, as they have left us. Leave them with their lives, leave them alone, leave them to their karma or whatever it will be.

I know it is easier said than done. I am still emotionally involved, somehow. I am still very angry.

◆◆◆◆

I've always thought that a married man who would cheat on his wife is someone who proves he doesn't have what it takes to live in a relationship and is a very, very bad bet.

◆◆◆◆

Do you really think that a new relationship will prosper unless the two parties do something to find out why they act the way they do? No, they will recycle old baggage in the new relationship.

That having been said, from all I have read you will be better off without this man. I know that you are still in agony and hurting so badly that you can't see that now. But the man you have described seems to be more than just midlife crisis... he seem to be a narcissist. (Notice my quantifier... the word "seems.")

Work hard on preparing yourself to take care of YOU. It will keep you so busy that you won't have time to obsess about him. Hard to do, I know; but it is the best course.

◆◆◆◆

My ex said to me that I wrongly assume that people are as thoughtful as I am, or on the same or a similar level of awareness. So they might be very happy about a so-called carefree, superficial, happy-crappy relationship. This might be their dream of a relationship. Doing things together occasionally, going on carefree holidays and seeing each other when they feel like it.

No commitment except the one -- and here the dark clouds are coming -- of controlling each other. Because both of them are obsessed with each other, more out of fear of losing each other, as they both have cheated on their ex-partners and still might think about cheating on their new partners.

So the only dark cloud it seems to me is not being able to trust each other. On the other hand, this is their modus operandi, as they have done this for quite a while. Maybe they get a kick out of it.

◆◆◆◆

I find that most people are not analytical (or if you prefer "thoughtful") and levels of awareness are highly variable but not usually high. Too much trouble.

Superficiality seems to be the order of the day. Just watch all the idle chit-chat socializing going on in workplaces. People blabbing ALL about their personal lives and families to veritable strangers. Leads to massive unproductivity AND in many cases office affairs.

If they were doing their job right and exercising appropriate boundaries; they wouldn't have time to develop deep intimate relationships at the office with inappropriate others. But THIS would require a deeper level of awareness of pitfalls wouldn't it?

◆◆◆◆

My ex was a very handsome, fit and intelligent man, he ended up being quite wealthy too. He had some stunning women chasing him over the years. He was never interested. He was known for his integrity and family values.

When the crisis hit, he became a very immoral man. Within two weeks, he began a relationship and moved out and gave away the life we had together. There had been no early warnings, no sign at all he was not happy. I thought we had it made, somehow, his reality shifted.

It was a very traumatic time for everyone, me, our children, family and friends. And ultimately even for him. His other woman was a skanky predator, that eventually died off.

Currently he is with a woman half his age, who I think seems sweet by all reports, but somewhat unintelligent and will be the submissive person he seems to need now.

The shelf life of this relationship may be short lived, and I suspect he is with her because of his low self-esteem and her availability. Other than a general muse about it I don't care to know more.

♦♦♦♦

Was I wrong to snoop?

When I was in the preparing-for-divorce-but-giving-him-a-chance-to-change period, I didn't stop snooping. I needed the snooping because my gut was telling me my ex was lying, and that makes me crazy.

What I did do was stop picking fights about it. I pretty much assumed he was lying about anything he told me, and unfortunately, I wasn't often wrong. Oh, he may have been technically telling me at least a partial truth, but it was hardly ever the whole story.

One of his complaints during The Speech was that I was too controlling. Ok, so whenever he informed me about what he was doing (truthfully or not), I had no comment. No opinion that I would voice to him whatsoever.

And that drove him NUTS. Totally bonkers. It's like he had no compass of his own to follow without me telling him how I expected him to behave.

Sometimes he would get really frustrated and rebel against how he thought I would have advised him. I didn't even need to be present in order to be controlling, I guess.

I hoped if I stopped being his moral prop, he'd be able to figure out right from wrong on his own. He never really did.

♦♦♦♦

I continue to snoop, and probably will. I can't help it. I can't depend on him to tell me the truth. Also, as far as snooping is concerned, I have texted phone numbers off of my bill that are suspicious and have found that every single woman I've contacted didn't know that he was married. They were told he was divorced with kids.

My husband told me that all he wanted was sex from these women. However, now that he told me that he's broken off all contact, some of the women I got hold of have texted him and told him that they don't care if he's married and want him anyway.

So now it dawned on me, late in the game that he needs to change his phone number. Why I didn't demand that sooner is beyond me.

◆◆◆◆

Don't demand he change his phone number. If these women text him, and he allows it to continue, you have your answer, don't you? Right now you have a way to verify the truth. If you insist that he changes his phone number, he almost certainly will, with a different carrier — and a new password. Or buy a secret phone and keep the old account as a decoy.

Let him think you're gullible and stupid. Don't tip your hand. If you verify his statements with his actual behavior, you'll have gut-level evidence that maybe he can be trusted now. But if you keep your mouth shut and your eyes open, you'll have the truth either way, right?

◆◆◆◆

We have a family plan with a carrier that has all of our phones together, a package deal. They have texted him. He hasn't responded at all. I am just bothered that other women have his number.

If he changes it, I'll still have access to the phone records. I have a separate login password to get into our account. What he doesn't realize is that I put myself as an additional administrator in that account.

Yes, he could go get a secret phone. He could have 1000 different emails. That's the world in which we live. He could hide stuff from me very easily. With that being said, I still want that number changed.

There's no way that anybody can track anybody else completely. I figure that if he gets a new number then I can track it easier because he will have to give that number out. So whoever texts him or calls him, I'll know from what date the number was given.

The number he has is the same number he's had for a long time now. It's going to be a big hassle to get his new number out to all the people that need to have it but ask me if I care.

Furthermore, I have texted these women and have received a lot of information from them. More than what he ever told me. I try to be non-confrontational in my texts as I come to assume that these women didn't know he was married. They have told me that they wouldn't ever contact him again.

One women wanted proof so I accepted her friend request on Facebook and I posted family pictures for her to see. Lots of them. We then instant messaged each other and she was shocked but gave me a lot of information that I otherwise wouldn't have had.

So my text messages go something like this: "I am the wife of ... and I am curious as to the nature of your relationship with my husband." They then text me back without being on the defense and I get information out of them.

I've become quite the expert. Sickening, isn't it! My point being, that if he changes his number, then these women really can't text or call him again because they won't have his new number unless he gives it to them. Then I'll have my answer as I have become an expert snooper.

◆◆◆◆

I know it feels "safer" for these women not to have his number, but it really isn't, and you're giving up the element of surprise. But, you have to do what you have to do, so good luck with it.

◆◆◆◆

I feel like the world's biggest fool for even considering reconciling with this low down, no good, cheating, lying, dog! What am I thinking! He has been lying to me for at least three years!

The more I snoop, the more I find. How do I stop the snooping! It's crazy! Yet, I feel that I have to know the truth. Now that I know what I know, I feel like a fool for trying to move forward with reconciliation. I didn't ask for this, deserve this, or want this. I'm just so angry and sad right now.

He said that he has stopped all communication (like I could possibly know that) and that he wants to reconcile. He says that since we have hit rock bottom that we can rise above and have a better marriage than before. Sounds great, but then I remember rule #1: they lie, lie, lie.

I asked him, rather told him, that I wouldn't get into his car ever again. We spent weeks looking for the perfect car and finally found it.

Now that he has used it to take his bitches for rides, I told him that I would never ever step foot in that car. He said he'd sell it.

Today I found out that he wants new rims, tires and other work done. I'm so pissed! He's actually putting that car before me! Time to wake up!! He's a liar!! Point blank!

So now I'm just sitting here ready to throw in the towel. I'm tired of all of this crap. I miss the man he used to be. I miss our closeness. We could practically finish each other's sentences. Now I sit here alone wondering what to do. I'm so pissed off.

♦♦♦♦

There was no "WE" that was screwing other women... there was only HIM. He's not ready to take personal responsibility for his actions. He wants to make HIS betrayal your mutual problem and let you shoulder a big chunk of the burden for his behavior. And that completely misses the point. Completely.

This is a deep problem within him, and that's the only reason your marriage is in trouble, really. You can't slap a bit of duct tape on your marriage, stop snooping, and think because the outside isn't looking cracked any longer the inside is no longer fatally flawed.

A chain is only as strong as its weakest link, and a marriage is only as strong as its weakest partner.

I was dumb. I had to have evidence, over and over and over again, that my husband couldn't face what he had singlehandedly done to our relationship, and kept doing to our relationship, and he never even fucked another woman as far as I know.

So I know that gut wrenching disappointment you have in yourself right now for thinking maybe this time will be different and of course it wasn't.

So sit with this for a while. Don't get into it with him just yet because he'll promise you whatever you demand explicitly without understanding why you need those things.

Figure out what you need for the next say, three months. Not from him, just in general. Be content to not divorce instead of thinking that you're reconciling.

If you focus on what you would like your life to look like instead of putting a lot of fruitless energy into a marriage he's really not ready to repair, you might save yourself some heartache and give him time to understand the problem is bigger than the symptoms.

♦♦♦♦

I totally understand the snooping because it is so important to know the truth even if it is self-destructive.

♦♦♦♦

Your obsessive need to know is NOT crazy. It is because you had a reality and now that lies shattered in pieces around your feet and now, what is real? So you go looking for the pieces of the jigsaw so that you can fit them together and get in touch with the 'reality' you had no idea you were part of.

♦♦♦♦

Got home and after snooping I found the cheap other cell phone. Knew it! He actually texted some slut while we were on our mini vacation/reconciliation road trip!

I was livid! Of course I got the same old speech (I'm sorry, blah, blah, blah). So now I have to decide what to do. He made a counseling appointment today. Don't know how I feel anymore. We actually were making headway, or so I thought. I'm so depressed and angry. He's a serial cheater and liar. NOT the man I married.

♦♦♦♦

Is he cheating if he says it's just phone sex with someone he never met?

Two years ago things began to change in our marriage. A year ago I went looking for proof that he was cheating. What I found were bills for two porn sites. We were in the process of losing our home and he's paying to be on porn sites.

Then I go looking into his phone and find three women's numbers I don't know. He claims they are from his poker site. Two months later he confesses because I have gone through everything and found proof he can't deny.

We have been in counseling and he now refuses to go because he doesn't need the help. According to him I need to continue going to get over MY anger issues.

This is a very abridged version of the story. He claims he never met up with these women only talked to them on the phone. I can't prove otherwise. He says it's not infidelity; counselor says its emotional infidelity I say it's cheating.

I guess my question is, would anyone else be willing to believe their husband? Am I too stuck to think straight? Is this infidelity?

◆◆◆◆

I agree its emotional infidelity and shouldn't be tolerated.

◆◆◆◆

I am sorry you are hurting. It is. No doubt. When you start looking, you will find. What is the point of your search? Where do you want to go? And where does he?

◆◆◆◆

Your gut told you to go looking. Trust it.

First, they omit the truth. Then they lie. When they're absolutely caught, they minimize. "Oh, I never fucked her, I couldn't go through with it. I wouldn't cheat on you." "We

were just talking — she was helping me with our marriage."
Yeah, yeah, tell me some more bullshit, buddy.

Even if he never broke the letter of the law, he sure as hell
broke the spirit of the law. And THAT is the real problem —
that he thinks he needs to find a loophole to go get attention
from other women.

♦♦♦♦

I wouldn't believe him. It is infidelity no matter how you
slice it. I've always said that men's mantra goes something
like this: Deny, deny, deny, then defend, defend, defend. I
think you already know the answer but if you need honest
feedback from those who have been there, I think you already got it. So sorry. What a damn drag!!

♦♦♦♦

If you think it is infidelity, by the terms that YOU had for
your relationship, it is. There is no absolute measure ... but if
he crossed the line you had for your relationship, then there
is no question. Unless you were okay with him having relationships with other women behind your back, be it by telephone, internet or any other means ... it is infidelity.

♦♦♦♦

Why do they turn it around and make it about us??? Last
night's argument was about how I'm always telling him what
he's not doing for me and that I'm asking for too much. Really! After 19 years of marriage the last two years of hell and
I'm asking for too much! I'm "too strict" I'm too "black/white
there is no gray area with you."

I appreciate the support, of course I see it as cheating. It's
just killing me to walk away. I have two beautiful children
who didn't ask for this crap. The guilt over hurting them is
worse than the thought of leaving my husband. I don't understand how he can just throw it all away.

Thanks for not telling me how stupid the question sounded. I feel like such a fool

♦♦♦♦

You are not a fool! So many of us have asked that question, it is not even funny! Hell, mine did not come home one night and there I was telling everyone on this board "No, my husband would never fuck around on me!"

Yeah right... Been asking myself for four years when is it my turn... When do I get to breathe... Well I never got the chance to breathe and I am pretty sure that I did not get any credit either... Now he is shocked that I finally served him with divorce papers.

Take care of you and leave him to his own miserable self!! It is going to be a long time before the meltdown is done!

♦♦♦♦

You are not a FOOL! My marriage vows said, I pledge myself to you, only you, til death do us part, period.

Not PS: We can have as many other emotional affairs, phone sex, porno site attending, etc. AS WE WANT!

I am in a similar situation where my husband has multitudes of "so-called" just friends on Facebook along with an "emotional affair" friend out of state.

I see this as "there is nothing to talk about until our relationship/marriage" is the only thing you are working on.

Stand tall and hang tuff, you need to make him think he may not get you back.

♦♦♦♦

The other thing I would consider is that there is more to this than he is saying. They almost always minimize. "Oh, I didn't SLEEP with her, we're Just Friends," or, like my wayward spouse said "it was only oral sex I got from just one hooker that I saw only three times."

It ended up being several hookers, way more than three times, and all kinds of sex.

And in marriage counseling during our false reconciliation, he gave the excuse that because of his erectile dysfunction he panicked and just had to "get it to work again" and thought an escort was the way to handle this, instead of going to the doctor (he was too embarrassed) or talking about it with me (again, felt too embarrassed).

I also found tons of porn on his computer where this was never an issue in our marriage. Hardcore stuff, too. I think my husband developed a sex addiction, or had one all along that he was keeping under wraps most of our marriage.

Bottom line, you can't believe their version is the truth, the whole truth, and nothing but the truth. There may be kernels of truth, but it isn't the whole story, I can guar-an-damn-tee you.

♦♦♦♦

My now ex-husband claimed that when he had phone and internet sex chats with people, it wasn't an affair because they were not actually together.

I used this to explain my point of view: "Would you have done what you were doing with these women while I was standing next to you watching/listening?"

He didn't want to answer so I said, "I'll assume that means 'no.' If you wouldn't do it with these women with me witnessing it, and would only do it if I was not around, then it is by definition CHEATING. You are hiding something from me, getting sexual and/or emotional gratification from someone else, and you don't want your wife to find out."

♦♦♦♦

How do I set boundaries and what should they be?

I need help with what the consequences should be without being too ridiculous and actually achievable. Preferably without having to leave my house with three confused kids in tow!

I know this sounds really stupid but I want to be told what to say!!

♦♦♦♦

A boundary states what YOU WILL DO if he does a specific thing. He may still choose to do that thing, in which case, you MUST be willing and able to follow through with whatever you said you would do. And of course, you have to be able to prove that he did whatever it was that violated the boundary.

So, for each item on your list so far, what would be the DESIRED behavior? What would be YOUR RESPONSE if he didn't perform the desired behavior?

♦♦♦♦

You can't change what he thinks OR what he chooses to tell others about you or the marriage. You can't stop him from calling the other woman, coming and going as he pleases, or leaving the door unlocked or reading porn on the family PC.

You can't make him help around the house, join you for dinner, share his phone messages with you, or even leave the phone outside the bedroom.

But NONE of those behaviors are things a husband would do. They're actually things one might do if one was trying to convince a spouse to leave the marriage! He may be trying to make you angry and miserable enough to divorce him.

Is he succeeding? WOULD you divorce him if none of these things changed?

If not, what WOULD you do, if you knew he was planning on continuing to behave this way for the rest of your marriage? For instance, would you look into living separately, getting an apartment so you wouldn't have as many household chores (such as a lawn) to deal with, and could lock your doors and know they'd stay locked? You also wouldn't have to worry about what he was doing on the family computer or with his phone, because it wouldn't be done right under your nose.

You still can't do a thing about what he feels or says about you, even if it's false. But he'd have a lot less reason to say anything if you were already out of the picture, officially.

And, he might take you a little more seriously, and treat you with a little more respect, if you stood up to him this way. He can continue to live his life this way, but NOT if he wants you to be a part of it.

But if you won't divorce him, and can't find a way to separate from him for a while, what can you change about your daily activities to be less of a spouse to HIM, until HE starts acting like more of a spouse to YOU?

Nobody can tell you exactly what to do or say; only you know your exact situation and what you are emotionally and physically capable of tolerating. We each have to find our way, and find our own strength to make the changes we need. All we can do is encourage you, and reassure you that, no matter how scary, difficult, or seemingly impossible it may appear, you CAN make changes that will eventually make things better for you.

◆◆◆◆

I've taken a few days to think this over, so I could be as honest as I can with you about my answer.

I really didn't do anything to save my marriage except detach. As a result of the midlife crisis "diet" I lost weight, I then went on to change the way I "live my life" i.e., I started finding joy in life again, despite him.

It was a long road back for him. When he came home, it wasn't all about "me" for over a year. And then we took baby-steps for another year after that. We're currently two and a half years into reconciliation and we're "still" a work in progress.

This is a long, hard road. It's filled with pitfalls, PTSD, stress of every magnitude... plus hope.

I don't know what your belief system entails, but I took great strength in God's promises. I never believed that I would end up without my husband. I always had faith that he would once again be "mine." I just couldn't let it (or him) go.

◆◆◆◆

How can I trust anything he says?

Everything was going along fine, regular sex, "I love you," physical affection... all the regular stuff. Then one day he says he just doesn't care if the marriage lasts or not. It's not important anymore.

We've worked on things, he blames it mostly on stress (which admittedly, he has had a TON of) but takes responsibility for letting it go downhill in his head without saying anything to me. I was blindsided by this.

So now, whenever he says anything to me, I wonder if it's true, or I over-analyze it. Like if he says he loves me, I wonder, "Really? Cause you said you loved me when you had one foot out the door."

If he says "Thank you for doing chore Y today" (whatever that may be) and I think "Well, is it enough?"

He'll say he's committed to the marriage because he has to be. And I think "So he's just doing this because he 'has' to, not because he wants to?"

I'll ask him a question, and regardless of the answer, I'm just questioning it. It may be a perfectly good and normal answer that a month ago would have been great, and now, I trust nothing he says.

I hate being like this, I hate being insecure. I hate being angry and hurt because of what he's done to our marriage. I do "forgive" him, I do love him, and I'm seeing a marriage counselor, but is there anyone who has forgiven their husband's betrayal (whether it was an emotional affair, physical affair, or anything else)? Do you feel like I do or did you at one point? How do you get over it and trust again?

♦♦♦♦

Basically I think what I've learned is to accept and detach.

Accept meaning take an honest look at him for who he is now without denying it or glossing over it (which it seems you are doing).

Then detach, meaning if his behavior is not healthy for you, get away. You decide how much you need to protect yourself; timeouts, separation or whether staying married is right for you.

Realize in all of this you have choices. The choices may not be easy to make, but recognizing that you are not at the mercy of his whims and moods and insensitive comments is very empowering.

Detach from him by drawing boundaries of what you need to protect yourself. When he's rude or moody, you can still be happy and upbeat. Choosing to live with him may mean you build your support network of positive people and leave him to stew in his negativity.

At first it's hard and feels like the rug has been pulled out from under us. Today your husband is someone who is stressed, unstable and not coping well. Take precautions knowing that fact.

I denied for too long accepting my husband for where he was really at, and making the necessary steps to protect myself. I wanted him to be the old him and that prevented me from opening my eyes, working on protecting myself from being hurt.

It may be you don't trust him. Living with someone "new" is not settling, there are too many unknowns. I cautiously stepped back and watched: how would he respond to me? If I didn't like it I pulled back. He noticed, but it was through distance, not trying to change him.

♦♦♦♦

For one, you don't really know there hasn't been any physical cheating. You believe him, and that's fine, but if I had a dollar for every spouse who came here and said he's not cheating because the other person is gay/when would he have the time?/I know he'd never do that, well, let's just say I wouldn't miss the $38,000 in back child support my ex owes me.

For two, he betrayed you even if there wasn't any penis-in-vagina action. My ex was choosing to spend time at the bar with his buddy instead of being home with his family. And I'm not talking an hour or so after work — I'm talking every day for hours. We would go weeks without seeing him awake. My home was his crash-pad.

He is not committed to the marriage for any reason. He hasn't left it yet because he is still getting something out of it, but that's not commitment. That's just being too weak to leave.

You are feeling insecure because you're in a very insecure situation. Don't try to talk yourself out of it... your gut is screaming at you for a reason. You would be very foolish to trust him when he clearly is only in your marriage for as long as it suits him.

I'm sorry. I know that's a bad situation, because I lived it, too. But that's what you have to reconcile yourself to for NOW.

♦♦♦♦

You can't really say that he betrayed you if he never lied to you. The fact that you're willing to accept a particular situation is your doing, not his. If he wants to leave, let him go. Do you really want him to stay because of duty or guilt anyway?

◆◆◆◆

He betrayed me. He did lie to me, both actively and by omission. But his betrayal was mostly taking attention that should have been given to his family and giving it to the weird buddy. And he's gone because I made him leave.

◆◆◆◆

After 24 years of a great marriage (so I thought), I have come to find out in the last two weeks that my husband has had an affair while deployed overseas. Now he's deployed again, state-side, and he has been fooling around with lots of women.

For the last two months he has had an all-out affair with two women at the same time. I called them both. He met them through a dating service. They were told by him that he was divorced with one kid. They had no idea. We have three and are very much married. I feel bad for them because they weren't out looking for a married man.

Now that all has been revealed, he wants to work things out. I'm appalled, heartbroken and confused. I've started counseling and he will start counseling as well this week. When he returns in two months, he wants us to do marriage counseling.

Sounds good but the problem is, I don't trust him. I don't know what to believe anymore. I'm so devastated and yet a part of me is hopeful. I guess what I'm asking from all of you is, do I try to work it out or is it just a matter of time before he does this again. Like they say, once a cheater, always a cheater.

♦♦♦♦

One of the things about being in a relationship where you're blindsided by betrayal is that you get a little bit of tunnel vision. You don't see things that are blindingly obvious, so obvious in fact that we often forget to take them into consideration.

One of those things is that you have as many options in this marriage as he does. I'm not saying you should go out and have an affair, too, no, of course not. But as he has already broken the marriage contract — the reciprocal agreement that defined the rules you agreed to follow while living together — your obligations are up for renegotiation, too.

So if you always were the spouse who took care of the home, you get to think, why? Why is this my job? I don't think I want this job anymore. It's all up for grabs.

You don't have to sit around and wait for him to decide what's next. You may choose to, but you don't HAVE to. If you look at yourself honestly, and decide, no, I can't ever trust this man again, then go ahead and walk away now. No one will blame you. It's OK, really. A lot of people on the midlife club forum wish they had done just that in hindsight.

There's another option, too. You can learn to live in a state of non-divorce. You don't actively try to repair the marriage, but you don't actively pursue divorce, either.

If he's still in the mindset of "I want to be married but I'm entitled to cheat," then you may want to consider non-divorce to see if his attitude changes. No point in going to marriage counseling with a man who secretly believes his only mistake was in getting caught, is there?

Most people panic and rush off to marriage counseling like it's a life raft. But that's not what marriage counseling is for. Take all the time you need to decide what you really want, and what you are likely to get.

♦♦♦♦

You shouldn't trust him now. He's proven he's not trustworthy. It is my opinion but I think you have a very difficult battle ahead of you for several reasons. One of which is that he's in the military and he travels for deployments, the other is that he didn't just cheat on you, he's a serial cheater.

Serial cheaters have less respect for women (in general) and feel more entitled to cheat for a variety of reasons. In your shoes, I know I wouldn't believe him.

I have a friend in a situation like yours (several children, husband in military, deployed and cheating) and she found out after digging that it was far more pervasive than he'd told her. I think you really have your work cut out for you if you want to salvage your marriage.

♦♦♦♦

I do have a lot to think about. On one hand, I have a chance to reconcile even if it's a small chance. On the other hand, I don't know if I could ever trust him again so why bother.

I have such mixed emotions right now and I don't know what to do. For the sake of the kids I think that I should take my chances at reconciliation. They would be devastated to see us divorce. I know that's not uncommon.

So I stand at a crossroads. I've never felt so alone in my life!

♦♦♦♦

With children it makes all of the thoughts and decisions much more difficult. I can understand your thoughts and it would be extremely difficult to trust a serial cheater—my first love (high school sweetheart) was just that and I ran into him years into our marriages and he was still cheating.

Don't fool yourself. It's their issues, their insecurities, their character flaws, that allow them to go to such lengths to meet some superficial need for acceptance, lust, false emotion.

My husband and I are in reconciliation after five months apart. We have three children. In an ideal situation for MYSELF I never would have taken my husband back. Sometimes, I still wish I hadn't, but our choices are never in a vacuum. There are many peripheral things to consider.

♦♦♦♦

I am three years + into reconciliation and I still don't trust him even though he has done everything right. He is in individual counseling, he has promised never to do anything that hurts me again, and he is trying to be a better husband. But he still doesn't own what it is he really did.

If I did not bring up the affair he would never mention it ever again. He just wants to pretend it is in the past and we can carry on our merry way.

The lack of trust isn't about his behavior although he took a woman he admired out to coffee last month which really shows me he doesn't get it. He can fuck and suck whoever he wants, whenever he wants. I just know if it happened again the shutters would come down SLAM! and that would be it.

It is because I don't know him. He has all these secrets and boxes and thoughts and emotions that he keeps to himself. That is why I don't trust him.

♦♦♦♦

I really, truly believe it's the day in, day out exposure to their bullshit that ruins any attempt at future reconciliation. We just stop "liking" them. And even if they eventually pull their heads out of their asses, it's simply too late at that point. Whatever respect and affection we might have retained has been stomped into the dust by then.

♦♦♦♦

I'm getting to that point that I don't "like" him anymore. The incredible lying is just too much. I told him that he's become an expert. He denies that he's a liar. Then he lies some more... how arrogant is that!

I told him that I don't know him anymore. He begs me to give him another chance. He says he'll do anything. I just think to myself "like I haven't heard that one before." He repeats the same promises over and over. When I point it out, he sees it but he doesn't know what to say about it.

There are bits and pieces of the old husband that come out every now and again. This new person is just so foreign to me. I don't know how much longer I can deal with this. I deserve a decent, honest and good man. I didn't sign up for what is before me.

♦♦♦♦

He's not capable of having a real marriage right now (if ever). For whatever reason, he's traded in his honor, integrity and manhood to become a sneaky, lying teenager who is trying to appease his parent so he doesn't get in too much trouble while sneaking out to party because it's a rush and it's fun.

If I were you, I'd completely detach and focus on just you for now. Is there any way you can ask him to move out?

♦♦♦♦

I've actually been thinking about when to ask him to move out. I have to be careful. Timing is everything. I know I'm not crazy. Just incredibly hurt and disgusted.

♦♦♦♦

Come to realize that my husband is just a big A**hole! As long as I keep that in mind then everything makes sense. For example, if he says something stupid to piss me off I just keep in mind that "that is what a**holes say."

I don't look at him the same and I don't feel the same. I'm just going through the motions. He says he wants to do marriage counseling with me and I told him that when he sets up the appointment, I'll be there. It hasn't happened. He expected me to do it.

Guess you can tell by now that I am completely ambivalent towards him. I promised myself and told my counselor that I would give this marriage a year. Don't know if I can last or not. Not really sure of anything anymore.

♦♦♦♦

Change that promise to "goal" and you'll be in a better frame of mind. It's emotionally hard to break a promise, even if it's to us. But we miss goals all the time, and THIS is something that needs to be re-evaluated often. There shouldn't be any shame in deciding you're done waiting for him to become different.

♦♦♦♦

Of course you don't look at him the same. You've learned some awful things about him that reflect on his character in a very bad way and he's hurt you. These are huge issues and I think they forever change the way we view our spouses, even those who try to repair the damage they've done.

♦♦♦♦

I guess goal is a better word. My husband is in counseling and so far so good. My main problem is that I just can't trust. He is trying the best that he can, I suppose. It just blows my mind how far he went to betray me.

Everything that I found out was because of my snooping not because he was forthcoming. That in itself is the reason I just cannot trust him. Anything he says, anything he does, I don't trust.

I guess I have to find a way to put this behind me but I'm having a real difficult time doing just that. How do I move forward with so much baggage? I've been in counseling and it's all very logical and makes sense but to actually put it into practice is a whole different matter.

I'm at the point where I don't know if love is enough. I'm still very much in shock. At least I'm at the point where I'm taking this one day at a time. For a long time it was moment by moment.

◆◆◆◆

LOVE IS NEVER ENOUGH. It's just not. If it were, Romeo and Juliet would have a happy ending, instead of being a tragedy about two flighty kids.

There's always the possibility that maybe his best really isn't good enough any longer. Our standards tend to change once we discover the truth.

You'll trust him again when, and if, he ever becomes trustworthy. And that's going to take a long time for him to prove.

◆◆◆◆

At this point I don't know if I can ever trust him again. It's just so huge. The lying is mind-boggling. I have a hard time understanding how my best friend could do something so horrible to me. Who needs enemies when you have people like this in your life?

Maybe today I'm just feeling very angry and hurt. Some days are better than others. Today I'm just having a hard day.

◆◆◆◆

I cry for the man he used to be and I despise the man he has become.

Yesterday was a bad day. I cried until I couldn't breathe. It felt like I was standing out in the middle of a hailstorm with no protection being pelted with several different emotions all at once. I lost it.

I cried for the man I miss. I cried for what will never be. I cried because while I'm home trying to tend to household chores and keep things afloat, he's out with his whore. I cried because I didn't see it coming and I partly blame myself for not seeing it.

I know it's two steps forward and one step back but it's those backward steps that it takes time to recuperate from. I miss him so much it hurts my soul.

He is not the man I married. He is cold, unfeeling, distant, and wants nothing to do with me. Sometimes the pain is unbearable.

Today was an "I hate that woman" day, but I'm learning to hate him too. That has taken some time. I am angry for the way he left me, angry for him not talking to me first, angry for seeking solace in another woman. He turned into a real prick — the type of person he used to despise.

I'm hoping tomorrow will be better, but I just had to vent. It was seven months today that he walked out on our beautiful family for greener pastures. Maybe the pastures are greener because they've got more manure in them.

♦♦♦

That's what's so mind-boggling about this. They become the very sort of people that they used to judge as "bad."

Keep that in mind when you have moments of blaming yourself. A healthy person doesn't make their morality and integrity contingent on someone else's behavior. When these guys blame us, they're essentially saying that they're justified in being immoral.

I'm sorry you're in pain. I hope you have some comfort knowing that there are so many other women out here who know exactly how you feel. We weep for you and with you.

◆◆◆◆

Yes, it is two steps forward, and one back. You are still one step forward, but that step back is a bitch. I am sorry. I know it hurts. It will get better, promise.

◆◆◆◆

The sad truth is that the past we knew, the family we knew and the values we knew are all gone, dead, and there is another life ahead of us. Not necessarily better, it's up to us to make the best of it, but not necessarily the end of the world either.

I so get where you are now and to me anger was a step forward. Becoming angry to how he treated me, becoming angry to how he left his family and child, becoming angry enough to fight for what i consider to be my rights.

Life is too short to waste it crying for a person that doesn't want us in their life.

◆◆◆◆

His whore skank girlfriend listened to his old voice messages and private messages that I had left him. He called ME upset that I had called her such horrible names in those messages. ME! After all, she never, ever called me such names.

Then he threatened that if the kids don't stop saying negative things about him and her that he will stop dealing with them.

He wishes that I would stop whatever I'm doing because it's only hurting the kids. Really?!

I'm still doing laundry, still making dinners, still cleaning the house and going grocery shopping, still checking in with them off and on all day, still making sure they have money for gas and hanging out with friends.

I hate the life that he has dumped on me. I loved that man so much and he has turned against me in a manner that I could have never expected from him.

AND he keeps telling me that if I had only showed a little affection and appreciation, he wouldn't have had to look elsewhere. Bastard.

◆◆◆◆

There is a saying, "If you don't feel loved enough, perhaps you are not giving enough love." He, of course will not see any truth in this with respect to him and his behavior. He is practicing projection.

He did not communicate his feelings of being unloved and then give you a chance to respond in any way that would have helped him feel loved... now did he?

Kool-Aid... and nothing more. Don't drink it.

◆◆◆◆

No, he never told me he felt unloved. He would say he couldn't do this anymore and something had to change but never elaborated. He would say it under his breath.

I guess I was supposed to pick up on the subtle clues but I didn't.

I thought he was not happy with his job — not his marriage. He has actually taken some responsibility for not telling me but he said that it was my personality — and that no one can change their personality.

♦♦♦♦

You can rant and rave and it will help you to blow off frustration, slice and dice this a million ways as we all have in an attempt to understand his bad behavior.

In the end all the analysis and definition does not affect their actions; they do what they WANT to do. Logic, rationale, morals, ethics, etc., etc. have no influence or bearing.

They have launched their ships into new seas and they see adventure ahead. We are not part of that scenario.

Acceptance of his new reality and the self-discipline to detach will bring you some much needed objectivity in which to take a breath, re-align your goals and begin to act positively on your behalf. That's what it comes to.

Know that we have all experienced this. It will save your soul, your heart and your sanity.

♦♦♦♦

Don't be surprised if he is unhappy with his job and everything else. Girl, quit beating yourself up; it isn't anything you did.

"Restlessness inside of me," "need to be free," it's all the same BS. He is looking for his happiness externally, which is a train wreck waiting to happen. Get out of the way.

♦♦♦♦

How do I tell him to leave until he has figured things out?

Two weeks after our 23rd wedding anniversary my husband informed me that he longer loved me. He wasn't happy and that he'd be happier alone than with us. (We have two teenaged sons.) He saw no solution.

His interest in not attempting to find a solution raised the red flag. Less than ten days after he dropped the news, I discovered there was someone else (married with three kids).

Began monitoring his correspondence with her to see how involved they were. Well, they were talking/planning like a couple of lovesick teenagers. When confronted about her, he didn't deny it. It was an old high school girlfriend.

After individual and some marriage counseling it was determined that he was having a midlife crisis. We attended a marriage counseling weekend. Less than six hours after returning home, he texts her "I love you. I miss you. I WANT YOU."

After two months of this nonsense I requested that he have "no contact" with her while we're sorting all this out. His definition of "no contact" didn't match mine. He just eliminated instant messaging and texting her. They continued to send emails and he has initiated phone calls with her.

They had stopped seeing each other prior to our marriage weekend. I asked how the "no contact" was going and he denied calling her. He did admit to sending her a birthday card.

The emails are getting "hotter" and more frequent. He continues to profess his love for her and that happiness is next to her. We're having a group counseling session tomorrow (the two of us and our individual counselors).

Once again, I'm going to ask about the status of his relationship with the other woman. If he isn't honest with me, I'm going to confront him with the facts (printed emails, phone log etc.).

How long do you tolerate the other woman? He seems like he wants to work on the marriage, yet he continues to keep his relationship going with her. When do you ask him to leave and come back once they've figured things out?

♦♦♦♦

He does not want to work on the marriage while keeping her. He's just keeping the marriage as a "safe" place he can fall back on if the new love doesn't work out with the other woman.

He's holding your hand until he learns to run and then he can let you go. Don't be that for him. He is not in your marriage, he's appeasing you which is all about his safety and it feeds you straight into hell if you let him keep it up.

Before confessing anything to him see an attorney to find out your rights, gather all financial and asset data you have and put it in a safe place.

♦♦♦♦

He is lying to you and continuing to cheat; if not physically, he is cheating you emotionally. I learned firsthand that you can't go to marriage counseling with another woman's boyfriend!

It is worthless to attempt to reconcile the marriage while he is still involved with her. It's like trying to treat an alcoholic while they are still drinking.

There is no magical time to wait for him to get rid of the other woman. This is NOT about you or anything you have done or he blames you for. He is on an escape! You have no control over what he does, but you can try to detach and try to figure out what you want.

Most of us don't want a cheating husband. Life is hard enough without losing our self-esteem to someone else's midlife crisis. He has the midlife crisis and I like to think I am making a midlife correction.

◆◆◆

He's saying he loves her, he misses her, and he wants her. He's not saying you. Why are you still with him? He's lying out his ass to you and doing exactly what his heart desires. And it's not you.

Get to a lawyer and then get smart. Cry as hard as you need to, but do it. It's a shit storm, but you'll get through it.

Rule number one: Don't love someone who doesn't love you back. Your dog or cat is nicer than that.

◆◆◆

Unless he goes total no contact with the other woman, there is no working on the marriage. Get all your financial ducks in a row BEFORE confronting him. See an attorney for a free consult right now.

◆◆◆

I discovered an affair with my soon-to-be-ex with a mutual friend by reading emails they sent to one another. He was away on a trip at that time.

I immediately went to a very good attorney and took his advice. Only then did I confront him when he returned from his trip. I packed his bags and asked him to leave.

He begged me not to follow through, said it was an emotional attachment not physical (lies — as if that made it any better) and said he would break off all contact with her (lies) and would tell her husband the truth as well (more lies).

As a few weeks passed it became clear the lies continued. Contact with the other woman didn't end. Her husband called me and asked for the emails and I gave them to him.

I would have wanted him to do the same thing for me. We were friends, the four of us used to vacation together, spent a lot of time together. He left his wife and she pursued my husband full force.

My soon-to-be-ex didn't break it off with her and after two months of this drama I told him I had had enough and had him pack a bag and leave. I deserve better.

Before you do any kind of confronting, interview attorneys and find a very good one. Take advice. Gather all of your financial information together, past tax returns etc. An attorney will want to have these in order to advise you properly.

Once you have a plan for yourself, then confront. I found that giving him an ultimatum did not work. He ignored the first ultimatum when I packed his bags for him.

When I discovered his continued lies to me I said I have had enough. I know the truth. I deserve better. It is time now for you to leave. And that's that.

We began a sort of separation since his daughter wasn't living with us but coming over for visitation. He stayed elsewhere when she was not there, and in the basement when she was.

This went on for two weeks. I did this to give him time to contemplate the consequences of his actions, yet another chance. Still he did not break with the other woman.

At the end of two weeks we split formally and four months later I filed for divorce. It has hurt, it has been difficult, but it has been so much better than how it was when we were living together and he was lying constantly to me.

Your husband is not in your marriage. He is holding your hand until he gets the strength or makes a plan to leave. That plan will not include you and will likely not be to your financial benefit either.

The time is now to protect you. The unthinkable has happened.

♦♦♦♦

Right now, it appears that he doesn't realize that you are aware of his emails and regular interactions with the other woman. Use this time to your advantage. While he's sneaking around, you get your ducks in order. Don't tip your hand.

When this was going on in my marriage, I didn't let him know what I knew. I instead would ask him questions. I watched him lie to my face.

When I saw how easily he would lie, how absolutely undetectable his lies were (no blinking, keeps eye contact, no physical clue that I could see that might indicate a lie), I realized I would never be able to trust my husband again.

To me, this is what pushed me to pursue divorce. Of course, I had no children.

Keeping what you know private for now is good advice. It's hard, but right now, you need to take financial and legal precautions while he's focused on keeping his affair secret.

See a few lawyers to get some legal advice. This doesn't mean you will divorce. It just means that you are gathering information and getting important advice that may be of great help to you in the future.

Keep a very close eye on all expenses. Watch to see if he is spending extra money anywhere, or if he's moving money out of joint bank accounts. Make sure all bills are paid.

If possible, set up your own private, separate bank account and put some money into it.

Get a post office box and do all legal and bank correspondence through this.

If he checks your cellphone records, get a cheap pay-as-you-go phone and use that for legal correspondence.

This may sound overwhelming, but you need to gather information and come up with a plan. He may work through his issues and come back to your marriage, but he very well may not.

It doesn't hurt for you to get legal info and take the time to figure out what it is that you really want.

I didn't reveal the extent of what I'd found (such as my husband's online blogging about his affairs and feelings about me) until we were deep in divorce negotiations. Revealing it was what made him suddenly sign the agreement we'd been working on for eight months.

Holding on to my evidence was useful, because he kept incriminating himself further for months because I didn't tip my hand.

♦♦♦♦

He is not working on your marriage, is he? How can you work on your marriage but bring the Trojan horse into it?

You cannot work with half measures now: he is either in, or out. Only you can say what is acceptable and what your boundaries are.

Personally, with my experience of midlife crisis and having thought things over and over now for several years, I would help him pack this very minute and wish him blessings in his new life.

He wants to fuck the other woman. And nothing can stop this (except the other woman herself if she doesn't want this). As long as he is under hormones, you are trying to stop a high-speed train without brakes coming at you at full speed.

♦♦♦♦

See an attorney; take all prudent steps to protect yourself and any minor children financially. Get a plan for this. Have the plan ready to execute immediately, and then expose him and the married woman to the whole world and her husband, right after you have filed for divorce on grounds of adultery.

You husband is an immature, irresponsible, "regressed to teen" little boy who is in the throes of "lust crazed dementia."

He is an ADDICT, and the only thing that is going to even begin to get his attention is for him to be hit by the big old freight train of consequences and experience pain greater than the thought of giving up the skank.

You are not a doormat, nor are you some second-fiddle, consolation prize. You are his WIFE, dammit. Your place is sacred... do you understand "sacred"?

Give him everything he THINKS he wants... give it to him hard, fast and with no mercy.

Some men just have to be hit between the eyes with a 2x4. I wish I had handled it that way instead of "guilt tripping around" and feeling sorry for my ex. All it did was cause him to disrespect me further, and gave him more time to fuck me over about the property settlement.

Let this man KNOW that you think way too much of yourself to put up with this shit. Kick ass. Take names.

Men do NOT understand love as women understand it; they DO, however, understand RESPECT.

Have great respect for yourself or he will continue to sneak around and walk all over you and it will just get uglier and uglier... and your hell will just be dragged out longer than necessary.

◆◆◆◆

I think what you decide to do depends on what YOU want. I had a very similar situation. Married 23 years. Teenaged children. Suddenly my husband says we have "grown apart" and no longer wants to be married. We separated and I found out after about a year of separation that he was having an affair with his secretary.

I always thought that would be unforgivable, but found myself wanting to save our marriage. I had to do a lot of soul searching and literally wrote down pros and cons of staying married.

Bottom line is I love him and made a commitment "for better or worse." A midlife crisis is certainly not what I anticipated when I said those vows!

I have spent the last year and a half of separation working on ME. I have started exercising regularly, planned activities with friends, joined a women's bible study, and (after three tries) found a wonderful counselor who is very supportive of my decision to stay married.

We got to the point where he had filed for divorce and we were working on a property settlement. I told him from the beginning that divorce was not what I wanted, but that I would get an attorney and protect my and my children's financial future... which I did.

And I finally was able to tell him that I would not spend any more time trying to work on things until he stopped his relationship with the other woman. And I prayed every day for God to change his heart and realize what he was about to lose.

And finally he did. Three months ago he called and wanted to talk. He told me that he did not want a divorce and had ended his relationship and all contact with the other woman.

We still have a long way to go and the road is not easy but we are happily working on our marriage together.

We are happier than we've been in years (most of the time) and have finally been able to have open, honest conversations. He has withdrawn the divorce petition and we are committed to repairing our marriage.

So my advice is to spend some time deciding what YOU want to do. Stand up for yourself and take care of yourself and your children.

Find a counselor who understands what you want and supports that. And surround yourself with friends and/or family who will support whatever decisions you make.

I know that the choice I made is not for everyone but it was what I wanted in my heart. And I am thankful that I made the choice to stay married. Good luck and God bless you and your children.

◆◆◆◆

I can tell you from personal experience I am riding the infidelity roller coaster as well. Expose her to her spouse, the sooner the better. The website by William F. Harley, Marriage Builders.com, goes through the plans. I have not done it and I regret it.

Do keep busy so you don't keep dwelling on it. Bible study, prayer, whatever works to get you through the emotional roller coaster that happens.

My wedding anniversary will be this next month and I don't expect anything from him. He told me he was not involved and nothing has changed.

◆◆◆◆

"Another woman's boyfriend."

That's exactly how I saw my ex, after 19 years together, from the moment I knew there was another woman.

I couldn't have touched him if I'd tried. Didn't want to engage on any personal level. Any personal talk would only go back to the other woman.

I felt with every fiber in my body that I didn't want to be part of a triangle with him and his married other woman! He had told me he wanted "drama" — I didn't want to help provide it.

So I stepped right back and started considering my own interests.

◆◆◆◆

In the end I hurt myself more than he hurt me because I refused to get off that rollercoaster.

Why would you do that?

Probably because like me, you are grieving, sad, scared, anxious, fearful, traumatized. Staying on it brings more of the same. Get off, do it now.

You know what comes next. And like me, it is not something you want to hear yet. But, when you have had enough you will hear it loud and clear. You will stop living in limbo and hope and you will begin to live again.

♦♦♦♦

I too am riding this emotional amusement park ride. Seven months later I am still in denial.

He is in full-fledged midlife crisis and has been in a hot and heavy affair. He came home briefly then ran back to her. He is addicted to the adrenaline rush when he is with her.

I refuse to file for divorce, not because I don't want to, but because SHE wants HIM to. So I figure the more she nags and threatens him, the more he'll regret his decision.

She has already said, "If you really love me you'll file for divorce," and "I'm giving you till such and such a date to file, then you're out of here."

He's stuck between a rock and a hard place. He can't come home again, but he can't be alone.

My ducks are in a row. I have an attorney. I have provided her with all of my financial information so if he does serve me with papers, I'm ready to go.

I have to tread lightly, however, because he's currently paying me more than he needs to by law. Once the papers are filed, the house goes up for sale, I lose that extra money and life as I know it is over.

I'm biding my time right now and waiting for her to push him over the limit.

♦♦♦♦

What does he mean when he says "I love you but I'm not IN LOVE with you"?

In general, it's the statement (NOT a two-way conversation) notifying the left behind spouse that there is Big Trouble Right Here In River City. Usually it contains some version of ILYBINILWY — "I love you, but I'm not IN LOVE with you."

And that often is because he's either IN LOVE (infatuated) with someone else, envious of someone he knows who is infatuated with someone else, or thinks he "should" be able to feel more for you than he currently does.

The Speech "may" include a laundry list of your shortcomings, a list of demands, or a notice that he's in love with someone else, moving out, and/or filing for divorce, or that may come later.

And some wandering spouses never spell it out this way; you just have to "read between the lines" to realize you've gotten The (psychic) Speech.

♦♦♦♦

My husband said "I think I am over you and I know you are over me..." huh?

♦♦♦♦

I got the old "ILYBINILWY" word for word as if read from a script or a cue card. He then went on to tell me that he had no idea "what he wanted to do with the rest of his life," AS IF after 31 years of marriage his life was a "do-over." Whatever he "chose" for his life, I was definitely not in the plan.

That was over three years ago — he did eventually come back to reality and I am happy to say that I am very much in his life and plans, at this time.

♦♦♦♦

I think I have been given a speech of sorts. Over the past six months every time I have said I love you he has said no you don't and he even said "well if that's your idea of love your love is shit."

He has also been telling me that divorce won't be so bad, that I can move on and be happy with someone else.

Whenever I discuss/argue with him it always ends up with him telling me how horrible I am and how it is my fault.

He believes and has told me that he has done nothing wrong our whole marriage and that he is a wonderful person and everybody likes him except me and that I am 100% to blame for our troubles.

All this is so unreal.

I have been trying to give him the benefit of the doubt regarding his ex-girlfriend that he is in constant contact with via Facebook and thousands of dollars in telephone calls.

I have thought for a long time that he is infatuated or even in love with her but because of the distance and that nothing could ever become of it I have been willing to wait it out.

I have been to lawyers. The bank had my house valued to work out my options financially to see if I can raise three kids on my own and it is all doable, but taking that last step is so hard.

I have asked him to leave and he won't go. He said he is going to hang around to see what happens and in the meantime is "going to tolerate me."

He is not asking me to leave. He is fine with me being part of his life, all the while hurting, ignoring and not considering me.

Is it all worth it, can I get through to him, will we ever be a family again?

♦♦♦♦

I got the speech word for word along with a lot of other emotionally abusive statements. I was in such confusion that I started searching for answers and a friend told me what was happening. I found this forum early on and followed the advice about not participating in his confusion.

It was really hard. I tried to leave him alone but he would constantly be angry with me for things that didn't make sense. Eventually, he couldn't be in the same room with me.

At this point I had been staying in a spare bedroom for four months because he'd said I was snoring and disturbing his rest. (I don't, of course)

I walked on eggshells around him and finally couldn't take the abuse and told him to leave. It took him two months. Once he left he never looked back.

Our daughters gave me the news of the other woman and it was a blessing of sorts because his behavior then made sense. We've divorced and I am finally away from his crap! This is really HARD stuff!

There isn't anything you can do for him. Take care of yourself and the kids.

♦♦♦♦

I never got the speech, just a text telling me he had left me. Ten months before he left he said he wasn't sure he loved me. He took it back the next day saying he only said it to hurt me because I found out he was with the other woman.

It's like they are all singing from the same hymn sheet.

♦♦♦♦

When will I be ready to let go completely?

I think I am getting much closer to deciding that regardless of his indecision, regardless if he decides the other woman is a mistake, I've had enough.

I don't want to be anyone's second choice, like a booby prize. How humiliating. He might not recognize my worth, but I do. If he has to "test out" some other girl to decide if he wants me... no, I'm not ok with that.

How much more humiliating would it be if I kept waiting only to have him tell me, "No, I've decided it wasn't a mistake after all, the other woman is worth it and you're not." I'd rather just end the humiliation now.

I've written all my feelings out. Listed the pros and cons of waiting. Wrote questions to myself about how I'm feeling, if I'm ready to let go completely, if I'll regret it if I tell him I'm not waiting and that I don't want him back regardless, how sad I'll be if I tell him that versus how sad I'll be if I wait.

I read it and reread it and edit it and add to it. It's really helping.

I am so close to being ready. At least I think I am. So close...

♦♦♦♦

Someone broke it down on the forum very clearly — "I'm am not an option. I am a prize."

♦♦♦♦

Being ready to let go isn't really a decision you make. It's more a point you get to when you've really had enough. You can't force it — it takes time.

It can also take a thousand and one episodes of to-ing and fro-ing in your head and your heart — reasoning, feeling, remembering, grieving, hoping, arguing with yourself and arguing with him (internally).

It can also take a bit of carrying on at your ex! It's all part of letting go so don't fight it too hard.

♦♦♦♦

He has chosen a life that is the opposite of everything you and he had. Not because its better, but that in his mind it is justifiable... and you, as others have told me about my situation, represent responsibility and stability.

You can't help, control, or fix what's ailing his soul. And if he did possibly come back, it could be too soon (run again) or too late (you have moved on with your life).

So continue to move on with your life. And deal with him when the time comes.

And it will HURT... yes it will. And you will lean into it and accept it or you won't grow.

You will go through this for a while but you will be fine. You will be surprised how many "punches" we can take.

♦♦♦♦

Yes you are clutching at straws. This is how it feels when you desperately don't want to give up what you are comfortable with, what your reality is used to. I was sad and in mourning for two years.

I didn't fight it, I didn't do the "me" work, I just waited. Everyone kept saying to do "me" work, but I didn't feel like it. My "me" work was mourning and thinking and reading.

Now I can step back and say that I will never choose to be with someone like that again.

I now have the will do some "me" work like eating right, exercising and making good choices when I choose to date someone again. I will never have the desire to be with my ex again. I could not see him for the toxic person he was, I just wanted him back.

Now, I can see that we are totally incompatible with the mindset I now have. His character flaws have grown into huge character deficits and that is finally not attractive to me in the slightest.

You need to grow, and wait. Waiting is a good thing. Embrace the waiting. Be good to yourself.

If anyone sounds like they are too harsh, it is probably because they finally have answers to their own situations, know how you feel, and are desperately trying to help your mind wake up to the reality they now have but did not when they were in your situation.

◆◆◆◆

You're sad that you made those decisions to invest in a relationship with a man who turned out to be a bad investment and resolved to move your life forward now that you know better. Good for you! Many, many of us have felt the same way.

The old saying is, when you know better, you do better, and now you know, right? So you can put the past to bed, gently, and take the lessons with you to your new and improved life.

◆◆◆◆

Why doesn't he move out and go live with her?

My husband's other woman has her own apartment, after her husband kicked her out. When she calls, he runs to spend a night with her, but it's only one or two days a week. Otherwise, he is "home" at his normal time and acting like he belongs at our house.

He disappears most Sunday afternoons as well, usually returning with the family groceries. As our son said "it doesn't take 6 hours to get groceries!" but I think he believes he's still fooling people.

I have repeatedly asked him why he doesn't just move in with her and get out of the house. If that's who he loves and wants to be with, why doesn't he just go? He always says the same thing "I'm not moving in with her."

I just don't get it! Is she not willing to have him move in? Is he not willing to leave us completely? What the heck is going on? I have asked him to leave many times. As of right now, he is holed up in a room in our basement.

♦♦♦♦

If I had two jobs, that were both paying me a salary, even though I was leaving my first job to go do my second, why would I quit? Especially if Job #1 KNEW that I was staying on the clock while I was at Job #2? What's my incentive? I clearly CAN have both full salaries for doing half the work, so why wouldn't I?

This isn't just his decision. He is perfectly content. It's YOU who has a problem with the situation. And I'm afraid it's going to have to be you who changes it.

♦♦♦♦

Because we don't control other people's behavior, we can only implement boundaries and consequences.

So, if you want to implement a boundary of "I won't tolerate you investing your emotional/physical/financial/time resources in an outside relationship," then you need to come up with consequences that he MAY decide are too uncomfortable to accept.

In other words, reduce his "salary." Make sure he doesn't get as much compensation for remaining in your house with the title of "husband" as he used to get.

And if your consequences aren't uncomfortable enough to inspire him to change his behavior, then YOU will need to leave the relationship, and, perhaps, with legal advice, the marital home.

There are ALWAYS financial implications, and for some, they're quite severe. But, you CAN find ways to deal with those.

Or, you can decide that your position description has changed from "wife" to "co-tenant," and reduce your job responsibilities, AND YOUR EXPECTATIONS, accordingly. That's tough to do, too!

Your choices may be limited and unpalatable, but you do have choices, just like he does.

◆◆◆◆

You're not in an ideal situation, of course, but who is when this happens?

If he DID decide to move in with the other woman, and take his salary with him, what would you do then? Because she could put pressure on him to do so, or he could decide to just bolt, and then you'd find yourself in the situation regardless.

It's not easy, it surely isn't. But better to do things on YOUR timetable than have to scramble when it hits you unexpectedly.

From the beginning, I planned on how to best position myself financially once I got The Speech.

That was probably the one thing I did right during this whole mess. It took me three years to get there, and I lived with my ex the entire time.

It sucked, seriously sucked. I had to keep my eyes on the prize, and remind myself that I *chose* to stay for good reasons and I could change my mind whenever I had to... or wanted to.

◆◆◆◆

I still live in the same house as ex.

Before the bomb drop I knew there was something going on with the married other woman, but he of course denied it. They went out a few times that I did know of, and when he was here he talked to her all the time through chat.

After the bomb drop and confronting him with evidence of her he feels like he has nothing to hide. He comes home from work, he eats something, he goes out to see her and comes home in the middle of the night.

Lately, there have been a few days he stayed at home. He walks around the house nervous and looks lost. The other woman may want to spend some time with her kids or friends. I don't ask. I think if it was up to him he would pack her bags and move her right in here with us.

She's still married (according to my soon-to-be-ex she's going through divorce now) and lives with her three kids and her soon-to-be-ex-husband. I guess they found a place where they can meet. I asked him if it was possible for him to stay there while I'm getting prepared to move out. He told me he can't. And that he doesn't want to talk about it.

I also asked him about their plans: is she going to live in "our" home? He told me they don't have plans. But she doesn't have enough money to find a place of her own (and I do?), and he doesn't want to sell the house.

I'm learning to not get involved. We just live in the same house and that's it. When he comes home from the other woman, I don't even look at him. I set some boundaries for my own sanity. Not that he cares, but I stick to them.

We don't talk, I don't want act like everything is normal because it's not. I'm not his friend, he doesn't help me with finances and all he cares about is her. He can't understand that it hurts to see him like this.

In a few weeks I will finally have my own apartment. I can't wait!

◆◆◆◆

I went to see a lawyer and suggested to my husband that we begin to get our financial affairs simplified with a view to getting the house sold and divorcing, since he can't seem to give his girlfriend up.

Throughout all of this he's maintained that he loves me and doesn't want to lose the marriage. Unfortunately he's also in love with her and can't give her up. He knows that doesn't wash with me and that if she's not going then I am.

Although he's cheated on me sexually/emotionally he's not done anything underhanded moneywise, and in my heart of hearts I don't think he will, other than try to get best deal for himself when we do divorce.

My dilemma is this. He now says he realizes he needs to get some counseling to try to "get his head straight." I know the situation has taken its toll on him, too, as he lost lots of weight and friends commented how awful he looked, etc.

He's asked whether I'd consider delaying any major moves financially for a few months to enable him to get the counseling he says he now realizes he needs.

He is awaiting a date for his first session from the doctor now. I'm just not sure whether this is a delaying tactic (just like when he told me several times the relationship was finished when it wasn't) or whether to take him at face value this one last time and give him the additional bit of time and space to get his counseling.

I know very well there may not be anything in it for me, i.e. he won't necessarily decide to reconcile with me, so I would really just be doing it for him, except that of course as I still love him I am thinking that there might be a tiny chance of salvaging the marriage which is what I would like to happen, but only if it is genuine and real.

With the help of this forum and the book *Love Must Be Tough* I've reached a reasonable place myself in terms of knowing what needs doing regarding my future. But I almost feel that if I don't give him this bit of extra time I will possibly be closing the door on a possible genuine last chance, and I'm reluctant to do that.

What do others think? I know I might just be delaying the inevitable but there's this niggling doubt I have about shutting the door on him at the moment when he is appearing to accept that he needs outside help and wants to get it. Please help me to decide!!

◆◆◆◆

While this may sound counter intuitive to saving the marriage, my opinion is that you should go forth (meticulously and fairly) with the division of the property.

He has played delaying tactics for so many years that he may subconsciously believe, "If I string her along... she'll capitulate."

You cannot keep on living in limbo. It is psychologically unhealthy for you.

Be calm, be fair, but don't waiver. Tell him you are delighted that he has chosen to work on his issues, that you applaud his courage, but that you must also do what is right for yourself to maintain your own emotional equilibrium and hold up your own standards of integrity with respect to marriage and commitment.

Therefore you will proceed with getting all the details in order for him to be a free and independent agent because at this point it is the fairest and most logical resolution that you can come up with.

Then don't say any more and calmly and firmly go about the business of precautions to protect yourself financially.

Eventually he will begin to get that age old message, "We don't get to eat and have our cake, too."

When I hear about these cake eating wandering spouses, sometimes the mental image of a greedy puppy comes to mind.

Have you ever seen a puppy try to hold several items in its mouth at one time when there is not enough room and one or more keep falling out, and the puppy frantically scrambles about trying to snap up and hold all of them... becoming more frustrated in the process?

It gets comical and yet it is exactly how these wandering spouses act. "I want it ALL dammit and I'll scuttle about like crazy to insure that I get it all." Never is it successful, and often they end up dropping and losing the most delectable item because greed makes them frantic.

Be calm, be rational, and be sweet even. But take care of YOU.

♦♦♦♦

Tell him you appreciate his good intentions, but that you have reached the point where you are going to run your own life now, and if he DOES "sort his head out," you can revisit the marriage at that point.

Anything else is just going to give him breathing space to keep right on dithering. Except, he's really NOT dithering. He has things exactly the way he likes them.

It's not like he doesn't know if he wants to be with you or with her. He wants to find a way to have you both.

♦♦♦♦

Just because you continue to move forward doesn't mean you couldn't still get back together.

If he really wants to be with you, he will find a way, even if you have sold the house and have gotten a divorce. Granted, that would be more expensive financially, but how much more expensive emotionally will it be if this ends up being just one more instance of cake eating.

♦♦♦♦

My ex tried the same thing after I "hung in there" for about four years while he lied and jerked me around unmercifully, tried to reconcile three times, only to discover more and more lies). I finally said "I AM DONE, got a great attorney and filed.

He flipped, begged, pleaded, asked me to see his counselor with him, said he would work on himself, etc, etc.

I said I thought that was GREAT, and after he did all the "work" on himself, please look me up, I would be eager to meet with him then.

But the divorce was ON, and was staying on, and I stayed true to my word. He did NOT keep his, and never sought any real help or looked seriously at his many issues.

I knew in my heart even then that it was one of his tactics to try to control the situation, and lo and behold, I was right.

I would negotiate a fair settlement and carry on, a divorce DOES NOT permanently slam the door shut on getting back together; it DOES protect you legally however.

♦♦♦♦

It's another delaying tactic and you know it but you just don't want to know it.

There has to be someone who puts an END to this misery. It appears to be you because he doesn't have the balls to do it. Weak people cheat. Insecure people cheat. Pfft to "love." This is not "love" anymore. It's co-dependency.

I'm 99.9% sure no one here is going to tell you to give him ONE MORE CHANCE after he's cheated for three years.

Another three years goes by but during those three years he gets cleverer at hiding his crap and fleeces you financially as well? Stuff that!! Get your ducks in a row and get legal advice on splitting the assets while they exist.

♦♦♦♦

Very early on I asked my lawyer that same question. His reply was to suggest that marriage counseling continue but that we separate (meaning he leaves) for a time so each can step back from the situation, leaving the idea out there that things might still be salvageable if he plays along.

The alternative if he does not agree is that we will proceed immediately to divorce with him living in the home. Under no circumstances am I to leave the home. It's an asset that my lawyer wanted to remain in my possession.

Now my lawyer knew my particular circumstances and tailored his advice to me. I thought I would share it with you.

The purpose of doing it this way is so that your husband hopefully won't become frightened and fight you. It's a separation, a chance for each to step back and get some perspective, marriage counseling continues, etc.

Then once he is out of the house you change the locks. In my state you may legally change the locks if a spouse moves out.

♦♦♦♦

Please explain why I'm not supposed to have a problem with the other woman.

Am I the only person on this earth who thinks that what he has done and the other woman has done is utterly despicable?

I am SO sick of "society" not batting an eyelid about this!! How can any sane reasonable adult think that any of this is acceptable and just shrug it off as "oh well, it happens"?? I just don't get it.

So, she steals my best friend, turns him SO against me that he hates me, destroys my family (and her husband), hurts my children (which is completely unforgiveable in my book) and then I'm supposed to be happy about my children being involved with her??

She continues to deliberately hurt my children by ignoring their wishes that they don't spend time with her when they are with their Dad, and there is supposedly something wrong with me for not being happy about any of this crap?!

She is introduced to the in-laws as if she is sweetness and light and has done nothing wrong. She is just plain evil. She should have horns growing out of her head, but why can't anyone else see that??

Sorry, I am very angry and upset tonight. My husband is the biggest jerk on the face of the planet and I am so sick of his Crap!! I can't take being blamed for his pathetic, cowardly inadequacies anymore. There is only so much I can take and I've copped a lot in the last 12 months. Why are they so blind and stupid and pathetic?

♦♦♦♦

Rectal cranial inversion.

A lot of people think what he's done is despicable. Many will come to their own conclusions based on his actions now and in the future, and also on your actions now and in the future. You know the truth. So do the people who matter most. You can't control what everyone thinks, no matter how wrong their conclusions might be.

People also do know about the whole midlife crisis cliché. I think there's an element of "back away from the crazy person" in all this.

However, when you don't know the details, you tend to assume that there was a rational reason for people's actions, that a marriage breaks down over the years instead of suddenly, and that a person doesn't suddenly up and change and run away.

I've always had contempt for men and women who abandoned their families in order to take up with someone new. As far as I knew, my husband did, too. A lot of people feel the same way even if they don't obviously show it.

When people don't know what to say or do, they talk platitudes. Thus the pious stuff about the good of the children, getting over it, and all that.

Your in-laws are in a tough position. They have to accept what's going on because the man is their son. So they are polite no matter what they privately think about the situation.

Unfortunately, since your husband is not physically abusive, you can't protect your children from his craziness. Let the skank dig her own hole with your children. They will see what's going on. It's not just the skank who is ignoring your children's wishes — the kids' father is fully complicit. I'm sorry; that's just the way it is. It will have consequences.

At home, give your children the stability and structure and attention they need. In some ways, they have it harder than you, while in other ways, you have it harder than they do.

I hope you can all pull together and become closer as you cope in your various ways with the destruction of your family. As people here tell us, you are building your new family, and it can be very good.

It really sucks. The anger and upset are fully understandable.

Your husband has competition for being the biggest jerk on the face of the planet. A lot of us have spouses fighting for the title.

♦♦♦♦

They are not blind and stupid. They are selfish, mean and arrogant. Not to mention immature and generally despicable. Nice people do not screw around on their spouses, and neither do people who are nice help them to do it.

To knowingly bed a married person is lower than a snakes belly as far as I am concerned. And I am interested in nobody making excuses for that. I would much prefer it if someone said I did that, I was stupid and I was wrong and I regret it, but never will I condone it. I may even understand or forgive it, but god help anyone that tries to tell me they never knew that was wrong.

And yes, you are quite within your rights to say it is wrong. A lot of people I know believe it is too, and they are still working on their marriages and putting their family first.

People make mistakes, but when trying to force feed those mistakes onto others, it is just flat out repulsive.

◆◆◆◆

You have no reason to feel anything but righteous indignation at his behavior. But you can't really do anything about it. So take care of you... and work on that better life. It is there for the taking.

◆◆◆◆

Thank you all for replying, I needed a sanity check. I know you all don't think that any of this is ok, we are all in the same boat and all our husbands are as selfish and despicable as each other. I was meaning society in general (the non-left behind spouses).

I know it's all his problem, I know that. But I just want to rail at the injustice of it all and slap all those idiots who just turn a blind eye and condone this revolting behavior.

I think that is why there are so many divorces. It's too easy. Just walk away and treat the person you owe at least some respect to as if they are worthless, because life with the other woman is shiny and new and that's so much better and worthier!?

They did the wrong thing (a very wrong thing, no getting away from that) and I and my sweet, innocent children are the ones who suffer. It's just not fair and I'm having a "screaming at the injustice of it all" moment.

I think we should go back to the days of scarlet letters on women's heads (and on men's too) so that the world knows they aren't what they pretend to be. Maybe then society would wake up.

I have to add that my in-laws are wonderful people, who are decent and kind and love me the same as they have for all these years and I know they will not turn their backs on me and they have said as much to him. They are appalled at his behavior, but have no choice but to accept things because he is their son.

There is a big part of me that wishes they would stand up to him and not allow her in their door, but I know I can't control that and I understand that they are scared of losing him if they did. It just really hurts that he gets to replace me so easily. Really hurts.

◆◆◆◆

There is no pain that compares with this. It is worse than losing a limb. Only losing a child could be more painful. We have to bear it, but we don't have to grin and bear it.

◆◆◆◆

I was assuming you meant that HE thinks you're not supposed to have a problem with the other woman. And of course what HE thinks about how you feel about the other woman doesn't matter one bit. You don't have to listen to it let alone take it seriously.

It sounds like he was whining to you about how mistreated he and his paramour feel because of the way you and, by extension, your kids feel and behave regarding his new life. Well, too bad! Talk to the hand!

I don't think "society" necessarily condones or even turns a blind eye to this sort of stuff. I think "society," in general, has simply become resigned to coexisting with it.

But there are plenty of individuals who FEEL the same way you do, even if they aren't in much of a position to do much about it. Count on that!

◆◆◆◆

It's very hard when you're in the middle of fresh hell to think "what's going to happen, one, two, three, five, eight years from now?"

Nobody can do that when they're a gaping wound ready to strike back at those who have broken up their family. That's a primal threat that happened and in prehistoric times we probably would have killed over it.

But now we can't, so what do we do with all this energy and hatred and massive adrenaline rush day after day after day? We want to know WHY.

Nobody expects you to NOT have a problem with the other woman. NOBODY. You have the right not to forgive your husband and her.

But remember one thing: those are still your kids, they still love their mom. They are confused but the chips will fall where they'll fall. I have a feeling that right now, you are still a gaping wound and need to be working out all there is to work out for the time being and set these boundaries.

She stays in the car when he picks them up. She is not allowed in your house! She is not to call you regarding anything about the kids visiting, etc. He must do all that work.

Make it very clear. You can barely tolerate seeing him but you will NOT put up with her being in your presence right now. Demand it.

◆◆◆◆

My sister's husband left her and married the other woman. The eldest son, then in high school, told his father that he did not want to meet the new wife EVER, and wanted nothing to do with any children he might have. His father has respected this, and to this day, has never said anything to the first family about the new family.

If he comes by for anything, and the new wife is with him, he parks around the corner, and leaves her in the car. He cannot take the new wife to first children's events, out of respect for his children. I can only assume how this makes the new wife feel.

I guess it has to do with how things ended. He divorced my sister to marry the other woman because she was pregnant. My sister says if he would have done things properly, divorcing her first, then finding a new girlfriend, it would have been a whole different story.

◆◆◆◆

Wouldn't we all have a different story if they had done it "the right way"? I've asked my husband that plenty of times. You couldn't have divorced me and then went and found this new "love of your life"? You had to cheat.

And his reply is always the same banal junk: I know that's what I should have done but let me come back a few times and mess with you when she's leaving me hanging.

I get really angry sometimes about how hard it is on me and my kids, and the two of them just figure it's fine and life will go on.

◆◆◆◆

Since when do parents have to quietly accept irresponsible and hurtful behavior on the part of their children?

I love my children, and because I do love my children, I will speak up when I feel that they are being self-destructive or not acting in the best interests of my grandchildren.

He'd get called on it at my house, and the other woman would be told quietly but very directly, "Your conduct is not acceptable to me, and you are not welcome in my home."

◆◆◆◆

It's eerie. My parents have just begun living this very scenario with my brother. Their hearts are broken and they're shocked, hurt, angry, confused, and sickened about his choices.

They openly state, to him and the rest of the family, that they truly hope he turns himself around (and believe that he can), but as long as he doesn't, consequences apply.

And the grandchildren's welfare trumps ALL, including sister-in-law's, although they are supporting her as much as they possibly can.

BOUNDARIES. LOVING DETACHMENT. Parents can have them, too!

◆◆◆◆

Is an affair a deal breaker with no second chances?

I used to think it was a deal breaker, but love makes you change your mind and try once more, over and over again.

♦♦♦♦

What it comes down to is that we made vows to one another, in front of our families, our friends, and our God. He violated them without so much as a second thought. To me that is a character defect of epic proportions, and a definite deal breaker.

I could not take back a cheater. I would spend the remainder of my life wondering when it was going to happen again. I do believe that it would happen again. You can't unring that bell.

♦♦♦♦

Looking back now, with hindsight, it is a deal breaker for me as well now. I don't regret giving him his chance because I was doing the best I could at that time with what I knew, but knowing what I know now, I wouldn't do it again.

♦♦♦♦

I'd always said that infidelity would make our marriage irreconcilable. To me, there is no excuse for such a thing. It is an incredible sign of disrespect and selfishness.

However, I did think about giving him a chance. When I knew he was lying to my face, and not blinking/looking away/doing anything to indicate he might be lying, I knew I would never, ever be able to trust anything he said again.

♦♦♦♦

The affair isn't the deal breaker for me, though, like so many others, I once thought it would be. I would have gladly worked to get past the affair way back when, if he'd been willing to put the effort into getting back together.

In my opinion, my ex wouldn't be willing to do the amount of work needed to attempt reconciliation. Now that he's "free" once again (unless, of course, they reconcile), he'll find someone else with whom he can share commitment to the depth that he's comfortable, which would NOT be sufficient for me.

There would be no "coming home" until WAY down the line. We sold the marital home and I bought my own house, which he has never — and will never — set foot in. I'm not giving up that safe haven, and the life I've built there, for "a chance."

◆◆◆◆

An affair was not a deal breaker; the things he said were. I can forgive him because I need to let go and move on but that trust will never recover. Of course it also doesn't help that he married the other woman 15 months after he moved out.

◆◆◆◆

I did give him a second chance when I first caught him with hookers. I don't believe an affair is a deal breaker with no second chances, and in fact, when we were in marriage counseling and I was seeing progress in both of us, I felt our marriage was stronger for having gone through all that.

Prior to going through infidelity, though, I would have said it would have absolutely been a deal breaker. I find a lot of people say that, but the reality is very different from the hypothetical. When you are in crisis, it's not so simple to just throw someone out that you've built a life with.

◆◆◆◆

No I think that people make mistakes and big ones also. I've seen families not talk to each other for years, I've seen friendships dissolve for no good reason but a falling out (yes this more than that but it's also a marriage and that is a special relationship) and someone somewhere made a mistake but forgiveness in life is essential.

I'm angry, hurt, upset and devastated by what my husband did but I do forgive him. I know he has huge family of origin issues and I know he doesn't like himself. But then why shouldn't he? H walked out on his family.

But you know as I write this, I feel this is a moot point, I know in my heart of hearts he's gone for good, I just hope I can get to a place where I can love again as it would be a shame to be done loving at this tender young age of 50.

◆◆◆◆

I know that mine would have to get some sort of help to figure out why. What would cause this ordinarily morally upstanding human being to throw it all away without a second glance?

He would also have to live alone for a while to see that he could be alone. Mine went to moving the other woman right in with him.

The reconciliation would be on my terms. It would be a slow process of getting to know each other again and feeling comfortable with each other.

◆◆◆◆

No second chance.

I always said infidelity would be a deal breaker for me but I knew that if I was put in the position I might think differently. And for the first 12 months, I probably would have given him a second chance, anything to turn back time.

Now I KNOW it is definitely a deal breaker. I didn't deserve the way he treated me, the lies, the nastiness, the persecution.

Apart from the other woman, he has treated me like something he stepped in and I can't even be friends with someone who could treat anyone like that.

It breaks my heart that I would stand in the way of my family being back together, knowing that is all that the kids want and I want my life back too, but not after this. Not that I think for a second it would ever happen.

But I know now that he wouldn't stand a chance. He changed and I don't like the person he became. Even if he changed back, I know what he is capable of and I don't want to have anything to do with it.

The trust has been smashed and there is no going back.

♦♦♦♦

I always said that it would be an absolute deal breaker. But the fact is, it wasn't. I spent 20 years with this man and shared two children. I loved him more than I thought possible.

But looking at it today I am not sure he could ever do enough for me to give him another chance. The pain and hurt that he has not only put me and our children through, but also the friends and family that have supported me along the way is so immense.

Even though it was only three weeks that he came back... things were so different. When I looked at him, he was not the same man.

I felt awkward around him and scared to be myself. I felt the need to walk on eggshells even though he was the one to cheat and leave.

During his emotional breakdowns I would comfort him and let him know that I would stand by his side. But the fact is, my heart needed him to be there for me.

I wanted him to tell me that everything would be ok and really mean it. I think he was saying it to try and convince me and him.

When he would say the wonderful and loving things I had been dying to hear, I doubted it. I wondered if he told her the same things.

I was struggling so hard to believe his words. But truth be told, his actions spoke volumes to his hesitation and insecurity.

I am terribly saddened to now be going through the process of divorce, but this journey has made me stronger and let me find a little bit of me separate from being a wife and mom.

♦♦♦♦

I used to think it was, but now I think it doesn't have to be. Maybe it depends on the kind of affair?

He told me he finally found the love of his live, and that he didn't cheat because there was no sex. I don't believe him, but right now I wish it was only about sex.

But who will know what it would be like if it was a physical affair, not an "emotional affair/physical affair." Maybe I would be just as devastated.

Living with midlife crisis is not "just" the affair, it's also the lies and the way they behave.

I don't know. The bomb drop was about three months ago and my head is still spinning. I don't think he will ever "give ME a second chance." I believe he thinks I messed things up. He says he's happy, and things with her kids are working out. He's on the road to happiness.

If it ever comes to him wanting a second chance I hope I can wait so I'm able to make a rational decision.

◆◆◆◆

The affair was not the deal breaker. It was the lying and cruelty I had to tolerate for no reason.

◆◆◆◆

Prior to getting married, an affair was a deal-breaker. I never stayed with anyone who cheated on me and never even gave them an opportunity to explain or apologize as I didn't want to hear it.

However, things are different now because (1) we are married and (2) have two children together. So, I've been willing to try to work through this betrayal in the hopes we could heal this and move forward.

He has continued to lie about his contact with the other woman which makes it harder for me to rebuild trust, which he thinks I should give blindly. That's not going to happen at this point.

My husband moved out a week ago and it's still too fresh and painful for me to consider taking him back.

I may be at a different place a few weeks or months from now, but right now, I'm not willing to give him another chance.

◆◆◆◆

When will I stop missing him?

He left seven and one half months ago but it seems like forever. I still have a knot in my stomach most days. I have tranquilizers that the doctor prescribed, but I do not want to rely on them or worse, develop a dependency on them.

Today is especially bad. Spring is almost here, a time when we would start our yard clean up and he would fertilize the lawn. He took great pride in his yard until last year around this time when he started his metamorphosis.

My daffodils have poked through the earth and what would have normally given me great joy is now a reminder that another season has passed and he is not home with us.

I get an adrenaline rush and the knot tightens thinking about him with her — the two of them enjoying spring together.

The robins have returned, but he has not. I miss my best friend in life terribly. I try so hard to get a grip on my emotions but sometimes they just take over. I want to pick up the phone but cannot. Strict no contact at this time.

I would like to talk to him about our kids but I know that she listens to his voicemails, reads his texts and his e-mails and then he fills in the blanks. I do not want her knowing anything more about me or our children than she already knows.

I guess what I'm looking for is reassurance that at some point the knot will go away. I will no longer wake up to the thought of him and carry it through the day with me.

Everyone says it will get better with time. I can only hope.

◆◆◆◆

I still have the knot too but I'm only three and a half months in. I don't have any answers, I just wanted to give you a hug and say I'm sorry you're feeling so sad and miss him so terribly... me too.

◆◆◆◆

I so remember asking all these questions in the beginning of all this mess. The feeling I was never going to be normal again — that there would never be joy in my life again. I wanted time to hurry and go by — just to stop the pain.

After eight years divorced — I was 55 at the time — this wasn't supposed to be happening at this time of my life. We had plans — 25 years together — we would be able to slow down and finally have the good things we had worked together for all those years.

Let me just tell you the knot does go away. We all hate to hear that time helps — but that's what it takes. Being together with someone you've planned your life with — then having it all change — takes time for us process all that has happened.

Will it ever make sense? I can tell you no, but there will come a point when you will accept this and make a new life for yourself. I'll admit it took me about five years to come to peace within myself. Then it was like I was reborn again and my life took on a whole new meaning.

I don't miss that person I lived with for 25 years — in fact unless I think really hard about it (which I seldom do) I rarely even think of the life we had.

You will come to a place of peace and start enjoying life again. It will happen even though we find it hard to believe when we are in so much pain. Let yourself go through all the emotions you are feeling — your head eventually catches up with your heart.

••••

I'm slowly finding peace within myself. I still believe we belong together but I too am forgetting what it's like to have him in my life. I'm at the point where I don't want anyone else in my life but I'm told that too will change. Time will tell but time will heal also.

Hard to have faith when you are trying to pick yourself up off the floor but I believe in adventures, the human spirit and in God – one of them should come through. My money is on God who will send the other two my way.

••••

I just wanted to say don't force yourself — don't force yourself to fall out of love with him. I tried that. I got so tired and weary that I stopped and told myself it will be what is meant to be.

I know all the new left behind spouses on this site struggle every day — I did too — as did everyone who has gone through this.

I lost so much weight in the first year — went on anti-depressants the first time in my life — I totally lost control of myself. Honestly I didn't believe I would ever get through this.

I just wanted everyone to know that there is light — you will be whole again — you will learn to laugh again — you will find the joys in life and put all this in the past.

I have not dated in eight years; I knew I had to find my way on my own. Now that I've come so far I know I don't want a relationship but that's not to say that someone special may drop on my doorstep (because honestly that's what would have to happen). If that ever happened I may open my heart once again.

But I don't need a man to fulfill me anymore — I'm happy where I am — and that's quite alright.

You're all getting to that better place — one day at a time — sometimes one minute at a time — nonetheless just believe in yourself.

♦♦♦♦

I'm still struggling. I know it was probably prolonged by living with him until late last year, so this is really fairly new still with being completely out of his life. But I don't have a lot of hope that things will be better for me.

I was told I'd feel much better once I got out of that house, but honestly, I was just distracted with the move and now that things have settled in, I feel worse.

I'm also kind of dreading spring/summer, knowing SHE will be likely planting in my garden (what was my garden). I wonder if my perennials will get ripped out and replaced just like I was.

They do all the summer festivals/concerts together and while I admit, I don't have to be quite so busy, my ex never suggested we do any of these things. I miss him terribly and am tired of my life not working out.

I have had too many losses, and just have a hard time understanding why other people go through life much more easily, have their families, have their husbands, and I am alone.

Yes, I'm having a "why me" moment, but I'm just tired of being alone without a lot of connections or support.

♦♦♦♦

At seven months I was still not myself at all. Now in a couple of weeks it will be two years from the bomb drop, twenty months separated, and divorce decree effective on the anniversary of the bomb drop. And I am feeling much much better.

It takes time, so be patient with yourself. Lean into the feelings when they come upon you, and try to stay focused on the present moment as much as possible.

Put all of your energy into planning a new life for you, work on letting go of thoughts of them. Put your attention as much as possible on what you can control, and that is your life, your family, your friends, your career.

It does get better, promise.

♦♦♦♦

The longer the marriage, the longer the residual knot. It's been four years and most days no knot. But it can be triggered by driving past the place where they worked together (and she still works). So, I take alternate routes most of the time even if it means going several miles out of the way.

Yes, time helps tremendously... you will learn not to hurt; you will find many other joys in life, and you may even forgive.

But you will NEVER forget nor will you ever condone. This is what unilateral breaking of a long-term relationship does to the blindsided party. It's called PTSD... and it just takes time and effort.

♦♦♦♦

The thought of the two of them being intimate together; being alone; missing him; stressing about the divorce and the unknown.

Knowing that I will never be intimate with him again; knowing that he has started drinking again after so many years sober.

Not talking to him when I want to or about things that I would normally have loved to share with him; knowing that he no longer wants me.

Sometimes it's just there and I don't know why. PTSD — that's exactly what my therapist said. I'm tired of being the strong parent while he spirals out of control.

This is not what I had signed on for. I signed on for better or for worse (can't get any worse than this and I'm still willing to work on it).

I signed on to retire with him, to plan our daughter's wedding together, to raise our grandchildren together and to travel.

I do not wish to do this with anyone else. Oh well, nothing I can do but suck it up, carry on and hope for the best.

♦♦♦♦

I'm not sure how much I want to know about the affair and the other woman.

I already know too much and don't want to rent her any more space in my head. I would want to know why he had the affair and who he was when he was with her.

♦♦♦♦

I think I'm a bit unusual in that I was never really interested in the other woman. Where he was and what he was doing seemed fairly irrelevant. What mattered was that he wasn't home.

There was also no chance I'd run into her, or them. They were in another country. If the thought of their sex life crossed my mind I didn't feel sexual jealousy, oddly, — I'd just think "Yuk - two cheats, cheating." But I rarely pictured them even having a cup of tea together! It just didn't seem to be the issue.

The issue was not that he wanted to be with her but that he didn't want to be with me. Still, I can't imagine I'd ever take him back because he was deceitful, cruel and lied.

And he has years of history and experience with her now, so the continuity of our relationship is forever broken. Some things cannot be repaired and our relationship is one of them.

♦♦♦♦

I really don't know. If we had reconciled early on, I'm afraid I would have wanted to know EVERYTHING — whether that was healthy for me or not.

I might still want a lot of details, but I'm not sure. I expect I would want to know why — after a relationship of four years and his leaving his marriage — she took these steps. I would also have to know that he really wanted ME and I wasn't just a familiar (more or less) rebound — again not just talk.

◆◆◆◆

I needed to know the how and when. I didn't need to know what they did together, I already could piece some of that together, pun unintended. I think I was looking for some insight into how I was feeling when all this went down.

Looking back, I knew something was going on, and I wanted validation that those feelings of mine were true. My warning system was fully functional; I just wasn't monitoring the reports adequately.

Those discussions made me stronger in myself, allowed me to trust my decision to give it a try even more. I knew I wouldn't ignore warning signs and I knew I could be okay without him. That gave me the strength to take things slowly, to not rush.

◆◆◆◆

At this point, it does not matter about his affair and the other woman. It would be very hard to decide if there was a chance of us getting back together but there is not.

No matter what my feelings were/are, that is his relationship, not mine. I'm sure there are things they share that we did/do not but I know what we had and that is something they will never have.

◆◆◆◆

I already know so much about the women he was with. I don't consider his "new and improved" girlfriend an "affair partner" but rather someone he pursued posing as a single man. I guess, technically, he was, as he had told me it was over and made the unilateral decision to end things.

The fact that I was still living at the house and he was giving me mixed signals didn't matter in his mind.

I think I'd still want him to tell me everything, though, because I would want him to open up about it and be forthcoming and transparent.

♦♦♦♦

Nothing. I have given her enough space in my head, I still hope she lands in hell but I don't want to know anything. Nothing will change that period in either of our lives and it will only add to my pain.

I'm not sure if that's because this is still raw but for now, no I don't want to know anything. I do know that try as she might, she won't measure up to me that much I know for sure. If she did, she wouldn't have gotten into an affair with a married man with two kids.

♦♦♦♦

He actually provided me with a lot of info about the other woman. Most of it I believe. However, he got really good at lying.

He thought he loved her and they talked about a future together. He completely entwined himself financially to her. Took her on vacations. Even entertained the idea of more kids although he had a vasectomy.

He is saying he wouldn't do that now. He said they just have a "connection." After he left me the second time, he went back to her again. I speculate that it was the easiest option. Both on the lease, little responsibility, etc.

♦♦♦♦

I found out way too much. I think it is best to know as little as possible. It was almost like he was a peacock showing off all his beautiful feathers. It wasn't for me that he was telling me everything. It was more for him.

◆◆◆◆

Originally, I wanted to know everything. All I knew was he told his sister that he was "in love" with the other woman, but did not act on that. She isn't even aware it reached that point on his side.

I would want to know if he was still obsessing about her and "missing" her.

I would want to know that she will not be around our children when he goes to visit his family (she's a close family friend on his side).

I would want to know if he's redirected his attention to another person in her place.

◆◆◆◆

Did he ever say he regretted cheating and wished he could undo the harm he had done?

He said he just thought to himself that he couldn't believe that he actually cheated. He said that his thinking was "what my wife doesn't know won't hurt her."

This has always scared me because what I have learned is that he does not feel bad about any wrongdoing as long as he doesn't think he will get caught.

♦♦♦♦

My husband apologized to me and asked me to forgive him. I asked him if he just expected me to separate and divorce without any questions or qualms.

He responded, "No. I would have come to my senses and you never would have known all this other stuff going on in my head, things would have gone back to the way they were."

Plus, what if I didn't learn of the emotion affair. Would it have escalated to something more? I wish I could hold a poker face because I should have just not let on until I had my "ducks in a row."

♦♦♦♦

It really is difficult to wrap your head around, let alone get your ego to accept, that you can be COMPLETELY off the radar where your spouse is concerned. But, in many cases, that is the absolute truth, at least the first time or so.

Once a cheater has to start working around his marriage in order to be with the other person, then you are at least superficially on the radar but more like the mountaintop he has to avoid crashing into, not a living, breathing, feeling human being.

You stop registering that way, because it's too emotionally expensive for him to do that. And if you persist in trying to break through that image, to demonstrate how human (emotional, unpredictable, etc.) you are, the more likely you're going to see him treat you like an object, a mere obstacle.

♦♦♦♦

My ex-husband told me that he did not see her in his future, however, he ended up marrying her, and still says he made a mistake. He also blames me for divorcing him. It looks like he is blaming me for marrying the bimbo.

♦♦♦♦

My hope is that he falls hopelessly in love with the whore that he's with now. I hope he invests time, emotions, money, dreams for their future and she dumps him like a piece of shit. Then, MAYBE then, he'll feel half of what I've felt for the past eight months. All in good time...

♦♦♦♦

My husband also had the idea that what I did not know would not hurt me. He knows differently now.

Our marriage counselor recommended Judith Spring's book, *After the Affair: Healing the pain and rebuilding trust after a partner has been unfaithful.*

My husband ordered two copies from Amazon so we could read it at the same time. We both underlined pertaining statements and then exchanged books to see what the other was thinking.

One thing that jumped out at me from the book were these statements:

"Women believe their affair is justified when it's for love: Men, when it's not for love."

"Women seek soul mates: men seek playmates."

"Women anguish over their affairs, men enjoy them."

Of course, these are generalities, but in our case, I think they rang true.

♦♦♦♦

We sat in my car when I confronted him about the girl-friend and when I asked him if they slept together yet, he looked me square in the face and said, "No, but we will this weekend."

My heart caught in my throat and I could barely breathe. I don't remember driving home but when I walked in the door and saw my grown son. I literally fell into his arms. I will never forget that moment, ever.

♦♦♦♦

Why is it they can treat us in the worst possible way, but we can't ever tell them EXACTLY how we feel? I did with my ex a number of times.

No, it didn't make a difference to him, but I wanted him to know exactly how I felt and was very glad I was at least able to say what I needed to say.

I realize no contact is the best way to go overall, but there are times (at least there were for me) when I needed to really let him have it and I did.

♦♦♦♦

The thing I would like to find out is: What is so great about doing this, that it is worth turning into a liar and a cheater?

Why is it when they are found out that suddenly they want the marriage, the women don't mean anything, they regret it hugely, they aren't the people they thought they were, blah blah blah — but they threw what they (now) want away like trash and can it ever be fixed?

I don't suppose there is an answer to that.

♦♦♦♦

Here's the deal about that. He wasn't planning on getting caught so he doesn't see it as hurting you.

It's about him getting his kicks outside the marriage. Honestly? He wasn't thinking about you at all.

Now that you've found out, which probably amounts to the tip of the iceberg, he's all about doing damage control. He wasn't planning on getting busted and that, despair, is what you have to deal with.

You have choices too. It's not his party anymore.

♦♦♦♦

When talking about stuff with my counselor about how they can continue to do what they know is wrong rather than stopping after their first fall, she said from what she's learned that once someone gets away with something like that, they tend to think they won't get caught.

They succeeded once, so it makes the second time easier. I intend no justification or excuses for behavior, just some explanation of how they can get to be so off kilter in their thinking.

♦♦♦♦

How can I stop having dreams and nightmares about him and her together?

He left seven months ago and I've been having vivid dreams and nightmares about him and the other woman ever since. I almost dread going to bed at night because I know they'll both be there haunting me.

The dreams always start out good; he and I are together and happy or are trying to work on our marriage. Then inevitably she enters the dream or he decides that it's not going to work after all and I wake up with my heart beating through my chest. I hate it.

Anyone else have dreams? If so, when will they stop? I can't remember the last time I had a good night's sleep and woke up not remembering a horrific dream.

♦♦♦♦

I, too, had the dreams. They became more and more infrequent and diminished to virtually none over a period of several years.

We know that those of you who are in the early stages of this get so tired of hearing it, but it takes time... and a surprisingly good amount of it to get through all this grief and pain. If you need it, get some medical help from the doctor for the sleeping.

♦♦♦♦

Yes I had/have the dreams three years into it. Mine are the same as yours. In the beginning we are happy and then he runs off with the other woman.

I can never fall back asleep. They do diminish when I have no contact with my husband. Whenever contact resumes, however, so do the dreams.

In counseling I was told to "dream" about my favorite movie star. It did not work. Only time with no contact.

◆◆◆◆

I had this issue in the beginning as well. I think it's common because we've been betrayed on a very deep level.

This is how I learned to cope with it.

Journaling -- I bought a journal and started writing letters to him and letters to her. I would get out all the feelings and pain on paper so they weren't stuck in my head.

This helped me to clear some of that clutter before trying to sleep. It also helped me to reach a place of resolve that they didn't deserve to haunt my day AND my nights. Sleepiness and exhaustion are culprits in self-healing.

Lucid Dreaming -- I bought a book on dreaming and started writing down as much as I could remember upon waking. I learned how to change the course of my dream so that I was in control of what happened.

I still had dreams about her, but I also "finished" the story in my dream so that I was okay and happily moving on with my life. I have used this technique for other painful memories that were cropping up in my dreams.

Meditation Music -- I have a Pandora account that we stream through the television. I play symphony music at night to help relax myself and our children. It works wonderfully.

I also bought a few self-hypnosis CDs that I listen to via earphones while I sleep. This has helped me to "drown" out the unpleasant thoughts and stream in positive energy and self-healing messages. I definitely notice a difference.

Please understand... I am NOT saying it's easy and that you should not feel the way you are feeling.

You are entitled to your feelings and they will come out no matter how hard we try to avoid them. However, I have learned that empowering yourself to not allow them to take any more from you is truly liberating.

Someone told me the following and I didn't "get it" at the time. Her message was: "It's never too late to live happily ever after."

♦♦♦♦

Even though (or maybe because) I'm feeling a little more in control of my emotions, I've noticed that for the last four nights, the nightmares are becoming more intense.

I have been awakened by nightmares of him coming back only to stay one night and then leave again. Each time, I wake up choking and gasping for breath and feeling completely devastated.

Is holding myself together and trying to let go during my waking hours "causing" me to have these more intense dreams and emotions while I sleep?

I'm not really looking for answers, I think I'm just posting as an outlet for my fears, pain, and sadness.

♦♦♦♦

My therapist said that I should think of things that make me happy immediately before I go to bed.

The subconscious holds onto these thoughts and those are the ones that come out in dreams. It would make sense because I think of him before I go to bed.

♦♦♦♦

I had a dream early after the bomb drop where I caught him with the other woman. My reaction was violent to say the least and I realized that detachment was necessary for my own mental health.

♦♦♦♦

Do I tell the other woman's husband about the affair?

When my husband told me about his affairs and the particularly obsessive nature of his current one (one and a half years and still going) I kicked him out. He has been out of the house for a month and hasn't looked back.

I just found out who she is. I want to tell her husband. I wish someone had done that for me before I wasted 19 years of my life being married to this douchebag.

Any thoughts?

♦♦♦♦

Are you prepared for the backlash from your husband and his other woman if you tell her husband?

Are you prepared to deal with this bringing the two of them closer together as it makes you the bad guy they can blame?

What result are you looking for by telling him?

♦♦♦♦

Do NOTHING.

First of all, you are not operating from your most logical self at this juncture. Keep the information and if at some time in the future it is of strategic value in securing your finances, bring it out.

I have made it my policy to wait at least 24 hours to respond to any communications from ex. That assures that IF I choose to answer I will RESPOND, rather than REACT. Often, after I've had some time to process whatever the situation is at that moment, I choose not to communicate back.

Think long term and high road; you can't go wrong.

♦♦♦♦

What's the point? It will make you feel better momentarily but in the long run, you won't.

If her husband doesn't know, who are you to tell him? Would you want someone to hurt you like that in the name of making themselves feel avenged?

The high road is the way to go. Because when you look back at this (and trust us old timers, you will), you want to look back with a good heart.

◆◆◆◆

Look, I'm real fond of the low road. But there's too many unknowns in this situation. You don't know this guy, and he has no reason to believe you. She could paint you as some crazy jealous type that's just trying to make trouble.

So... in this case... I wouldn't tell him. It will feed into the vortex of drama too much and you really don't have anything to gain but satisfaction from it.

So write your tell-all letter to the other woman's husband, and save it on your computer. It will make you feel better without giving the lovebirds anything new to bond over.

◆◆◆◆

Depends on your style and inclination.

If you feel you want to drop a grenade into your husband's affair, and this man's life, go ahead. If you prefer to step away from the chaos your husband is generating, don't do it.

Only you can decide whether to take action or not. Good luck.

◆◆◆◆

That man's unfaithful wife is HIS problem, not yours. Your unfaithful husband is your problem, and that's not the other woman's husband's problem to solve for you.

Besides, he can't keep his wife in line any more than you can keep your husband in line -- they're free adults who are CHOOSING to do this despite their spouses and potential consequences.

◆◆◆◆

I've done it. But the circumstances were a bit different: My ex had an affair with a friend of mine. The four of us, including her husband, used to go on vacations together, etc.

When I learned of the affair, I didn't go to her husband. I told my ex to tell her that she needs to tell him the truth. And that if her husband asked me for the emails I would give them to him. But I would not actively seek to destroy her marriage. Keep in mind her husband is a friend of mine.

She and my ex together lied to her husband using a story that my ex cooked up for all of us. Her husband called me, told me her lies, and asked me for the emails.

Ironically it was my ex and the other woman who told him there were emails that I discovered. I gave them to her husband. Within an hour of reading them he had packed his belongings and left her permanently.

She cried and cried to my ex, and he blamed me for the demise of her marriage. Blamed me.

It had the effect of bringing them closer together, ex told me that he was "responsible" for her because his actions in seeking an affair with her brought down her marriage.

They bonded closer together against the rest of the world and my marriage ended.

She and my ex were telling all of us lies that it was an emotional affair not a physical affair (as if that made it ok) and would have continued to lie and see each other regardless.

I realized later that once my ex became involved with her he wasn't going to stop. He admitted to me that he is weak, and failed me, and continues to say that to this day.

The only reason I shared any information with her husband is because he is a close friend of mine, a very good friend still, because we were and still are, part of a larger friend group. And even then I wouldn't do it unless he called me and asked me point blank.

My reason for doing it, I told my husband, is that were the shoe on the other foot, were it me calling her husband to give me the emails I would have wanted him to give them to me.

I still stand by that today. But, it was very messy for quite a while. And contributed to the end of my marriage, but I believe that would have happened anyway.

You posted this question asking for opinions. Here is one from someone who actually did reveal an affair to the other woman's husband. In your case I would not do it.

It will not change your circumstances any with your husband; it will likely hurt you more than help you. It seems that to me for you to do this with someone you do not know would be an act of vengeance and will reverberate back against you in ways that I believe you will regret later.

Your husband is having an affair and it either has caused or will cause the end of your marriage. Focus now on you. Your life, your future.

I know you are angry and have a right to be. Just be aware that actions taken out of anger will not help you. And they will suffer the consequences of their actions. They will.

◆◆◆◆

The only reason I'd be doing it is for kindness to this guy. He is young and can have a better future while still young that I only WISH someone had given me. I DESPERATELY WISH that someone had told me years ago. I would pay all the money I have to be doing this 10 years ago.

I am not doing this to stop the affair (I couldn't care less who he is with) and I'm not doing it to save the marriage (I don't want it). In truth, if they bonded over this and stayed together I'd be thrilled because I truly believe she does and will bring him misery.

However, I will take the high road.

♦♦♦♦

Get your settlement in place FIRST.

♦♦♦♦

Agree... get your settlement in place FIRST!!

Like you I wish someone had told me, it was after the fact that people were saying oh my we're so sorry we knew, blah, blah, blah. I know people don't like to get involved, and really would things have changed, I can honestly answer NO. Financially YES but emotionally NO.

It will just give ex and the other woman more to talk about; she obviously doesn't care about her husband. Karma will get them I promise you!

♦♦♦♦

Well, if you consider that NOT telling the husband is "taking the high road," that sort of implies that your motives for telling him weren't necessarily for his own good -- they were on "the low road." Which is understandable, but all the more reason not to go there.

♦♦♦♦

Get your financial settlement ironclad and legal. Then IF there is proof and you still feel this strongly that this young man should know all there is to know about his business... find a way to get it to her husband.

All I know is this: The great majority of people whom I know who have been betrayed by a cheating spouse, wish to high heaven that someone had clued them in early on so they could take steps to protect themselves. In this world of STDs... anyone needs to know about a cheating spouse.

Perhaps your use of "taking the high road" was a turn of the phrase used in your post... as opposed to you holding any retributive motive for telling this young man about something he really ought to be aware of? You and ONLY you can examine your motives and decide if they are benevolent or not.

♦♦♦♦

I would echo the advice to get your settlement in place FIRST.

However, I will share with you that some kind soul did let me know about my cheating husband. And they did it anonymously by sending me a sympathy card in the mail.

The cool thing about doing it anonymously was that it forced me (and my husband) to focus on the message rather than the messenger. I will be forever grateful to whoever that anonymous person was.

♦♦♦♦

Yes, to clarify, my use of "high road" was just using the phrase you all were using about this situation. I was actually surprised that few people felt the way I do about telling this guy and were focused on vindictiveness as a motive.

I feel very strongly that this person has a right to know and if his wife won't tell him, someone should. I am harboring rage about the fact that some people knew about my husband's cheating for years and never told me...

I do feel like I really wasted great years and love that someone would have valued on a person that I now realize is so narcissistic that he told me what I wanted to hear but wasn't actually capable of real love.

I like the idea of sending an anonymous note and will consider that for the future.

◆◆◆◆

I think he has a right to know, especially given the STD issue. I would do it anonymously. I know I would want to know if it were me.

◆◆◆◆

"Wanting to know" is a very personal and individual thing, and there's no way to know if someone does "want" to be told. They may already know or suspect anyway. So, you're applying YOUR preferences onto someone else with no idea what they might want.

That's not "wrong," just realize that that's what you're doing. You think it's best "for them" because you know it's best "for you." Your intentions are "pure," at least, even if it turns out this isn't appreciated by the other woman's husband.

But some left behind spouses "tattle," to share the pain or try to embarrass or punish the other woman (or the wayward spouse, if she thinks he'll get confronted by the other woman's husband) or in a vain attempt to break up the affair. The other woman's husband is basically just a pawn in these scenarios.

And some of those left behind spouses kid themselves that they're doing it for somebody's own good, when at the root of it, it's just lashing out.

So it matters that we each decide how to proceed based on our actual motivations, not the cover story that might make it sound better than it is.

◆◆◆◆

I found out a lot when I called the other woman's husband. His first words to me were, "I thought of calling you and wondered if you would ever call me." He knew way before I did. He helped me accept just how far gone the whole situation was.

We called each other back and forth as both our divorces progressed. Keeping each other apprised of what we did know, to help us in our divorces. He was a nice guy.

He said he felt so ashamed he stayed with her. He told me my ex was number four that he was aware of.

It was odd, but it made me feel better. I didn't need to compete against her. She was a bar whore. My stupid ex was just lame ass number four who fell for her shit. Good riddance to bad rubbish.

◆◆◆◆

There were people who knew what my husband was doing. If they had told me, several financial decisions would have been much different. The whole situation would have been different.

If you know the truth, then it is up to each person to decide what to do with it. Secrets are unfair to those in the dark.

◆◆◆◆

You don't know this guy. You don't know if you make him more evil than good by telling it. Or he might even know it already and doesn't mind the situation. You wrote that they are living in separate towns, right?

I think I would tell such a thing only to a person I know. In fact I did have a talk with married woman's husband, and it turned out that he had some clues and did not give a damn (he had his own agenda and own mistresses at the time).

Then there is also the trust issue: if someone completely unknown to you would contact you to tell you something bad about a family member of yours, how would you react? I would be suspicious at least and quite incredulous.

There are of course benefits in knowing, and I wish I had known earlier from some close friends that had their doubts. But I wouldn't have trusted a complete stranger, unless he or she would have sent me proof such as pictures of them.

And then it's also an issue of what you gain. On one hand, you may wish to open his eyes. But he might not see it this way. He might even become violent and kill his wife and her lover, aka your husband.

His kids, if any, might not see this knowledge as a blessing because this might imply divorce of their parents. There is a potential Pandora's box that you might re-consider opening.

On the other hand, what's in it for you by telling him? Would you not feel worse than better at longer term knowing that you interfered somehow in your husband's life, trying in a way to control it?

Good luck with your decision.

◆◆◆◆

I wish someone had told me long before I had found out, so yes I would tell him. I called the other woman's husband

and he refused to speak to me about it but he had known months before I found out.

My husband was the reason she left him and set herself up in a house waiting for my husband to leave me.

So I gained nothing from it but lost nothing either.

♦♦♦♦

My husband was calling his emotional affair married other woman from work every day. At least a half dozen people knew what was going on, but nobody said anything to me. I had to discover everything on my own.

I was/am absolutely humiliated that so many people knew what was happening, I feel like they were all laughing behind my back. I really wish someone would have let me know what was going on.

♦♦♦♦

I see no problem in informing other woman's husband. I wish someone had told me what was going on. As a matter of fact, when I found out I struggled with the decision to tell her husband and then when I did, I found out he knew it for months, or suspected at least.

That hurt a lot... we were all friends too and I have always wished he had told me about his suspicions. But he didn't. Exposing the affair sometimes takes the air out of it too; all of a sudden it isn't a secret.

♦♦♦♦

I know how the rage feels. Eventually, you may get to a place where you aren't so angry. Where you can let it go.

I will tell you that anyone who KNEW and who did not tell me, is no longer anyone I consider a close friend. Lost a few "so called" friends through this.

♦♦♦♦

I have no use for "friends" who will entertain or even appear socially with the cheating couple, in effect condoning the infidelity.

But I really don't think other people are responsible for keeping me informed about my spouse's questionable activities of ANY sort, and I don't blame them for being leery of getting involved in something that could blow up in their faces as well. I certainly don't feel angry about those who keep silent.

Then again, I grew up in a small town where everybody involved themselves in everybody else's business and I hate that.

The anonymous note, preferably with verifiable evidence of some sort so it doesn't appear to be a prank, seems like the middle road -- only if you genuinely are concerned for the betrayed spouse, not to serve some purpose of your own.

♦♦♦♦

I don't understand: how can a friend or a neighbor or a complete stranger know something FOR SURE about our wayward spouse that we did not know.

I am pretty sure all my "friends" who imagined something might be going on between ex and the other woman could not have known for sure.

You cannot know for sure unless you see them making out in public or at least kissing passionately. That's why I feel it's hard to judge who really knew and who not. If the wayward spouse fooled us so well, most likely he also fooled others.

And I would not feel comfortable to tell to any friend anything if I only had some suspicions, but no real proof.

I would tell someone close to me only if I also had the proof to give them. And again, sometimes ignorance is bliss, not for the left behind spouse but for any children involved.

♦♦♦♦

I would also advise, get your settlement first. You don't want any action, even an "anonymous" one to come back against you.

The other woman and your husband aren't stupid and are likely to figure out it was you. So get your settlement done.

Then send the anonymous note.

♦♦♦♦

Thinking it through, I couldn't expect more from his community of single cheater guys who partied with him and his other women. They are "dead to me" and my family but I don't need to engage with them to tell them that.

But there is one person that I did expect more from who is a good person and someone I worked with and spoke with weekly. He never told me.

Right now the steps I'm making toward my healing are deciding who I am going to be able to take with me into my future and who I want to leave behind. I've deleted people from Facebook and my contacts in Outlook (mostly his friends).

I realize, though, that until that one person comes clean with me about what he knew, when he knew it, and how he dealt with it, I cannot make an informed decision about whether the relationship has potential.

I have no room in my life for "relationships" that are full of distrust and lack of honesty. I'd rather lose people I care about forever than bring that negative energy to me upon contact with them.

My soon-to-be-ex put this person, who is a good moral person, in a no-win situation but that is not my problem and I won't accept that as a reason to keep this person in my life.

It will be sad to lose him but I'd be better off without him than having a relationship that is full of distrust and betrayal.

Did you all also shed those people who knew and didn't tell you?

◆◆◆◆

A close friend of mine was informed by the other woman's husband that her own husband was having an affair. She was very grateful to this man for telling her, as it propelled her forward to ask him to leave, and to protect herself settlement-wise.

She kept the info to herself for a period of time, but has always said she was thankful that this man thought enough of her to tell her what was going on. She also thought something was going on, but did not have proof. He provided it.

So, unless you have verifiable proof, I would not tell anyone anything. Could be serious blowback on you. Who needs that on top of everything else? Every circumstance is different; evaluate yours, and then decide.

◆◆◆◆

We're just starting our divorce. It'll be a while before I'll have the opportunity to do it. I do have proof that she was with my husband.

But I do not know her husband at all and I agree that I don't know what he'd do, which is risky. I also don't know what his wife would say about who I am. Additionally, my husband is not the only one she cheated on her husband with... there were many others.

I still feel strongly that I should have been told, but more strongly that those who knew me and who spoke with me should have done it and I will never forgive them. Good riddance to bad rubbish.

♦♦♦♦

I think it's a good choice. You conclude your dealings/ divorce with your husband, then you offer the information to her husband for whatever he wants to do with it or not. But it doesn't wrap back against you.

♦♦♦♦

I would tell him. Why should you care if they all get pissed at you? Your husband is already gone; her husband has a right to know and she deserves what she gets.

♦♦♦♦

I told the other woman's husband.

I had a strong conviction that he deserved to know. I felt that I deserved to know the truth and so did he, for many reasons. What he did with the information was up to him, but I wasn't going to be a party to a lie to a decent, trusting person (too many people had done that to me).

He apologized to me! She had left him a month before. He was devastated, but so grateful that I had contacted him and that it all made sense, but he felt awful that he didn't tell me four months before when he found evidence of their emotional affair. She'd told him that my husband was pursuing her and it was one-sided and she would tell him to back off.

My husband and the other woman were furious! And furious that someone had told me! "How dare they" was his reaction. He denied it but I had evidence. Being furious with the messengers was a pure deflection of their guilt.

I will never forget how I felt when I found out, and I'm sure her husband won't either. We have corresponded a few times and he was as devastated as I was.

I thought long and hard about telling him for a couple of weeks, but I couldn't live with myself knowing that he was probably as confused as I had been before I found out.

I know that I felt better once I knew, and hoped it would help him too. I took a risk as you never know how someone else will react. But I didn't do it for any reason other than I felt he deserved to know the truth.

Obviously each situation is different and each person's view of things is different. I'm not saying you should do it.

I made the decision that I could live with, not wanting to lash out and hurt anyone, but wanting to reach out to another human in pain and let him deal with the truth, not the lies they had been living.

But take care of you first. I wasn't anywhere near any kind of settlement with him then, he had only just left. But I agree with everyone else, get all your stuff sorted first if you plan to do it because you just never know their reaction.

I find it laughable that they made so much noise about people outing them, and denied they were anything other than friends.

She left work because she couldn't handle the fallout (they worked together) and took a vacation by herself and then the second she came back they were together and introducing her to the kids. Did they think we were all stupid?

◆◆◆◆

I can't think of many situations where the other betrayed spouse should not be told. If it were you, you would want to know. Why keep their dirty little secret?

♦♦♦♦

I'm not sure who I agree with at this point. The other woman's husband had called me because of an anonymous letter he had received at work one day.

This was after he went to his wife's work and made her come out to her car and read it with him. They felt that the letter was from me, but it wasn't signed. It had some very intimate details of my husband and his wife's relationship.

It really hurt the other woman's husband. He had no clue what was going on. So, he called me at work, as she claimed she didn't have a number for me.

I always answer my phone at work, so I picked up and when he told me who he was and asked me about a letter, I just told him I didn't know what he was talking about and that I was hanging up.

He called me a few days later, and left a voice mail, begging me to please talk to him about this letter. I still had no clue what he was talking about, so I didn't call him.

When he called me a third time at work, I gave him my cell number and asked him to call me later at home. He was so distraught and upset.

So, he ended up calling me later and we talked. He explained the letter and he believed that I had not written or sent it, but he wanted to know why someone would.

I had no answer. I didn't really tell him anything, but as he guessed certain things, I would tell him what my husband had told me. I also told him that my husband had emails that were very descriptive and told him that I could give him a copy of some of those if he wanted them.

Even through all of this his wife kept lying to him about the extent of her involvement with my husband.

I found out much later that the letter was actually sent by my husband. How sick is that? He started all of the drama, and he did it on purpose to hurt her. Not only that, but now he wants to be with her again, and she's going to take him back after what he did?

Did I mention that she blames me for her divorce in process right now? And that her husband is rich and that she'll get half?

Maybe my husband is the one who is using her for her money. That is always the subject of most arguments. It sure isn't for her looks or personality or intelligence. He's admitted that.

So, I didn't tell her husband directly, but I was involved in a way. Sucked in might be a better term. My husband orchestrated the whole thing to get rid of her, but has now run back to her.

I'd love to tell you it's interesting to watch, but afraid not.

◆◆◆◆

Should I tell my husband I know who the other woman is and more?

My husband left two years ago and I discovered recently he was seeing the other woman more than two years before that I know of because of documentation.

Even though I know he really could give a hoot, I feel a strange sense of relief that I let him know I know. Anyone else get that?

I've had people on this site say don't let him know, especially since you're still in the divorce process but it just seemed so crazy to me that I didn't say anything because this woman was my former friend. Our teen daughters know that they're dating and it's so odd for them.

Another reason I'm glad I said it is because afterward, he acted a bit guilty and was overly friendly. It was fake but it helped at least temporarily in his attitude toward me.

I kind of wonder if some men have less respect for you if you don't say "Hey, you SOB... you hurt me badly with those lies and you WILL reap what you sow!" I think for him, it's a Catholic guilt thing.

What also amazes me is that I asked him about his vacation schedule because I wanted to see if he'd admit he was going on a company cruise. He said it got cancelled because his company is not having a good year. Yeah right!

See the things you can get out of them if you confront? More lies.

♦♦♦♦

Yes, it is freeing to realize that one is not crazy, that there really was something behind it all. And it suddenly makes all the puzzle pieces fall into place.

As for not telling, sometimes it is wise to keep something up your sleeve especially if you're in the "discovery" phase. If a cheating spouse knows that you know, he might get better at hiding things. But after a certain point, it doesn't matter anymore.

I told my ex when I caught him in that lie. His comment? "I 'wanted' you to find out" The ass. But he was one that had his head so far up his ass that it was simple for me to continue to discover stuff. It was pretty obvious, and he was pretty stupid. Others do a better job of hiding stuff.

He is STILL lying, only this time, he lied to the courts... and I have proof.

♦♦♦♦

The purpose of not saying anything is in the cases where you are not sure yet which way you want to go... or to give you time to get your ducks in a row.

If he is out of the house and divorce is in progress, and you have nothing to lose, there is no point, in my opinion, of not saying you know if you feel like it.

I knew it was an either/or situation so he got the ultimatum on divorce day. I knew what financial things I was dealing with so did not have that many ducks to line up. Others don't say because it is to their advantage. No advantage, no reason to not have your say.

♦♦♦♦

I've never been in the position of knowing about a secret other woman, so I'm not sure how I'd deal with it. But given my inability to "fake it" on most other things (you'll never catch ME playing poker!) I highly doubt I could keep my mouth shut or otherwise not give myself away, unless there were some major benefits to biding my time, as others have pointed out.

But I think it IS a huge relief when they know you know, and don't have to hide any more. They can afford to be nicer. Personally, I'd rather he was nicer to me because I knew what was eating at him, than have him be nasty to me for a reason I couldn't imagine (hiding another woman).

To speak up, or not speak up, should be decided based on what is best in YOUR situation, for YOU. There is no universal right or wrong way, or time, to do things.

◆◆◆◆

I didn't have to "confront" him with the truth about his affair, I just proudly listed all of the adulterous charges he made on the company account in my court documents.

I had to prove that he's been spending money like he's a Rockefeller, while telling me and the court that "he has no money" to provide for his kids.

He now knows that I know about where he was going for months including our anniversary when he said he didn't have "time" to make any plans to celebrate, and around the holidays when he dropped the divorce bomb on me saying how he was so busy working.

Do you think that he came and apologized for spending our life savings on his selfish secret lifestyle? Nope. Was he nicer to me from guilt? Nope. Did he start becoming an even bigger ass to fight me for everything? Yep!

I am pretty sure that from his actions (no remorse, no empathy) that my husband is nothing but a Narcissist. Even his kids were tossed into the trash along with me and our marriage.

I rejoice for this divorce! What a blessing to be free of such an evil person! I deserve so much more, and he deserves the kind of twinkle twat he left me for!

He can try to pull the blanket over our kids' heads by making up stories about how he and his "roommate" were "friends first, but now they're more than that" when they see pictures of them hugging each other in his apartment. But, mommy has made every truth about his charges known to them.

Every time he gives the impression that he's broke, I tell them how much he's been spending on his own lifestyle.

There is no reason for me to "protect" their father's sorry ass for being a deadbeat and a selfish coward who ditched his family for a life of his own.

Gee, I think I'm still holding a tad bit of resentment... maybe if he did try buttering me up with guilt niceness I could let it go faster. That will likely never happen.

◆◆◆◆

There is something so liberating about finally getting them "outed" and it's even more refreshing to hear that others echo my sentiments.

Keeps me focused on the big picture and I can't wait for The End to appear sooner rather than later.

◆◆◆◆

My husband kept denying the other woman for months but I also have documentation that it started before "the speech."

Just a couple of weeks ago he admitted the affair. Guess he finally figured out it wouldn't make any difference in the divorce or child support so why not out it?.

Everyone in town knew about it anyway, it just made him look like a dumbass for lying about it.

◆◆◆◆

If you have copies of charges husband ran up with the other woman like gifts purchased that you don't have, etc., does it help in court? Can you potentially get reimbursed? I'd like to bring up all those "purchases" with him, but am biding my time.

◆◆◆◆

That is definitely something to discuss with your attorney, but I think that communal property spent on someone else during an affair can be recovered.

In my case, my ex was more than generous in our settlement so there was no need for me to use all the proof I had.

I would've if I had to though and it absolutely infuriated me that he spent OUR money without my knowledge on the other woman. Come to think of it, it still does!

◆◆◆◆

Is his emailing cheating or an addiction?

A few years back my husband had an affair with another woman. The affair ended and we got back together and I thought we have been happy for the past three years.

Just yesterday, I discovered that he has been replying to posts on craigslist of women wanting to get together just for wild sex. He states in his e-mails to these women that he has a conservative wife and wants something new and exotic.

He asks in his e-mails what will they do and how will they dress. He always says he wants to meet up and do the "act," but I never see anything where he has followed up and actually met these women.

I also see where he has contacted cross-dressers on craigslist. When I told him last night that I found these things, the laughed and said that he was just fucking with them and wanted to see what they would say. He and a buddy were goofing off and e-mailing them.

He said that he would never, ever do anything, that he loves me and swore that he has been faithful. He said that if I left him, that he wouldn't want to live.

So, I know that he does love me. But is this an addiction? How do I know if it is something he really wants to do? He has gone to porn sites on occasion, but not a regular thing, that I know of. He has had erectile dysfunction with me the past two months.

I just don't know what to do. Is this something he can get help for or should I just be done with him? I do love him and know he loves me. He is very affectionate all the time. I just don't understand why he is contacting these people.

♦♦♦♦

Yes, it does sound like he has a problem with porn and fantasy.

I'd say he's either in denial about this or he's knows full well he has an issue but desires to carry on with it. Either way he's taking away from his relationship with you. Not putting enough in as he should. He WILL know this.

Basically, he's addicted AND cheating. What YOU do about it is the issue here because HE won't do anything if he doesn't think he has an issue.

I'd suggest you state clearly to him that YOU consider this infidelity and that YOU require him as your husband to stop this bad behavior.

If he can't or won't then you have to make some hard choices. An addiction isn't healed without serious work from the addicted person but first he has to realize and admit to the problem.

Sorry for your confusion and pain. This isn't your fault or possibly even his, but it's his to deal with and sort out if he wants any kind of healthy relationship and life.

♦♦♦♦

What should I do? Where do I go from here? How does he fix this? Can a counselor really help?

♦♦♦♦

Until and unless he admits/accepts that he has a problem and he COMMITS to work on it there is, sadly, nothing to be done for him. No matter how much you want it for him, he needs to want it for himself.

You need to focus your energies and attention on YOU and what YOU are going to do with this reality.

♦♦♦♦

One thing I noticed that you said was that he states in his emails that his wife is very conservative. Have you considered NOT being so conservative?

Instead of worrying about what he is doing and what is wrong with him, why not try finding out what kind of "wild and kinky" sex he'd like and giving it a shot?

♦♦♦♦

I'd say that is an individual call. What might not be a problem for one might be a problem for another.

Personally, I would consider it a "problem" if my husband were talking about/listening to sexual fantasies with other women. Period. But, to each his own!

♦♦♦♦

It's a "problem" because she is uncomfortable with her husband having this type of interaction — even relatively anonymously and only "in theory" — with others, especially because of their recent history. This behavior represents a threat to her.

And, in these messages he describes her disparagingly, as if her being "conservative" was a bad thing or a lack or drawback, a "problem" for him.

He is blatantly stating that he is not getting something he desires from his relationship. That may be just more of the fantasy talk, but it still hurts to hear it or think he'd say something especially if it wasn't true.

But if HE doesn't see it as a problem HE is responsible for addressing, there is nothing she can do about that. His lack of consideration for her feelings becomes a second problem — one that is entirely hers to address.

♦♦♦♦

His desire for it isn't the "problem" though. And who knows if he actually desires the action? Perhaps the thrill is simply in talking about it online — which falls within HIS definition of "ok" behavior.

Apparently it is NOT "ok" with the most significant person in his life, however.

We can't determine for her whether this is "cheating "or an addiction. She can't even determine if it's an addiction; only her husband can tell if he's doing this compulsively and to his own detriment, and if he is unable to stop.

He may just not want to stop, because he likes it and doesn't see anything wrong with it, even if his wife does.

Only she can determine if SHE considers this cheating, and if SHE says so, then for her, in her relationship, it IS. Then, she gets to decide what she intends to do about his cheating — whether he, or we, consider it that or not.

♦♦♦♦

I have a problem with him on many levels.

He is being disrespectful to women all across the board. He is being secretive, seeking titillation, and being crude.

I doubt that this is innocent and anonymous erotic flirtation. He is out there circling the pond and cruising his options, and she knows he has previously had a compulsion to do the wrong thing.

I think this is the tip of the iceberg. His wife knows it. Now she has to decide what she is going to do about it, which in essence may amount to nothing, or she may throw the book at him.

I would not tolerate him soft soaping me or convincing me there was nothing to it.

♦♦♦♦

He is communicating his "desires" to strange women online; he is denigrating his wife to them AND he is trying to hide it all.

No one is saying that there is something "wrong" with his DESIRE for a spicier sex life. What I see is "wrong" is that he is discussing this with other women, in detail.

Wanting to "meet up and do the act" goes far beyond just "desiring" a spicier sex life. Not something I'd be willing to accept in my marriage, that's for sure!

♦♦♦♦

He's not looking to spice up his sex life with his wife. He's looking to spice up HIS SEX LIFE. Period. He might take what he can get from his wife but he's definitely looking for more action.

He's a filthy sneaky lying little love rat. Set a trap, catch him in it and let him die a long slow miserable death.

♦♦♦♦

Well, I have to tell you, I do spice it up for him from time to time, although, not often. I am having a hard time believing that he didn't meet these women in person, even though he swears he didn't.

AND, there is something else I didn't post, simply because I was mortified over it. I caught him e-mailing cross-dressers (who sent him pictures) and also a man who wanted someone to watch him and his wife having sex, and possibly join in. I am SO embarrassed! What kind of man does that?!

When I asked him if he really was interested in that lifestyle (cross-dressers, etc.) he said absolutely not. I asked why he does it and he just doesn't have an explanation. He says he doesn't know. But he is begging me not to leave him and if I did, he wouldn't want to live.

Can a straight man look at that kind of stuff and not be bi?? I am thinking more and more that he has an addiction. What do you think?

♦♦♦♦

There is something about the *general* doldrums of midlife that inspires lots of people to explore aspects of sexuality or take other illogical but thrilling risks that they never considered before and don't make a habit of.

So this doesn't necessarily mean he has been or will become any of the things he's investigating right now. In many ways it's like being 12 or 13 all over again, rediscovering the world outside your safe family cocoon.

The trouble is, he is playing with fire, and like so many teenagers, he could end up burning himself... or you.

You can't stop him from doing whatever he chooses, especially since this time around he's an adult and you're not his parent.

But your boundaries are just as important as the ones his parents set (or should have set) the first time around. They will protect you, and "may" inspire him to reconsider some of his choices and/or acting on his impulses.

♦♦♦♦

Don't be embarrassed, we have all discovered many horrors in these types of situations. His problems are no reflection on you.

It's difficult to know what's going on with him but he's out of control. In my opinion, you need to set limits if you are both going to work on saving this relationship.

If this was my husband I would be saying:

1. He breaks all contact with his various email buddies.

2. He takes this problem to his own counselor.

3. You agree to a timeline to work on any problems in the marriage, with professional help if need be.

The only other thing I'd say is that sometimes online stuff gets way out of hand. It's almost as if some people feel that because it's online it's not a real betrayal or affair.

The other thing is that you avoid showing any signs of permission or collusion. If he can't live without you then there is only one choice to make: Clean up his act and work at getting back on track. Anything less isn't a real commitment, in my opinion.

I found out my husband has been having an affair. He presented it to me in terms of him leaving and us remaining friends, going on holiday and all the great stuff we do. I left. He was shocked and now he's miserable.

I don't concern myself with what he is doing in his life. He said we were the 90% and she was the 10% that was missing. Now, using his own analogy, he gets 10% family time and 90% he's out on his own.

If he is allowed to continue with this behavior I don't think you have any chance of saving your marriage.

PS: I was in shock for three months and like jelly for six. It all takes time but the best thing I did in the early days was to set limits on what I was prepared to accept.

◆◆◆◆

This advice really has helped. I especially never thought of the timeline. I guess that makes a lot of sense. He can't go on with years of counseling, obviously.

Why can't I just have the faithful husband and happy family like so many of my friends do? I am so jealous of them.

◆◆◆◆

We can never be sure what others are actually living with, just based on what we see. We couldn't even see our own situations brewing!

Try not to expend too much envy on what you THINK others enjoy. Save the energy for dealing with the facts of your own situation. It's a much better investment!

◆◆◆◆

How do I keep no contact going with him?

I am going to initiate no contact again for the third time. We have never lasted longer than seven days.

I am afraid. I don't want to do it. I don't want no contact but I know it's the only healthy thing for me and that I must do it.

I want to be stronger, healthier, braver, and happier. In the long run, I think no contact is the best way to get to those goals.

It is so hard to maintain no contact because when we try he tells me how much he misses me, how I'm his best friend and he doesn't want to lose that, and how he doesn't know if breaking up is what he wants.

He also tells me he doesn't know if he really wants the other woman. And he cries, a lot. It sparks this false sense of hope. But what am I really hoping for anyway? All I can see in continuing this relationship is more pain.

♦♦♦♦

Keep no contact until the other woman is gone from his life for good. Otherwise, you will go crazy. Be firm with him on that. It's for your own good.

♦♦♦♦

Let him tell the other woman he isn't sure he wants her or not... you don't have to listen to that drivel. it's VERY hard, very hard and my husband and I have young children so when he left we still had daily communication.

He returned and even now when one of his texts begins to be a "rant" I just delete, don't even read it, and when he comes home at night, I don't even address it.

They are all caught up in themselves and I have NO idea why we get so caught up in THEM too.

Be strong. Right now he has her and you by a string — and the outcome is unknown, it really is.

Blessings for peace and resolve as you go no contact (they don't realize the first day or two or three... that you are no contact, (it's all about THEM remember?) but he'll get the picture eventually. Do this for YOU.

♦♦♦♦

Ok, so you've spotted the pattern. When you distance, he pursues until he gets his way. He knows the "magic words" to sweet talk you into caving in. Now that YOU know that, those magic words should lose their power.

Besides, what is he REALLY saying? HE is uncomfortable (missing a person is uncomfortable) and he "doesn't know" if breaking up is what he wants. (But, he might anyway... he just isn't sure.) So it's all about what's best for HIM.

Oh, be still my heart, is that the most seductive thing he can come up with? Repeatedly?

But what do you mean by "trying no contact"? No contact isn't a tactic or some sort of trial, it's what you do when you realize that contact is harmful to you.

Once you truly realize that fact, it's not so hard to control the urge for contact. You don't need help doing it, although supportive reminders about the damage that contact causes can be helpful.

♦♦♦♦

I know it isn't a tactic or trial. I truly realize that contact is harmful as it prevents me from getting over him and it prevents him from letting go of me. But it is hard to control the urge when I miss him like crazy and I miss him like crazy all the time.

Twice before I told him we needed to stop talking, texting, and emailing unless it was about selling the house, unexpected home repairs, or medical emergencies, things like that.

The first time he texted me after five days and I caved and said we could see each other.

It was great hanging out with him for a few days until I realized it wasn't doing anything to get me to a better place emotionally. I told him again we had to have no contact or I was going to be in this limbo forever.

That time it lasted seven days. On the eighth day I ended up calling him for help. Again, after he helped me, I caved when he asked if we could hang out. Dumb dumb dumb.

We stayed in contact again that time for two or three weeks, talking and texting and hanging out. This may sound crazy but it felt good having my best friend back while we were together. When we weren't hanging out though, it was horrible.

I have always known that I need to stick to it but I'm weak and being apart is so painful. The worst part is that I know he considers me his best friend and wants to hang out and when we do it's fun. In the depths of sadness, when that kind of "relief" is dangled before me, I'm ridiculously susceptible to caving.

So tonight I told him I really need to stick to my guns and we really are not going to hang out or talk or text or email any more. He asked me for how long and I told him until I move or until he breaks it off with the other woman.

I told him I was disgusted with myself and feel like I'm the other woman now. He told me several times that he doesn't know if he wants it to be over with us, as if that would make it somehow ok to be with both of us.

He seems shell shocked. When he left I could tell that it had only half sunk in. He told me if I ever want to hang out that I should call. I told him that unless he tells me he's ended it with her, I won't be calling.

As he was leaving, he turned back around and grabbed me in a tight hug and hung on like I was a lifeline. I know it's the best thing but it sucks anyway.

◆◆◆◆

Good for you that you've told him you're not his second option after the young girl he's screwing.

This sentence had me saying "Ouch": "He considers me his best friend and wants to hang out and when we do it's fun."

If you relent and go back to hanging out, you'll be setting yourself up for more heartache despite the initial "fun." The fun is strictly on "his" terms.

The left behind spouse tends to view hanging out in a friendly fashion as the wayward spouse moving nearer to her. The wayward spouse, though, tends to view it as the left behind spouse accepting that she's now just a friend.

Great! Who wouldn't like to use the ex they left, who knows them so well, for a bit of casual contact now and again, as long as it's no hassle?

But when we're in love with a person it's hard to be their best friend while they're dating someone else.

My ex came and went for six months after he left. He stayed in an apartment in our home and I didn't sleep with him. (He was another woman's boyfriend now.)

He wanted to hang out. He wanted to hold hands and sleep with me. (No.) I was trying to figure out what to do about finances, our home and so on, so I accepted him visiting.

One day we went to the coast because he wanted to check out hotels in case he decided to go there in the summer. I didn't think much of it as he had been coming to see me on his own, without the other woman, (obviously!).

We went to one hotel and he looked at a room. Then we went to another hotel. The receptionist asked: "Would you like to see a room with single beds or a double bed?" He said: "Oh a double bed! Of course!"

He was planning his summer holiday with the other woman.

To him, that meant nothing. He'd told me our relationship was over. I knew he was with the other woman. He wanted me to be his friend. He wanted us to hang out together. On "his" terms.

And of course a pal of his wouldn't have minded traipsing around with him while he looked at hotel bedrooms for himself and the other woman. I "did" mind!

You accepted your ex's relationship with his other woman for some time — a situation you probably thought you would never accept. Don't let him jerk you around now you've put your foot down!

♦♦♦♦

Do you see the flaw in the logic here?

"Until I move... OR until he breaks it off with the other woman." Why is it ok for him to contact you once you move?

And can he contact you as soon as he and the other woman have a fight and "break up" — even if they make up a few days later, or he's in the midst of pining for her and needs your soft shoulder to cry on?

I only point this out because I made the same mistakes myself. It leaves you both with loopholes and leaves YOU open to the same old toxic stuff as soon as you hear from him again.

If it were me I'd tighten those boundaries a bit. Why not try writing it out to make sure you've covered all your bases and have a clear and enforceable policy?

Then when you're confident you do, email it to him — and don't respond to anything he does after that, that doesn't meet your criteria.

◆◆◆◆

He has repeatedly said there was nothing wrong in our relationship that we couldn't fix. That he still loves me. That he thinks he might be making a mistake with this other woman.

That he would like to move back in and see if we could be happy again, but that it's "too complicated" because the other woman would find out. And now this, out loud, that he wants us both.

Not that it wasn't obvious, he has always tried to keep me in the picture and said things to keep me hanging on.

What is wrong with me that I still love and want this man, or should I say boy! He's a little boy living in fantasy land. On top of all that he keeps saying he just wants me to be happy again... Again? Here's what I hear when he says that, "Please be happy so that I can stop feeling guilty for having crushed you to pieces for no good reason and get on with my life and be happy with my new girlfriend."

It's only the second day and already he's texted me. He wants to come over after work (around midnight) to get some things from the garage.

I can't imagine what is so important that it can't wait and feel like he's just testing me. On the other hand if he really does need something, I don't mind if he lets himself in and out and keeps it at that.

I want to know what it is he wants so badly but, in the interest of minimizing contact, have refrained from asking.

My real problem is that even though I don't want to see him and that I know if I do I'll just end up feeling bad, there's this stupid, stupid, weak part of me that won't/doesn't want to resist the urge to see and talk to him.

How do I resist the urge? I know I will have some regret whether I resist the urge or not.

I'm going to tell him to go ahead and get his things and let himself out but that I can't see or talk to him. I just need to harden my resolve to follow through that way.

I was doing so well today too. Why'd he have to go and wreck that? I feel like I'm going to throw up.

♦♦♦♦

It's a pretext. He IS testing you. So, now what? This is where you need to lay the groundwork BEFORE you try to enforce a boundary.

What is your legal situation regarding him accessing the property and/or taking objects? Until you get that ironed out, he can probably legally show up every hour and take one item at a time until the place is cleaned out!

If you've already signed a separation agreement then he should have a deadline by which he either picks up his things (at an approved time) or he relinquishes them to you.

If you don't have a separation agreement, then you need to get one in place ASAP.

♦♦♦♦

Look up "extinction burst." He is doing what has always worked for him in the past. If you cave, you will have given that behavior of his more power and it will be even harder next time.

Think of your kids in the checkout at the grocery store and those darned candy bars.

♦♦♦♦

I did it! I didn't cave. It was so hard though. Resisting wasn't really hard. It was just emotionally hard in general. I felt like I had taken a tiny baby step forward yesterday before he texted and then a step back after.

He didn't show up until I had already gone to bed but woke up when he texted me. He wanted to know if I wanted him to come through the house so opening the garage door wouldn't wake us up.

Yeah, my and my daughter's bedrooms are over the garage and when the door opens, it wakes me up, but NO! I didn't want him to come through the house! Things were hard enough as it was.

I only had one break in my resolve... when the garage door closed and I knew he had left, I started crying and sent him a text that said, "That was hard." He said he was sorry and that it was hard for him too, thanked me and made a sad face. I should have resisted even that.

So this morning I'm struggling not to cry and fall apart again. And I pray he doesn't pull that on me again any time soon.

He wants someone else! Why does he torture me by deliberately doing things to keep me hanging on too? It's cruel and heartless.

◆◆◆◆

Yes, THAT makes sense! They really can't see how transparent they are. But even when we can see right through them, our brains can't always over-rule our emotions, so we respond with an equally useless text.

Until, that is, we finally BELIEVE the things we've heard and read, that make sense but go against what we want so badly.

Once you truly believe that he's not the guy you want him to be right now, you'll find it's a lot easier to not give in to the urge to reach out to THIS version of him.

But you have to get disappointed enough times before you can believe yourself!

◆◆◆◆

You were right, of course. It hasn't been hard to control the urge for contact. That actually has surprised me. That's not to say getting through the day hasn't been hard.

It has been horrible, but... it IS getting easier. I'm shocked to say that. I know I shouldn't be, but I am.

The realtor came over today to take room measurements and get the ball rolling on selling the house. Apparently my husband still doesn't want to sell the house.

He has told me all along that the house represents our relationship and how good we were/are together and he doesn't want to let that go.

I am sure that the fact that it's going to take a big chunk out of his wallet when we lose money on the sale has at least as much or more to do with it than wanting to hang on to the memory of "us."

It's just one more thing he should have thought of when he decided he couldn't resist the candy grinding up against his fly.

♦♦♦♦

He says I didn't give him what he needed so he found someone else who would.

I can admit that family life has been a little rough in the last few years, but I thought my marriage was the strong point. My husband would complain about sex, the house being a mess, the kids not listening, but to me that was just life.

My husband turned angry and then started to push family, friends, and everyone else away. I stopped including him in decisions with the kids and the household to avoid his anger. Because I chose to avoid dealing with his anger he feels/felt that it was all right to look elsewhere for acceptance.

The other woman came into the picture about 18 months ago. It started out as them just being friends. Then they started to share how miserable they both are/where in their marriages.

I discovered that he had been texting her all the time. There where pictures of her on his cell phone. He talked about her and her child all the time. He could not stop talking about her. I confronted him when I found out about all of this.

He made up excuses about the text messages, about the pictures, about everything. He made me feel like this was all my fault. I am the one that pushed him to get comfort from someone else. Since then I have been doing a lot of soul searching.

Just his past week I had the "moment" when everything finally came together. I believe he loves her. I have told him that I believe he loves her. He did not deny or agree, but he said everything by not saying anything. He has agreed to go to marriage counseling.

So now I just wait. What I really want is for him to admit his feelings, his true feeling.

♦♦♦♦

He chose to go outside of the marriage. THIS IS NOT YOUR FAULT. You are not responsible for his actions.

My husband also had an emotional affair. It went on for three years before I found out. He then blamed me, treated me badly, and justified it all in his head because "I wasn't there for him."

In my opinion, marriage counseling does not work until they realize they have done wrong and want to do the work to reconcile.

♦♦♦♦

I understand that it was my fault for not paying attention to him. I get that. I cannot change the past, I can only change the now and present. And it is his fault for going somewhere else. He is married, for better or worse.

♦♦♦♦

My ex would complain about the messy house, too. Trouble is, he was the slob and didn't do a damn thing to keep it clean. Yet somehow I was supposed to work full-time, do 98% of the child care, AND do ALL the household chores?

He's been renting a room from one of his bar buddies. He was hospitalized last week, and needed his family to go get his medications but the bar buddy wouldn't let them in the house to get the meds until they agreed to clean up his room. He's a 45-year-old man who couldn't/wouldn't keep a single room clean enough to satisfy another middle-aged drunk.

But there wasn't a thing wrong with him bitching to me that the house was a mess. That was "communicating his displeasure."

How come you never hear women use "messy house" as one of the reasons they cheat/leave a relationship? Cause the odds among my acquaintances are that it's the men who are most likely to live like pigs. Not 100%, but that's the way to bet.

For some reason, its men who think they're entitled to live in a home that looks like a spread from *Architectural Digest*.

Do NOT buy into that. Do NOT. Please, let's not regress into some mythical that a woman and a woman alone is the determining factor in a successful marriage.

It's not your fault that he DECIDED to cheat. He CHOSE to do this. Never forget that. The rationalizations always come AFTER the cheating.

♦♦♦♦

You can't change the past. However, it's a common thing that the pre-midlife crisis signals get overlooked. I do think that complaining about 1) the messy house, 2) the dominance of children in the house, and 3) sex, are clear indicators of an upcoming midlife crisis. I also get that you didn't know that, none of us did before we got here.

Life can't be all about the kids. It's also about the two of you having a relationship, having your own living space in the house, having sex, enjoying life and your relationship together. It's the kind of thing that tends to be forgotten, and when one spouse needs those things less than the other, they tend to think its okay the way it is. But it's not.

But you're also right, that once he started getting his needs met elsewhere, there's nothing more you can do about it. That's his fault, and he is wrong for doing so. You are married for better and for worse.

◆◆◆◆

I, too, am in the same mindset that I pushed him away. However, when I look back, it was me who did 95% of the house, the kids and all of that. I made it too easy for him to stray. He had more freedom than I did.

These are things I blame myself for but it is no justification for what he's done. I'm just saying that I won't be making that mistake again. Whether we reconcile or not.

◆◆◆◆

Someone said that it was the person who gave less that was more apt to run away. Less investment in the marriage, the household, the intimate side of things, expecting the other spouse to keep picking up all the slack — those are the real warning signs.

Complaining about the messy house without being willing to help — maybe that sense of entitlement is another warning sign of the lack of commitment, the lack of empathy and appreciation for your spouse.

The other spouse ends up doing more and more, and getting less and less of his/her own needs met. And in the end, it's all the same – midlife crisis spouse says that the other spouse is at fault for not listening, not doing enough, etc., even though the other spouse is just about doing backflips in an attempt to keep the marriage and household functioning. Or would be doing backflips if they weren't too busy doing everything else.

At least that was how it seemed to work in the last few years of my marriage. No doubt my husband's version is quite a bit different. What I've heard sounds just like all the other midlife crisis husbands' complaints.

Well, he didn't really complain about what was wrong until after he left (and most of that seemed like rewriting history).

Before that, it was what he felt he was missing, what he wanted to seek. And most of what he craved was drama, excitement, and illicit sexual experiences with a new person.

◆◆◆◆

While I am a firm believer that there are always two sides, and think it is good that you acknowledge that you have a joint role in your marriage, your spouse has a joint responsibility, too.

Yes, he may well have needed more attention, but HOW did he communicate that to you? If the kids were becoming too much, what was he doing to lessen the load? If the house was messy, was he in there rolling up his sleeves to help you?

If the sex wasn't what he needed, was he doing anything to improve the tone/add more romance into your marriage?

Your story is similar to mine with my husband having an emotional affair with a colleague and he claims he "ended up there" because he was lonely and she understood him.

My question to him has been, did he ever stop to ask whether maybe I was lonely too? Did he ever look at our situation and ask himself what he could do to improve things?

I'd moved so he could pursue his dream career, gave up mine to look after our kids, ran myself ragged trying to keep the family afloat in a foreign country while he just came and went as he pleased.

When confronting reality and the challenges of domestic life with a young family in a foreign country didn't turn out exactly as he thought, he ran outside to stroke his ego when he realized that someone 15 years younger and who admired him would feed his ego better than his wife who, yes, expected him to be a grown up and take his responsibilities as a husband and a father seriously.

Yes, we are both responsible for making our marriage work. However it takes only one party to destroy it. Going outside the marriage is a choice, with repercussions that the wayward spouse can't even begin to image.

The choice to have an emotional affair was his and his alone. You did not "push" him into it. He chose it all on his own.

♦♦♦♦

But what if the house was tidy, the kids are grown up and leaving the nest, and your sex life was great AND they still cheat?

They leave to be with another woman who has small children who are demanding and noisy and she has a messy house and a messy life with two ex-partners?

♦♦♦♦

Damned good and right HIS INFIDELITY IS HIS FAULT. Infidelity is a CHOICE not some kind of affliction that leaps upon one. She did not put a gun to his head and MAKE him do it.

We are talking about a marriage not dating where people can be picked up and dropped at will like changing one's underwear. Don't even come here with this load of bull or you will find yourself in a huge shit storm.

If he was that unhappy with the order of priorities in the marriage, then he should have COMMUNICATED that there would be a discussion, a resetting of the priorities, and the resolution of conflicts OR he would have to get out. Not go sneaking around behind his wife's back looking for the "perfect, mind-reading woman" who DOES NOT EXIST.

An affair and the subsequent destruction it brings on a marriage is one of the single most cowardly, passive-aggressive things one spouse can do to the other. It smacks of being a spineless weenie who is too damned lazy to learn to resolve the inevitable differences and conflicts that arise in a long-term intimate relationship.

◆◆◆

When a six-year-old whines and complains it's not tolerated; why would it be tolerated from a grown man? Complaining is not communicating, this is adulthood 101.

He was looking for a reason to take the easy way out and he created a reason for himself. If the house had been tidy and the kids gone he would have just given different reasons for taking the easy way out. It was not your fault!!

I'm in the beginning stages of anger with my situation so forgive me but if the house was a mess and the kids didn't listen to him why didn't he pick up a mop and clean then sit down with his kids and really connect/parent them so they would be better listeners?

I will bet all the money I have in my wallet right now they listened better to their mother because she spent most of the time parenting them.

If the couple needed more alone time why didn't he get the babysitter and make a night of it?

What about the other woman makes his life better? Nothing... he just leaves it behind for someone else to clean up.

Why are we to believe that a midlife crisis allows a grown man, with responsibilities to his family, wife, and society, a free pass to walk away leaving a wake of destruction in his path? Then as he's walking out the door to turn and say "oh, by the way, this is your fault too." I don't buy it!!!

♦♦♦♦

Everybody focuses on the infidelity (and that IS the most egregious offense we can SEE) but what about this part? Why push "everyone else in his life" away, if his wife is the root cause of his unhappiness?

Maybe he did "communicate" his unhappiness. Why is it his wife's responsibility to fix that?

You wouldn't want to do things to undermine HIS EFFORTS to change the things in his life that are upsetting him, but why take responsibility for the whole thing for him?

He did take responsibility for "fixing his unhappiness" — he CHOSE to cheat, be angry, and push everyone away. That is 100% entirely his choice of resolution to his problems. There were plenty of other options he could have exercised.

Sure, you could have dealt with his anger directly. Not by appeasing it but by confronting it, putting up a boundary about it. In hindsight, there are things like that a lot of us might have done, if we had it to do over. But "at the time," the path we chose seemed the most appropriate one, given our entire circumstance. All we can do is learn from it.

♦♦♦♦

See this is where I get a bit confused. Isn't some of what is described just called "life"? Kids that misbehave, a messy house, less sex... it's life. And the words "communicate" or "communicating" get thrown around a lot.

My ex never came to me and said, I am unhappy in our marriage and here are the things I am unhappy about; if they don't change I'm afraid I cannot stay married to you anymore.

Isn't that proper communication? Trying to communicate isn't the same thing as communicating.

◆◆◆◆

My husband and I have been going to marriage counseling for a few weeks. This past week he told the counselor that he only loved me because I am the mother of his children.

This was not a big surprise since I had been thinking this for a long time but to hear those words come out of his mouth I really felt like I was just hit by a train.

Over the weekend I put myself back together and I am going to ask my husband to leave the house. I deserve to be loved for who I am, not just because I am someone's mother.

I have not asked or looked to see if he is still talking to the other woman. It is time I take care of me and my children.

◆◆◆◆

We don't have a crystal ball to see the future. I am working hard now to claim today as a good one, for me and my kids, regardless of what my husband does.

◆◆◆◆

My husband also tried to tell me he had told me his unhappiness and, yes, it was based on the messy house. That JUSTIFIED him finding Little Miss Admiring and All Her

Options to completely wreck our lives. I guess fake admiration and being told how fabulous he is, is more important than loyalty, truth and integrity.

Now he is in counseling. Guess what it focuses on? HIS conflict avoidance, HIS poor coping skills, HIS inner void, HIS mother, HIS lack of boundaries, HIS passive aggressive behavior. Not a lot of messy house in there.

Marital problems are 1. inevitable, and 2. require commitment and communication to solve. NOTHING to do with the CHOICE to run away, lie and betray.

Good luck, stay strong. Stay No Contact. DON'T respond to any of his texts, phone calls, blaming or justifications. Stay away from his insanity.

♦♦♦♦

Today has been a good day, made it an hour without crying. It is a small victory, but it is a VICTORY.

He is still sleeping on her couch. So he says. Not my problem. Every time he chooses her, it makes the decisions easier. He made those bad choices not me.

Trying to deal with anger with the kids. My son is having a hard time coming into our house because his dad is not there. I told my son he can still talk to his dad anytime since he has his own cell phone.

♦♦♦♦

How do I stop obsessing about the other woman and how betrayed I am?

How do I stop obsessing about this woman? How do I stop thinking about how betrayed I am? I'm so tired of being angry! I am not naturally an angry person but I can't help it.

Tonight I asked about a strange phone number on our bill and he didn't know who it was and he'd find out tomorrow and get back to me. I'm a patient woman but not these days. I told him that I'd call and find out.

He was furious. He's tired of the inquisition. And I can't help it. I can't trust or believe anything he says! So if that is the case, why am I still asking him questions? It's insanity!! I don't know who I am when I get like this. Is this normal?

♦♦♦

It's absolutely normal. You've been made to feel crazy, to question "yourself" for so long, that it's completely normal to keep probing and testing for the truth.

You finally figured out that despite his repeated assertions, the sky really isn't orange, but it's going to take a while before you trust your own senses again.

He's sick of the "inquisition" because it makes his life inconvenient. Tough luck, bucko. Consequences.

You'll stop obsessing when you feel like he's trustworthy again. Right now he's not.

♦♦♦

You are unique in the universe. If he truly appreciates that and wants that special gift in his life, he will meet YOUR terms. If he doesn't appreciate or want that badly enough, he won't accept your terms. Then you have to decide whether you're willing to live with HIS terms. It's as simple as that.

♦♦♦♦

Sometimes I send him texts knowing that she's going to read them: "When you come to the house next week, I'll be home doing laundry. Come on in." or "I found another T-shirt you left here." or "Call me, I have a question about XYZ."

♦♦♦♦

You can stop yourself. Turn it around. If he said, "I just can't stop contacting the skank," how would you feel about his lack of self-control? So don't YOU be that person.

It's understandable, yes. And it definitely takes practice. But knowing that you CHOOSE whether or not to play games is very empowering.

♦♦♦♦

You're obsessing because your whole reality just got re-arranged. It's very, very typical, so be gentle to yourself. It's not wrong, it's just a stage you have to get through and there aren't any shortcuts.

Rarely does having evidence of adultery make much difference in a divorce in this country. The only advantage is that you could try to recover "dissipated assets" as part of your settlement.

Sometimes it provides you a psychological edge because these idiot men often want to protect their skanks from being named in divorce papers. Otherwise... it hardly matters at all, I'm afraid.

So now you know the truth. Your sense of control will eventually return because you won't be trying to reconcile his lies with what your gut is telling you.

But definitely give yourself permission to grieve. The level of betrayal is stunning and you need to process that.

♦♦♦♦

Finding out about the lies, the deceit, the violation and betrayal is one of the hardest things you will go through.

You're right, the adultery won't do much for you legally. I could have sued for divorce on the grounds of adultery in my state, but it's far more expensive, there is a large burden of proof, and ultimately the end would be the same. I would be divorced, and all the people I care about would know about his infidelity anyway.

Right now the best thing you can do for yourself is to take care of you. Eat healthy foods. Get regular, gentle exercise (or vigorous if you're in decent shape). Try to get as much sleep as possible. Avoid alcohol and other drugs. Reach out to a true friend and talk.

Once you're feeling like you can take some sort of action, make some appointments with lawyers to learn about your legal picture. You don't have to be ready to file to talk to a lawyer.

I had my first consultation six months before I could think of filing. But it did help me get my financial information in order and to negotiate a separation agreement before he moved in with the other woman.

◆◆◆◆

I can't stop obsessing either. I get mental pictures in my head that won't go away. Images of them having sex. Images of them kissing and holding hands. Images of them cuddling on the couch.

My therapist says with time it will go away. When? I have a knot in my stomach from sun-up till sun-down. I keep asking myself how I couldn't have seen it. What could I have done differently? WHY ME?

I stay home and maintain the house, pay the bills, do the laundry, go to work, the list goes on. Where's he? At his whore's house or out to dinner with her.

At least I can keep food down now. I've lost 40 pounds (a plus) and I've found out that in our state if you can prove that he bought the other woman ANYTHING while he was still living in the marital home (jewelry, dinner, clothes, whatever), he is required to pay you back half. Unfortunately, my jackass husband did everything in cash so I can't trace it.

◆◆◆◆

I also found out my husband was lying to me, pretending he'd ended it with his married other woman when he was still seeing her. He didn't know that I found out the truth (I found his online journal and he once left his cellphone behind with text messages and saved recorded messages).

It was mind-numbing and painful. I decided to stay calm and not confront him with my knowledge until I could use it to my advantage.

I kept talking with him about what he was thinking and feeling, while he spun out in his midlife crisis craziness and kept sneaking around and journaling, thinking I was clueless.

I used this time to meet with lawyers, to come up with my plan for survival. I wanted him to keep thinking I was oblivious so that I could plan my next steps, and I could ask him questions to see if he would lie — and he did.

The fact that he could look me in the eye and lie repeatedly without the slightest blink of an eye, twitch, look away from my eyes, etc., told me volumes.

I knew I could never trust what he said again; because there was literally no physical clue he was lying to me. Even when I put him on the spot and he had to pull a big lie out of his pocket.

This may or may not happen for you. You might ask him questions and be able to see when he's lying. You might start to make your plans going forward with your life, and he realizes what he's losing and ends that relationship, works on himself, and you reconcile.

The key is to not tip him off as to what you know, however tempting it is. You can use this knowledge to gather evidence, so if you DO decide to divorce, you can use it to your advantage.

I did that, keeping my mouth shut until we were at a point in divorce negotiations where I decided to tell him just a little bit of what I'd found months earlier.

He was literally devastated that I had found this information, and he suddenly agreed to our divorce settlement.

Finding the evidence is so painful and shocking. But, in a sense, it is better to know what is going on rather than to wonder and question your own sanity.

◆◆◆◆

Use the info to keep reaffirming that getting rid of him, and her as a friend, is the right thing to do. And get on with your life. They are not nice people to you. Delete!

◆◆◆◆

After falling for the dangling carrot of a possible reconciliation I've found out in the last two days that in fact he's bringing his whore to our house (I'm not currently living there) for sex after he takes her out for dinner.

Trouble is I don't know when they're going to eat and I'd sort of like to know. I'd like to be there waiting for them when they get home for sex, just to see the look on their faces, or maybe just be at the same restaurant! All just a fantasy of course.

Think I must be entering the vindictive phase when I wish them both ill; sentiments like that are not usually like me at all.

I'm currently trying to figure out questions I could call him with that he wouldn't be able to answer unless he was at the house but haven't come up with anything yet. Seems pathetic I know, but I'm sure I'm not the only one going through these feelings.

♦♦♦♦

Save yourself the emotional turmoil of confrontation and find a way to stop financially subsidizing their "recreation." It sounds like you are making part of the notes on what WAS the family home. Can you push hard to go ahead and have a property settlement? Would that be viable in your situation?

♦♦♦♦

I do understand your feelings. So much so that I went to the trouble of getting the information I needed to have confirmation. But I wasn't able to use it.

I confronted him, and since I wasn't able to use the information I had gathered all I could say is that I knew the truth and what that truth was. He denied, and denied over and over again. It became rather ridiculous. Whatever.

So I filed for divorce. We are nearing settlement now. He still has never admitted to it and it doesn't matter anymore. What matters is me and my life now.

So, before he detaches from you completely, get yourself protected somehow. Get a settlement as soon as you can, while he may still feel some guilt about what a low down ass he is.

◆◆◆◆

So do it. I've done it. It's actually pretty satisfying to catch him in a lie. Not because it "gets" him in any sort of "gotcha" way, but because it proves to YOU that your truth is real.

I caught my ex in so many lies I couldn't even count them. All it did was make him argue and justify that much harder, about how he HAD to lie because I was so controlling. I wasn't controlling, but I also wasn't a moron and he was really bad at lying. I could always tell.

Eventually, you do stop caring. You just assume they're lying because history has taught you well. Even when it was thrown in my face, I just couldn't care enough to argue any more.

What have you got to lose? A little time, a little energy? The first couple of times you'll get some satisfaction, but the thrill will wear off, eventually.

◆◆◆◆

I've caught mine in a lie by way of his bank statement. He neglected to change his address to his new address. He'll remember to do it soon I'm sure, but in the interim the bank statement came to my house. I of course opened it.

All of his caterwauling about being broke is nothing but bullshit. He has several thousand dollars in the bank and plenty of cash going into his account every week.

So I just go about my business, making believe I believe that he is broke. Wait till I subpoena his bank statements and IRA's. I swear he thinks I'm stupid.

I may have been blindsided but they say hell hath no fury like a woman scorned. Wait til he tells his whore girlfriend that he has to pay me permanent alimony and that I found out about the cash. She'll head for the hills. She wants his money and doesn't want to have to share it with me.

He wants me to get weaker with every day that goes by. His loss. I'm getting stronger and angrier.

♦♦♦♦

It turned out to be very easy to catch my husband in a lie. He provided a good clue — his lips were moving. But really, he left so much evidence around. In spite of his bare-faced lies, I could usually find independent evidence about what was really going on.

Not that it matters. It helped me detach more quickly, as my respect for the man turned into contempt. It also helped me move quickly when I found out about his financial plans that would have screwed me over even worse than ended up happening.

I did not confront him on the lies because I did not want him to become more secretive and better at hiding his tracks.

Other than for your own protection, who cares? People having affairs are liars. People having a midlife crisis often lie. It goes with the territory. They lie to you, they lie to their affair partners or friends or family, and they lie to themselves.

Most won't admit the truth even if you have airtight evidence. They will continue to lie after that.

I'm sorry to say that your spouse will no doubt continue to provide evidence of his current asshole status. It goes with everything else.

♦♦♦♦

I guess my most sensible course of action is to get the legal stuff sorted while he still has any sense of guilt, which I think he still does presently.

Potentially catching him "in the act" with his whore will just anger him and may make him more difficult to deal with.

But, I can't help smiling when I think of the look of utter disbelief that would be on their faces when I strolled into the bedroom when they thought no one knew where they were and what they are up to!!

I'm glad I found out about his latest episode as it has given me the kick up the ass I needed to decide to get rid of him.

Tonight is going to be hard for me as I'm fairly certain they're planning to meet up at our house for sex (after he's taken her out for a meal using money I supplied for a different purpose of course).

♦♦♦♦

What if he wants to reconcile but I don't?

I convinced myself that love could conquer all. I was kidding myself. My husband has had a problem with pornography since the day I met him.

It was a huge red flag but I didn't realize it then but I do now because that is precisely why we are in this mess.

It was the perfect storm. He's deployed for a year, too much time on his hands and no responsibilities to his family (at least in his mind because he's not here).

He admitted to me that he was back on pornography and then he decided it wasn't enough. So he acted on it.

I can say looking back that I'm not surprised. The shock for me is that I didn't think he'd go all out crazy!

I still have no idea how many women he has slept with. He says around ten but that's only what he admits to. So I say double that number! It all comes down to lack of character.

I went through photo albums last night... for hours. I would see certain pictures and remember that he was mad because we were in the picture together and he wanted one all by himself. Like the one in Las Vegas with these beautiful showgirls. I was in the picture and he is clearly mad.

Then I looked at many more and realized that he was in a hell of a lot of pictures alone. Then I re-read the post on lack of character. Bingo! It was always there. It's never left. I can't deny it any longer.

He starts counseling soon. I don't know if this problem can be helped at this point. He wants to reconcile. He wants his family. Thing is... I don't want this problem of his to be a part of our marriage anymore. The damage has been done. I won't go back to that again.

He needs help but I know that I'm not the one that can help him. So where does this leave me?

◆◆◆◆

Are you sure he wants to reconcile in the way you might consider reconciling? For many of them, they want the marriage AND the candy. And they see no reason why they shouldn't have both... after all, what you don't know won't hurt you, right?

If you aren't ready to split — and that's perfectly fine of course — then go about your business as usual but PREPARE for divorce. If it doesn't happen, great. If it does, you'll be in a better position. Then you can see how he behaves when he gets back.

◆◆◆◆

You can't do anything about HIS character, but you can do one hell of lot about your own... and become a self-actualized and even more beautiful person than you are now in the process.

HE does not realize what he has, "looked past." You, however, live in the skin of that treasure.

"We can change without growing; but we cannot grow without changing."

Change you into what you want to be... and the rest will take care of itself.

◆◆◆◆

I've been working out for years but now my direction has changed. Or should I say my mind. I've lost 15 pounds so far and I'm on the road back to who I really am. I'm doing this for me. I cannot wait around to see if he is going to change.

I've signed up for school full time and am pursuing my degree in a new field of study. My title is no longer "stay at home mom," "wife of so & so," or any other title. I will always be my kids Mom but I can no longer be who I was.

These things I have to do for me now whether we reconcile or not.

I'm trying to keep my head up and my eyes wide open. It's difficult but I believe it is the healthy way to go. I know some days will be great and others will be difficult if not downright horrid.

This is the lowest I've ever been. Now I know that only I can pick myself up, dust off, and take flight. I believe this is also what the Lord has for me to do. I surrender to Him. It's the only way I know. I have to go forward.

♦♦♦♦

Only you know yourself and him and only you can decide if you still want to believe in him or not. Follow your gut. If you still see something in him worth fighting for and if he proves to be sincere in his wish of reconciliation, why not try to see what it comes out?

Ask yourself also if you can live with him knowing what you know now, even assuming that he will never stray again.

♦♦♦♦

I know that I can't change the past but he crossed a boundary that never should have been crossed. I go round and round about that. I still don't know the answer.

I do have faith though. I know that nothing is impossible with God. With that being said, I have to prepare either way this thing goes. I didn't ask to be put on this ride but here I am.

My therapist said that I have two choices: modeling for my children forgiveness or modeling for my children that they don't have to put up with this crap from anyone... ever! I can relate to both.

To be honest, if it weren't for my kids, I do believe that I'd be gone. However, it's just not that simple now. I have invested my life to this marriage and to this family. Yes, I understand that he's the one that threw us away so he could act out his fantasies or whatever. I got dragged into it.

I know that I'll survive either way. I continue to read, research, and pray every day. It's all I can do at this point. I can't tell my family until I make a decision. This is by my choice. I just need time to think this all out.

◆◆◆◆

So my husband has come home for a week. It's been hard. I'm so confused. He wants to start over and fresh. How? I can't seem to move forward when I'm still in a state of shock and disbelief. Then again, how do we move forward without... moving forward?

Help me. I'm going crazy with all of these emotions. I can't stand it.

◆◆◆◆

He wants to start over and fresh. Maybe he should describe what that looks like to you.

If it involves forgetting everything that happened and pretending you can turn back the clock and forget he fucked around, then... no.

If he's willing to be honest and completely transparent, fine, as long as you want that too. But first I'd want to know what he considered a way forward.

◆◆◆◆

In my opinion, he wants to sweep the shit under the carpet and carry on his merry way without any serious consequences.

Personally, I don't think he should be back in the home because now you do not have your independence from him. It also lessens your personal power in campaigning for change in him.

In my opinion, you've sent the message he can act this way and not lose anyone or anything of importance. WHY is he going to change? He has NO incentive to. He WILL continue his current lifestyle but be more careful about it.

♦♦♦♦

Of course he wants to start over and start fresh. Both of those imply he wants you to forget that he's been cheating on you with multiple women for god knows how long.

The trouble is, that won't work. I don't care how strong you are, how much you love him. You will not be able to love and care for him and trust him knowing what has happened.

He may be remorseful he got caught because that was never his intent but that is entirely different than being remorseful for cheating on you or using the women he was cheating on you with for his sexual gratification only. He has very serious issues with a lack of respect for women.

There is no way to move forward without dealing with what has happened. That means intensive counseling for each of you individually and marriage counseling as well.

The only way out is through. You have to work through what happened to heal and grow as a couple.

Right now he's proven he is not trustworthy, he is not honorable and he has abandoned his integrity. That doesn't change back overnight.

He now has to prove by his actions over the long term that he wants to regain those things by being trustworthy, honorable and acting with integrity. Only over time can his actions show you he really has a desire to be faithful and loving to you.

I personally think that he has no idea of the gravity of what he's done and he's in instinctive damage control mode to mitigate the effects of what happened for HIM, not you.

◆◆◆◆

I've struggled with this whole mess. I'm so tired of it. I wake up every day and the nightmare starts again.

It's been difficult. I'm tired of fighting, questioning, etc... I don't think he's realized how much he has hurt this marriage. I'm still on the fence. It could go either way.

He has begged for reconciliation, wants to go to marriage counseling when he gets back and he's promising to continue individual counseling as well. So far, he's kept his end of the bargain.

I guess I just don't trust him anymore. Will this pass if he keeps his promises or am I just a fool? I love this man and I want to fight for our marriage but at the same time I don't know if this will happen again.

He promised it wouldn't. I really don't know. How I hate this whole thing!!!

I am wondering if reconciliation is even possible. He hasn't done anything that I haven't asked. I have his email passwords, his phone lock password, and I have access to phone records, etc. My mind, however, tells me that it isn't enough.

Am I overreacting? Am I going nuts? I just don't know if reconciliation is worth all of this headache. Today I'm just feeling without hope and for no apparent reason. Other than what's happened. Which is enough. Am I making sense?

I can't get images out of my mind or conversations. I'm being haunted. I am in counseling and plan on marriage counseling. Until then, what?

♦♦♦♦

Do you have the feeling that he's following the "letter of the law," but not really understanding the spirit of it?

My ex, when he was trying to prove his serious intentions to me, would do every single thing I asked exactly as I asked him to (for a while, anyway). But if I didn't spell it out... it didn't occur to him.

He wouldn't apply ANY common sense to his behavior or consider how it might be perceived. And that put me in the position of being more warden than wife, which is a pretty terrible feeling.

♦♦♦♦

That's exactly how I'm feeling. Like he's going through the motions but doesn't really get why it's so important to me. Is this going to continue for years like this?

I don't know if I can do this for months on end or years on end. I'm trying so hard to be optimistic but I'm tired. It's so damn exhausting.

I don't want this in my life. I do feel like a warden instead of a wife, a partner, or even a friend. For crying out loud!!

♦♦♦♦

He can give you all those things that give the appearance of trust, but there are many free phone services and emails on the internet. You cannot possibly keep track of him and he would know it.

You have to make a decision to trust him, or to say you don't. If you trust him, then back off on the snooper vision, and rebuild yourself. Wait and see what he offers in terms of a marriage with any quality that you could stand to live with.

If you do not, then it's time to accept he is a narcissistic dog in heat getting a huge supply of sexual gratification elsewhere, playing all ends off against the middle.

I would be telling him "you get into counseling and peel back all the layers as to why you are doing this and keep me fully informed of that, or you don't come back. And you don't come back while you are doing it to stay here."

This is a man in full hormonal beast mode. That beast needs a good smack on the nose to command his respect.

♦♦♦

Well I made a deal with him the other day. Since we are apart, (he's deployed but comes back in a month) that we wouldn't discuss this mess until we are together and in counseling.

Meanwhile, I would deal with this in individual counseling and he would deal with it in his individual counseling.

My reason for such a deal is because I think we should be dealing with this one way and he wants to deal with it another.

We are not on the same page and all we do is argue which doesn't get us anywhere. He can't understand where I am coming from and I can't understand him. I think that's a fair deal but then again I know that I'm dealing with someone who isn't fair. I just can't stand arguing on the phone all the time. Too mentally exhausting.

Another thing is, I can't trust what he tells me anyway. I have rules and rule number one is: he lies, lies, lies. So when I inquire about things and he tells me whatever he tells me, I always go back to rule number one. So it's a waste of time being on the phone arguing all the time.

♦♦♦♦

Can I ever get past the betrayal?

Even if you do reconcile with them how do you get past the betrayal? I mean, it is not like it was just a one night stand. They went out and had a full blown "I'm in love" relationship.

How do you ever trust them again? Is it possible. Do they ever really get over the other person?

♦♦♦♦

I don't think very many betrayed spouses can recover from that break of trust. I know that I cannot. I would love to believe that I could but I know I could not.

♦♦♦♦

It is like an adolescent. My husband is seeing another woman who is either around the same age or older than I am. But he says she makes him happy like when we were first dating (he was 19 then).

I didn't even bother to mention that when we were first dating we didn't have years of history and issues and baggage together or that we didn't have kids to worry about, or bills, or real jobs, or houses to maintain, or aging parents to take care of and bury when they died, etc.

We are not at the point where he has decided to even try yet. But, I have the feeling that if he did come back the first time we had a fight about anything he would be saying, see, I knew it wouldn't work.

♦♦♦♦

Affairs are not about the betrayed spouse but the spouse who did the betraying. They are lost and need validation because of something going on with them.

I know my husband had a two year affair with another woman but I would look past that. What really gets me is the abandonment, the fact he walked out on us with little explanation and he was a monster. That's what is hard to get past, the destruction of abandonment.

◆◆◆◆

Not that it could possibly happen, but I think what would be harder to get past than the actual sexual relationship that he had with the other woman is the cruel and horrible way that he treated me.

I think if he had accepted any kind of blame and not said some of the absolutely horrid things to me during the divorce that I could have gotten over or learned to accept the affair and move on.

Instead he was mean, nasty and took her side over me and the kids and it is the way that he treated our children that draws the final line in the sand that I cannot cross.

◆◆◆◆

It is not the sex that breaks the deal. It is the lying (which destroys trust in relationships) and the sudden abandonment complete with the rewriting of the marital history (self-justification). The inability to simply say, "I was wrong as hell and I'm sorry as hell." (Pride.)

Those are the deal breakers. And, the longer it goes on the more broken is the deal.

◆◆◆◆

I often wonder if my ex wants to come back, could I, we, make it work?

I guess I won't know until, or if, he wants to come home and then how hard he tries to make it right.

But, yes... it would have to begin with "I have been totally cruel, selfish and rotten. I have absolutely no excuses. This was my entire fault! Please forgive me."

Any attempt at justification would probably be the last straw for me.

◆◆◆◆

I don't know. I guess I'm worrying about a point that I'm not even at yet anyway.

My husband is still living at home, still seeing the other woman and being torn about what to do. I said I would give him two weeks without talking about us so he could think.

I know this is going to be the longest most difficult two weeks ever. I guess the other woman is also demanding that he make a decision.

I just feel like he is going to leave. I can't compete with the rush of a new love high that makes him feel like he did with me at 19.

◆◆◆◆

Nor should you have to. If the years of love and devotion you have doubtless shown him don't count for something, what the hell is he going to get from a new relationship with a total bimbo?

Do not attempt to compete with this tart. Be the woman / person you are.

Remember, all new relationships are fun at first because it's a novelty. Once the mask slips and you see the real person then it's down to the serious business of trying to make it work.

Guess what, all you wayward spouses out there? Your new love breaks wind in bed, picks her toenails, will be irritable, bad tempered and unfair on occasion, and golly, gosh she isn't bloody perfect! Because no one is.

He... like my ex, and all the rest, are in for a serious dose of reality check which will be administered in the form of a quick kick up the backside!!

Do not change for your husband. By all means, try to be patient and understanding, try to give him space, but under no circumstances let him treat you like a doormat.

The more you allow him to walk over you... the more he will do it (believe me I own the t-shirt!).

I also think you shouldn't let him live under the same roof while he makes up his mind. That's totally cruel of him.

I know you don't want to provoke him into the wrong decision but maybe if you gently suggest he get a hotel room and give you both some space for the next week, but keep in regular touch.

Follow your heart by all means, but temper it with common sense and keep your self-respect.

◆◆◆◆

I don't know why he always threatens to leave but never does. His other woman is single. Which is why I was really surprised that when the whole affair was admitted he didn't just go stay with her.

I guess my husband assumed that when he admitted the affair that I would just say that he and I had problems and we would get divorced. Then he would live happily ever after with her and remain "best" friends with me. I guess it is not going according to his fantasy.

He said at one point he talked to his mom and told her he was unhappy and we were having problems but that he had found a "friend" to talk to about it. He said his mom cried. I'm sure his mom was smart enough to figure out what he meant.

◆◆◆◆

It sounds to me like he's trying to provoke you into kicking him out and forcing you to make the decision. As is always the case you / me / all the other betrayed spouses are the ones to blame!

No doubt at that point he can run around town telling everyone: you kicked him out! And he has found solace in the arms of another much more loving and understanding woman who merely started off as a friend and a shoulder to cry on!

But he can't torture you like this. Like I said, maybe he could rent a room for week or two.

It's hard I know because we are damned if we do or damned if we don't.

Just try and maintain your self-respect; love and understanding are fine, being abused is not.

◆◆◆◆

You will get past the betrayal but the wounds will leave permanent scars, which will from time to time "ache." You simply learn to find other joys in life and minimize the ache. Put it in perspective and regard it sort of like an old battle scar.

Much like residual arthritis from old bone injuries, we take our Advil and keep on doing the things that DO bring us joy, peace, and serenity.

And we put it all out there and love the people who will let us love them. Nothing about life is perfect, so we learn to accentuate the positive.

♦♦♦♦

I got over the betrayal enough to go on to a happy new life.

I would not have been able to get over it and reconcile though.

For me, personally, I could never continue a marital relationship with the man who threw me and our children to the curb for a piece of ass. I'd never respect myself again.

♦♦♦♦

Do they really and truly love the other woman or is it just the rush of new love? If they say they love you but are not in love with you anymore can they ever really fall in love with you again?

♦♦♦♦

I think they think they do love the other woman — mine did. I think it was a rush but thankfully it didn't last too long. Depends if you decide to stick around to find out.

My husband didn't ever say he wasn't in love with me I think he just found something new, different and more exciting in the other woman.

I don't think you "fall" in love again. It is more a case of loving me all along but having fallen out of sync with me and finding someone more exciting who was giving him the attention he desired which she should have been giving her own husband.

♦♦♦♦

It is possible to get past the betrayal? Yes. Well it was for me anyway. Like other losses in life you learn to live with them.

It isn't something you will ever forget. Hopefully in time it will move to the back of your mind rather than center stage.

♦♦♦♦

I get the whole "we are living like roommates speech." This just breaks my heart that I am losing my husband, the person who I thought was my best friend all because some other woman without all the responsibilities wants him.

Yes, I know my husband is the most to blame here, but I just don't understand how another woman thinks. What goes on inside their heads to make them think getting involved with a married guy is an okay thing to do??

I also hate knowing that there is some stranger out there who probably knows so much personal and private stuff about me and my marriage.

♦♦♦♦

I wish I had an answer but my husband cheated three years ago and it is still tough to get past. His was his ex and he justified it because they did not actually have a sexual relationship since he supposedly got cold feet at the last minute.

But I did go through his emails and the other woman was looking to completely take over my life. Talking about how she would be a great mom to my kids and such.

I forgave my husband but it still lingers in the back of my head sometimes if taking him back was the right thing to do.

♦♦♦♦

It all makes me hurt so much that I can't even think. I can't possibly imagine how I would feel good about myself being some guy's secret lover.

Sneaking around, not being able to tell people. Having some guy call me up for a booty call. Giving your love to someone you know goes home every night to a whole other life. I just can't even imagine how that would make someone happy or feel good about themselves.

♦♦♦♦

I wouldn't want to (and won't) spend the rest of my life looking over my shoulder to make sure he's not texting, calling, meeting up with or contacting another woman.

The trust is gone. He was my best friend for 30 years. Best friends don't do this to each other.

Unfortunately, I have had to make choice to move on with my life, start divorce proceedings and figure it out from there.

Was it the life I wanted? No. It is the life I was thrust into and had no control over. I can however, work to control my emotions and feelings going forward.

I can say this; I will NEVER let it happen again. It will be a long, long time before I trust another man, if ever. He has ruined it for me.

I wish I could get past his betrayal, but I do not believe I can.

♦♦♦♦

I don't think I could ever trust someone again either. Which makes me ever sadder, because he will go off with his new love and I will be left alone and feeling even more like a loser for being alone.

Their cheating not only stole our husbands, our family, and our way of life, they steal from us the ability to trust or make us ever vulnerable to another person.

♦♦♦♦

At some point you just have to make a leap of faith and CHOOSE to move past it.

Does trust come back 100%? No. I don't think there is one of us who are in reconciliation who can say that we 100% trust our husbands; that boat has sailed.

Are we comfortable enough with the amount of trust we DO have to continue in our marriages? Yes.

Yes they can and do "get over" the other person. It doesn't happen overnight and sometimes they come home while still harboring feelings for the other person. They just have made the decision or choice to remain in the marriage and we made the choice to accept them back.

Sometimes they don't even admit to themselves that they aren't totally over the other person or the thought of another person.

♦♦♦♦

I am really struggling with this because I could never ever ever ever be with my husband again. Not after what he has done to me and to our family (not that he would ever want to come back anyway).

My struggle is as I move toward the future. One day I hope to meet someone and I hope to be able to trust him. I think it will be okay as I will not hold my husband's sins against another man, but I would be lying if I said that this won't be difficult for me. Once bitten twice shy...

I guess what I am saying is that after having gone through this nightmare, I wonder if there is anyone out there who is not capable of going completely crazy and violating my trust.

Never in a million years would I have expected this from my husband. Never. So what does that mean? Am I capable of trust?

Maybe it is me that I don't trust.

♦♦♦♦

Do you think you will ever 100% trust another person like you did your husband again? I won't.

Does that mean I can't be in a relationship ever again? Nope.

All it means is that I don't think I will ever 100% trust him again.

♦♦♦♦

Playing devil's advocate here, don't you think that at one point even though this is tough you can learn to love again? Trust will come with time but we won't have the same vulnerability. Maybe that's fairer to say? Trust is innocence? Being less innocent and less vulnerable is key?

I guess I came from a marriage where I did the majority of the work. Found out a long time ago if I needed something, I would have to find it within myself, I couldn't count on him, I couldn't trust that he would come through.

I've had to be self-sufficient in many ways. Maybe that's different than what the rest of you experienced. Right now, I feel like I won't ever date or open my heart again and not out of bitterness just because it's just too much work for what you get back. Selfish? Maybe, but maybe it's about time.

♦♦♦♦

I don't know. It is just way too early to think about it. All weekend my friends were telling me, it is his loss, you are a beautiful woman and you won't stay alone long.

But even if this ends I am in no hurry at all to rush into another relationship. I went from my mom's house to my married life. I've never really been alone before.

I've always had people to "fix" things for me in life, never really had to do it on my own. Plus my self-esteem right now is rock bottom. So, I can only imagine till I get my self-confidence back I would only make a bad choice in a man right now.

♦♦♦♦

I think we have forever lost our naiveté about romantic love. Trust is a choice, blind trust is a part of naive youth that we surrender to the truth revealed when we go through such a deep betrayal.

In the end, you realize that if someone you've been with for 10, 20, 30 years can blindside and betray you then blind trust is a drawback rather than a virtue to be sought.

♦♦♦♦

I can't see ever mixing assets with someone again. What's mine is mine after this.

♦♦♦♦

I think the type of person we choose to be with after going through this experience affects us too. If we let ourselves be with someone who is like our ex then I think we are more likely to experience the same type of feelings.

I think that if we step back and really think about what type of person we would like to have a relationship with; let ourselves be with that type of person; we can learn to trust again. I have to believe that.

♦♦♦♦

I hear what all of you are saying. I'm having a hard time wrapping my mind around trusting again. After what my husband has done, I don't think so.

We are reconciling, which is harder than I thought, and I don't think I'll ever look at him the same and I don't think I'll ever trust him like I did. After all, he betrayed me so deeply, something I never thought he was capable of, that there's no way I'll ever trust anyone like that again.

The one person in my life that was supposed to have my back, yet lied and lied instead. Myself, I'll never recover.

Is this a false reconciliation? Don't know. All I know is that I am doing the best I can and we'll see how it turns out.

I continue to work on me and read, read, read. I love that man but is this love that I have enough?

Don't know. Perhaps one day I'll see things differently. For now, one day at a time is all I can handle.

◆◆◆◆

The question was posed and that was my answer. Yes, I am trying one more time. It's extremely difficult. I read so many who say that they wished they could've had a chance to reconcile their marriage.

Let me tell you, it's the hardest thing I've ever had to do. To be betrayed, have your husband take your problems to a stranger, let her know our business (I didn't get that), and to then try to work this mess out. I never thought this could happen to me or us. No clue.

It's so devastating. I read all the pain everyone is going through on this forum and I'm just floored that people can be so damn cruel! Least of all your own spouse who you've given your life to. Who you'd take a bullet for. Just mind blowing how painful this all is.

◆◆◆◆

That is what my husband keeps saying. "If we get in a fight in the future you will just throw this up in my face."

My feeling is if we get in a fight how do I know he won't say or think he should have chosen her instead or that he won't go running to her?

I told him I can't answer that. The only thing I could tell him was it won't be easy and if he doesn't think he can or doesn't want to put in the hard work then he should just leave.

312 | Adultery At Midlife

He keeps talking like you know no matter what I will be there for you.

I have to keep reminding him that if he chooses to go with her that no, he won't be there for me. That we will have no contact after that.

I told him there is no way we are going to stay friends if he goes off with this woman. If he goes with her I want to get on with my life and that life will not include him in any way, shape, or form.

That I deserve the chance to heal without him and his new love in my life. So I can heal and maybe meet someone new someday.

This seems to upset him. I guess he thought I would just settle for going from his wife to just a friend and that should be enough for me for the rest of my life.

◆◆◆◆

More projection, more blame. I got a similar line of BS from my ex when he told me he wasn't seeing hookers anymore and I expressed disbelief.

Then I got "SEE, we could NEVER get back together because YOU would never trust me about anything or believe anything I ever tell you!!"

No, jackass, you just can't SAY something, you have to demonstrate through your actions that you are trustworthy, and actively work towards rebuilding trust, which is a long, hard road.

It was not that I would never trust him again, it was that he was entirely incapable of working on rebuilding trust.

So what if you threw it up in his face? It would be up to HIM, then, to reassure you, or have a conversation about fighting fairly if it became an ongoing thing that you constantly brought up.

These guys act like they can just wave a magic wand and we are supposed to just forget about everything. Once again, they want to bury their heads in the sand and not be reminded about what they did. Incredible.

♦♦♦♦

I would like to think that I could try to get past the betrayal.

BUT, I would need his acknowledgement of the ingrained personality traits that lead to this, his willingness to face whatever it took to address those issues wholeheartedly and without reservation individually, and together (and my own issues, of course).

As a coward who was unable to face any of that before he dropped the bomb, I don't see him summoning up what it takes to do that, even after the glow fades off the married other woman. I see him as accepting that he just has to stuff his feelings the rest of his life and putting up with it.

He would have to totally change his way of thinking, and I wouldn't presume to ask him to change if I thought that was working out for him, but this passive-aggressive nice guy crap has caused him to totally break down mentally and morally.

In my opinion, something's got to give. But maybe I under estimate his staying power on the self-delusion.

♦♦♦♦

This is a tough time for you and like they say somewhere here, "Reconciliation ain't for sissies."

In one or two of the many books I read it was found men are less tolerant of betrayal than women.

After three failed reconciliation attempts, I knew in the end I couldn't do it a fourth time, always wondering if I could trust him and WHEN would he do it again. Then, if and when he did, I would possibly end up doing jail time.

The divorce was best for both of us, my sanity and his safety!!

♦♦♦♦

I guess it depends on what you mean by "get past." Is it possible to move forward in a healthy, compassionate and positive way? Absolutely it is, with or without your wayward spouse.

But, if by "get past" you mean "forget completely" or "live as if it never happened," then, for me at least, the answer is a resounding NO. It happened.

There is no changing the past, not even by trying to erase or forget it. It informs the current me. It is a part of me. I refuse to pretend otherwise.

I think the key is not to let it take over your life in a negative way. I think so often we are given these challenges and we get to choose whether to let them hold us back or propel us forward.

I will never ever trust someone so blindly like I did my husband before his infidelity was revealed. It's just a fact.

Do I miss that naiveté? Sure I do. But, heck, I miss not having the responsibility of paying bills or going to work every day! I wish I could just play all day long like when I was a kid!

So, I trust my husband enough, but not 100% or blindly like I did before.

It works for me.

♦♦♦♦

I agree that there is no living as if it never happened, it did and that has to be integrated into what the future looks like. For me, "TRUST," in the sexual sense, was almost easy. I know that sounds odd but I learned to trust my gut.

It turned out that my husband was actually as transparent as glass and I'm comfortable that if he were to betray in the future, I would know it almost before him.

I also agree that if I broke up with him, I would likely not ever combine finances with anyone ever again. I'm simply too wary and self-protective (I have a decent cash stash to this day).

I see naive trusting women with a mixture of envy and pity. I feel like I understand a harsh side of life that they haven't even imagined yet. I don't know which of us has the worse position.

My husband's words and actions in early reconciliation did 90% as much damage as the original misdeeds.

This betrayal seeps into every single facet of life, poisoning as it goes, and proof of it will continue to be uncovered for years to come.

It has helped me to believe that IF my husband had actually known the pain and damage that would be caused by pushing the "send" button on that first email that crossed the line, he would have sooner cut off his arm than send it. But sin is like that.

I will never trust my husband 100% ever again. But neither will I trust anyone 100% again, so I'm just as "safe" with him as in a new relationship.

I've also become very jaded about super-duper lovey-dovey relationships. People get into them thinking that the intensity of their early courtship is some guarantee against later betrayal.

I think that over-the-top romance is a desperate attempt at self-soothing and it can (in an unhealthy circumstance) be little more than mutual emotional masturbation.

So I'm not interested in going out to find some new, exciting, assumingly-reliable love. I will admit that every once in a while these things work out, but I'm VERY skeptical.

♦♦♦♦

In my experience, I was able to get past the betrayal, because in my mind everyone is human and we all make mistakes. For me it wasn't easy, and I am sure if you ask my husband he would say it was extremely difficult.

But I was able to hold on to the love I had for him, and just continued to try to get through. Time heals all wounds sort of thing.

Now, sad to say, I am faced with it again. I feel so stupid forever believing that we could heal! In reflection, I know that I had forgiven him and was moving on.

Unfortunately, he was never able to forgive himself. He never felt he could rectify his mistake, and I think he just got tired of trying. He has decided it is easier to cut his losses and run. Easier to start over.

He told me once that I was better than him. My response was, no I am not better than you. We are just different.

Reminds me of another old saying though, quitters never prosper. But, I guess it is time to let go.

♦♦♦♦

I think the ONLY way to move forward, eventually, will be to trust again, to be vulnerable again. That's easier said than done, of course.

My soon-to-be-ex has told me that he can't come home because "It wouldn't be fair to you (meaning me)."

Not sure what that means.

a) That I would have to spend the rest of our marriage trying to get past his betrayal?

b) That HE would have to spend the rest of our marriage trying to get past his betrayal?

c) He doesn't love me and it wouldn't be fair to come home just because he's comfortable here?

d) He is so disgusted by his behavior and I have been clean and celibate and he has not?

e) All of the above.

I try in my mind to get past his betrayal, not only of our marriage, but he betrayed our children by lying to them while he was having an affair.

To me, he's dirty now. Our sacred, intimate marriage now has a huge scar that will never heal.

Much as I'd like to, and as much as I try, I don't think I'll ever move past it. I wish more than anything that I could, but I don't think I can.

♦♦♦♦

I want revenge! Am I nuts for feeling this way?

Have any of you ever had the urge for revenge against your husband and the other woman?

I know in time my husband will see the other woman for what she truly is, but sometimes I would like to do something to accelerate that. Not to get him to return, but I think so he can feel a little pain.

I won't do anything and plan on taking the high road, I was just wondering if anyone else ever had those thoughts or am I nuts.

◆◆◆◆

You are not nuts. I think all of us have felt that way at one time or another. Especially, those that now have teens or adult children and feel that we have been with our spouses through the tough child rearing times and were hoping to now get to retire and travel together.

My ex is doing that with the other woman and it makes me want to scream.

◆◆◆◆

Oh, most definitely. In fact, I just found out this weekend that his other woman has been emailing and Facebook messaging with another married friend of ours begging him to come and visit her for a weekend!!

And when did it all start? The week AFTER she was in my bed with my husband. Wonder if he knows that about her.

Would LOVE to say something but as with everything else he is doing these days, it's none of my business!!

◆◆◆◆

It just really pisses me off that she gets the rewards of our hard work. My husband will have one bill every month and the rest he can spend on her.

♦♦♦♦

I feel resentment, too. I raised his daughters and now that it was coming to a point where we could share our life together he takes off with someone else.

We were one year away from the youngest daughter going off to college. Now he has the life of fun and no responsibility that I did all the heavy lifting for.

Yes, I do hope he suffers.

♦♦♦♦

I have to say that my revenge fantasies were really creative... I just didn't do any of them. I'm glad now, but I still think "I date married men" would have looked good spray painted on her BMW.

♦♦♦♦

He filed a claim with our insurance company to fix the pock holes in his truck after a hail storm. He has a white truck with black trim, and the other woman has a white car.

I was going to get black spray paint and spray CHEATER on his truck and WHORE on one side of her car and SLUT on the other. I decided against it.

♦♦♦♦

No matter how bad things get, taking the high road always feels better. Sometimes that's the BEST revenge.

♦♦♦♦

I did in the beginning. I don't have the urge anymore. I think he and she are one big mess and I feel lucky to be free.

Sometimes my ego feels bruised, but I am learning to identify that it is just my ego, and not that I actually miss him. I miss who he was years ago, but he is not that person.

I don't know if I would call it revenge, rather than something I did when I was hurt, but anyone who called, I told them, "here is his new number at his girlfriend's house."

I also wrote her parents a letter detailing how she wrecked my marriage and told me my kids would, "get over it." I thought at least I could ruin the chance of her innocently introducing him as her new boyfriend.

It didn't work, though. He is friends with her dad on Facebook. It probably helped him, because, although he would have started out lying to her parents, I made him face up to it right away and air it all out in the beginning. But the truth is the truth. I am still glad I sent it.

So not really revenge, but truth telling right from the start, which he hated.

◆◆◆◆

I have thought about doing a lot of things, but the only thing I did do was rub pink fiberglass insulation into his ergonomically engineered gel bike seat — right inside the notch where his tiny balls gently sit.

I am not sure of the exact result, he didn't appear itchy and scratchy last time I saw him, but I will never know. Either will he!

◆◆◆◆

At the beginning, yes, I made a lot of "revenge" scenarios in my head. Once the tears and depression periods became more distant, and I did more reading (on this forum and books about recovering after betrayal), I tried to put a stop to revenge thoughts every time they came in my mind.

Now I am no longer wishing him or the other woman bad. In fact, in a way I wish he finds his happiness, so that he could teach our young daughter something useful in the future. He is a better father now than he was when we were together, probably because he is seeing her less.

My inner pride also tells me that the best "revenge" is what he did for himself. He chose a woman full of problems and empty of moral fiber over me and our daughter. I am sure that sooner or later, once the "love hormones" weaken, he will realize her faults too, and will have a hard time dealing with his choices.

Of course, it's also possible that both he and the other woman "grow" in this process and become better human beings. But this should make me content, because it's nice to live in a world of good human beings.

◆◆◆◆

I think about revenge a lot. I even asked everyone if they could give me some ideas on hurting the other woman. The general consensus is to take the high road. I'd rather not, but I probably will.

But sometimes the pain is so unbearable it doesn't feel fair that we're hurting so much and they aren't.

◆◆◆◆

YES, SO BADLY... I believe in karma, what comes round goes round.

◆◆◆◆

I would love to see what revenge would do on her, but... she has small children and a husband and I don't want to see them get hurt.

This woman has broken up several marriages and seems to be a serial adulterer. (I got this from the private investigator's report.)

◆◆◆◆

I have had my little revenge fantasies, like putting his precious sports car in the backyard pool.

It was fun to make a list of things that would make their lives as miserable as they were making mine. As I detach and create my own new life, I care less and less about them.

I do believe in Karma, and reap what you sow, and no matter what happens to them, I choose to be happy. For my kids' sake I have taken the high road and earned the kids' respect.

I think the best revenge is that now they are stuck together, living with all those flaws they were able to hide from each other when it was just an affair. No more sneaking around, lying, secrecy = boring!

He snores really loudly and only thinks about himself. He has gotten fat and smelly. She won the booby prize, and she will be stuck with him since they are "soul mates."

Revenge is a dish best eaten cold.

♦♦♦♦

I think about it... I have some pretty good revenge fantasies that can help me get my anger out but I would never do them.

Some days I wish I was the type that would put his credit card info on an adult entertainment website or something but I'm just not.

It's frustrating watching him living the life, spending money, going on trips. I would love to derail that somehow but hope it happens on its own in its own time.

Maybe someday I will be able to wish him happiness but I can't do that right now.

♦♦♦♦

I fantasized about spray painting "Fuck-me-mobile" on her sports car. I also fantasized about contacting her parents. That one I was more serious about but never did it.

I think it is hilarious and he did it all by himself. No intervention on my part required. Sometimes I believe in Karma.

It can be healing to just think about what you could do, even if you don't really do it. Just don't be obsessive about it.

♦♦♦♦

In the beginning of all of this, I used to have very vivid dreams (when I had actually managed to fall asleep) about beating the living crap out of her. They don't happen anymore now. I try not to think about her anymore. She isn't worth my time.

It's hard and there are several things that I would have loved to do — including confronting her — but I also believe in Karma... and she is a bitch. One day they will both get bitten by this.

In the meantime, I feel proud of the way I have handled myself, I feel proud of the compassion and understanding and patience I displayed to him while he was trying to make up his mind.

I feel proud of myself for getting out there with friends and working on finding myself again... and all of that is the best revenge for me. Looking good and feeling good helps me project more confidence, more independence, more of the attitude that attracted him to me in the first place.

And it's not about getting him "re-attracted" to me... in fact, it's just the opposite! It's about ME now.

♦♦♦♦

Best way to get revenge? Live a happy life!

♦♦♦♦

Revenge never seems to come at the right time anyway. It always seems to come after you have gotten over it.

No, no revenge. What could I possibly do to her or my ex that would be anywhere near as hurtful as what they did to me and my family?

And why would that make me feel better? It would make them say "crazy ex-wife" and I will never allow that to happen.

Dignity is worth so much more than petty revenges. And I truly got the best years of that man; she can have the rest.

♦♦♦♦

I thought about screwing with them at their work. My ex always seemed to make an enemy or two wherever he worked and I knew the name of the lady who was his enemy of the moment.

I was really tempted to contact her some way anonymously about the affair. I even had one person tell me I should call his boss. However, I would never have done either.

I needed him to have a job and have some money. And that dignity thing is important although it's still fun to think about!

♦♦♦♦

Oh, yes. It occupied my thoughts for a very long time. In my case, my ex has had plenty of time to see the other woman for "what she is" and apparently he likes it just fine.

For me, one of the things I really struggled with was the complete injustice of being betrayed and abandoned by my husband. Without realizing it, I had a belief system that if one did the right things, played by the rules, was a good person then you would be treated in kind.

I didn't realize how deeply I believed that, but I did. Now when I think about it, I can see that millions of people all over the world have terrible, unjust things happen to them, things they did nothing to deserve. Still, the injustice of it can be terribly hard to take, and I think that's where the revenge fantasies come from.

I'm now glad I didn't have the opportunity to do any sort of real harm to the other woman. I fought for my marriage, yes. I tried to drive her away, yes. But for me to cause her harm in some way out of revenge would (in my own opinion) lower me. I don't want to be a person who causes harm to anyone. I try not to be.

I am not in any way a spiritual person but I do believe that negativity feeds and creates negativity, and revenge is a negative. That's just my opinion.

There was a time when I actively and obsessively looked for some way, any way, to harm her and had I found one, I would've. I'm glad I didn't. Now.

♦♦♦♦

I had horrible thoughts of revenge against my ex and the other woman who was a friend of mine.

But really the best revenge is to carry on like they never existed, look great, and feel great. I know it bothers ex that I have managed just fine without him around.

♦♦♦♦

My sister saw the other woman at the store for the first time and thought she was going to die she was so ugly. My sister said she was scared that the girl was going to be okay and that she would have to tell me because she doesn't lie about reality. She thought she was hideous — which she is, but no one believed me until they saw it for themselves.

I found out that she got fired because of the affair. We are in a very conservative state and she committed a crime (alienation of affection and criminal conversation).

Revenge is bittersweet. It doesn't change the damage they did, but it is somewhat comforting that my children and I weren't the only ones who got punished by their disregard of everyone's lives.

◆◆◆◆

I went two months without paying the house payment. I got the house in the divorce. Granted, I dropped my credit score, but I destroyed his.

I've had loans and cards that have built up my credit over the years, all he had was the house payment. Poor guy found out the hard way that his credit was in the toilet, I'm sure that impressed the other woman.

I've remarried and it's made him mad that there's another man in "his" house. But, he left the door wide open when he walked out and another man came in and closed it.

My daughter rubs it in that her step-dad has her car running great and has done repairs on it, ones ex was too lazy to do.

And worse thing is my grandchild calls my new husband, grampa and we post family pictures on Facebook. Even though he don't have Facebook, his family members do and I'm sure they pass it on.

Revenge comes in small, subtle ways. I've enjoyed it. Covers all the pain that he caused when he thought he'd just step out of one life into another, and that grass wasn't as green as he thought. And he can't come back!

◆◆◆◆

I think it was one of the veterans on here that said... the best revenge is YOU being happy!! I keep repeating this in my head... so true!!

♦♦♦♦

I enjoy reading the intelligence and mastery of resolving feelings revenging on giving what he or she was so easily "dumping" by the side of the road as I wrote in one email early on to him.

That was the feeling my adult children and I felt... and that is almost two years ago. They stopped calling him "dad" and now call him by his first name. They also have not seen him for almost two years.

I can just picture his apprehension and nervousness at each corner and crevice wondering where he will "run" into us. That is great feeling also.

♦♦♦♦

I often have the urge for revenge, probably too often. I have had plenty of opportunities to humiliate ex and howorker but my voice of reason always tells me to take the high road.

My sister worked with her boyfriend and his other woman. My sister got her hands on the other woman's coat and put a few shrimp in a tiny little hole in the pocket of the coat so it ended up in the lining. No one could figure out why it smelled so bad!

♦♦♦♦

You betcha I wanted revenge!! Even his mother was thinking of stuff we could do to the other woman!! Painting her car (bitch, slut, you get the general idea), egging their vehicles, dumping garbage in her yard.

328 | Adultery At Midlife

I'm just waiting for him to catch an STD or something as she is also a serial other woman.

♦♦♦♦

Each and every day. However, I know I am the better person and always remember when you lay down with dogs (or pigs in ex's case) you get up with fleas.

♦♦♦♦

The other woman had moved into our house and I found my husband with her. I kicked her out (she didn't figure out the necessity on her own — go figure). There was an interim period before she could extract her possessions, so I dug out the choicest pieces from her lingerie chest and BBQ'd them out on the back deck.

♦♦♦♦

I think it's only natural that we have an urge for revenge once we've been so wronged; but in the end, to do any revengeful act just lowers us to their level.

We all know we are more dignified than that. And why give your ex the satisfaction of knowing he is still able to get under your skin like that??

I did have a dream about meeting the other woman after an email I sent to my ex telling him I accept that he's with another woman but I never ever want to meet her. So, I dreamed that night that I went to some event and he was there and he talked to me a bit and then moved over and there she was.

She reached out to try to hug me — and I held up the palm of my hand, and said "Oh, no, you don't. You're not worthy of touching my skin." Wow — that was my best "dis" ever and it came from my dream!

♦♦♦♦

Certainly I do. I think I'll be following Ivana Trump's advice in the movie "The First Wives Club." Don't get mad, get everything!! I think I will... at least more than my husband was bargaining for!!

♦♦♦♦

A friend of my husband's had an affair with one of his employees several years ago and when his wife (who had access to his work email account) found love letters to another woman, she forwarded them to everyone in the company. It is the stuff of legend around here with all the affairs going on in this small town and that company.

When I found the love letter from the married other woman to my husband and he started blaming and spewing filth at me, I reminded him how reasonable I am as I had not pulled a "name of husband's friend" on him. It shut him up quick.

I told him and her that my biggest revenge would be for them to end up together and then have to go through the pain I went through as they wondered who the other was constantly texting.

♦♦♦♦

I also considered rubbing poison ivy in his boxers, but I didn't go through with it.

♦♦♦♦

I have been thinking about that for days. Getting my husband to come here and mow the lawn and stuff. I know when he is here she will be freaking out the same as I did.

I am feeling a lot of anger towards the other woman. She has done things to hurt me. Putting stuff on her Facebook for people to find. Doing it on purpose. I really feel the need to get back at her.

♦♦♦♦

Wasn't just an "idea." I held the poison ivy in my gloved hands and stared at it for a few long seconds after picking it and then made myself throw it away.

A friend whose husband left her for a "trophy wife" ten years ago sprayed Roundup on his vegetable garden the day she moved out. Ten years later, he is now begging her to get back with him after "trophy wife" found an even younger "trophy husband."

◆◆◆◆

I too wanted revenge, but took the high road and did nothing. But, I kept thinking Karma would get them!

Two months ago, I got a phone call from ex (we have been divorced over five years now). He wanted me to know how sorry he was for treating me the way he did. That I never did anything to deserve that treatment. That it was the biggest mistake he ever made in his life!

He then proceeded to tell me that they were getting a divorce! She told him "I love you but I'm not in love with you" and that she hadn't been happy in over two years. Now where have I heard that before??

He then asked if I would meet him. That's when I told him, "Sorry, I don't date married men! I know some women do and think it's ok, but I have better morals than that!"

He got quiet and said, "I guess I sort of expected that from you."

Am I sorry I didn't hook up with him? Hell No!!

◆◆◆◆

Thought long and hard on this one. I did get the guy fired at the phone company who fixed my husband's phone records so that the whore's phone number was no longer on them (he just happened to be one of the whore's friends).

And I did call child and family services to tell them what an unfit mother she was. I wanted to put a cup of sugar in her gas tank so that she would have to buy a new engine but haven't been that vindictive yet.

◆◆◆◆

I thought about taking Roundup and writing whore in her yard and because it is fall it would not show up until next spring. No I did not do it and won't because they would know it was me.

◆◆◆◆

Ex knows that I hold two very incriminating DVDs of him and the married other woman. I probably will never do anything with them now... but THEY don't know that... or what her trusting husband could get if she ever leaves him. Can't be fun, but then what they put me through was not fun either. Suspense... the best revenge.

◆◆◆◆

I've thought about it, but as hurt as I am do believe in the high road here. But it's okay to think these thoughts and get them out of you.

I agree that karma will get her. She's a waitress and my revenge dream was to go into the diner when she was working, order, and be polite until it came time to leave her a tip. I thought that then I would write on the back of the bill "Invest in single men."

But again, it would serve no useful purpose. She's an amoral creature and I wouldn't lower myself to be in her shoes.

◆◆◆◆

I really enjoyed reading this. I've had many thoughts but didn't want to live up to the typical "crazy ex" stereotype!

However, I was sick of 19-year-old other woman befriend-ing my young teenage daughters on Facebook and sending them messages about their dad's future plans with her and asking for their approval.

It upsets them that they have to hear this from her and then when he's confronted, he just lies.

My oldest daughter has lost so much respect for her dad so she decided to tag both husband and the other woman for all their friends and family to see.

We got a good laugh seeing the comments and how pissed off they were that other co-workers now knew about the af-fair. They lost the respect of everyone at work as well.

They untagged themselves within a day or so but I left it up on mine so all our mutual friends could see. She blocked my girls as well. Too bad she didn't get the approval she was looking for from the kids.

My husband and the other woman are so STUPID, they will just self-destruct, that will be my revenge!!

♦♦♦♦

The only revenge thing I did when I found out about the only other woman I had evidence of (there were probably others though) was take out $100 from the bank in one dollar bills and write her name and cell phone number on the back of each one, with the phrase, "I sleep with married men, call me for a free BJ!!" and then spent every last one of them.

♦♦♦♦

I, too, have taken the high road and last week finally stopped myself from obsessing about my husband and the other woman, researching on Facebook, etc. I put a tick on a chart every day that I don't do this and have to tell my friends if I mess up, just as if I was a kid with a sticker chart. Childish as it is, it is working and I feel a lot better for it.

As the other woman is married, I don't know how much the affair is coming out at their workplace — we've only been separated two months and the last I heard she is still with her husband.

Good to know we're all in the same boat. Take a deep breath, count to 10 and concentrate on our lives, our careers, hobbies, kids and happiness — much more productive.

♦♦♦♦

Drunken idiot husband had explicit sex pictures and videos of the married other woman that I found on his computer. Also pictures of trips they had taken together and pictures of her children.

I had them for about six months without telling him. During one particularly bad argument where he did something stupid and blamed me for not stopping him, I decided to give him a video show.

I had never seen him so panicked; pale, sweaty, obsessive swallowing. He had no clue that they were on his computer! As I said — drunken idiot husband.

I felt no joy in this. To intentionally hurt someone was not me. I decided then that his midlife crisis was not going to change my basic character. I am and will continue to be a good person. I never want to do something that I will look back on in shame. The next day I gave my husband the downloaded copies and expressed the above to him.

♦♦♦♦

Yes often, but in the end sanity prevails and if I ever did anything I would not be the better person. I also believe that in the long run karma prevails.

334 | Adultery At Midlife

♦♦♦♦

I had a revenge fantasy of contacting my ex's employer with printouts of all the emails he had sent saying that he had to go take care of sick kid, or leave early to deal with a repair person. And refuting every single one of them as lies.

The man never picked up our daughter when she was sick or took a day off work to look after her.

I think there was one occasion, in 20 years together, when he missed work because of something needing fixing at the house. And that happened because I was out of town and couldn't handle it and it impacted his personal comfort.

I never did, though. And later I discovered they pretty much knew he was lying anyway, and fired him for it. It wasn't just me he was fucking over. I was just first in line.

♦♦♦♦

My revenge is to forget the bad years of recent the past, and go forward with my life, knowing that he can NEVER recover completely what he lost.

Even if he never knows it is revenge... it is going to be enough for me to know that I am living a life true to my values, principles and dreams.

I will admit this is a shift... for a while I did want vengeance, but I don't have enough time to waste on him now.

♦♦♦♦

I am entertaining thoughts of paying back myself. Not really revenge; I tried to imagine bad accidents happening to ex and other woman, but those images did not sit well with me, and I realized that I highly prefer that they do live in good health and get confronted with the consequences of their actions.

And here, about the "consequences," I discovered I do have a say. I am no longer powerless. I can impose rules and I can retaliate if rules are not obeyed.

I would gladly live without any drama, but we are forever entwined because of our daughter. And as much as I would like no contact at all even between her and him, I know she loves him and needs him in her life.

◆◆◆◆

I fantasized about rat poison in his coffee. Or wiring his nuts to the national grid and flicking the switch.

I wanted the other woman to drop dead or drive her car into the nearest obstacle that would just kill her so she would stay away. In the end I got my revenge.

She had been a serial adulterer that our community thought was a sweetheart. She took my husband. I took her reputation and smashed it with the truth to her colleagues and friends that I know.

He once told me I had really upset her. REALLY? Tough shit.

◆◆◆◆

Seems like it's always one of those mousy little eyelash batters who are sneaking around with other people's husbands. The little floozy involved with my ex has been one of those, too. Fools her husband and family... fools her friends... but not me.

She acts so meek and demure but has been seen by too many doing too much, especially where she has worked. It seems that these people never get what they ought to get.

So, my kudos to you for helping the process along and knowing that at least one ho-worker got a good kick in the butt.

◆◆◆◆

I love that phrase, "I took her reputation and smashed it with the truth."

Kind of like I did to my ex. And I'm SO glad I did.

Let everyone know what kind of "man" he really is.

♦♦♦♦

That's exactly the kind of woman my soon-to-be-ex left me for. She was a prior sweetheart, but since the old days she cheated on her husband and even had another man's child. She looks harmless, rather mousy and with no style. But she's a serial adulterer.

Makes me feel bad for those women who get judged as that type simply because they look overly sexy. It's the mousy ones you have to watch.

♦♦♦♦

I watched the Jezebel work her magic on my husband for three years. I would try to tell him about it hoping he would see her for what she was doing. They hooked up for the last four years until I caught them via Facebook.

I am so angry and hurt. I only did one thing and that was drop a trash bag in front of her house marked with her name and "adulterer" on it.

Unfortunately, nothing came of this but I feel closure on her. I am now waiting for her to get hers through karma.

♦♦♦♦

I spent plenty of time thinking about revenge. Then I realized that even thinking about it left me feeling awful, stirred up, anxious and angry. My heart physically hurt.

I chose to take the high road. It made me feel more peaceful and calm, and that is what I wanted more than revenge.

♦♦♦♦

I have that urge all the time. I would love to carry it out see how it unfolds and then erase it. But since I can't, I just take the high road.

I can't say it is easy, but I try to tell myself that rather than focus on how humiliated I feel, I will focus on how those who know me and my struggles will respect me for how I have chosen to conduct myself.

My favorite thought is to email his boss the phone records and love notes between the two of them. But then I realize that if he lost his job, it would hurt my stepdaughter.

I do believe in karma. I know some day regardless of what happens to our relationship he will regret the person he was and how he treated his wife. To me that is the worst punishment to hate yourself and what you did and know you can't do a thing about it.

Still, a baseball bat to his new car and one to her car would feel so good!

♦♦♦♦

Oh do I want revenge. In a perfect world I would grab him by the back of his hair and pummel his face into the sidewalk while chanting, "You m-fer, you m-fer." But that's not legal.

I want him to die in a room — alone. I know my kids won't be there and I know I won't be there. It will just be him and her and whatever manifestation of a new life they scramble together.

I do get revenge... every month when that little shit has to write an alimony check. I know how much money means to him. Thirty years, gone. POOF! His kids don't talk to him, he lives hundreds of miles away.

I own his house. He has his clothes and his memories. There are no pictures of the kids to hang on her house walls.

While it may not be the revenge that I wanted, for me, losing my past would be a far greater hell. But, that was his choice. As we teach our kids, there are consequences for actions. You wanted a whore, you got her. I got your history.

I told him in the only counseling session he went to with me that if he did it he would lose 30 years of memories, me, a shitload of money, half his retirement, his house, and, most importantly, the respect of his sons.

And I asked him, "Is it worth it?" He looked at me and said, "Yes, it's worth anything to get rid of you." Well, he did. And everything I said to him came true.

The funny thing with all this, though, is he's so narcissistic that he doesn't feel pain like a normal person. My idea of what would be revenge to me is not what it is for him. He can't feel emotions like a normal person. How sad.

◆◆◆◆

My soon-to-be-ex said something similar, but not quite as cruel... something to the effect that "Yes, I want out. I'm willing to be broke to end this." What can you say to that?

And you're right about the narcissism. If they don't think like a normal person there isn't much you can do.

◆◆◆◆

The mousy other woman re-invented herself in chat rooms with sexy avatars, all big boobs and bums. In reality she wears a heavily padded bra and is nearly anorexic.

My friends say she looks like a piece of dry paper, all wrinkled and mousy. Ex has paid for an expensive hairdo so now it is mouse with make-up and golden blond long hair like an angel.

I have this theory that it is mouse's revenge. She always wanted to be a cheerleader and now she takes away the husbands of former cheerleaders: successful, nice, intelligent, honest and beautiful women.

I actually really have this theory that it is about envy and really low self-worth.

◆◆◆◆

Yes, yes, yes. Revenge is exactly what first crossed my mind. Actually, I could get revenge quite easily. My husband's other woman is active military, is married herself, and it is against the rules to have a relationship with another person on base.

I could have her brought before her superiors, but that would do nothing but hurt my children. The drama would be way too much and there would never in the future be a relationship between the children and their father.

My husband does not want to be married anymore, but he does not want a divorce either — so I sort of think the other woman will not be at family get-togethers in the future, but just in case I need to take the high road as well.

Besides he would be busted down as well and lose money which translates to hardships for the children as well as me.

My revenge will come in the form of living well; it is really the best revenge.

I plan to do as George Strait's song says, and "let myself go" on a cruise, to the spa, back to school, shopping for new clothes, and allowing my husband to cover all the children's expenses per the agreement he has signed.

I realized he does not deserve to have my power any more. He has drained my energy for too long.

◆◆◆◆

I am so glad to see that I am not the only one. Sometimes I get upset with myself and worry that my thoughts will become actions.

◆◆◆◆

I did. I did tell my ex I was emailing his boss. He said go ahead you can't hurt me, I have resigned. I saw red over that so I did, asking that the other woman be fired.

They responded that they were very sorry but would not interfere in a personal situation. I was left feeling sick and it makes me cringe thinking about it.

I did it because although I had kicked my ex out he was coming back saying he wanted our marriage to work, was 100% committed, swearing on his father's grave there was no one else, and then going back to his apartment with her.

I hired a detective; that's how I found out for real. I was so angry at the time and hadn't found this website then.

Not something I am proud of.

◆◆◆◆

I've been divorced now for over two years. And in my own little way I still get revenge. Every now and again I get an email to the "family" email address from a head hunter looking to recruit for various companies. It's always people he has interviewed with before and somewhat knows.

When I get these emails my reply is always the same — "Dear Mr. Headhunter, Mr. X is no longer at this email address. He and I are divorced. He is now living with the woman he left his family for. He can be reached at... Please remove this email address from your data base as his contact."

Trust me, no corporation wants someone who left his wife for a whore. And I know how these headhunters network. I'm sure tongues will be wagging.

Oh well. As the saying goes, karma is a bitch that has been dumped.

◆◆◆◆

I have thought about it, but, in the end, I would rather hold the moral high ground. In my mind, he has had his just desserts anyway. He lost ME, a genuine, nice, honest, caring person, who stood by him when he has lost everything to his gambling addiction.

He was on his knees, crying like a baby, pleading with me not to leave him. He had lost everything and I stayed and helped him and supported him.

And that's a rare quality in a person. His loss, loser that he is.

◆◆◆◆

Odds are high that they won't become actions because obviously you think about consequences for others. Too bad your cheating spouse wasn't raised to have the same level of character as you.

◆◆◆◆

Every day on my drive home from work, my mind wanders into all kinds of revenge to exact on ex and the other woman. I have been divorced for four years and you'd think I would be over the revenging idea.

He ended our marriage five years ago this month. He never looked back or apologized. He lives in a nice three bedroom condo behind my neighborhood.

He lives by himself. The other woman visits as she is still in her house with her kids. I am doing all the heavy lifting with regards to raising our kids. He is your typical uncle dad.

The half full glass would see this as his "karma," my "revenge," in that he has no real relationship with his kids. He has not moved forward in his relationship with the other woman (as in marrying her). He is alone.

The half empty glass would see it as damn, he is living the life! He has no one to clean up after; his girlfriend comes to visit but doesn't live with him. No lawn to mow, driveway to shovel, house to paint, etc. He is living a pretty swell life!

I do not know the other woman. I do not know what she looks like. I have yet to cross paths with her. What she doesn't know is that I am big Law & Order fan. And the main theme of that show is the ball always comes rolling back to you. Isn't any karma thing, just reality.

If I could figure out how to get revenge without the ball rolling back to me...

♦♦♦♦

Yes, wanted to call all of whore's neighbors and tell them not to let their kids play with hers because they would all catch an STD.

I would never do it, but when I was telling a friend at work, we laughed about it and created a whole afternoon soap opera around it. It blew off steam and gave me a great laugh.

I want revenge to stay thin, to set up that new successful business, to fall in love again with someone who will take me into account this time, not just himself.

Nothing out of the realm of possibility and far more delicious than anything bad that can befall either of them.

♦♦♦♦

I hunger for revenge. Retribution. So far I've gotten an excellent separation agreement that nails him to the wall financially. And he barely has a relationship with his teen son.

He recently has had back problems from a partially herniated disc that he never got treatment for. I can only hope that is making it difficult to satisfy his twenty-something whore's carnal urges.

I feel there will be more karma to come for him. My mom always told me, "If you're patient enough, they (your enemies) will get their just desserts." I think she was right. Also from my grandmom: "Patience is a virtue."

The trick is being patient and (as so many others have said) taking the high road. It isn't easy, but in the end I have to believe the universe bends towards justice.

♦♦♦♦

I love the tag line I saw recently on someone's posts here: "When another woman steals your husband, the best revenge is to let her keep him."

♦♦♦♦

A few weeks ago, my co-workers came up with this idea: we would build a snowman in the other woman's front yard. We'd put a tank top on the snowman that one of the girls saw at Walgreens. It had a martini glass on it and said "grandma's sippy cup."

We would put a poodle-hair wig on the head since the other woman's hair is a frizzy mess. We'd top it with a hat from the company my husband works for.

Or we would just leave a flaming bag of dog shit on her porch. But, with my luck her house would catch on fire and I'd end up on the wrong end of the law.

♦♦♦♦

I think my revenge is going to be the other woman herself. They have only known each other a little more than a month and she is already pushing pushing pushing for life-long commitment and public declarations of love.

He's telling her he's all in with that but thus far they both have kept the affair secret from everyone for reasons of their own.

To me, all indications are that she is slightly imbalanced. As a former drug addict she might have some residual issues. He wanted passion and chaos in his life and she may give him both.

♦♦♦♦

About a year before I found definite proof of adultery, I actually caught my husband on a secret cell phone. (Ok... slow learner here. Yes, that is definite proof but shit... I was in denial City.)

So when he said they are just friends and told me her name I said "Who is that?" He reminded me when we went to a party at her house and I said, "Why are you talking to her on a secret phone? She is not even pretty. She is actually mousy."

♦♦♦♦

My soon-to-be-ex used to repeatedly say, "I'll leave this marriage without a cent" until I finally said "Okay. Thanks." He does not say that anymore.

♦♦♦♦

I haven't thought it through too often, but I have thought that when I contact the other woman's husband, he and I would connect... and get ALL the kids (she has three, I have five) and then cheating husband and married other woman could suffer together without their children.

♦♦♦♦

Those feelings are pretty normal when you're in the worst of all this but they go away.

There's a whole transition period after The Speech/Separation/Divorce where the left behind spouse still feels her life is intimately bound to that of her wayward spouse.

If he's spending money on the other woman, it stings, because he should still be spending it on you. If he's taking her on trips, it feels maddening because he should be taking you.

But after a time, and maybe a long time, it doesn't feel like that anymore. You detach and get into your own life where what he's doing doesn't have very much meaning. You eventually just stop seeing your life in relation to his, or theirs.

If you're not there yet or not even anywhere near there yet, don't worry. You'll get there and it's much more comfortable once you do.

◆◆◆◆

Do any of you get the urge for revenge, even if you've reconciled? My husband and I have been in reconciliation for almost a year and I am still real mad at her.

I still want revenge. I keep telling myself that I should be grateful. I got what I wanted, a reconciliation.

And I know that a lot of you, who aren't in reconciliation, will probably feel like that.

But, that ho gave my daughter two anxiety disorders, and put the rest of my family through hell, because she was so selfish. I still harbor so much anger toward her.

◆◆◆◆

What makes you think that it is her that gave your daughter the anxiety disorders and not your husband? Did she put him in some ropes and keep him near her? Did she force him with a gun at his head to come in her bed and her arms?

I understand your wish to put your blame and anger on someone, preferably on the outsider, but let's not forget that, despite the pompous name, midlife crisis is not an illness, not a handicap of reason, not a justification for the betrayal imposed on us by a cheating spouse in midlife crisis.

Now that you forgave your husband, I believe his other woman has as much right at your forgiveness as him. In every relationship between two persons, there are exactly TWO persons that make this relationship work (unless, of course, she did force him with the gun at his head).

Try to listen more to your husband's point of view, to how he saw his other woman during his "fog" or "hormones speaking stage" and try some empathy towards her as well.

I believe you'll never have a truly peaceful relationship with him again, as long as you hold a grudge towards his other woman.

♦♦♦♦

I got my revenge/closure when I bumped into them both at the supermarket. I said my piece and walked past with my head high, killer heels, and looking good (in my opinion anyway) and they scuttled away.

My soon-to-be-ex looked like I'd actually caught him in bed with her he was so shocked and couldn't move.

I brought a bit of reality to their day and to me it was revenge. I walked away laughing because I found the whole situation comical.

♦♦♦♦

Harkening to the comment about him leaving without a cent... the many, many people who told me "once he sees how much this will all cost him, he'll wake up." Is it a knock to my self-esteem that he did lose some money, but she still got the guy? Jury is still out on that one.

Reality bites knowing I will have to work another 30+ years, likely at hourly wages, in order to retire with some money while other woman and ex have great jobs and make excellent money now.

I want justice/revenge, which ever pays monetarily the most.

♦♦♦♦

Unfortunately, neither makes up for having a huge irretrievable chunk of your life stolen by an ingrate. Many of us know the feeling of having to work much longer than anticipated because of situations as yours.

Kind of makes you wish you could go back and do it over knowing that looking out for number one should be job one.

Despite all their protests to the contrary, marriage has always been the better situation for the man from the point of what he receives in intangibles.

Sorry you find yourself in this situation. If you have daughters, be sure they understand the realities of not having a profession or allowing a man to define you.

♦♦♦♦

This has been a HUGE wake-up call for me. I knew a lady on another forum who would constantly counsel women to "have a Plan B....always."

If I have anything to do with my daughter's outlook on life, I hope I can impress upon her the importance of having that Plan B. Have an education and have work experience.

As much as I was grateful to be a stay at home mom for much of my children's lives, I'm more grateful that I was able to transition fairly easily into employment due to my skillsets obtained through education and previous work.

♦♦♦♦

I only daydream about revenge as I have not found out who the other woman is or truly moved into anger yet.

But I fantasize about ex's Facebook page. He set it up but has never used it and I have his password. I think the Facebook page from hell might be my ultimate revenge.

Every detail of what he has done and then request everyone I can find on Facebook to be his friend. I wonder how long and how many people would see it before he got wind.

♦♦♦♦

I know I started this thread and I really thought I was over the revenge scenarios, but now my husband wants me to pay him the difference in value of the assets he is keeping versus what I am keeping.

SO I am to pay him for lying, cheating, humiliating the family for a serial home wrecker. Needless to say I WANT SOME REVENGE!!!!

♦♦♦♦

My husband left with one little overnight bag to start his new life with his ho. Like most cheating spouses he was so excited to be leaving, he left most of his things behind.

I noticed he left his Cialis in the bathroom cupboard. I pondered on those expensive little pills for a day... then flushed them down the toilet. If felt great!

He came back several days later pretending to pack his clothes, but what he was looking for desperately was his pills. I just smiled and walked out of the room. I had not contacted an attorney yet, so I was not admitting to anything!

♦♦♦♦

Once when my then wayward spouse (we're reconciling now) came over to see our daughter, I took his bottle of Viagra out of his gym bag. Bet he and married other woman didn't have any fun that night!

♦♦♦♦

Now that you are reconciling have you told him about the things you did?

♦♦♦♦

Hell no! He would probably be mad, even though he would understand.

I figured if we're still together on our 50th wedding anniversary I am going to tell him everything that I did. Including tossing his very expensive cell phone in the lake, after reading his and married other woman's lovey dovey sickening texts to each other.

♦♦♦♦

I'm getting past the need for revenge as I go along. No I can't get back the years that I lost and all the investment emotionally and financially.

But... I can see how lucky he was and how I will get on with a life I never would have had otherwise. I know I'm going to be ok.

Maybe the other woman is better than me, better for him? I have no idea, but one thing I do know is if I can keep going forward, and I will, one day this will be just another bad experience.

Him, on the other hand, I hope he does end up with her and I hope that she is a nightmare, which would be enough revenge for me.

Be afraid of what you ask for you might just get it.

♦♦♦♦

Ditching the ED pills must be a common scenario. I too flushed a couple of hundred dollars' worth of Levitra, after replacing them with baby aspirin look-alikes.

♦♦♦♦

Wish I could have done that, after my husband got ED last year and said I should get him some Viagra as he would try it. I did and it worked for us.

The sex was emotionless though. He got hard but he had no technique, (heart wasn't really in it, I suppose).

♦♦♦♦

I flushed his stash after he left me. Found them in his medicine cabinet and did the deed. He did not need them when he was at home. Perhaps they really do have performance problems with the other woman.

♦♦♦♦

I found out about the affair a year ago. He hasn't been with her for almost a year, since it came out in public. I had a bad day yesterday when I heard about her from a friend and thought maybe ex was with her again. Why should I care?

I think of revenge still because I know where she works and lives. Fortunately, time does heal though I hate having bad days that still pop up.

I think I will always have those days, but fewer and fewer in time. And I strongly believe, that if I don't do any sort of revenge, I will be happier with myself in the long run.

♦♦♦♦

I would love to take revenge on the other woman, but sadly lack the opportunity. And when it comes down to it, thinking about her gives her power over me that I don't want.

But, I do have a deal going with my best friend. Next time I see the slut on the bus I'm going to text my friend who will call me. I will then launch into a long (and untruthful) description of how soon-to-be-ex has contacted me about getting back together and how he's not happy with the slut but can't leave because she's supporting him (which is true).

If I work it right, I should give her enough anxiety to last a few months, and she definitely deserves it.

♦♦♦♦

While he was still living home and didn't come home one night, I got suspicious and drove my car to his office in the middle of the night. I banged on his door, but got no answer. I saw his brand new car outside.

I was so mad and upset that, using my car key, I engraved "friend, trust, honesty" and x-ed them out. Later he found it out and felt badly hurt because friendship was the foundation of any relationship for him (and he had killed it!).

I also ruined some of his stuff that he was going to come back to take with him. When he send me a message saying not to destroy his stuff, I answered that I only destroyed "stuff" but he has destroyed everything I had cherished so dear for so many years.

Now I'm done. I want to use my energy to better myself.

♦♦♦♦

I have considered everything from a baseball bat to his and her vehicles, and when I'm really pissed to their heads but have no wish to be in jail for him.

I hate what he has done to me and our trust and marriage and lots of scenarios have crossed my mind. But in the end would it matter? And it brings me down a notch.

So as someone said, take the high road, be intelligent and get your digs in where you can.

♦♦♦♦

I didn't have dreams of revenge. I had dreams where I made sure he knew he'd simply ceased to exist to me and was no more than a boil on the arse end of humanity that needed to be lanced.

♦♦♦♦

I just finished a book that had a chapter about revenge. Interestingly, it made a couple of good points: knowing that we are wired to want to punish socially unacceptable behavior means that if we set the expectation of extreme vengeance, we may deter the actual transgression.

They described an experiment to see if men and women had different notions of fair revenge. Men were much more vengeful. Women wanted vengeance, but they were not as likely to go to more extreme levels to enact it.

So much for "a woman scorned"!

♦♦♦♦

Interesting... the myths of feminine evil that abound. And the myths of our "power" too.

My ex used to make the smart-ass remark, "Of course women are more powerful than us. Women control over half the world's wealth and the entire world supply of nookie. That is what I call power."

My reply to him was always, "Now that statement tells me what is really most important to men." (In retrospect, perhaps I should have believed my own rejoinder.)

♦♦♦♦

Honestly? Now I just want to go forward and have the most beautiful life... full of love, friends, success and real happiness. I'm working on all of the above.

Daughter brought her new boyfriend over one evening earlier this week. During dinner she mentioned how ex had not met new boyfriend, and openly referred to the other woman as his "slut."

I will just leave ex and other woman to reap the rewards of their actions, and I can reap the rewards of mine.

♦♦♦♦

That's the rocks, scissors, vagina logic. According to guys, vagina always wins. Just depends on which flavor they are seeking at the moment.

♦♦♦♦

I have been considering revenge with a 21-year-old who finds me attractive. I am 43 and the mother of two teenagers.

My husband has been unfaithful for the past several months and has no remorse. He had an emotional affair with a 31-year-old who still contacts him with total disregard for me. He admitted he still wants an affair with her.

My heart is so broken and my trust is completely gone. I want him to hurt the way he has hurt me. I don't want a new relationship I just want to get back at him so bad!

♦♦♦♦

A revenge affair won't do anything but make you feel worse and cheap.

Just go ahead and swim this river of shit to the other side and find a decent guy with some honor. They do exist; unfortunately most of them are married and are (or should be) off limits to women with a sense of honor.

♦♦♦♦

Sure, a zillion times, but have never acted on any of it. There is a website where you can order animal dung, different varieties and the company will deliver. Of course, ex would know who had it sent. Or just pay some kids to throw dog shit at the other woman's house.

Been really angry this last couple of weeks about what ex has done to me and our once together family. Have to rehash in my brain all of ex's nasty notes, text messages, and phone calls to realize that he is a bitter old man now.

Have to say to myself over and over again, you selfish asshole and your slut girlfriend, how dare you destroy what we had. How dare you walk away from a perfectly great marriage?

I think about what I would do when one of our kids gets married and ex and I met at the punch bowl. I just want to say to him, "You fuckn', selfish, asshole. When you told our kids you were leaving their mom and that you had issues, why didn't you seek help with the issues instead of causing all of this pain and heartache?"

◆◆◆◆

Someone emailed me a link to a revenge website. It was interesting and all the ways to get revenge were anonymous. They have some interesting stories in the members-only section that people wrote what happened after one of the revenge tactics were used.

Has anyone here thought of doing something like this?

◆◆◆◆

Someone sent me a link to cheaterville.com. They said that it was featured on Anderson Cooper's new talk show.

If I ever did something like that everyone would know it was from me. I am sick of the High Road. I am sick of my kids crying and their feelings not being taken into account.

He and his girlfriend and her kids are all happy as can be.

◆◆◆◆

I've thought of revenge, just a little, to let people know all the lies he says and to muddy the other woman waters.

Do these sites really keep it anonymous? Has anyone tried? It would just stir a little trouble; God knows we've had some.

♦♦♦♦

Revenge? I think about it a lot but don't want to get my ass thrown in jail!

The other woman drives a car with a plate frame that reads "I'd rather be golfing." I have special ordered another custom frame that says: "I'd rather be sleeping with married men."

I'm going to change the frame while she is at work. Then I'll be done.

♦♦♦♦

I love that. Just make sure that as soon as the plate arrives you wear gloves so there are no fingerprints.

♦♦♦♦

The other woman stalked me, called me, and even put dog shit on the handle of my car. She convinced everyone that I did it to myself.

Do I want revenge? YES. I lost my husband, an intact family, financial security, my health, my home, and even my dog. She lost nothing.

He bought her home and is remodeling it. Bought the kids a big plasma TV; buys her whatever she wants. I struggle to pay my bills.

After more than thirty years of marriage I was put in the trash. He has his 40-year-old and her kids.

♦♦♦♦

I thought about getting revenge, too. But in the end, I figured the guilt of what I had done would be far worse than the harm I could ever do to him. I figured my ex would do more harm to himself than I could ever do to him.

I think living the good life and being happy is probably the slap in the face that he will get from me. I also thought if something bad happened to him, he would point the blame at me.

◆◆◆◆

The license plate frame has arrived, but I am NOT going to put it on her car. I was wasting way too much energy on this woman.

I was even practicing taking off and putting back on the frame on my own car so I could learn how to do it the fastest way possible.

Other women are not worth this kind of energy!!

◆◆◆◆

He wants to come home. Should I give him a second chance?

Does he really want to come home and stay married? Or is it just that the fantasy has not worked out on a day-to-day basis and he doesn't want to give up assets in a divorce?

Mine kept coming back and forth for years but didn't want to reconcile the marriage; he just wanted to keep what he has earned.

My husband fought the adultery divorce, but would never stay out of the house for the required separation divorce our state requires. He liked being in control, felt entitled to a wife and a mistress, and wanted to squat at home without making any changes or taking responsibility for his actions.

I gave him multiple second chances, only to be betrayed over and over again as he kept going back and forth to the girlfriend. It was just more fun to sneak there and keep fooling me. It made him feel so smart.

◆◆◆

Ex had his second chance. He came home six weeks after running away. I didn't know about the other woman. He left to go back to his job after a few days and called the next night and said: "I don't want to have a relationship with you."

Sometime later his credit card bill came to the house. I opened it and saw that, the same night he called, he'd had dinner in a nice restaurant and the total made it clear there were two diners.

A year after running away he asked about getting a third chance. No. I knew now that me-or-other-woman-me-or-other-woman was just part of his instability. I didn't want to play games and I didn't want to hand him the chance to run away again.

♦♦♦♦

When I first learned of soon-to-be-ex's affair, he maintained it was only an emotional affair and begged me to give him a second chance. I did.

Then I learned that he lied from the start, it was more than an emotional affair, it was a physical affair from the beginning, and all of his promises that he would give her up and wanted only me, none of them were true.

I felt such a fool to have believed him, to have trusted him again. I was in a state of shock, because we did not have a "bad" marriage. He told me he was happy, that he loved me, and so on.

♦♦♦♦

He would have to be honest, committed, and willing to work on his issues, then our marriage.

He would have to listen to me and treat me with respect.

He would have to know that he had an incredible mountain to climb in order to regain my trust.

He would have to understand that he didn't get to call all of the shots whether we stayed together or not.

He failed all of these... and he would have had to meet all of them in order for me to consider it.

♦♦♦♦

I might consider it. If I remember that I spent a third of my life with him and we have so much shared history (not to mention two shared children), it makes me think that I should be open to the possibility even while I maintain the ability to shut it down at any time. And, quite honestly, I would love to feel "un-rejected."

♦♦♦♦

I did give him a second chance. My ex had an affair ten years before this one. He said it was a drunken one night stand and I believed him as he got his best friend to come plead for me to take him back.

He opened up his phone, his laptop, everything. Said she was blackmailing him that she would tell me and his boss. I bought it all. He insisted we go to a counselor as my behavior wanting to see everything was abnormal in his book.

Roll on ten years and another young girl at work. She and friends calling the house asking if I knew where he was, who he was having coffee, dinner, drinks, with, etc. When I asked I got "someone causing trouble."

Then see a text from her. He didn't know her, knew who she was at work but didn't know her. Four months later catch him in the bathroom texting her. Told him to leave; that took two weeks, and he blamed me to kids, said he didn't want to go, it was my idea.

Until he moved out he was still trying to convince me nothing was going on, and would lock his laptop and phone in his car every night.

Even after he was introducing her to mutual friends as his new partner, he was telling me she was just a friend, no future with her, just someone to hang out with.

Counselor suggested we each have a list of questions we ask each other. I went back to affair ten years previous, found out one night stand was actually a year long affair. He had promised her he would leave me but he was never going to. Admitted that second time was same scenario.

There was no going back with this one. I felt if he had stayed I was giving permission for him to keep having affairs, if that makes any sense. Felt I would have been weak, and no trust left at all.

This last time was different though, he was different, he was nasty, abusive, crying, begging, all these emotions but never gave up the other woman. I think he had to have backup, and it wasn't going to be me. He showed what sort of man he was by marrying her while saying it was not what he wanted and it was all my fault. He is a coward.

When I took him back the first time, I outlined what I needed to know, that he was 100% in our marriage, he had to be transparent, show me anything I needed to see, he had to answer any questions I had and be honest.

The counselor also said that I may well ask for one month, one year, or forever. That people have their own time limits to get through it all, and my behavior was totally normal. He did not want to go back after that.

He was never honest, not even with the counselor, but I didn't know that at the time and I still loved him.

Would I ever take him back now? No never. Even if he turned up tomorrow my ship has sailed. He had his chance the first time (fool that I was), no second chances here.

First time I still loved him, this time I don't anymore, that made it easier.

The lying is what I could not get past. I hate the lying.

♦♦♦♦

Personally, I don't see a one year crisis a complete deal breaker on a 23 year marriage.

That said, my husband would have to have some understanding of what he had experienced and be prepared to work on himself.

He would have to be truly over the other woman. He would have to agree to attend a six month period of pre-reconciliation counseling. He would have to love and want me and me only.

I wouldn't settle for anything less than complete emotional integrity and honesty about where he was at. I knew when he wanted to be here and I knew when he didn't.

To be honest, when the pain and the anger have passed, the details of the crisis don't matter that much to me. I know the connection that existed between us and if that came back everything else could be dealt with.

Everyone gets to fuck up once in my book. We have weathered crisis before but this is the first time it has involved a third party.

Suffice to say, there is no sign of any of this happening. (PS: 10 months in. When does your heart stop breaking?)

♦♦♦♦

The last time, I was more cautious than ever. I knew I didn't want what we did before. He was either really in it or I wasn't interested.

We spent a lot of time talking about what was different, what we both wanted. He had to be invested in those discussions without disappearing again.

I needed to see that he wasn't going to vanish the minute it got stressful. He had to be patient and give me time to watch him walk his talk. I needed to feel like he wanted me in his life. I had no interest in being his out-of-town woman.

♦♦♦♦

It is so hard to answer that question. I did give him a second chance when I first caught him. But he begged me to

362 | Adultery At Midlife

"work things out" and agreed to marriage counseling, which was started right away.

I wanted him to be totally transparent, though, and he never was, and I wasn't demanding enough in that regard to insist upon it.

I suppose it should have been a red flag to me that he wasn't opening things up to me totally, but at the same time, I know he could have shown me everything (laptop, cellphone, etc.) and could have still had secret emails or phones I was not aware of.

Even given all that, I often wish we could reconcile again, but if the opportunity truly presented itself, I don't know if I would/could give him another chance. Assuming I would, though.

♦ ♦ ♦ ♦

Personally now after four years and lots and lots of hindsight I'd say hell no. But only because I know what I know now. That he didn't hang the moon.

I have two rotten ex's and I wouldn't take either of them back. The familiarity of second ex was powerful. It was a good so-so life but I know now it wasn't true love by any means.

Being in a current relationship now and loving in such a grown up way is very different. It rises above everything I've ever experienced.

It honestly makes me uncomfortable familiarity-wise. It's too good to be true, but it keeps being true. My fear is he will find out my secret flaws and dump me. Cheat or just walk away. Like ex two who found me not "enough" and went elsewhere.

The dynamic of trusting again is huge and applicable. Daring to love with fear and calculated risk I guess.

So the question seems to me to be, why do I want to choose to love this man? He has hurt me or he has the potential to hurt me. How do I balance that with the desire to love him? Why do I want to love this particular man? I think that is every woman's question.

If you give the familiar another chance — there better be a damned good reason to — for the rest of your life, to commit to him again. He better be pretty damned special. A wise, objective, eyes wide open woman's heart and mind.

The forgiveness comes after that thought process I would hope. And we have to own our choice. It's never about safety and security.

We are big girls now. We can make our own money and survive and thrive quite nicely. That was actually ex two's parting words: "You'll be just fine without me."

I am. Thank you.

Sometimes this is a blessing in disguise.

♦♦♦♦

I would give him another chance (have given him one already) but he would have to truly invest and I would have to matter to him and not feel like the last thing on the list of "activities," like golfing, going for a run, playing a computer game, and so on.

He would have to make me feel safe; I haven't felt safe in a long time in this marriage.

But before it all, I know how selfish he is and has always been, he would have to turn over all his equity to me if he were to leave again and it would be signed by both of us in an ironclad legal document prepared by my lawyer. I'd know for sure then if he was for real or not. For him money is king. I think that would be his deal breaker.

♦♦♦♦

I can't honestly say one way or the other, as I can't predict what my response to whoever he is now would be.

If he seemed to be who he's been for the past few years, a repugnant person to me, I wouldn't even let him in the door. He is toxic to me and that person is no one I care to expose myself to ever again.

If he seemed "different" and my instinct told me it was safe to spend time with him, I might hear him out to gauge my own response.

That would mean checking my visceral responses to him continually as to what was being answered in me by the changes in him. (Does that make sense? It does to me.)

At THIS point, on THIS day I'd be loath to even open the door to him. It's only been four or five years and I think he's still spinning. I'm feeling so much better than I did even a year ago that I'm unlikely to step onto the thin ice that is disrupting my progress.

I am very protective of my progress and my new strengths and level-headed thinking that took so long to achieve after the cataclysm.

I would rather be peaceful and clear on my own than with the wrong person, no matter who that person might be.

This truly, is all that we make of it.

♦♦♦♦

He actually did come home. As much as I had said that it was over and I could accept it, his words were what I had waited for.

All I wanted was a chance for us to work on things. I wish I would have put more thought into what I wanted from him. What I accepted was a wonderful week of dates and phone calls and secretive chats (not telling our girls yet).

Then we went out for an afternoon together (it was amazing) and that evening he told the girls he wanted to be with mommy.

He moved back in and that is when things changed. He almost seemed out of place, uncomfortable in his own skin. But he couldn't put his finger on it.

In the end he said how much he loved me but just couldn't get past that feeling that there should be a great spark and passion. This coming from a man who had just spent eight months with a 22-year old girl.

♦♦♦♦

My take on this, as it was from the beginning after I found out about his affair, is that it takes two major things to happen so that I might be willing to ever give him a chance:

1) That he grows up emotionally and learn from his experience how to and how not to treat people around him.

2) That I also find a new man in my life with whom I have more than adventure but still that relationship somehow fails or ends.

In my opinion both of the above conditions are very likely to never happen, so my answer tends to be towards "no other chance" and "yes, the affair is a deal breaker"

From personal experience with a couple of divorced female friends, I found out that those who are more or less financially ok after a divorce are much less inclined to give him a second chance.

I believe it's also a decision dictated by a person's own survival instinct.

I also know several women in what I would call a "bad marriage" who say the thing they fear most is the lack of money and the financial crisis if their husbands left them.

♦♦♦♦

Even though he and the other woman broke up and he is slowly starting to act more like a human being, and is being a better father, he is not even close to being someone I would want to reconcile with.

He does not believe that he did anything wrong (though he doesn't want anyone to know what he did).

In order for me to take him back (purely theoretical because he is "happy" alone with the peace and quiet away from the kids.)

1. Acknowledge that what he did was wrong.

2. Honesty, lots and lots of honesty (I don't think he has ever been capable of this).

3. Counseling, both individual counseling and marriage counseling. I went for years to help me through this.

4. I could never trust him completely again, he would have to be ok with this and help me deal with this.

I do not know if I would take him back even if he wanted to come back, because do I really want to be with someone I can't trust?

But the fact is that I do still love him, that I haven't even been able to consider going out with the other guys who have asked me out. So I think that I am either all alone or he will have to work his way to the other side.

♦♦♦♦

I gave him plenty of chances over the five years this has been going on with the other woman. When he is away from her completely, he is a noticeably different person, so much so that I would equate it to the man I married.

But the horrible person that he becomes when she has influence over him is a complete monster I don't know. It's a real Jekyll and Hyde.

After all those chances though, I can't imagine a time when he wouldn't go running to her, so I don't see any more chances at this point.

The only thing I think that never happened all those times that I wish had, was that I get to stand right there when he looked her in the eye and told her to get out of our lives.

Then, I wish there would be complete transparency. But, at some point, you have to realize when you've been duped one too many times and walk away.

◆◆◆◆

My situation is a bit complex in that my husband's behavior is being fueled by our geographic proximity to his family.

I would require him...

To resign from his job and find another one farther away so he can't just go to have them coach him in hurting me.

To give me a full written apology with an action plan (with measurable checkpoints) on how he will change his behavior and make amends for all the damage he's done.

To go to marriage counseling and tell the truth so we can address all the issues. He would also have to read the books I bought and make time to talk about issues on a regular basis instead of avoiding everything until it explodes.

Give me full access to his email accounts and cell phone records so I can watch for signs of him talking to his "support team" for long periods.

I can't or won't keep him away from his family (and never have) but I have a right to be concerned about the topic of discussion since he's already broken the promise not to bring them into our marriage again.

He has to submit to STD testing and accept a no physical contact rule until I know he is clean and safe. I'm not risking my life for anybody.

He would have to seek counseling for his passive-aggressive behavior so he can learn to talk about issues without undermining and blaming me.

He would have to spend three hours each week taking me somewhere alone, i.e., dinner, a movie, a picnic, etc. We've grown apart since the kids were born and that was our primary issue before he compounded it with an emotional affair and becoming enmeshed with his family.

◆◆◆◆

I really hate the Other Woman!

How is it possible not to have any morals? Am I jealous? Hell yes, but I'm mostly heartbroken, sad, trying to be strong enough to file for divorce.

Sometimes I think: is it worth it, to let a whore destroy my family? Maybe not. But then again, it was not really her, it was that pig that I still call my husband.

The only thing that keeps me smiling is that he is doing the same thing to her that he did to me. He is sleeping around with other women besides her, and she thinks she is keeping the big prize? Don't think so! I should call her to thank her; she is taking the bastard away from me!!!

These are the things I should be thinking every day; to be sad and heartbroken is not taking me anywhere. Is the depression ever going to go away?

♦♦♦

I don't know how it is possible for so many other women/other men not to have any morals. To knowingly go into a relationship with a married person is beyond me. I guess that is the big difference.

My husband and his other woman were together because they didn't have a very good moral compass.

All I can say is that I thank God that I am not that kind of person. I don't think I could look at myself in the mirror knowing that I was the cause of so much hurt to so many people, especially my children.

The day I go to see my maker I will know that I was honest with a very good moral compass and that I should be proud of myself for that.

Funny thing, my counselor told me that one day I will look back on this period of my life and actually want to thank the other woman for her help in removing a compulsive liar, cheater, and non-emotional, non-communicator from my life.

That I will want to thank her for her part in my being able to find a full and fulfilling life. And you know what? Some days I am actually starting to believe her!!

♦♦♦♦

I hate that skank ho that he's been with. That whore KNEW he was married, KNEW he was living at home, KNEW he had two children but went in for the kill anyway.

Any woman with any class, dignity and self-respect would have said, "Sorry, honey. I don't do married men. I won't even do separated men. Come back when you're single, divorced or widowed. If you're divorced, bring your divorce papers."

She has infiltrated his family as if it was her own, going to family gatherings and outings, stopping by for coffee. All the stuff we did when we were together. And he is loving every second of it!

She loves to be the center of attention and they hang all over each other like they're lovesick adolescents. I hate that slut whore with every bone in my body. He keeps saying, "You have no reason to hate her. It's not her fault, it's mine."

I went back through my computer and found that she had reached out to him several times since early last year and he finally took the bait.

She told him everything he wanted to hear. He was sexy, deserved to be happy, she liked to do things spur of the moment, she would be with him through thick and thin, he was an amazing person, blah, blah, blah.

Unfortunately, as much as I'd like to seek revenge on this trollop, I cannot. I have to sit back and take the ridicule, gloating and embarrassment that she has caused me.

She talks shit about me behind my back. Imagine that. She takes my husband then talks shit about me. What a skank.

He came home earlier this year and left six days later. He admitted that she was controlling, manipulative and cunning.

She put his phone in her name so she could check to see who he was calling and when. She put his PO Box in her name so she could monitor his mail. She put his cable in her name so that if they had a fight she could unplug it and take it (which she did.)

They had a huge fight and she took his phone (he couldn't call his kids), took the cable box, and put all of his clothes at the curb. Six days later he ran back to her like an asshole.

He gave up our marriage, home, two kids, friends, family, money, and the comfort of knowing that everything he needed was right here. He worked his whole life for everything he gave away for a six week affair with a slut.

So yes I HATE the other woman. But karma will get them both. It won't happen today, it won't happen tomorrow, it may not happen next year. But they will both get theirs — and I hope I'm around to see it.

◆◆◆◆

I hate the other woman with every fiber of my being. I knew her when she and her husband were casual friends of ours. She walks like a guy, can drink any guy under the table, tried it on with two other guys who turned her down before she made a move on my husband and is a manipulative, controlling, depressed, bitch.

I swear to God, if I ever see her in this town again there will be hell to pay. I KNOW she worked my husband for all she was worth and in his addled mind he went for it.

Yes, I know he is to blame too; they were both married and should never have crossed the boundaries they did. And I told him that.

Her husband left his first wife for her. Boy is he kicking himself for that. He realized the pain and torture he caused his first wife and his kids at the time.

He told me that he feels so bad for leaving a good woman for skank and knows now what he put her through because his skank wife put him through it with my husband.

So between them they decimated two marriages. Skank doesn't have kids so she stole my husband who does have kids and he left without a backward glance. If I ever have her in my sights...

◆◆◆◆

I wish I could hate him, I really do. But I don't. I still love him and I hate her!! I still love the good man he still is.

He is not mean to me, he is still giving me his financial support, and every time I ask him for help with the kids, he is there to help.

I hate the other woman because she knows that he is married, he does not want to divorce, and she is still there, texting him, opening her wide legs for him.

I saw some of her pictures in Facebook, and it's not because I hate her, but she is not younger than me, she is fat with a huge belly hanging out (and her boobs too). She is ugly. Reading the stuff she posts, she spells horribly, so I don't think she is very educated.

But you know what? She is always available for him, any time, any day; she is there, telling him how much she loves him, how funny, how cute. Of course she thinks there is money for her! She is not letting this one go.

The funny part is that he still spends lots of time in the house with us. He pays the mortgage, some of my bills, and gives me cash whenever I need it.

He claims that he misses me, but he is confused about what to do with his life, that he is not ready to come back to the house yet.

I do believe that he is not in love with her; she is not the reason why he left the house. He is seeing other women too. He calls them "just friends."

I think this is all about him doing whatever he wants, no explanations needed. He wants freedom, to feel single, young and be a player. He also spends lots of time with his single male friends.

I know she is not long term (unless she gets pregnant), but I still hate her because she is fighting to destroy a family.

The day after I found out about the affair, she posted "tell me that you love me" in his Facebook, knowing that my daughter and all our family was able to see that (what a bitch!).

She tried to humiliate me, and she did. He stopped her the next day, and she has never posted anything back again.

I don't know if he is in a midlife crisis or not, and I don't care. He is hurting me and my girls, and he knows it, and he keeps doing it.

I feel like I will file for divorce, despite the fact that he is the love of my life, I don't deserve to go through this. If we are meant to be together, we will be together. I feel like I deserve some love and respect. He can fuck around all he wants, I will not stay there to watch it.

♦♦♦♦

Why is it that they hook up with ugly fat dumb women the same age as them? I know in my heart that she was working him, flattering him, listening to him as he told her how shitty his life was and needed to find himself.

They are two messed up people feeding each other garbage... or for all I know they are soul mates and destined to live together forever. God I hope not... I want him back warts and all.

Not that I couldn't find another man but why would I? I know him down to his bones (before all of this). He is the father of my kids.

We have history and I know all his baggage. Some other guy will have just as much baggage, maybe more and could I trust him any more than I would trust my husband if he returned? Probably not.

So far, my husband has put nothing of him and bitch on Facebook because I told him his kids see that page and what would they think? So far nothing and he is listed as "single."

♦♦♦♦

My husband has also taken up with a tramp stamp, motorcycle riding slut with a mattress label stuck to her (it got stuck there because she's on her back so much).

She's got a nose like Jimmy Durante and a horse face. I used to call her Secretariat. Now I call her Strawberry Shortcake because for some reason, this skank ho chooses to dye her hair pink. I guess she thinks it makes her look innocent and virginal. I don't even think her shoes are virginal.

I have already warned my soon-to-be-ex, my kids, and my friends that if I ever see this sorry excuse for a woman out in a public place such as a diner or such, I will have 911 on speed dial because someone is going to get their eyes ripped out and shoved up their ass and it won't be me.

I DESPISE that fucking whore.

♦♦♦♦

I have chosen to take the high road, much as it kills me. I will come out of this with class, dignity and self-respect.

I cannot slash her tires, put a brick through the front window of her business, etc.

My only saving grace is knowing that both she and my husband are aware of her past and that she is a manipulative, conniving, cunning, husband stealing whore.

His entire family does not accept her. He has lost the respect of his children, family, friends, etc. I think he has even lost respect for himself.

My son says he walks around and stares into space like he's on drugs. And all the time she's screaming at him, "When are you gonna get divorced so we can be together forever?" It's only a matter of time till they crash and burn.

I think the adrenaline rush of puppy love is starting to fade and reality is setting in. He has to continue to convince himself and anyone that will listen that he has done the right thing and he deserves to be happy.

His happiness is dependent upon me and my kids' misery, as well as that of his family. The only one he has right now is that slut. Good for them.

I have a front row seat to the show and am just sitting back, eating my popcorn and waiting for the final scene.

♦♦♦♦

The only thing as pitiful as a chronic philandering whore (with loose elastic in her panties), is an old saggy scrotum lecher who can't even remember the name of the women he has banged or even IF they were all women.

Sex is an incredibly wonderful, pleasurable, and thrilling thing when engaged in by committed people who truly love each other. Under those circumstances it can rock our worlds.

In other circumstances it is in the same league as scratching a nagging itch... there is only momentary relief from that nagging stimulus that never seems to go away.

♦♦♦♦

Has anyone ever heard the saying, "Women cheat up, men cheat down"? So unbelievably true in my case. She is a walking, talking, leg spreading STD. She should have a tattoo in her inner thigh that says "High Traffic Area."

♦♦♦♦

If anyone asks him, she's a nice person. She's kind and generous and wants to get to know the kids. She bought them Christmas presents to be nice. I think she bought them to "buy" their approval.

It's not her fault, it's his, and everyone needs to just give her a chance, especially the kids. She feels terribly guilty about her role in this, you know. She can barely live with herself.

He must think I'm a complete idiot.

♦♦♦♦

He hasn't seen the real her yet, only the projection of what she wants him to see.

Just wait until the reality of daily life hits him and her for that matter and they see each other warts and all.

These men think the grass is greener as it is all so new and wonderful. It is not a real world they are in because they have been keeping it a secret, never have to deal with bills, work, cooking, cleaning, it is all fun at the start.

Don't waste your time or energy hating the other woman. You do at the start but as time goes on you stop thinking about her.

I blamed the other woman at the start as well. She knew he was married. Who in hell did she think he was sleeping with, and making love to when he left work and came home? It was my choice to kick my now ex out. It was the right decision for me.

Found out later he told her we had separate bedrooms and we had been over for many months. None of it was true, nothing he had told her. He also told her he had left me, yes, that accounts for the nastiness from him the last four years, doesn't it, and the not wanting to settle.

The lies they tell not only the other woman but other people will get to you if you let them. I found myself justifying every lie he told at the start, then one day I had enough of the shit. I just don't care, that was the start of my healing.

You ladies are still raw, very raw, and it is early days. Your husbands made the choice to cheat, yes she helped but put the onus where it should be. And while you are doing that, get the best possible settlement you can, as soon as you can, as their guilt wears off after a while.

◆◆◆◆

He has seen her sadistic, selfish side — knows all about her sleeping with other guys when they were together and in between, has taken verbal and emotional abuse from her repeatedly, has told me all of her shortcomings and made a pro and con list about her and me that was so lopsided that the paper wilted.

Seriously? What a freaking idiot. I think he is more afraid of being alone, but this is that hard to choose? The other woman has a large nose, jutting chin and reminds me, minus the green coloring, of the Wicked Witch of the West. And no mattress marks, but the car seats of many vehicles have left a large dent!

Sometimes this dissing feels so petty — but darn it's fun and makes me laugh. Couldn't we all use a good laugh... and at their expense? Hang on — should I be pissed because I'm definitely the better choice and he chose her? Hell to the no!

◆◆◆◆

Even in the movie "Fatal Attraction" many would say Glenn Close (the other woman) was less attractive. At least she was well educated, dressed classy, had a decent apartment, and spoke perfect English with a great vocabulary (except when she cussed him out on the tape).

I don't know why these guys go for these hos that could shatter a mirror if they walked by, I just don't know. And even those that have money, still dress like hookers from the 70's and look like them as well.

The rest of them weigh 300lbs and insist on wearing short, tight pants, leotards and tank tops with their hair piled sloppily atop their pudgy peasant faces. If they wear makeup — God help them, it only looks worse.

What's the world coming to? The other women are no longer the "femme fatales" but the dregs you see feeding their faces while they wait in line at the grocery store.

If only the other woman did look a smidge like a classy woman, we'd really be more scared than just plain pissed, wouldn't we?

◆◆◆◆

First Aid For Betrayed Wives | 379

I've heard a lot of theories around here as to why the cheater chooses who they do (and often date down), and I think there's truth in all of them.

There are so many reasons, whether it's because that person just happened to be the first person who said yes and tells them how great they are. Or because they are in such a warped, crazy place that they meet a warped crazy person and think "soul mate!!" Or that they have such awful self-esteem that they choose someone who expects less of them and for whom they don't feel as beholden.

Lots of reasons that have everything to do with the cheating spouse and nothing to do with the betrayed spouse, as usual.

It bugs me from time to time, and I was talking to my counselor about it because I really don't compare myself to her. I see what the bizarre crazy thing is between them, and I don't want my husband anymore because he's such a train wreck, and yet it still bothers me! She said, "Well, yes because it's a bit insulting."

Yes, it kind of is. You always think if you get left for someone it's going to be because they find someone better— and in a way they do— they find someone "better-suited to their crazy train of a messed up psyche."

I was reading one of my books last night and in it they had a quote by Ann Landers that I need to remember at times when I start getting miffy at the mess of a person husband is dating: "Hanging onto resentment is letting someone you despise live rent-free in your head."

And that's the truth. Hating her, or being insulted he dates her, just gives her space in my life and in my thoughts.

In my more rational moments I also just look at it and think, good, she can have him. The whole one-sided, take everything and give nothing back, anger laden, frustrated, depressed, shallow, procrastinating, lying, non-trustworthy package.

She can sit at home and wonder where he is at night knowing that if he's doing something she wouldn't like he won't tell her and there's no way for her to know.

She can try to have those emotional conversations about feelings etc., which go nowhere and get him angry so he lashes out. She has taken all of that off my hands and left me free to take care of myself, be in peace, and open my heart to all of the good energy out there.

She's like the Salvation Army of emotional detritus. I've cleaned out my house and it's now cluttering hers.

◆◆◆

I just got back from my counseling session and asked my therapist, among other things, what type of woman would date a married man?

I could never in a million years ever knowingly date a married man. Why would my soon-to-be-ex's mistress date him knowing he was married for so long and had a family?

Her answer? This woman has no empathy. She has a low self-esteem and is in desperate need of male attention. The reason I couldn't do it is because I have morals and self-respect. I have compassion and empathy for others.

I said she had been married two, if not three times and my husband may be number four.

She explained that the other woman has desensitized herself to certain emotions such as compassion, empathy, remorse or guilt. She is not in this for the long run — it is a short term fix then she will be onto someone else.

Sometimes, she said, it's the thrill of the chase. These women live on an adrenaline rush. Once the rush is over, they move on and leave catastrophe in their wake, to which there is absolutely no guilt or remorse. Some of them "get off" knowing that their man left his wife for them.

I don't know how these women can live with themselves, but like my therapist said, they have become desensitized to anyone's feelings but their own.

♦♦♦♦

She may be a scum-sucking, despicable piece of trash, but this is all your husband's doing. If it wasn't this woman, it would just be some other woman, you know?

She didn't break up your marriage, your husband did. It takes two to tango, so even if she was just constant with advances towards him, it wouldn't have made a bit of difference if your husband had morals and/or loyalty to you.

♦♦♦♦

My husband's other woman is his first girlfriend who spent two years trying to track him down. They now live on opposite sides of the world but she still managed to reach him at the wrong time in our marriage and he now thinks she's his "soul mate."

Their contact has been by email and one meeting but he can see no wrong in anything she does. She's currently on her second marriage but assures him she should have spent her life with her.

Her first marriage ended when her husband became violent towards her which was "all his fault and terrible for her."

Now my husband is violent towards me and it's all my fault because I say things to make him angry — go figure!

Do I hate the other woman? Yes I do, because their shared history is something I can never fight against.

◆◆◆◆

Not all cheaters want to leave, some just want to CHEAT. And to do that requires someone "permanent" to cheat ON.

Some cheating spouses go to great lengths to hide an affair from the wife, which is where the real lying begins.

If the marriage ends, the affair just becomes another relationship, which defeats the whole purpose.

◆◆◆◆

Ex's ex-other woman had a high paying job, luxury car and a gorgeous house. I sometimes think though, that he fell in love with her money instead of her. But she played that "damsel in distress" card to the hilt.

◆◆◆◆

When I was still so pissed I did send married other woman a note reading, "Thank you for taking out my trash."

◆◆◆◆

Just found out that soon-to-be-ex's humping partner has been married and divorced three times. If she marries my man, it will be the fourth.

She's almost fifty. You'd think that dumbass husband of mine would see the red flags. But it must be true love. I'm gonna puke.

Good for them. They've finally found the love they've been looking for. She'll be wearing the big scarlet "A" pinned to her wedding dress. Skank.

◆◆◆◆

The way I look at it, I had thirty years of filet mignon. She has the doggie bag leftovers.

◆◆◆◆

Soon-to-be-ex told me that the whore he left me for feels so bad that she contributed to the demise of our marriage that she is in counseling.

She is having trouble with the guilt. After all, she's never done anything like this before. She's as chaste as the virgin snow.

What a joke. Bitch has a tattoo on her inner thigh that says "high traffic area."

I've been in counseling for six months but he seems more concerned about her mental state than mine.

If she felt that guilty about it, she would have risen to the occasion and said I can't do this anymore. But no. They're still together, drinking, dancing, cavorting and generally enjoying themselves.

Guilt my ass. Neither of them could feel guilt if it was presented to them in a gift wrapped box with a bow on it. Maybe she'll give him the clap.

◆◆◆◆

I bet she does feel guilt. She should feel guilty and unless she's a true sociopath I'm guessing she does.

That doesn't mean anything and guilt is not remorse. It's not even close to the same thing. I'd also bet money that she has no idea what remorse is let alone be capable of experiencing it.

I think some people use guilt as a way to self-judge so they can let go and forgive themselves without changing. "If I feel guilty, I must not be a bad person, right? A bad person wouldn't feel guilty, right?"

Truth is that what they mean is remorse, not guilt but what they feel is guilt, not remorse.

♦♦♦♦

I've also had to teach myself the difference between regret, remorse, and guilt. Not really even interchangeable.

She tells him this so that they can stay together. Their love is real. They're soul mates and she's working on herself so that he won't leave her.

Theirs is a co-dependent relationship because neither wants to be alone. She's filling a need in him (the need for validation and appreciation, supposedly) and he in her (the need to feel important and loved.)

They're both sick. They should both be in therapy.

♦♦♦♦

Okay, so he says she "feels badly" and is seeking a way to stop "feeling badly." What she wants to change is how SHE FEELS, because it isn't pleasant FOR HER. You could say the same thing about nausea.

Where does remorse come into that? What does that have to do with YOU, in any case? Why does HE feel you need to know this "from him"? (Probably because HE would feel better if YOU thought more highly of the other woman, right?)

♦♦♦♦

My state is a no fault state and I can only file irreconcilable differences first, with adultery second. Then I can have the slut listed as a co-respondent in the complaint and served with the same complaint.

My only saving grace is that her name will be listed in the complaint as an adulteress, along with her mailing address and once the complaint is filed, for the rest of her life, her name will be in the Court of Records in the county that I reside in, as an adultering, slutty whore. Forever and ever. She should be forced to wear a scarlet letter.

I'm not sure if when she goes for a mortgage or someone does a background check on her if her name will pop up and she'll have to explain why she was listed as a co-respondent, but I can only hope.

Let us not forget, though, she feels badly and has to see a therapist. I wonder who's footing the bill for that, the slut or my soon-to-be-ex.

Damn, I am starting to hate the high road.

◆◆◆◆

I'd like to have just fifteen minutes alone with the other woman!

I think many of us know the other person is a symptom of the problem with our spouses and not the real issue but if you could have 15 minutes with the other woman, uninterrupted, to say or do what you want and there would be no consequences, what would it be?

My complaint with the other woman was her selfish, calculating, predatory nature. She set out to find a meal ticket because hers was leaving her. He claims he is done with her but I don't know. She really manipulated him and some women play some damned awful, mind twisting games.

We also know that many men are not led by their intelligence; other body parts take over. I know she is not the reason things happened with him, but she was a catalyst and she didn't help the situation at all. Supply and demand in this situation is no different than any other supply and demand situation.

Now if I had 15 minutes with her, I'd let all my anger loose and warn her that if she ever goes after another married man, especially one with kids, I'd take her out. I would tell her that there are two camps of women, those who build and those who destroy, and if she kept up with her predatory, selfish game, she would rue the day.

I'd happily cross over from building to destroying if it meant saving another woman the grief I have had. In the meantime, I figure I'll just let Karma have at her, which will be more than enough.

♦♦♦♦

It wouldn't have made any difference... having 15 minutes or any time for that matter.

She didn't/wouldn't have cared about anything I had to say and it sure wouldn't have made her change her mind.

♦♦♦♦

Nothing. Absolutely nothing. There'd be no point in saying anything to her. Nothing would be resolved nor accomplished for me.

I'd be wasting my time and validating a person I have no respect for nor any desire to acknowledge.

♦♦♦♦

I think I would say to her, "you poor, poor thing."

♦♦♦♦

When it all started I would have lashed out. I would have unleashed the devils of hell and damn the consequences. Now I would look at my watch, stand up, give her a slight smile and say, "Be careful what you wish for," and walk out of the room. I would not waste any of my precious time on her!!

I do not want the person he has become and she is paying a heavy price. She wanted my life, and she got him! If she is prepared to settle for so little then she is welcome to him — water has found its own level.

I realized just yesterday, as I was playing with two of my grandkids and we were planning a combined holiday next year, just how much he is missing out on.

My pulse doesn't even rise if I think of the other woman. She has him, and that is punishment enough (that is something I have only learned with the passage of time).

♦♦♦♦

I actually ended up sitting across the table from her at a restaurant at an impromptu surprise party for one of "the gang" when then-husband and I were trying an emergency midlife crisis/first reconciliation attempt post-speech.

Luckily ex was extremely attentive to me and held my hand under the table the entire time.

I intentionally totally and completely ignored her, including when she greeted me. She was, and remains, a total nonentity and beneath my notice.

And ex followed my example; lucky for HIM.

♦♦♦♦

All of you are taking the high road and I would want to get Medieval on her skank ass. I feel bad.

♦♦♦♦

Don't feel bad. A lot of us are way down the road from you.

There was a time when I wanted to burn that stupid fucker's house down, and thought endlessly about ways to do it without getting caught.

♦♦♦♦

Oh, I don't know — I think being treated as if she was invisible was about the worst thing we could have done to ex-other woman. She'd have gotten off on any sort of attention!

♦♦♦♦

Nah, for me, it's not about taking the high road. Honestly, I just don't consider justafriend worth my time.

Didn't like her before she and ex got tight and now? Well, I just think of people like her as space-takers; they mean nothing to me and really and truly aren't worth the effort it takes to acknowledge them.

And... YES! With the passage of time, healing and growth, what once seemed so important just no longer does.

There's no reason to feel bad about acknowledging your feelings… just put yourself on Pause before you react to them!!

♦♦♦♦

I'd take her for a nice drive... There is a farm I know with a nice deep pond... It's a lovely place to sit and chat and have a glass (or seven) of wine and take a refreshing swim.

♦♦♦♦

I ended up writing to the three women my husband had long term affairs with.

I did it FOR ME, not because I thought it would have any impact on them. And, once I did that, I was able to "let go" of all that "what if" stuff rambling around in my brain.

Like all of this midlife crisis brouhaha, you have to sort out what works for YOU.

♦♦♦♦

My answer has changed over time.

At first I'd probably end up putting my hands on her and beating the crap out of her. Not something that I'm proud to admit, but it is the truth.

I had a lot of anger directed at her because of her actions towards me. I'm not talking about her indirect action of fucking my husband but her direct actions towards me.

Later on, I don't know, probably be horribly verbally mean to her. I don't know how long this stage is or was… I know I had a lot of pent up anger towards her and at the same time a lot of pity towards her too.

Now, I don't think I'd talk to her at all. I might look at her… but probably not… probably I'd keep her in my peripheral because I don't trust that bitch.

♦♦♦♦

I'd send this message: A woman who cheats with a married man, then gets that married man, then marries that man is married to a man who cheats.

I'd tell her to be sure she has a pre-nup in place as this is a man who goes from woman of means, to woman of means, to woman of means. That would be a good litmus test as to whether he really loved her, or if it was just her assets he's kissing.

But of course, I won't do it. All of that will make itself apparent in time anyway.

High road, high road, high road.

♦♦♦♦

I'd bring my sons and let her see what she didn't "give a rat's ass" about. They are more than a "rat's ass." They are strong, healthy men... something she'll never have.

We are all doing fine; "diner waitress" is still slinging hash, no husband, no meal ticket.

Me, I have no desire to meet the woman. She got what she deserved. But what if husbands didn't tell them they were married or still lived at home?

♦♦♦♦

I'm not sure if my ex's girlfriend is technically another woman. He pursued her under false pretenses as a single person (in his mind he was from the moment he gave me the bomb drop). When he finally broke down and told her I was still living at the house, I'm sure he told her it was over between us, he was just doing me a favor letting me stay there until I found a suitable place, etc.

Still, it pissed me off that she stayed involved with him knowing full well he had not tied up all the loose ends with me and was technically still involved with me. For that reason, I think she's a woman of little to no integrity.

I wouldn't need 15 minutes with her, though. My message would simply be "get tested for STDs." My ex was with hookers for months when they were first dating, and he may still be seeing them from time to time.

Then I think, why should I do her any favors. She thinks she has "Mr. Wonderful" in her life, didn't think twice about what it was like for me to lose my home and marriage, and I'm quite sure she was putting a lot of pressure on my ex to get me out ASAP. So screw her.

◆◆◆◆

Over time my feelings are shifting. At first, I'd likely get my hands on her and they'd need three very strong men to pull me off.

I'm still at the stage where I would give her the tongue lashing of a lifetime to the point where she would be a grease spot on the rug.

Hopefully that would crack her in two and she might think twice before she hits on the next married guy at the PTA meeting.

I want her self-esteem to take a thrashing just like mine did. But then again, she has gone through a divorce and my ex dumped her. Don't they learn playing with matches burns you?

More than anything I'd like to believe I would put my energy in helping the next woman whose husband she put her talons in instead of taking it out on her. Truly it serves nothing.

◆◆◆◆

Laugh because I know what she's in for, but I'd refuse to spoil the surprise.

♦♦♦♦

I don't have much to say to her. I put 100% of the blame on my soon-to-be-ex.

♦♦♦♦

In the beginning I wanted to tell her what a low life she was and wanted to blame her for everything my husband did. Then I found out he knew she had been married three times before to men who were married when she came along, and that she was a ho. Now I give him total responsibility for the actions he chose.

♦♦♦♦

My husband's other woman was one of my best friends. We knew each other since we were in middle school. She has to live with that every day and every night she has to sleep next to her husband as they are still keeping it a secret.

I could have told her husband any time but I am not going to do her dirty work for her. She can suffer every day and night until she has the guts to leave her husband.

Having said that, if I do ever get 15 minutes with her, I will tell her exactly what a low life, disgusting, excuse for a woman she is.

♦♦♦♦

I'd have to say thanks. Even if it would gall me to be nice to her. She'll never be my friend, but she did do me a huge favor. Then I would "not" buy her a beer. It would only take me 1.5 seconds.

♦♦♦♦

I'm afraid I had already told her all that I had to say. She used to be my friend. Not that this changed anything or made her stop pursuing her selfish goals. Now (at least for the present) I don't feel anything against her anymore.

I am sometimes wondering what's wrong with me that I cannot see her responsible for any pain upon me.

All the pain came from my ex's part. He is and has been the main culprit in all this. I don't care that she threw herself in his arms; he was definitely very willing to receive her. Besides, she has behaved well with my daughter so far and my daughter even likes her (so she tells me).

I am content that my daughter is healthy and safe and I pray that this continues, no matter if the other woman is or not in her life.

If you asked me two years ago about this, I was thinking that I would never reach this stage of don't care towards her. But with hindsight, she is yet another victim-to-be of ex's selfishness.

♦♦♦♦

I guess I'm currently in an angry stage because I would rip her eyes out.

I KNOW he is responsible for destroying our family, but she is a major factor in that decision. She helped destroy my family and cause untold grief and hurt to my children and now expects them to accept her and love her so she can have the family she always wanted!?

She is a bottom-feeding troll who knowingly and consciously caused (and is causing) grief and pain to innocent people. Nobody does that to my children and gets a free pass from me!

Actually I revise that: first I'd spit on her and then rip her eyes out!

Really, I wouldn't rip her eyes out, I'm not violent or mean, and in reality I'd probably do nothing. But, it was nice to dream and vent that! I feel better for getting that out

♦♦♦♦

I have never given her headspace and I certainly don't have anything I want to say or do to her. Perhaps back in the day IF she had been forced into my company I MAY not have been accountable for my actions.

If I hold any attitude toward her it's cold cold cold so the likelihood would have been icy disdain.

♦♦♦♦

In my case the married other woman was my "friend" and the emotional abuse she and my husband put me through was like they cornered me in a dark alley and stabbed me over and over again while I was crying and begging them to stop. Then once I lay there with everything gone and almost dead, they laughed and threw me in the trash.

So I guess I would like to show her what that feels like. But then that would make me like her and I'm better than that. So I would leave it up to karma, fate and God, and just walk away and live a beautiful life now that she and my husband are no longer around me. I can't wait for the day when I will forget I ever knew them... I pray for that.

♦♦♦♦

1. Shake her hand
2. Shove him at her and tell her to keep him
3. Go in search of some hand sanitizer

♦♦♦♦

Yes, what we would do changes over time.

Initially, I'd have insisted on having both her and him there... broken both his legs, broken both his arms, given him a concussion that resulted in a permanent vegetative state… and then REALLY hurt the woman. Fantasy of course.

Then I subsided to the stage where I'd probably have just told her off and called her names and threatened her.

Then I reached the stage where I'd have done the "haughty momma" scathing-scorn stare.

Now (and any meeting would be purely accidental as I have no desire to interact with her) I think all I'd say is, "I have forgiven you. But I'm not the one you have to worry about. GOD requires not just saying you're sorry but actually changing your ways."

As for my ex? His eye-contact avoidance, being the peripheral, wistful wraith at family functions, and playing the victim because he has to pay me alimony, gives me visions of a scenario where my foot might need to be surgically removed from his rectum. I mean GROW UP!!!

◆◆◆◆

I woke up to a dream of the other woman telling me she would forgive me. I was sputtering, and wanted to grab her by the shoulders and shake her until her teeth fell out of her head.

I thought I'd gotten further down the road. I guess it's back to working on me and getting her skanky self off my "hit list."

◆◆◆◆

I'd probably say "you can have him and his foul moods, his narcissism, his snoring, his impatience. I had his best years; you're welcome to what is left of him."

But to ex I'd say: "If I meet her I'll box her in the nose, so just don't let it happen."

◆◆◆◆

No consequences??

I would beat her until she couldn't breathe. Then I would use a defibrillator, bring her "back" and beat the shit out of her some more.

I know I will eventually get to that place of not caring anything about her and really don't right now. She is a non-entity to me and completely worthless; certainly not worth my time or energy.

But if given the opportunity, with no consequences, I would damn near kill her. Fucking predatory bitch. She deserves everything she gets including my loser of a husband.

◆◆◆◆

Sadly for the other woman, I have worked her out. She is an immature drama queen who needs the public forum to acknowledge her love of "her man." Not for his benefit but for her own. She flaunts it at her ex and she needs the external validation that she is important.

Well, little cherub, as God is my witness, I will never, ever give you that validation. You are nothing to me and I will never acknowledge you in any way, shape or form.

If I felt inclined to respond to her, I would go up to her and say "I am so sorry for you" and then walk away laughing. I think she might physically and verbally abuse me if I did that though.

◆◆◆◆

The first time the other woman and I met, she said "What's up with his snoring?" which was so shocking to me that I just said, "There are some things I don't miss" and walked away.

She honestly believed that I was "healed" from the trauma that had happened to me. It was eye opening to say the least.

Actually, I think she did not understand what a trauma it was for me. She is an only child with narcissistic personality traits.

I don't give her much thought anymore. We're such polar opposites that we would never "get" one another. Different planets, for sure.

♦♦♦♦

Yes, the answer to this has changed over time.

At first I wanted to punch her in the face and add to that some public humiliation.

If I was in a room with her now, I would say: "So let me get this straight... you were engaged the whole time you were seeing my husband. You let my husband get all wrapped up in you until he treated his family like SHIT all the while you kept him a secret from everyone in your life. I would like to tell people in your life that you are NOT the woman they think you are. They think you decent, I know you are not. You need to spend every day for the rest of your life scared that you will come home one day and I will be sitting with your family explaining what you did in great detail."

♦♦♦♦

I called her. I read the love letter I found from her to my husband. She said they were "just friends." I reread a part of the letter, "I love you with all my heart." She said, "I told him to go home and work on his marriage."

I reread this back, "I will just keep my distance until the dust settles. I don't want us to be together by being caught." This went on until she said, "You're not going to let me say anything." I told her there was not anything she could say because I now have the evidence.

And I said, "I also found the condoms." She said, "Those were not for me." I said, "When my husband tells me who those were for, I will show up at her door with the condoms and tell her husband and if he doesn't, then I'm showing up at yours to tell your husband." She said "I am so sorry. I am so sorry." I told her husband.

Nope. Didn't make a difference in the situation. She and her husband separated but are back together and she and my ex have lunch together every day.

Would I do it again? YEP.

♦♦♦♦

I never felt any interest in contacting either of the other women that I know about. They were fantasy/bizarre "characters" in some weird-ass parallel universe he created in his head. Both were married and middle aged.

The first one, if I can believe what he told me (which is highly doubtful), was basically looking for a walk on the wild side, and was just out for some fun on the side. He probably wasn't the first or the last (if I can go by what he told me).

The second one, bipolar crazy woman a little younger than me with kids and ready to blow up her own family (she was caught... maybe accidentally on purpose by leaving emails to my husband open on her computer and her husband found them). She seemed to enjoy the drama and the excitement of having two men fighting over her sorry middle-aged self. There was a lot of Jerry Springer-world drama with frantic phone calls and texts like teenagers, promises made, promises broken, promises "slightly" broken.

As her husband said in one of the messages he left on my voicemail, "They are acting like lovesick teenagers and it has

GOT to stop." Or he was going to DO something about it, dammit.

She was obviously crazy, maybe in midlife crisis herself. What would be the point to talking to her?

The first one just seemed like an idiotic fling. Again, what's the point? I had no interest in either of these people... no contact worked for me!

♦♦♦♦

Give her a huge hug and thank her!! (Five years later.)

♦♦♦♦

Ok I admit. I did it! I called the other woman when ex first left. I played the desperate wife role to get information. When I got what I needed, I told her if I ever saw her she better run as fast as she can the other way. Not because of my ex but because of what she was doing to my kids.

I used to text her "do you like my life?" I called her a whore and got out what I wanted.

Did it change anything, NO. Do I regret it NO. I would have done more if I knew what my life was going to end up like. Now I'd hug her!

♦♦♦♦

I called the other woman, too, when I found the messages in his phone, and got her answering machine. Called her every name I could think of and I'm sure I made some up. I think I used swear words I'd never heard before.

Her teenaged daughter picked it up and was upset. My husband was upset. The other woman was upset. Did I care? Not an iota. Would I do it again? Yes.

♦♦♦♦

I told her, "I'm leaving him and he's yours now." They are going to LOVE wondering who the other is texting all the time since they are both philanderers. So have fun when that starts up.

I told her, "He's your responsibility now." She said, "I am NOT going to leave my husband for him."

I also told her about the second suspected married other woman. My ex said, "You told (married other woman) about (other married other woman)?" all pouty.

Yes. Lots of drama. Not proud but I'm not ashamed of it either. Still glad I did it.

♦♦♦♦

The bimbo was one of my friends.

When he left, he left everything he had behind... everything. She thought she was going to have everything she didn't have with her husband of two years only now she has even less. She bought herself a house and he doesn't even have the tools to help her fix it up.

My ex's family will have nothing to do with her, nothing!! I am very close to his entire family and do things with them often. She is not ever allowed in their house.

She has no friends, I still hang around with them all. Oh, but there is nothing going on; even after two years, they are still only friends.

In my book, she is not worth the words or the dirt she will be buried with. I am going to just sit back and watch the show and be grateful that it isn't me in her footsteps. She will end up with nothing in the end and so will he.

♦♦♦♦

I did take the high road, BUT I could write a book about the things I wanted to say and do to her and to him also.

♦♦♦♦

I would ask her if I should believe everything her ex-husband would tell me about her and if not why would she believe what my husband told her about me?

At the beginning I would have loved to beat her to a pulp, and at the time I think I would have enjoyed it.

I would have liked to write WHORE on her lawn in Roundup so it would show for a long time.

I would have posted her face on a billboard announcing her to the community as an adulteress and home wrecker (and that would cost her job and all community respect).

She went after my husband with a purpose, she was about to age out of her child support and she was looking for a meal ticket.

And, no, I do not for a minute not hold my husband responsible for any of it. But she fed into him and I believe she gave him the "courage" to believe he was so unhappy with me. She took information from him and tried to get me fired from my job.

I have no love lost for her. I truly hope I never meet up with her in a dark alley with no cameras and a good alibi because I am still not at a point where I do not know what I would do.

I am truly working on it.

♦♦♦♦

I think I'm the minority here, but I don't, and really never had any major anger towards the married other woman. I always saw her as a victim of my ex.

In all likelihood, he pursued her relentlessly. He was obsessed with her. Or maybe I am just naive... and she really played a game.

She wasn't his only indiscretion. HE is the despicable creature, not her. Oh well, I think I've hit another anger phase. I hate the sonofabitch.

◆◆◆◆

For some reason, I have truly not given the other woman much thought. I could tell from the cell phone records that she definitely preyed on him and he fell for it hook, line and sinker. It's the new math: Predatory woman + vulnerable midlife crisis man = CHAOS!!!

It was still HIS choice to stray but we might have had a chance if she hadn't worked so hard to convince him that I was the cause of all his problems.

The most I have thought has been about her teenage children. What kind of a woman lets a married man move into her home in front of her teenaged daughter and son?

If it weren't for her kids, I might be vindictive enough to do something. I hope if I actually saw her in real life I would simply make eye contact to show her that I know who she is and then walk away because she isn't worth the time or the energy to even think about confronting in any way.

◆◆◆◆

I had my moment and I attacked her. Was it one of my best moments? NO... Would I do it again?? YES. I don't regret it for a minute. I just wish I had more time before my husband broke us up.

◆◆◆◆

She is not worth anything. Any woman who goes after a married man and does this to another woman has no respect for herself. I would not put myself in a room with her at any time.

I don't respect her, have no opinion of her. She is a non-entity and she can have my leftovers as I had my husband's best years and she is getting my scraps.

♦♦♦♦

It has taken a long time to get here and some days are still not good. My feelings changed the day my husband told me that I am a bad person.

I will no longer allow people with no moral values or integrity clutter my mind. I am worth so much more.

I believe in karma and what the Bible says, you reap what you sow. I just want to make sure that my kids are always treated well. She is a ho and an adulteress who deserves men like my husband, weak, self-centered assholes.

♦♦♦♦

I just could never get past the reality that ex chose to be involved with another woman. HE CHOSE.

I couldn't figure out how I could blame or despise anyone for playing him or playing into his searching.

HE was the one who was ripe and ready and, obviously, looking for something.

If he didn't want to compromise himself or US, he wouldn't have done as he did. How could/can I blame anyone else but him? That's all.

♦♦♦♦

I don't like/admire/respect his ex-other woman on general principles; she's one messed up, spiteful mess who has intentionally inflicted a LOT of pain on others.

But she wouldn't have been able to do that to our marriage if HE hadn't allowed it.

Then again, that's his biggest hang-up these days. Not that he's DOING anything about it.

♦♦♦♦

If there were no consequences I would really like to slap her face, just once, for how she hurt my children. I just cannot find it in my heart to forgive that.

She plotted to get my husband and our teenaged daughter went to her house and confronted her. She couldn't stand seeing my pain any longer. It broke my heart when she told me that she had gone over there.

That ho was so defensive and snide. You'd think that she would've hung her face in shame. But, no. She defended their love and then told her to blame her father! And, yes, he is to blame. But you'd think that she could've been a little more compassionate with our teenage daughter.

♦♦♦♦

They are trashy little sluts. They don't know what compassion is. They don't care about our pain or our children's pain. It's all about them and what they want.

I asked my husband one day how he could look at someone who hurt his family so badly.

I said if anyone hurt my kids like that I would never talk to them again I would be so disgusted. But that's because we are all loving, caring compassionate people. They are not.

I would have never let someone come between myself and my family.

♦♦♦♦

I don't "blame" the married other woman as my soon-to-be-ex has been having affairs for years, lying to the women that he is single with no kids (this woman as well). She eventually found out about the kids but clearly she didn't care enough about us or about the fact that he is a liar.

The last two years he was in midlife crisis and his affairs worsened which is when he "fell" for the married other woman. This really is about him and not about her.

But, that doesn't mean I wouldn't like to hurt her and I would be meaner than any of you if I had 15 minutes.

♦♦♦♦

I would like to knock her block off. Sorry I can't rise above this and be the better person. I think if I had the chance I would knock her into next week. She did set out to play my husband and groomed him into it.

I know he was responsible as well but to be honest she worked so hard to get him. Phone stalking me. Got a little cottage in an area that he loves all set up waiting for him. Pays for everything so he doesn't have to think about money.

My husband was no match for his other woman. She really is an expert whore and set her sights on him and was never going to give up until she got him. She did create a perfect world for him to step into. She is a sicko but good at what she did with no expense spared.

♦♦♦♦

Who knows how long this other person was tempting my fucked up husband. He was messed up a long time, and she was "there." But, they actually deserve each other and have far more common priorities, attitude, and lack of values than I would want in my life.

So I would not give her the time of day IF she continues to treat my daughter well. If she does not, I will move on it then.

In the end, it was my husband, not her, that placed us where we are. His weaknesses, his selfishness, his lack of integrity and character. She now gets to deal with all of that and all that he is from here forward. And that sort of evens it out.

◆◆◆◆

I know that my husband chose to engage in an affair. I know this and he is responsible for this action. I love my husband and will work toward reconciling our relationship and our family with him.

I also know that ex-other woman "knew" we were together and yet she agreed to engage in an affair with him. I hold her responsible for this action. I've got no love for her, never had, but I work toward forgiving her for myself.

The kicker for me as it relates to my anger toward her is that I went to talk to her and she lied to me. She sat there, watched me cry, HUGGED ME, and lied to my face about everything.

Then all the nonsense that went on afterwards instigated by her. That's a hard one for me to forgive, to put to rest.

◆◆◆◆

I probably wouldn't say anything to the other woman. I agree with some of you, ignoring her would probably cut her the most.

However, if I had to say something, anything at all, I would thank her. I would tell her how my life has changed and I am much happier now than ever before. My only regret is that my divorce didn't happen sooner.

And I really mean it.

◆◆◆◆

I have been thinking of sending my husband and the other woman a thank you letter. I now believe I am better off and scum deserves scum. So still figuring out how I can send something like that.

It would be nice to send something to her family so they know that they are both adulterers and cheats.

♦♦♦♦

In general, I refuse to give their relationship the time of day but if I met her I would be sorely tempted to punch her in the face... just the once and walk away.

After the affair began, this smug piece of work wanted to call me to show me her compassion. I think one slap on the chops is warranted and he has already had his, several times, in fact.

♦♦♦♦

I figured the best revenge is to live a good life. I guess there really aren't any words to impart on the other woman. I wish her well and I am thankful it is her and not me.

The ex does make a lot of money, but I figured not all money is good money!

♦♦♦♦

I really hope in time I'll be as strong as some of you. But I just found out so I think it's for the best not to talk to her at all. Her husband and kids don't know what's going on.

I know the married other woman and we spoke not that long ago. I now know that they were getting pretty involved at the time. I think because her marriage is not that good, supposedly, she couldn't care less about me or her family and made a choice.

♦♦♦♦

I still want to brand her ugly face with a huge scarlet letter "A," so that everyone will know her for the lying, cheating whore that she is.

♦♦♦♦

My husband keeps telling me how much she likes me and cares how I'm doing. I've never met her nor do I care to. I'm sorry but I can't seem to get past my anger towards the other woman.

What she did to my boys, tearing apart our family! She knew he was married with kids. I would deck her in the nose without a second thought. Call her a few choice words and probably spit on her!

My anger and bitterness is still so profound. Yet I seem to be able to let him off. Narcissistic charmer. They belong together. Karma and God will get them both!

♦♦♦♦

Husband broke up with the other woman. I would like to talk to her and ask her if her heart is broken and, if so, how does it feel? Maybe this is just desserts for what she did?

I'd like to sarcastically thank her for going after a married man and breaking up a family just when hers had fallen apart and she knew firsthand the pain of the dissolution of a family while she tries to keep her family together. I hope she feels it was worth it.

He will just go on to another one, I'm sure. I'm so tired of all this, so tired of his lack of maturity, his anger, and his destructive nature towards me.

As for the other woman, I wish her the luck she deserves. But she obviously has no scruples at all, so I'm sure it's a matter of time before she goes after another married man.

♦♦♦♦

I haven't exactly let my husband off the hook. I have slapped him on the face on three different occasions. I just don't feel as much anger toward him. I actually feel sorry for him. This whole thing sucks, but things will get better over time.

◆◆◆◆

Although it was my husband's choice to cheat, I feel the other woman is also culpable. If I were to be in a situation where I could speak to her, I would ask her what it is like to suck a married man's c**k while knowing he is having un-protected sex with his wife.

◆◆◆◆

I have been in reconciliation with my husband for about six months. After five years of him living away from home denying there was anyone else, to me to my kids, I finally found out the truth, there was another woman he was with for over four years.

The day I found out I went to her home, rang her door-bell, and demanded to know what she and he were doing. That ended the relationship, except for a few phone calls. I gave him a choice, her or me.

He chose me, but I called her and told her that this is what he was telling me and I wanted to meet up with her, along with my husband, to see if this was true.

We did a three-way phone conversation and she answered every question that I had, found out all the lies that he had told, and that has been the end of their relationship.

Since he and I are in repair mode, since I have learned the truth, I do not have the same feelings for him. I learned that I am a lot stronger than I thought I was and if this ends to-morrow, I will be ok. No, I will be more than ok.

◆◆◆◆

Knock her out and tattoo on her forehead: Caution - Wide Load - Home-Wrecking Whore!

◆◆◆◆

I did, at one point, have a situation that forced me into the same room with the other woman because she worked for ex, and he and I had business to discuss. She had to take phone calls while ex and I met with financial people in another room, with the door open.

She was a nobody then and she's a nobody now. A complete non-entity that doesn't deserve a shred of time invested by me. If I would have said anything to her, it would have been that I thought she was pathetic. But didn't need to do that. I know it and don't feel I have to point it out to her.

◆◆◆◆

I have nothing to say to her. I actually ran into her a few weeks ago at the front door of my ex's house when I stopped to pick up mail. She knocked; I asked her if she would like me to open the door with my key. She wasn't sure where to run and hide.

I am angry with her because she trampled on the boundaries I had with him. I have disgust for her because she is selfish. I have pity for her because she thinks she "won." But the very fact that she enables his addictive behavior tells me she doesn't have a clue what she is getting into.

But most of all, I just cannot stop wondering what kind of a desperate woman whores around with a man who is in a committed relationship for seven years, with the hope of someday getting more than his drunken time at the bar?

She had no vacations, no holidays, no sleepovers, so how far below the bar is your self-esteem when you continue to hang onto that?

I heard a quote one time, "There is a special place in hell for women who are mean to other women." When I found out about her, this was all I could think of: honey, you will get yours and ending up with him may very well prove to be your "special place."

♦♦♦♦

I have nothing to say to her. I think she already knows that she won the booby prize! My friends think I should thank her for taking him off my hands. I just keep thinking: Be careful what you wish for, honey. Karma is a bitch.

♦♦♦♦

I'd run. She's manipulative as hell.

Apart from that I feel, they've earned each other; both are lying, manipulative, and immature. I wish them the best of luck suppressing the facts.

The only thing I'm having a hard time letting go of is that they're both in victim-mode. I'd love to pillory them — literally — and shout the truth out to the world around them.

Instead, I'm taking the high road. I will never ever again exchange so much as a word with her or him. They're fundamentally dishonest people.

♦♦♦♦

Yes, 15 minutes! I'd rather be cleaning the fridge! Or the stove or even the shower recess!!! At least then I would feel like I had achieved something.

My grandmother warned, "You can stoop down and pick up nothing."

♦♦♦♦

I have never met or spoken to the other woman/new wife. I have no desire to. She is never invited to family events. Ex is invited, but chooses not to come.

However, I semi-acknowledged her once when ex was in contempt of court. New wife emailed me and pretended to be ex and threatened to reenlist so my half of his pension would stop.

I played dumb and emailed back like I thought it was him. I said, "Go ahead, the contempt charge will be waiting." And then I said (knowing that it was her), "You used your deployments to cheat on me and I am sure that you will be just as faithful to your new wife as you were to me."

Needless to say, he didn't reenlist. I have been lucky, as ex and I have been to court three times. I won twice, so now he pretty much follows our divorce decree.

◆◆◆◆

Well, I didn't directly talk to her... but I DID take her to court and I had her deposed. And she was really a bitch! Even the judge told her she was a liar! It was actually quite fun now that I look back on it, but it was expensive. But it also cost her bundle since she had to hire an attorney.

It was really interesting to see her squirm under oath and still she lied. If that is the sort of person he wants, well, he will have a ton of fun!

I don't need to talk to her. She gets a person she can't trust, who has seriously reduced financial circumstances, and he gets a very used up ugly other woman.

Now every month she gets to help him hand over cash that she thought would be hers!

◆◆◆◆

I would make the ho look me dead in my face for the first ten minutes. The last five I would explain that you cannot build happiness on another's misery. It will come back to haunt you the rest of your life.

Then I would ask why she has been married three times, has had multiple relationships, and cannot seem to keep lasting relationships with a man. I had my man for 30 good years. She's had him for six months. She dangled her goods in front of him and he dropped like a fly. Jackass.

♦♦♦♦

I would only need five minutes to tell her that I wish her luck! That he didn't leave me or choose her. I left him no choice and refused to take him back when he begged me to. He had nowhere else to go and no one else that wanted him.

Then I would give her the letters he wrote and my responses that verify this.

In actual fact should I ever meet her, I would say nothing and rise above it. But hopefully my dogs would pee on her or, worse, lick her to death!

♦♦♦♦

I have class, dignity and self-respect. She has none of those character traits. She's a man eater and has been through many, many men. Good luck to the both of them. They will never truly be happy.

Relationships that begin with lies, deceit and adultery are extremely unlikely to ever succeed.

♦♦♦♦

I think the other woman in our marriage is an effing idiot. I would have to speak to her slowly in one and two syllable words so that she could understand.

"Listen, Ho, you broke up my marriage. You aren't worth the shit on the bottom of my shoe you miserable slut. I would have used the word paramour but I don't think you'd understand so slut works just fine. Oh, and here's a dictionary. Go look up the other words you don't understand." Bitch.

♦♦♦♦

I would not so much want to confront her as I would like her to have to confront who she is.

I would love to post a sandwich board on her and make her stand in the busiest place in the city where she spends her time trolling for unsuspecting men.

Then I would love to post a video of those 15 minutes on YouTube, so she could run, but she couldn't hide.

I know her soon-to-be-ex and older kids wouldn't mind. They know her well. They wouldn't be surprised.

You wouldn't believe how many times she wanted to meet with me and "talk." She thought I'd say no, but I always told her sure.

She found so many excuses never to show up... and she texted me to call me a chicken. Did I mention infantile?

◆◆◆◆

Things well-meaning people say that I really don't want to hear.

Maybe I'm crazy, but there are some things that well-meaning people say to me regarding my husband's infidelity that I really don't want to hear.

Do these words bother anyone else?

1. You deserve better
2. You'll find someone else
3. You're so much prettier than her
4. I don't know what he sees in her
5. He'll come back begging (when? It's been 7 months)
6. It'll get better
7. Be strong
8. Do something nice for yourself
9. He'll get his (see 5 above)
10. It's a shame he didn't talk to you before having an affair
11. Get out and meet people
12. Go on a date
13. You need to move on

Please feel free to add any others.

I'm hurt, angry, sad, depressed. I don't want to go out yet. I don't want to date. I want my husband, my best friend in life, and my companion, back.

If you want to help, call me and say, "Let's talk. Tell me how crappy and sad you feel." or "I'm here for you and I love you." or "If you want to call me and just cry, I'll listen."

Maybe I'm just bitter. How do you all feel? We were married for 29 years and he left me for a trollop that he had a six week affair with because he "found his soul mate" and "he loves her." I want to puke.

Yes, I've been in therapy for almost seven months.

♦♦♦♦

Most of the time people will say stuff like this, not knowing what really happened or how it makes you feel. They don't understand that it is not "only" the infidelity, but it is also about everything that comes with the midlife crisis. And that it takes a long time to recover and figure things out.

There's not a button you can push and everything is fine. They think by saying this, it will make you feel better. You know that you didn't deserve this. And you know that there are more men out there. But it doesn't help pointing that out, right? I don't want to hear it and it bothers me big time.

But I have to tell you... sometimes you will get some really good advice on this forum. And it's from people that really understand what you are going through.

If someone at work tells me that the future will be brighter, or that I should be glad not to be with a man like that, I don't listen and do my best not to explain that this is not helping.

But when I don't know what to do or think anymore and I'm in tears, it really helps to have someone here that tells you to act strong, straighten your shoulders and do something nice for yourself. They know; they've been there.

And they will not try to "comfort" you with "that sort of thing happens all the time" if you want to talk about how you feel. It's all about who the person is that's giving the advice I think.

♦♦♦♦

I completely hear you. I feel very much the same way. I'm tired of the clichés as well. It's not something that anyone can fix and the one person that has the magic words is a stranger after all these years. It's the most devastating thing I've ever been through.

♦♦♦♦

People who shovel out such tripe have never had this happen to them... but if they live long enough something equally traumatic will. Gives a whole different perspective.

We know your pain. We also know that it will take time and working on you to diminish it. Never be ashamed of having loved deeply.

♦♦♦♦

I prefer to think that people who offer these tidbits mean well but have no clue WHAT to say and don't realize how these things not only don't help, they often aggravate us!

So, try to be thankful for them that they DON'T know what they're talking about. I mean, you don't wish this sort of experience on others, right?

And that's the ONLY way they'd really be able to know what they should or shouldn't say.

♦♦♦♦

What I really want to hear someone say is that they have talked to him and he says that he loves me and wants to come home. That he regrets his decisions and hopes that I can find it in my soul to forgive him.

I want him to say that he was confused. That he never loved the other woman, that he was just using her. I want my old life back with my awesome, kind, gentle, loving husband. I don't know who this man is. Neither does anyone else.

At least my in-laws are compassionate. They say things like, "It'll never last," and "She's not you. We'll always love you and the kids." His own brother and sister think he's acting like an 18-year old and an ass. I hate this.

♦♦♦♦

Re-examine what you wrote and you'll see that there are people whose compassion comes through even if they don't necessarily chose the exact correct words.

But then again when someone is going through this kind of pain, words just can't suffice to make the pain go away. But I agree with you that they CAN leave off most of the original 13 that you posted.

Besides, even those of us who have gone through it don't necessarily say the right words at times. Sometimes people are in such pain that words just aren't helpful; they need for someone to just "be" with them.

Somewhere on this forum some pain-riddled woman was pouring out her heart, and somebody came along and gave out a few well-modulated, prissy schoolmarm platitudes, and then concluded by saying, "Welcome to the wacky world of midlife crisis."

That last has stuck with me because it was the most inane comment, almost like something a movie reviewer would use in describing the latest Jim Carrey movie. I almost barfed.

Here is this woman feeling like a gunned down and gutted deer hanging over the tailgate of a truck and bleeding out due to her husband's cruel behavior, and all that can be said is, "Welcome to the wacky world of midlife crisis"?

Sometimes, it's just better to say, "I feel your pain," and then let it go.

♦♦♦♦

Thank you for such a heartfelt and authentic post.

I am nine months in and I am still in pain but trying my best. I think I heard most of the things on your list. Some of my friends even try to change the subject. I guess I have had my time quota with some folks.

I have moved on inasmuch as I am not sobbing my heart out on a daily basis but I am far from being over my husband.

I have heard most of the comments on your list and I agree, they can be hard to hear. The one I struggle with most is when people tell me he will be back but I will be so far down the road that I don't want him.

All of a sudden everyone knows my life and my future. The other is, you'll meet someone better. It's as if no one can bear to be real.

Personally, I am tired of trying to get over it and going through the motions of doing new things and meeting new people. It's exhausting and I miss being a family and no amount of art classes, or having control of the TV remote, eating when I want, or job satisfaction, makes up for that.

◆◆◆◆

I couldn't have put it more beautifully. It's like you're in my head. As he grew out of love with me I grew more in love with him.

I have beaten myself up for six months now. How could I not see it? What could I have done differently? What does she have that I don't have?

I am happy being in denial for the time being. It's safe here. Does he think of me every waking minute like I think of him? Does he dream about me like I dream about him? I still dream that he'll appear on my doorstep and my life will be back to normal again and that this was a nasty nightmare. He was awesome, sexy, kind, gentle, generous, and spontaneous, and the list goes on.

We would snuggle on the couch with a cup of coffee and watch American Idol. We would sit on the deck in the autumn and watch the deer eat the apples. We'd get up before the kids and go for a cup of coffee at the diner.

I don't want to love another man like I loved him. I miss his smell, the way he feels, the way his car sounded when it pulled in the driveway after work.

I miss my best friend (I'm crying as I write this). I cringe at the thought of another woman holding his hand, running her fingers through his hair, and snuggling with him.

How could he do this? I thought we were happy. I've been scratching my head for months now.

◆◆◆◆

Did you grow more in love with him, or just go through that automatic "no you can't change my world that much I'll cling tighter" reaction?

I was scared shitless when I got The Speech, and it didn't make me love him more, but it made me more desperate to hold on to what I had.

That's pretty normal. And it's pretty normal to feel like a blind clueless loser, too.

But that phase wears off, and you realize that you don't love him more after all. He's being a dick. A stupid and immature dick at that, and dickishness does not make a person more lovable.

You really don't like this new guy very much. If he were a stranger and you found out he ran away with his soul-skank, you'd write him off as a loser. You also realize that all those terrible personality flaws you have that must have driven him away, aren't so bad, and are actually very normal.

You miss your old husband and your old life and you want both back. But that guy is gone for the foreseeable future, and he may never return. It takes time to see it that way, though.

♦♦♦♦

I didn't grow more in love with him after he left; I grew more in love with him the longer we were married. I still got goose bumps sometimes when he walked in the front door or grabbed me from behind and kissed the back of my neck.

I looked forward to being able to do more things with him as our children got older. This was to be our time together and I couldn't wait to see what exciting things fate had in store for us. If he grew out of love with me, he'll grow out of love with this slut loser too.

What type of woman must she be knowing that he left a 30 year relationship for her? I would never want to be the other woman.

Going forward, should I ever decide to date, I will ask for divorce papers up front. I could never unleash the hurt that an extramarital affair has on another woman and her family.

This has hurt not only me and our kids; it has hurt my parents, my sisters, our friends, his family, his friends.

He doesn't see it. He's entitled to be happy and he'll shout it from the rooftops.

The kids hate the slut and he keeps shoving her down their throats (and everyone else's for that matter). If they would just give her a chance, he says they will grow to love her like he does. It's been just under seven months but this asshole doesn't get it. The kids need to grow up and we all need to move on, according to him.

Please, give your poor family a chance to heal. What a dick. I still love him because I can't turn off that feeling like a water spigot. With time people tell me I will still love him, just differently. We'll see.

I hate this but it's comforting to see that I am far from alone. Everyone's stories look exactly like mine.

◆◆◆◆

Every left behind spouse, pretty much, goes through that period of yearning for things to be like they were. You want him to come back, say it was all a terrible mistake, pick up the threads of married life and carry on. (Which some do.)

Many fight to retain their love in the face of outrageous emotional abuse because it seems like a betrayal of "what was" to let go like the cheating spouse lets go.

He may trash the love you once had but you want to preserve it. That's natural at first.

I remember when I came to this forum years ago feeling incredibly frustrated with people who'd ask, "What is it you want?" or "What do you want to do for you?"

It just seemed obvious to me that what I wanted was him and our "old" life. I wanted my life back.

Bit by painfully slow bit, you realize that "waiting" for them to get through midlife crisis is a waste of time. Where does it leave you if he remarries and lives happily ever after with the other woman as some of them do?

Bit by bit, most realize that the old husband and the old life, are not coming back any more than our teens or our first date are coming around again. That part of life — important as it was — is over.

It's just my opinion, but I don't think healing can really begin until the point where a left behind spouse stops wanting her husband back. Then, she can get really involved and absorbed in the life she's rebuilding.

I'm not saying that an end to yearning for the runaway husband can be forced. It's something that comes with time and reflection.

For a long time our hearts cannot "see" what our brains know — that this guy is not our friend any more, not our lover, and not worthy of our love or time.

He cheated, was deceitful. "But I love him," the left behind spouse cries. Actually, she probably doesn't really — she loves the experience she had with him pre-midlife crisis and she wishes she could have that back.

Slowly, you get to a place where you don't love him or want him anymore and neither do you hate him or feel like dispensing curses on him and his other woman. You simply glide into indifference and get on with all the things in your life that claim and engage your attention.

To newbies, that seems impossible and undesirable. The love must be kept alive at all costs! But couples break up every day and, yes, it happened to us too. And, whatever anybody says or doesn't say, we do eventually get over it, in our own time.

♦♦♦♦

I never knew my husband to lie. Over the past few weeks the lies have started to come to the surface. He has been hiding money. Telling me he has no overtime, no cash coming in. He's broke. His bank statements prove otherwise (he does not know that I have them).

Now my attorney has to subpoena all of his banking records and 401k statements so that my alimony is properly awarded.

I am entitled to permanent alimony so long as I never remarry due to the length of our marriage. He is livid! Says he cannot pay that and will not pay that, that I can put him in jail.

You are correct, my brain is telling me that he is a lying, cheating scumbag, but my heart still skips a beat at the thought of us cuddling on the couch with a hot cup of coffee.

I hate this so much. Unfortunately, fighting him is going to cost money so I'll have to take a loan. In the end it will be worth it because I refuse to give up what is mine by law without a fight.

Next time he threatens to withhold money which he already has or otherwise, I have been instructed to say "whatever" and hang the phone up. Same with texting.

I am also going to ask that he reimburse me for my visits with the therapist. I would not have had to see a therapist were it not for him. So far I have spent $1,500 and still go every week.

I'm so glad I found this forum and the women that this has happened to. It was NEVER going to happen to me. How dreadfully wrong I was.

Someday I will smile again.

◆◆◆◆

I'm so very sorry you're in so much pain. I completely understand.

May I add these to your list?

14. I never liked him anyway (my family and friends).

15. He's just fallen out of love with you. You have to accept that (his family).

He's someone masquerading as your husband. He's NOT the person you married and lived with so happily for so many years. He's not your friend.

♦♦♦♦

Some of us have been members of the forum for a while and this conversation is helpful to all of us. It reminds many of us of things we forget along the way.

Our friends and family want us to look at the reality and just to move on but you don't move on from 29 years of marriage overnight. And reality is very frightening.

The one I got was, "Well, it's ok because you have your kids." Like that made it alright. Those kids are hurt by what has happened.

We are a splintered family but only for a while, we do reknit together again. But that is the one that really got me. Like all this is fine because in the end you have kids.

But you lost your life's partner and that is a huge tragedy. Even worse, you deal with issues of self-esteem, abandonment, going to events where you are the only single person or single parent.

Your dreams come crashing down and your heart is in a million pieces with some shards too small to pick up and glue back again.

I heard the same thing, most want to come back but by the time they do, we are way down the line. That made me hang on far longer than I should have because I was also told by his sister to trust the love he has for me. Talk about false hope building in your heart.

This sister was like his twin. I trusted what she told me. Instead, I should have listened to my heart and what it was saying, and to my head.

I knew he didn't have what it took to sort himself out and he has not gone for any help either. Instead he hangs on to anger instead of looking for the good in what we had and the love we shared.

Twenty five years of marriage wasn't enough and, if I wasn't enough through all this, I'm at a loss to figure out what would be enough. I'm too tired to even think of what more I could have done for him.

But I took great care of him and now I can transfer that love to me and, wow, will I get spoiled!! Sounds funny but if we could only manage that same level of love, we would be ok and then some.

People say things meaning well, they don't know what to say and we are not a good society for deep conversations or uncomfortable discussions.

Think of going to a funeral parlor, what can you possibly say to someone to take their pain away or to even lessen it? And this is a death in many ways.

Some books tell us that what we experience is worse in some ways than losing a spouse to death as we have no choice but to accept it when they die. We have good memories and, in some cases, the one left behind doesn't have the same financial issues to deal with.

None of this is easy but you sound strong. We are all sorry you had to find us but it's a good bunch who truly care, and there is genuine empathy, great advice and caring. Some days when you can't keep going, this forum picks you back up and gives you the support you need.

There is a cheering when one of our own has a good turn of events too. I'm told over and over that we will come out of this and thrive but we have to take it one day at a time and put one foot in front of the other.

Thank you for starting this conversation, I think it helped many of us. It sure helped me. I hope it helped you too.

♦♦♦♦

You took the words right out of my mouth... and brought tears to my eyes about the sound of his car in the driveway and all of the other things I miss about my old life. Spot on.

And yes, people have tried in their way to help by saying things to me but it really doesn't do much for me and sometimes makes how I am feeling worse.

They don't know any better given that the advice is coming from happily married friends of mine who have the comfort of going home to their husbands at the end of the day.

Oh how I wish he was home with me. It has been a year since he moved out and he has been living with skank whore for six months. But they were an item before that, just kept it hidden.

This year has been hell, absolute hell. He seems to not have a care in the world and I am the one seeing a psychiatrist every two weeks, taking anti-depressants and Xanax.

Tell me how this works when he is the one that caused the shit storm and walks away to his shiny new life and I am the one left to deal with the kids (older so a little easier), the house, work, trying to be happy, getting wood for the stove, you know... all those little chores we used to share?

And then someone says, "Oh, you need to go out on a date." Are you kidding me?!

♦♦♦♦

The worst one for me is: "He will come back begging." It's been nine months for me.

Another one for your list? "Be positive!" How? My heart is in pieces, how can I be positive? I see my girls crying for daddy, and I need to be positive? Yes I do. But how?

I understand that people mean good, they are trying to make me feel better, but nothing they say can make me feel good.

All I can say is that I learned a great deal of respect for the women who are going through this. I cannot judge anyone if they decide to forget the bastard and take him back. That's my dream!

A little advice? I mean, it's working for me. I found CODA (Codependents Anonymous) and I have attended their reunions. This is a 12-step program to help me take care of myself and let go.

I'm still in a lot of pain, but I found some wonderful women who don't judge me. They hug me, listen to me, and smile at me. Go online and find a group near you. They're everywhere.

♦♦♦♦

I see him everywhere — in the patio we built together, in the garden he painstakingly planned and helped me plant, in the kitchen he remodeled for me, in the smell of his dirty greasy tools still sitting in the garage.

I miss the smell of his clean hair when he came out of the shower and the sound of his work boots trudging up the stairs after a long day at work, and him asking, "What did you plan on having for dinner?"

That fucking whore will never love this man the way I did. No one ever will and he'll see that as he goes through life. They may think they love each other, but they don't. They are each filling a void in each other's lives. One day it will come to a screeching halt.

♦♦♦♦

My psychiatrist (I have been seeing one for a few months now) asked what triggers set me off. Holy shit. Where do I start?

Anything and everything: Couples buying groceries, the beach, the house, some of his clothes that are still here, and, yes, even his tools in the garage that we finished the renovations with as he was deciding whether he needed to move out or not.

♦♦♦♦

I don't know what is worse – the adultery or the abandonment.

I'm wondering what is worse, the adultery or the abandonment. For me, the abandonment and subsequent cruel treatment of me and my sons was far worse.

If he had been in the affair, decided it was over and truly tried to work through things, it would have been tough but I believe we would have worked through it. But the abandonment is extremely tough to recover from.

♦♦♦♦

The abandonment. The callous behavior. The blatant disrespect of me as a person. One affair is not a deal breaker, IF the cheater experiences remorse and expresses it. Why? Because that is the HONEST thing to do. It could have been forgiven and repairs made.

The deliberate deception, lying, patronizing my intelligence, gas lighting me and purposefully setting about to make me question reality was far, far more damaging to me emotionally and to my estimation of him as a decent human being. And the greed to try to retain the lion's share of what we had accumulated together simply put frosting on the cake as far as "deal breakers."

He'd have to go far to win my trust again. When absolute trust is broken, it is broken absolutely.

It indicates a lack of character that I had not perceived and has caused trust issues with the opposite sex that will take me years to resolve.

♦♦♦♦

I wonder if the damage is just too far gone to ever recover from. You know how it goes, the longer you are on your own, the more used to it you get. I'm only now understanding the devastation of abandonment. Up until now I've been just trying to get through the days.

◆◆◆◆

The abandonment. The casting aside of what I thought we valued, the rewriting of what I thought was shared history, the emotional and physical abandonment. It's very hard to crawl out from under the heavy press of being abandoned.

◆◆◆◆

My husband had an affair that I found out about five years ago, almost to the day now. It blew me out of the water, as I had no indication, absolutely none that he was capable of this and had noticed nothing in his demeanor. I caught him.

My world was rocked, and honestly, I think I barely moved for several days. We talked and talked and talked and I decided I could get past it, that I loved the man, and that he was a good man. He was working on figuring out how he had done this and he said all the right things to me to make me feel confident that he still wanted me and the marriage.

It took many months of extensive talks, but I felt like this was just an awful blip on the otherwise really rosy world and marriage that we had created. I really believed this. I felt like this was now a part of our story. Of imperfect humanity and how nothing is black and white.

One and a half years later he turned into the cold shark-eyed jackass. That version was ready to abandon us with no warning and no qualms to ride into the sunset with other woman #2, the bipolar ex-married other woman soul mate.

When that didn't pan out, I spent months talking to the irrational shit of a man that he had been become.

I can say without a doubt that I know this about myself now... I could live with infidelity if there were true remorse and transparency and love and caring.

The abandonment is a wholly different thing, conducted in a completely bizarre manner by a person with no morals or values or conscience.

♦♦♦♦

The abandonment. I could get over the affair; we could have worked through that if that was all it was but the abandonment of the marriage was an unrecoverable event.

♦♦♦♦

The abandonment of the life we created as if none of it mattered. Moved on in weeks to set up house with the other woman and her kids. Nothing more starkly shocking than that even if you realized it needed to be done and over.

♦♦♦♦

I actually got over the affair pretty quick (to an extent) to try and save the marriage. It was the abandonment that did me in! The irony was he said he could not continue the marriage because he had the affair and could not live with the guilt. I smell a rat.

♦♦♦♦

The abandonment, and all that went with it. The gas lighting. Being totally blindsided, after much effort was made to shower me with diamonds and dream vacations while planning for our future.

This was mentally, the cruelest, as my brain tried to decipher what was happening. Then the ups and downs of the emotional roller coaster of trying to adjust and believe what my husband saying while he was doing something completely opposite. While he was trying to manage his fence walking and do his cake eating. And now, the past two years of trying to pick up the pieces of a life that I thought we had, while I forge ahead to create a new one, on my own.

No. Walking out and abandoning me would have been less painful.

♦♦♦♦

I don't feel "abandoned," actually. Maybe that's because I'm blessed with lots of friends, family, and other sources of "belonging."

And maybe it's because he abandoned "the marriage," his previous life and friends, and most of his belongings, not just "me."

That's why it was so awful, though. If it had only been "just" boinking some bimbo, there would have been something left to work with.

♦♦♦♦

The affair was never an issue. What confused and hurt me to the core was also not the sudden abandonment per se but the sudden resentment, the sudden anger, the sudden derision, the sudden blame and the total and utter disrespect that went with it and that I got no chance to discuss with him. It still feels like an execution.

♦♦♦♦

No doubt the abandonment. It made me question his values regarding our relationship, our children, our obligations — everything.

♦♦♦♦

The total abandonment. I felt like a toddler whose parents took her to the deep dark forest and just left her there to fend for herself, not giving a damn whether she survived or not.

♦♦♦♦

Hands down, the abandonment. In fact, I had pretty much recovered from the affair when we had a false reconciliation and were in marriage counseling. I thought my ex and I were back on track and our marriage was stronger for having gone through that.

Then, whammo, I was hit with the bomb drop eight months after we started marriage counseling. Ever since, this has been a nightmare.

Being left for someone else and losing my husband, home, future plans together, etc., has been far more painful than him screwing someone else on the side.

♦♦♦♦

I didn't know if there was another woman for a year, and the fact that he is with her now is less painful than being abandoned.

In my therapy sessions my counselor said that being alone was going to be tough for me and she was right. I have felt abandoned on many levels by people throughout my life, but this one was the most severe because I was left with so little and in a worse place than when I started.

♦♦♦♦

The lying, constantly. I knew, people he worked with knew, everyone knew. But no one said anything. I didn't say anything either, to anyone.

I wasn't about to give him an easy out. If he wanted to end our marriage he was going to have to grow some balls and tell me directly that he wanted a divorce and then come up with a decent settlement.

Of course the longer it went on the more fearful I got that she would force him into a decision. And fear of abandonment was with me every day that they stayed together.

I didn't confront, acted totally clueless while I gathered information I might need, and patiently (yet terrified) waited for it to end. It did and he hasn't cheated since. But I still carry the scars and I don't think they'll ever go away.

♦♦♦♦

I was in denial about the abandonment. The affair I could have worked through. I was sure he'd come to his senses and come home.

Now that I've been alone for almost eight months and the denial phase of grief is pretty much gone, reality has set in.

He has told me that sometimes he stays with her not because he wants to, but because he doesn't want to be alone. Now I understand. I sleep alone every night.

When the kids aren't home, I do the laundry alone, tidy the house alone, do my yard work alone, watch television alone, make and eat my meals alone. It is devastating. He will never know the torture he has put me through.

It's not just physical abandonment, either. It's emotional, psychological, sexual and mental. He made me question my role as a wife and a mother.

This house is not the same nor will it ever be. The comfort of a warm body next to me on the couch watching television or having a cup of coffee on a Sunday morning before the kids wake up has been obliterated.

I hope one day she walks out on him and he feels half of the devastation he has put me and my children through.

♦♦♦♦

The affair for me was the final straw since he had another affair ten years before this one. I took him back then, this time he was out the door.

The nastiness started when I filed and he realized I was serious.

I didn't feel abandoned, it was the lies I couldn't handle and there was no way he was getting another chance after already having had one ten years before.

If anyone got abandoned it was our kids and neither they or I understand that. It's his loss and he will never get that back the way it was.

I was used to being alone with the kids as he traveled frequently for work. Four years on, I don't miss him at all.

◆◆◆◆

I'm also in the affair #2 situation. But for me it's still the abandonment. Make no mistake, if he had decided that he wanted me and the family more than the whore it would have been really tough to recover from.

But the fact that he did that and didn't care, just up and left, and is now planning to marry the other woman, it's definitely the abandonment.

The interesting thing is that if he hadn't left, I don't think I would have had a frame of reference for how badly I COULD feel — I wouldn't have known that him leaving was so dreadful.

◆◆◆◆

Exactly the same here — all that went with the abandonment.

I never thought I could forgive an affair, but that was easy when it came down to it.

I can't forgive myself now for still wanting him back. Eight weeks and counting.

◆◆◆◆

The abandonment. Of our life, our children, our vows. Two years out and I am still shell-shocked, to some extent. I have the television on all the time, even when I am not watching it, just to hear the sound of a voice in the house.

♦♦♦♦

I'm with everyone else — abandonment, betrayal, cruelty, lying, and everything else. Everyone else listed aspects of it that I could have also written. The affair was, in this context, a mere symptom or aspect of the greater betrayal and abandonment.

♦♦♦♦

Yes, the abandonment... the absolute hole that is left in your life. It makes you question everything about yourself and your life together.

But even more than the abandonment from me I feel so much worst for my children. How can someone go from being in someone's life every single day to maybe seeing them once a week or sending them an occasional text saying, "I love you?"

While my girls are handling it better than I ever thought possible, I still feel overwhelming sadness at the loss of the relationship between them and their dad. While it may someday be repaired, it will never be the same and they will have to carry that with them every day.

So I will pick up the slack and be the best mom and dad that I can for my two beautiful girls.

♦♦♦♦

The abandonment and the accompanying helplessness and hopelessness, which I have trouble understanding because I was very independent before I met him. I feel like my independence has been sucked out of me.

Thanks to those who recommended the book *The Journey from Abandonment to Healing*. I picked it up a couple of days ago. It helped to read and understand that abandonment is a very basic primal fear and the biology/psychology behind it.

I feel frustrated that this continues to affect me so deeply, but now that I understand that I have survived and am surviving one of the most catastrophic events emotionally —it helps me to be a little more patient with my recovery and healing time.

♦♦♦♦

For me it has been the abandonment. I know part of it is guilt that he has walked away from me, our friends, and most of our life together. He has walked away from everything.

It has hurt the way he has treated me, the way he shows no emotion for what he has done. The way he has completed vanished... simply it is so cowardly!

He would rather fade away and build a new life than do the work to repair the one he had. A whole new life has no expectations to meet and he can pretend to be someone he is not to all those people who don't know him. I am certain that is why he loves online dating.

You look at his page and he looks like a decent looking guy who was in a long-term relationship. All the women out there meeting him think they got a winner and he was the one who got away.

It all says something about the character of the man I married and the character of who he is now.

He is willing to walk away from a decent life, a family, and being a part of his daughter's everyday life because he doesn't want to face me.

He knows he has wronged me and our daughter. He is so ashamed he stays out of contact with his extended family and took our daughter to a football game instead. Said he was starting a new tradition when everyone knew he was making excuses to stay away.

As for the affair he never admitted to, the first time I found out about the emotional affair (a bunch of texting was all I could prove), they both apologized and she and I were not friends for five months because I thought it wasn't a good idea.

We got back to being friends and within six months I had a feeling something was back on. Now both families are broken up and they are not even together.

The more I am away I begin to understand how to him the other woman is a drug. I realize I thought if I told him no, he could turn her off like a light switch, which he couldn't do. He walked out and that was the last we talked about us!!

♦♦♦♦

Above even these, the hardest part to get over was the hatred. When did I become the enemy? WE were always a team, kids and all. All for one and one for all. The cruelty of his actions and words, that was the worst.

♦♦♦♦

My ex could not understand my animosity. I said, "Your name used to mean love, affection, laughter, safety. Now, your name means betrayal, rejection, abandonment, and humiliation." That about says it all.

♦♦♦♦

What requirements should I have for him to come home?

If he had asked to come home, I now realize I would have required that he prove to me that he ended the affair, he would need to get individual and marital counseling to work on the marriage. He would have to show some genuine RE-MORSE for what he had done, empathy for my feelings, and willingness to make amends WHATEVER they might be. Then I might give him a second chance to be the man I thought he was.

♦♦♦♦

Total honesty and transparency. Love and commitment. Appreciation. Medical tests for STD's. I would want him to sign the divorce papers, and I would hold them in my safety deposit box in case he ever cheated again.

♦♦♦♦

I told him then, and nothing has changed: There are three key things he'd have to DEMONSTRATE, not just promise: Honesty. Fidelity. Commitment.

And, those things would have to be demonstrated not just to and about me. I'd need to see GENERAL honesty, fidelity, and commitment to ALL aspects of his life: family, friends, career, beliefs.

That would be the absolute minimum before I'd consider anything more, with him or any other man, for that matter. Love, affection, humor, playfulness, etc., could all follow (and would NEED to follow, eventually) but those have to be the foundation.

I'm not as interested in who he was, as who he is, or strives to be, NOW.

As far as the other woman? Unless there were legal or moral reasons (read: HIS proven biological children) why he had to maintain contact, I would demand NO CONTACT OF ANY SORT with any woman he'd been romantically involved with. And he'd have to behave in such a way that I wouldn't have grounds to suspect otherwise. (Transparency!)

And if there were biological children? I'd have to think long and hard about whether I was up for sharing him that way for the rest of his life. If I decided to accept that fact of his life, I would need to share in that "fully," just as I would share in ALL aspects of his life.

As his wife, I would expect to be involved as if they were my own children, and treated with the same respect by the kids and their mother. Since that's a pretty tall order, I wouldn't count on that actually happening.

But that's the boundary: if you want me as a wife, I'm all in, or all out.

♦♦♦♦

At one point during our pre-divorce discussions (when I knew he was cheating and lying about it), we were talking about our needs, and how I felt mine were never on his priority list.

After a lot of thought, I came up with the following list of things I require in a healthy relationship. I asked him to listen to them and spend a few days thinking about whether he was able and willing to meet these core needs.

1. I need to be treated with respect.

2. I need to be somewhere on your priority list. My needs should be apparent to you, and you shouldn't disregard them. (I don't have to be #1 on his priority list at all times, but I should be somewhere on it.)

3. I need to feel desired, both romantically and sexually.

4. I need to feel appreciated.

5. I need to feel truly loved. (All of the above four points are obviously components of this).

His initial reaction was, "Where did you get this list? Did you read it somewhere?"

I told it that it came from my heart.

Two days later, we discussed it, and he said he didn't know if he was able or willing to meet these requirements.

I asked him what his requirements were, and he said, "I need sexy."

I made appointments with lawyers the next day.

♦♦♦♦

He'd have to:

a. Never NEVER be in contact with the other woman again and allow me total access to phone, email accounts, etc., if I needed it.

b. Show some understanding and a lot of regret for the damage he did.

c. Find a way to convince me AND our daughters that he is truly sorry. (Walking the walk, not just talk.)

d. Do some serious counseling to stop the physical affair behavior, to discover what family of origin stuff lurks in him that was at work in our life, to become able to deal with conflict in a healthy way, and to learn to communicate openly and honestly with me.

e. Work with me in marriage counseling to see if we could learn to be together as equals in a new relationship.

Plus I'd want him to provide me with some solid, specific plans to equalize our relationship re: household chores, recreation, etc. It would be too easy to slide back into old patterns.

I'd probably want to attend some kind of marriage seminar — and to have a recurring "tune-up" with a marriage counselor, maybe every year or so.

He'd have to agree to this and take responsibility for arranging some of it. And I'd want him to provide some ideas for re-establishing our relationship, so it doesn't become just my "job."

◆◆◆◆

The other woman, gone. Any time she tried to get in touch, I needed to know immediately and I needed to know how he resolved it. That meant that I got to read a letter she wrote to him and saw pictures of them together on vacations. It was painful, but he was standing true to his word to be transparent. She finally just crawled back under her rock.

He needed to answer any questions I had. That doesn't mean it had to be on my timetable. There were questions I had about the other woman early in the process that he asked not to answer. He was having a difficult time knowing what he did hurt her and her child and he wanted to give her very little head space.

He did tell me he would answer all those questions in time and he did. I know some people will think, so what if it hurt her? For me, it meant a lot to know that he realized his actions had consequences. He was an active participant in the affair. He made choices.

I needed to tell him I was hurt as well as what was going on with me while he was gone. I needed him to hear me without getting defensive or angry. That was difficult for me too.

At the beginning of this, I wasn't ready to be that open with him. I honestly thought if we talked it all through once, it would be over. That isn't realistic. Those damned triggers needed to be talked through for a while.

I had to understand that that is what they were. It is a PTSD reaction. You get this trigger and it washes over you like a waterfall and you feel out of control. You are once again in the hurt and pain.

Gradually, you learn to say, "This is a trigger. These feelings flooding over you are feelings. Is there a reason now for you to feel this way?"

Then you start giving yourself the time to explore what is going on, look for other possible reasons for what triggered you and figuring out what it means for you.

Sometimes as a result of that process, we would discuss what happened. Sometimes, I owned my own reaction and the responsibility I had to heal me. He could never have healed all of my hurts, I had to work too.

I guess that is the bottom line. I needed him to help me heal and I needed to be able to help him heal. I used an analogy once about a house after a tornado. Even though it is horribly painful, you have to go through the debris.

You find the stuff you treasure, the stuff that you want to take with you and you make a pile of the stuff you want to leave and then there are always the boxes that you aren't sure where they are going to end up when all is said and done.

We found that we wanted a lot of the same stuff we had, we still valued a lot of what we built together. We also had lots that we didn't want. We are still going through some of those weird leftover boxes.

I know some people want to know when reconciliation ends. I've given it a lot of thought lately. I think it is over for us. That doesn't mean we don't work on our relationship every day, it doesn't mean that we are complacent.

I don't think I will ever get back to that place and I don't want to. The attention to us makes us stronger. I've also realized that while I enjoy our time together, I also enjoy my time alone.

Living in two places works very well for us. There isn't an end line to cross, there is today.

♦♦♦♦

We would have to get married again. In all honesty, I don't think there would be anything he could do. It isn't a matter of what he can do but what I am willing to accept.

If we had not gotten divorced, I might be answering this differently. I would be answering that we would have to go through counseling, date and see how we felt about each other. That we talk, that we do things together, and make time for each other.

♦♦♦♦

Complete and total transparency, complete and total honesty, and he would have to be in serious counseling and really "walking the walk." I would want us back in marriage counseling as well.

I think, though, I would still have a hard time trusting him because it is so easy to have secret lives nowadays and if I felt I had to have him on GPS or somebody monitoring him all the time, that would never work.

♦♦♦♦

That he stays in his apartment for at least six months until I'm sure he's sincere and working at things. See a counselor and get a full medical checkup. Work with me with an

446 | Adultery At Midlife

IMAGO therapist and do all the exercises. I gave him the book but I doubt he read it.

Find a way to make amends to our sons. He has to fix what he broke. I'm far more willing to give him a chance than the kids are by a long shot.

♦♦♦♦

If I had it to do over I would want him to live on his own in his own place for at least six months. He has never been by himself. I would want him to have no contact with the other woman for at least three months. I mistakenly thought a few days was enough.

I didn't realize the pull of the other woman and how they feel the loss of that relationship. I now know he was not over it. I would want him to go to counseling to actually find out what is happening with him. He is a completely different person than who he was.

I would want him to spend quality time with his kids trying to reconnect. I realize now that when he came back he did not make that attempt. This from a man that was so close to his kids.

♦♦♦♦

I would want him to have to face everyone he cares about, his parents, my parents, and our children, and look them in the eye and tell them what he did. I've come to realize that I outed him once to my parents and a couple of friends, but he has never told anyone to their face.

Maybe if he had to admit what he did, it would make a difference. Probably not. Also, counseling and marriage counseling and the counselor and I would decide when it was "all good," not him.

♦♦♦♦

Should I expose his affair to the children?

After 25 years of marriage, I caught him and the other woman together. I want to expose the whole affair to our two grown children more than you know.

What have been your experiences?

♦♦♦♦

IF, big IF here... IF they ask, don't lie... but do NOT embellish or go into detail... the less said the better. Behave with dignity and honor. You can say it caused you tremendous pain, and end it at that. Make tomorrow brighter than today.

Just because their father sinks into mire, does not mean their mother should follow. It does not serve the children well.

♦♦♦♦

Is he waiting for you to tell them? I think he is. So he won't have to look at their faces and see shock and disappointment. No, let him tell them.

If they ask you, just say "That is a question you must ask your dad because mommy really doesn't have anything to do with it."

And you don't. Who knows more about his affair, you or him? He does. So let HIM spill the beans. Put the burden on him. It's not your responsibility how he and his children are to be toward each other in the future when the cat is let out of the bag. This really is between him and them.

They've got to hear it from his lips. That will determine their future with him from then on. If it spirals downhill, guess what? He has no one else to blame but himself. He can't blame you.

Just remember afterwards, be careful about how you talk about him around them. For example, if you call him an asshole and they're within earshot, they'll think, "Well, that's my dad, so maybe I'm an asshole, too."

You never know what goes through their minds or how much responsibility they take on by themselves.

♦♦♦♦

The children may know more than you think. I also say if they ask, answer truthfully and factually. If they don't ask, perhaps it's because they'd rather not discuss it.

♦♦♦♦

Well, my experience, when my husband's relationship with the married other woman came to light, I asked him to disclose sooner rather than later to our sons, as her youngest son and mine go to same high school and I really did not want him hearing about it in the hallway.

I also asked that he step up and disclose to his parents, as until he did I could not see them. It's an important relation-ship for us, they are old, frail and love me very much.

So he did, to his credit.

He did do a few wonky things with it in my opinion, like telling teen son that the married other woman, "hoped son would still like her and wouldn't be mad at her." Son knows her pretty well as papa's coworker. Older sons, he coupled the disclosure with asking if they wanted to meet her. This with his parents, also.

So far, no one does, though I have been clear to all that this choice on their parts does not need to be made "for me."

The message I feel we both are giving (to greater and lesser degrees, as he wants everything to be "ok"), is that we are there for them, and they don't need to feel any way about all of this for either of us.

All we want is for them to just be true to how they feel and reach out to us for support, and that how they feel will shift and change and that's all ok.

◆◆◆◆

My experience has been that pretty often the kids already know.

◆◆◆◆

Although my husband said in an email to the other woman that he has told our children about her, he has not. He has not told anyone. The only people that know about his adultery are the people I have told. Even his parents don't have a clue.

I also have not told our teenagers because they have not asked or brought up why this is happening. Is this a good time to sit all three down and explain that there is another "woman" in Dad's life and that she may start coming to things with him?

I don't want to be blindsided, but I'd feel worse if my sons were. I think the oldest might have started to guess the situation, but the two younger boys I don't believe have a clue.

I'm afraid of ruining the boys' relationship with their dad unnecessarily. At this point, my only thought is of my boys and what is going to make this as painless as possible for them. My shell is getting stronger every day. They are just kids.

◆◆◆◆

There's no way to make this totally painless for your children. I'm not sure you're doing them a favor by even trying. Answer questions honestly (and age-appropriately), but maybe don't volunteer any information? That would include trying to prepare them for their father's girlfriend. I would just "deal with it when it comes."

But that's me. I definitely believe that the children's relationship with their father is his to manage, for good or ill. He has done a lot of damage already all by himself, so there's very little left for me to protect them from. My answer might be different if your kids were a lot younger.

◆◆◆◆

Yes, I would tell your kids. I would make it as casual as I could, to let them know that you are aware of the situation, and that you are dealing with it. Something like, "Hey, I'm not sure if you know that your dad is seeing someone. I don't want you to be surprised if he brings her to the soccer game." And then take it from there.

If they ask for details, I would be honest but not provide too much information. "Oh yeah, she's part of why we split up but that's really between me and your dad, so you don't have to worry about it."

It's the truth but also tells them you are NOT trying to align them to your "side" in the situation.

◆◆◆◆

You do not need to protect your husband from his own actions. His relationship with your kids is his to manage and as your children are older they do deserve to be given some information so they can prepare themselves as well.

Supporting lies and deception is not what you want to model to your children, I would imagine.

◆◆◆◆

Had a very long talk with my oldest son tonight. He knew about other woman but didn't want to admit it because he didn't want to be the one to tell me that his dad is a cheating asshole! After we figured out we both knew it really took off from there!

He has known for a few years, and he said he hated her from the get go. I suppose, if your dad promises to take you to play racquetball while your mom and younger brothers are having a birthday party in another part of the facility, and a woman walks up to your dad, whispers something in his ear, and he asks you to walk away for a minute, you might get a little suspicious.

Poor kid has been carrying this around for so long and didn't want to say anything to salvage my feelings. My son agrees with most of you. He says I should just deal with it when it comes up. Smart for a teenager. And here I thought he took after his father so much.

♦♦♦♦

I'd be livid that my kid was put in that position. Oh, man, would there be verbal hell to pay. I wouldn't even care that he wouldn't "get it," because he'd be raw and bloody from my tongue lashing.

♦♦♦♦

What makes it even better is that oldest son has never really let on to his dad that he knows and has been very polite and kind to him all this time. I told him how much I admire him for that.

I hope he feels lighter, although I'm a little afraid that he is going to start to take on the role of "man of the house" and that will be a huge burden on him. I wish I knew how to take that away, but I feel like the damage is already done.

I still couldn't get out of younger boys what they might know already.

Did I also mention that oldest son was going to call his dad and let him know that if he "brought that slutty bitch, there'd be hell to pay?"

It took me a while to back him down from that or "kicking his ass!" Maybe I shouldn't be so proud, but his reactions and behavior make me feel like I'm doing my job as a mother pretty well.

♦♦♦♦

Has anyone discreetly checked to see if your younger sons know about their father's "friend"?

If so, it would be a huge burden for them to believe that they have to keep the secret. It was good for your older son to have an honest discussion with you. Your younger sons may well be equally observant.

Secrets can be toxic.

It can be difficult to find the balance between truth-telling and over-sharing or bad-mouthing. But, given that your oldest already knows more than you realized, it might be wise to give your youngest boys a safe space in which to talk.

You can still deal with the original issue if and when it actually arises.

♦♦♦♦

You tell your son that you're proud he has morals and standards but this isn't his fight, and that you are the parent and you won't let him be cheated out of HIS youth.

There doesn't need to be a man of the house, just a family in the house.

You may have to lovingly remind him a few times that you are the only one in the position of leadership, but he will be secretly relieved when you do. Tell him you will support everything he does to maintain a healthy relationship with his father (mild emphasis on the "healthy").

As long as you are open and honest with him from here on out, I think you can undo some of that nasty secret-keeping business his father put him through.

♦♦♦♦

When I received "the speech" I had no idea about midlife crisis or that what he said was absolutely typical and almost verbatim of others' speeches.

He said he was moving out, swore there was no affair, and yet over a year later, and many hurtful "conversations" and arguments, he is still here.

I finally figured out he was having an emotional affair and called him on it, but, of course he couldn't see a problem. I have been checking his schedule, text messages, and trying to access his email account. I finally found evidence that it had become a physical affair.

I confronted him, told him had to move out, and what my terms were. A huge argument ensued and thanks to reading this board and the book *How to Survive Your Husband's Midlife Crisis*, I was prepared.

He tried everything under the sun to blame me, put it back on me, and cut me down. But I was able to keep my head and not let his mind tricks get me. My only regret was I let him see me cry.

I wanted him to tell our three teenagers but I don't trust him to be clear and direct. "We" (I sat there in shock, while he babbled) told the kids that we were having problems and they left confused, without really understanding what was happening.

I also don't trust him to be unbiased. I'm thinking I should tell them, but I'm at a loss. Does anyone have any suggestions? I want to be unbiased, but my emotions are screaming at me to blame it all on him. I won't though.

I thought that I would tell them (as a group) that their dad was moving out because we couldn't make it work despite our efforts. That it had nothing to do with them and that we still loved them and wanted the best for them.

Then, tell them if they had any questions, I would talk to them individually. I will direct them to ask their dad questions also.

I so want to tell them that their dad is leaving me for someone else, but I know that isn't fair to them and won't do it.

Here is where I need more advice. Is there anything else I should do or say? They are already in counseling, but it's sporadic. I plan on informing their counselors, and the school counselors. I want this to be as easy as possible for them, with the least amount of disruption.

The only bright spot about this is that their dad travels a lot and they are used to him being gone. So, on a day-to-day basis, nothing major will change for them.

◆◆◆◆

I guess I am of the school that you tell the kids the truth. That you are having trouble in your marriage, that their father is seeing someone else, and that you won't tolerate it. You still love him and you hope he can sort himself out, but that you simply needed him to move out given the circumstances.

Be brief. Be clear. Be calm.

◆◆◆◆

I think you have the right train of thought. I cannot see how the children would benefit knowing their dad has another woman. If dad wants to tell them about her, let him do it. You could say, dad has made a choice that he no longer wants to live as husband and wife and we both agree he needs to live somewhere else.

I honestly don't think any couples' marital problems are the children's business nor should those problems be discussed and shared with the children. I can see no reason that they would need the facts and details. Never forget that they are in the middle of this and they love both Mom and Dad.

Given time the children may figure it out about the other woman. I just don't think they need to be thrown into more emotional turmoil than required on the outset of this life changing event.

◆◆◆◆

My kids are much younger and I've stuck with "Mommy and Daddy can't live together anymore, it's for adult reasons that have nothing to do with you and we both love you very much."

Some advice I've been given, especially since he has been telling them Mommy wasn't nice to Daddy and he couldn't talk to me, that he wasn't happy and doesn't love Mommy anymore, is to say that Daddy was unhappy. He chose not to tell Mommy he was unhappy and Mommy didn't have the chance to talk with him about it. Daddy has decided that he will be happier if he lives somewhere else. It's not the kids he was unhappy with but other parts of his life.

I think my son has some idea about the other woman given he has already introduced them to her and they know they live together, are buying a house together, and go on trips together. He hasn't made all the connections yet and I have the feeling he's trying not to.

Your kids are older and may figure it out on their own. I would suggest keeping the reasons for your husband leaving fairly neutral like you wrote. If they come to you with questions, answer them honestly, but they don't need details.

♦♦♦♦

I vote for the whole, simple, unbiased truth using age appropriate wording. Makes no sense to gloss over why their parents are splitting up the family especially when you've nothing to be ashamed of.

You don't have to go on and on negatively about your husband to the kids; they don't need to know details. But, I think they do deserve the honest truth put as gently as possible.

Lying will one day come back to bite you in the arse — it always does. And then you'll have to deal with their lack of trust in you to tell them the truth about anything else.

I will never regret honestly sharing the truth with my children especially because they later came back and said they'd known about their dad's exploits long before he left.

Respect your kids enough to be honest with them.

♦♦♦♦

We told our teenaged sons together that we were separating, and I made it clear that I wanted to work on the marriage, and that their dad did not.

This was a very hard thing to do because it was such a shock to all three of us; it was very surreal at the time. I also did not know about the other woman at the time.

In hindsight, if I had known, I most likely would have said something to them. I know how much it killed me when I did find out. With the shock and all, I probably would have.

He was not very present in their lives for the next ten months after he walked out, and the boys suffered. One son was depressed, late or absent for school every day, and his grades plummeted.

When I filed, I sued for full custody. Right around the time my husband found out I was suing for custody, our oldest was in a car crash. Our son is okay but that was when I told my husband that he had only seen our son for about six hours in the past six months which he did not believe.

Anyway, I'm not sure if it is the custody, or realizing that he really has not been there for his sons, or what. He has really been around for them much more, and the change in our sons is remarkable.

My point being, that if having a dad who is present in their lives is going to be better for them, then I will keep my knowledge of the other woman to myself because I know if they find out, they will reject him.

I guess my advice would be to look at your situation from all sides, and figure out what is best for you and your kids.

♦♦♦♦

My ex wanted us both to tell our kids (teenagers) and I agreed. He told them it was a temporary separation, I was having a hissy fit, and everything would be okay. Our son asked ex if he was having an affair and if there was somebody else. He said no.

What ex and I didn't know at the time was our youngest daughter had heard me telling him to get out, that I couldn't handle him having the other woman in his life with him denying she even existed. So ex moved out and the next day was caught out in the city with the other woman by friends and our eldest daughter.

If my kids came and asked me something I told them the truth. All they got from their father were lies.

By the way, my ex didn't recognize an emotional affair as an affair; it didn't count at all even though he spent over $1000 on a Christmas present for her that I didn't know about until the discovery process in our divorce.

She was "just a friend." I did ask how he would feel if I had spent that on a man who was just a friend. He didn't like that at all. Double standards anyone?

Your kids are in counseling already and you have told the schools. I did the same at school. Good move on your part, the schools need to know. Can I suggest you ask your counselor how to handle it?

My youngest teen daughter went through a really bad first year after we broke up. Talked of suicide, scared me silly, but now, two and half years later, is doing brilliantly. Top of her class, involved in sports, and with her friends.

My other two were older and handled it better but certainly told their father how they felt.

The sad thing in all of this is the fallout with the kids and mine all have a tenuous relationship with their father now. It will never be the same.

I do think truth is better than making excuses for him or letting the kids think everything would be ok like my ex did. It hurts them even more in the long run.

◆◆◆◆

My kids are twenty-something adults. When I first found out about the other woman I asked him if he was planning on telling the kids and he brushed me aside saying he did not know.

My kids, all still at home, knew something was wrong. My husband was coming home late and he was not as affectionate as before. I started to snoop around trying to find out "things." I was acting strange, but they never asked anything.

When my other daughter came home for spring break I asked him to tell them. I thought we would sit down together and tell the three of them, but he only told the girls one day when he took them out for lunch. When I found out he had not told my son I decided to tell him everything myself.

As it turned out, my husband had not told the girls about the other woman, he just told them he was unhappy. I did not know that and so when they told me about their talk I asked them how they felt about the other woman, which was obviously a surprise.

After it was all out my kids said they were very angry and disappointed with me for not trusting them with the truth. It made them very upset that they were being "nice" to their dad while all along I had been hurting the way I was.

Two of them don't want to talk to their dad now. This is their decision alone. My other daughter is still talking to him as they were always very close.

To this day he has not said a word to my son about anything. Not even a goodbye... which he did say to the girls the day he packed up and left.

I was trying to protect my kids from hurting the way I was; we were such a close family.

I wish now that I had confided in my kids sooner, because they are young adults and they are capable of making their own decisions.

This has actually brought us closer together. They comfort me when I am sad and it's easier not to have to hide it since sometimes it is so very hard to do.

They are actually taking this better than I have. They are great kids.

◆◆◆◆

You have to consider the age of the children. I would tell my adult kids things I wouldn't tell a ten-year-old.

When my husband told my teen daughter he was moving out, she was sobbing. She looked at me and said, "You said you wouldn't get divorced." I told her I would gladly work on our marriage if he wanted to.

She didn't ask about another woman then and I didn't tell her. When she did ask if there was someone else, I told her that there was.

I didn't want to lie either. Honesty has always been important in our family and just because he had changed his standards didn't mean I had to.

◆◆◆◆

My daughters knew because he accidentally texted older teen daughter a love message intended for the other woman. So there's the secrecy all gone.

My other daughters, in their twenties, are informed about him, because he blames me for not coming back, and I tell them that he's not home because there is the other woman.

My daughter found a hair, not belonging to us, in his car. She showed me the hair, and I said it was the other woman, because the other woman was in car the day before.

My kids have handled it very well. They see their dad and still love him. But, I really, really think, that this is because their dad walked out on the family long before I kicked him out. So when he finally left, nothing really changed for them. They got used to it.

I believe the kids should know only given the circumstances. I believe the fewer people that know, friends and family included, it is much better.

This way, your husband's conduct is his own, no blame game.

◆◆◆◆

As others have said, I think it all depends on the age of your kids.

If I had known, when we separated, I would have insisted that the kids be told. As it was, one of my daughters saw my husband driving with another woman in his car.

She asked me about it and, at the time, I knew nothing and told her she needed to ask her dad. He, of course, denied everything. And we all know that it is the lying that is the most difficult to deal with.

I think your kids are old enough to know the truth. And, if you don't want to tell them when you talk to them, tell them that you will answer any questions they have truthfully — then, if they ask, tell them the truth (without editorializing).

◆◆◆◆

The day my soon-to-be-ex decided he wanted to spend the rest of his life with the other woman was the worst day in the world. It wasn't the cheating; it was how was I going to tell my teen daughters. So I gathered my strength and told them that their dad wasn't coming home again and that he was going to move out.

My eldest daughter was the one who came out with, "Did he cheat on us"? She used the word "us" not "you" which in reality is what he did. He cheated on us as a family. I had no option but to say yes. I could not lie to them, so I said yes without going into detail.

My younger daughter said that she knew he had another woman as she heard him talking openly about what he was going to do with her sexually in graphic detail when I wasn't around.

Who knows what else the poor kids have heard. The sad thing is that my daughter had known more than I knew and had carried this around with her for more than three months. She was too scared to tell me in case it split us up.

This was the part that hurt me the most, that he had no decency to even hide his affair, even though he knew his children were at home and in earshot. It was a relief for my daughter to finally be able to let it all out and is now on her way to recovery and has been attending counseling.

I was asked the question about the cheating and had no option to tell the truth. Sometimes I think of what my grandmother used to say, "What you don't know doesn't hurt you."

It's tough on the kids to think that their father lied, cheated, betrayed and ran away from them just as much as he did to me. It's a tough one.

♦♦♦♦

I think age, personality, and emotional maturity, all come into play in deciding whether or not to tell kids. My daughters were in their early teens when their dad left and they were completely blind-sided. Their grades suffered and they had to get extra counseling.

I didn't have the confirmation of the affair with a woman who had been my friend until last year when he told my daughters they just started dating. "Sure..." my youngest said to me sarcastically. She sees things in black and white.

My oldest still wants to believe that he just started dating the other woman a few months back, not years before when he moved out. Deep down, I think she knows. She just isn't ready to come out and say it. She'll say "I don't want to know." That scares me because he's managed to manipulate her.

So I guess it really depends on your kids. I don't believe in lying. Look where it's gotten my soon-to-be-ex? They have lost a lot of respect for him because they know he isn't straightforward with them.

When you think about it, by lying to teens or young adults and covering up for your ex, are you really helping them? Sometimes the truth hurts but in in the end, I think it allows them to grow.

◆◆◆◆

If the kids ask, by all means tell the truth. Lies come back to bite you. Look at the relationships the kids have with the wayward spouse. Do you want that type of a relationship with your kids?

I don't, and I have a better relationship with my kids than he does. Up until he pulled his disappearing act both of us had very good relationships with our kids. Now only one of us does... guess which one?

Treat your kids with as much respect as you expect them to treat you.

◆◆◆◆

The excuses and reasons he gave me for cheating.

I almost laughed as he looked at me and said "You, you, you, you, you." That was seven months ago, and I found out the other day that it is still my fault... per him.

♦♦♦♦

I got blame, because I "allowed it to occur." When I did try to stop him, he went to his lawyer and told him I was "threatening" him.

♦♦♦♦

Mine was cold and flat when he gave the speech and told me he was leaving, that our marriage was a sham. Everyone knew it was over.

He hadn't loved me for years and when we went away for our 15th anniversary he planned to tell me it was over. We had gone to our honeymoon location several years prior to speech day and had a wonderful time.

The pictures from that trip show us both just beaming and him holding me close, kissing me. The children would be happier because they knew the marriage was over.

♦♦♦♦

I got "the marriage was already over" and I even got the words "it's all your fault."

♦♦♦♦

He never made an "excuse" for cheating. Always knew that was absolutely wrong and confessed it when I'd never have been able to find out myself since he was stationed overseas at the time.

Fully expected me to divorce him on the spot, and when I wouldn't, was very fair and as responsible as possible when he decided to end our marriage himself, years after the affair ended. He did struggle to find a reason behind his behavior, and the best he could come up with is the "it's all my (his) fault" line of reasoning.

That there was something inherently and, therefore, unfixably wrong with him. For a very brief time he believed that the "right" woman could fix/prevent whatever that was, and I simply and obviously wasn't the right woman for the job, but that passed pretty quickly.

For a while I thought he was using that as an excuse to not fix things, but I've come to believe that he actually does believe this. It's sad.

♦♦♦♦

There might be some explanations of why someone allowed themselves the act of cheating (crazy and false as may be). But there are no valid excuses.

♦♦♦♦

"She thought I was 'fair game'." Fair game? A man who lives with his kids and sleeps in the bed with his wife is fair game? What did he tell her?

♦♦♦♦

My husband said, "She has nothing to do with our problems; she is just a by-product of our issues." What a crock; he checked out of the marriage when he started with her.

♦♦♦♦

Mine denied, denied and denied. And still denies three years later although he is living with her. But I was told:

I feel trapped.

I want passion in my life and I don't feel that with you anymore.

Why don't you just find someone and fuck them, I won't care.

You don't take care of me anymore like I want you to. (Well if you would have ever been home and not with her all of your free time I could have taken care of you.)

I could go on and on but we have all heard just about the same things come out of their mouths. They all read the same "speech book" together.

◆◆◆◆

I got a whole stew full of reasons...

I don't love you anymore.

We've never been right for each other.

I never wanted to get married.

I was never in love with you.

I'm not happy.

I haven't been happy for years.

I never meant to hurt you.

It just happened, I didn't mean for this to happen.

I especially loved the last one. I asked him if she tied him to the bed and forced herself on him, and if so then we needed to call the police. Well, he wasn't forced. Guess he needs to accept responsibility for his actions like a big boy.

◆◆◆◆

He denied to everyone for the year after he left me and of course, said she was "Justafriend" which was how we referred to her until he married her.

Anyway, he said (1) he knew that I didn't love him anymore; (2) he hadn't been happy for years; (3) I never asked him how his day went; (4) I loved the dog more than him (now this one is true).

◆◆◆◆

I heard:

I don't love you anymore.

You deserve better.

You put on too much weight (well, I'm not 20 years old anymore).

I'm unhappy (but only after the other woman came into his life).

I need some space (it's hard to talk to the other woman when your wife is in the same room).

And I'm still hearing we're just friends (yeah, right).

♦♦♦♦

"I'm unhappy." Like others have said, this was only after the other woman came into his life. Two months before she entered his life, he wanted us to have another baby and was all excited about the future.

"I don't feel the same connection to you that I did in the beginning."

"I almost feel like I need someone to talk some sense into me." Followed by, "I don't believe in marriage counseling."

"Marriage and relationships are something that should come natural; you shouldn't have to work at it."

"We're just friends." Silly me, of course, all friends talk to each other on the phone for three hours every night around midnight.

When asked how he'd feel if I had started connecting with an ex-boyfriend, "I wish you WOULD reconnect with one of your ex's."

The other woman is his ex-girlfriend who cheated on him twice during their relationship. She has two divorces under her belt already.

He said this to my father, who owns multiple guns by the way: "She's just going to have to accept the other woman."

"Marriage was your idea." Definitely not! He spent two years trying to convince me!

After a weekend trip when he said he was going to be just two hours away at a buddy's house and ride bikes, but his car was found at the airport because the other woman was living in a different state. "It doesn't matter where I went, because we're getting a divorce!"

Followed two days later when I served him with divorce papers: "But I don't even know what I want yet."

♦♦♦♦

What WE would accept as a reason but not as an excuse, they may be offering as justification (excuse).

But reasons don't necessarily make logical "good sense" either. For example, people get murdered by random passers-by or stray bullets. That's the reason they died, which is not logical at all!

♦♦♦♦

"I'm responsible for her." Nice.

"I didn't feel important anymore. You had your weekly get-togethers with your girlfriends."

"You gained 20 pounds." Well I've lost them now and will make sure you never get the benefit of it.

"You haven't worked since you got your degree." Oh so that's why you got together with the other woman who you describe as a child, unable to take care of herself.

"You don't need me like she does." Wait, I thought I didn't work and was too dependent — although that was a joint decision we both made so we could travel more together now that our daughter is older and almost in college? Now I'm too independent in the same breath?

"I don't know why I did it. You were perfect." Really?

"You gave me everything. You deserve better." Now that's a fact.

♦♦♦♦

"I never loved you."

"I didn't want to get married." (No, I didn't hold him at gunpoint)

"You have gained weight." (Yes that happens when you are pregnant with twins.)

"You tricked me into having children." (Seems to me, I was the one who asked you to get a vasectomy, and that you should know what happens when you have sex.)

"She is just a friend."

"We are just talking." (For at least four hours every day.)

"You don't need me." (No I don't need you, but if I knew that you were leaving I might have planned differently.)

"You don't cook big meals." (Well, I work full time and have two-year-old twins and was pregnant again, so by the time I got home I was pretty wiped.)

"I deserve to be happy; the kids want me to be happy." (No, the girls were two and I am pretty sure they just wanted their daddy to come home. After he left and didn't see them for three months they were making up ways that he had died.)

♦♦♦♦

The relationship got too familiar and it was easy to get lost.

A man wants to be a rock in the relationship but sometimes he can get too overwhelmed with finances, work, stress and his family hence not realizing what he is doing he will try to find an escape even if it is a little while.

Sex got boring; wanted to try a new flavor.

She raped me.

She seduced me.

You were too controlling.

You never appreciated anything I did for you; no matter what I did it was never enough or good enough for you.

♦♦♦♦

None — soon-to-be ex-husband denied it. Made up stories for all the cheating charges. Then he moved in with her immediately and forced our kids to accept her within a couple months.

He is a coward, and can now offer that to the other woman.

♦♦♦♦

I never heard an excuse for cheating. He said it "just happened." He said nothing was wrong with our marriage and he still loves me. This just makes it much harder for me.

But he says the reason he is gone and is not coming back is because he wants a baby. We were married for twelve years and never used any type of protection. We weren't trying to get pregnant but we decided we would be happy with whatever happened.

I never got pregnant in all those years (and I should add we had sex a lot). So he has left me for a baby which he doesn't even know he can have.

And he tells me how important it is for him to have a baby after I go through menopause. Thank you very much!

Maybe the baby is just an excuse to be with her but last week he told me that he may not even marry her unless she gets pregnant. I wonder if he has told her that. Wow. I think he is so selfish to use people like this.

♦♦♦♦

The sad thing is that he said these excuses, and then announced outright that he "deserved to have an affair or a mistress."

I don't know if the speech happened before the affair started since he had just started and working a thousand miles away, leaving me home with the four teen kids.

My husband had lost a parent, a friend, and two jobs in the previous year. So the best and last excuse/reason for dumping me was: "I need to have sex every day or my testosterone level rises and I get aggressive at work, which caused me to be fired. So it's all YOUR fault I lost my two jobs because we didn't have sex every day."

My husband then went on to be involved with the same other woman for the last seven years. He has also had six jobs in the last seven years, so, I guess she's not putting out.

Excuses are the best way to offload feelings of guilt and shame! I just choose not to pick up what he's putting down! I am finalizing the divorce after years of him coming back and forth and feeling "confused."

◆◆◆◆

It will be really good if a husband would admit to cheating... mine did not... he's just lying over and over.

◆◆◆◆

He told me I was intellectually intimidating (this is after 30 years), we had nothing in common (after 30 years), and a whole bunch of other crap.

My excuse for him cheating? Very simple. He couldn't keep his teeny weeny in his pants.

◆◆◆◆

He told me he loved her, sex was great, she understood him, and she was just an emotional woman because she could not decide if she wanted him or the other married man she was officially engaged to.

He was hoping she would pick him eventually. She did not. She lied to him every time she went back to the other man as well. And he constantly took her back.

I was completely caught off guard when he said he needed to talk to me one day. We sat down and he told me he was never coming back because he totally loved her and was sure she would eventually choose him.

Not long after this he asked me to wait while he had a relationship with her again, to see her full reality, and then he might come home, this was highly possible but not probable... and on it went.

Wish I could say I took the high road, emotionally, spiritually, academically, but the reality he was left to deal with was I told him to fuck off!

◆◆◆◆

He told me that he had one of the highest testosterone levels his doctor had ever seen. So, of course, this justifies having an affair with one of his secretaries who is much younger.

Does high testosterone mean lower number of brain cells?

◆◆◆◆

Mine was having erectile dysfunction issues and claims it freaked him out so much that he just HAD to "get it to work again" no matter what.

He thought going to a "professional" would fix it, and then realized the sneaking around was a thrill for him, too. This is when I caught him and he agreed to go to marriage counseling. As far as I know, the behavior stopped, but then he started up again with his girlfriend escort, and when he dropped the bomb, he tried to tell me she was a legitimate girlfriend that he met through his work.

I found out she was an escort and he told me all sorts of nonsense. He was "in love" with her, she made him feel appreciated (well, yeah, you're paying for that!), she was really a "nice" person, he didn't like that when he came home from work I was watching TV in the evenings, everything was always what I wanted to do, and he made all the sacrifices in our marriage, etc., etc.

I now believe he has a sex addiction and wonder if he wasn't seeing hookers all along during our years together. I think he may have been doing it very infrequently or "white knuckling" for many years with the midlife crisis causing him to fall off the wagon.

♦♦♦♦

When I found out it was, "We are just friends and co-workers," then, "I trust and care about her. I stopped caring about you long time ago." Now it's, "It was all her fault. I didn't know that she was looking for husband number four. I thought we were just good friends." (Sure… he kept her a secret for three years.)

♦♦♦♦

When I found proof of an emotional affair, he said "I'm glad you found those text messages. Maybe you will become jealous and show me some attention."

Yeah, like my no contact due to his emotional affair is really giving him more attention.

♦♦♦♦

"We were nothing more than roommates toward the end. I wanted a wife, not a roommate," and, "I wanted to find someone who liked to do what I liked to do, and I found her. She said she wasn't happy in her relationship either."

Fast forward to, "It just happened. It's so out of character for me but you never showed me any attention."

All crap. And the infamous, "I deserve to be happy. I'm almost 50. How many years do I really have left?" Not many by the time I get through with you, jerkoff.

♦♦♦♦

Like a few others here I never got an excuse, because he never cheated. He told me he'd always been faithful and he met married other woman a few weeks after leaving me.

He told me he had his emotional affair with her five days after leaving me. So, gosh — how can I possibly know if he cheated?

♦♦♦♦

Did anyone get "you never paid enough attention to me, you were always so busy with the kids" or "you have put on so much weight, it's pretty repulsive, that's why I can't get it up" or "we were just way too young (twenty years ago) when we got married."

Really? He needed to waste twenty years of my life to make that decision? It's pretty amazing. I am pretty sure that I have heard all of these at some point. So, none of them are very creative?

Is there a handbook they all get that we don't know about? Can you see that infomercial?

♦♦♦♦

I believe there is a handbook floating around. Only those persons possessing the XY chromosomes can get their hands on it. They don't start reading at chapter one either. They skip around through the book looking for affirmation that what-ever situation they are in is normal and they need to act on it.

Then they practice "The Speech" in the mirror or some even practice "The Speech" on each other.

I'm sure my husband was disgusted that there were no pictures or cartoon characters in the handbook. He probably just dog-eared the pages pertaining to sex or internet porn then highlighted the areas he wanted to go back and read. Jackass.

♦♦♦♦

Some of his reasons were that I tricked him by getting pregnant (our kids are five years apart) and that I am a Christian.

♦♦♦♦

Obviously these were his excuses for cheating to HIM-SELF, because at this stage I had no idea about the other woman (please feel free to shout "Bingo!" when you have a full house):

I need to find the love of my life (my personal favorite).

I've been unhappy for a long time.

I want someone who can come with me when I do all my sports (we have three children and I always thought I was doing him a favor by keeping the home fires burning).

I've tried to tell you what was wrong but you just wouldn't listen (ummm... no).

I've just fallen out of love with you — and I don't know why (really??).

I don't want to lie on my deathbed and have regrets. (But you will, sweetie. You REALLY will.)

When the other woman emerged from the woodwork a full year after he'd met her as "justafriend" who he "bumped into" when out with the children, these mysterious comments started to make sense. Not a lot of sense, but I could at least start to join the dots.

♦♦♦♦

How can you tell someone you love her and tell her she's the most important person in your life, and at the same time make plans for a completely different life with the other woman?

To be honest, I do think that all the things my husband told me are very real to him. But a lot is BS, lies.

♦♦♦♦

One of my husband's main excuses was that I encouraged everyone to drink water when we went out to eat for budgetary reasons (we had recently dug ourselves out of a mountain of debt).

He was tired of drinking water so he had to leave. That and I didn't support his every whim to live beyond our means when we finally paid everything off.

Now he's flat broke, but in love with a whore. Oh well. It's his happiness that truly counts, isn't it?

♦♦♦♦

There is nothing unique about adultery and the lying, sneaking, and betrayal of trust and destruction of family bonds that accompany it.

Adultery is as old as mankind. Regardless of the names, dates, and places, the behaviors are incredibly similar. Regardless of names, dates, and places the devastating effects on marriage and family are remarkably similar. And, whether in German, Sanskrit, or Martian, cheaters make the same tired old excuses for their BAD behavior.

♦♦♦♦

Mine says it wasn't his entire fault. He never wanted to cheat. I just never showed him any affection or appreciation so he had to look elsewhere.

So basically, he had no choice, as his new humping partner shows him plenty of affection and appreciation.

In return, he has to clean up after her houseful of dogs and cats — including fecal matter when one of the dogs craps on the floor.

Ah, the price we pay for a roll in the hay.

◆◆◆◆

How do I handle running into the other woman?

Wish it had been me, but my good friend bumped into my soon-to-be-ex at a restaurant tonight with the other woman. Funny thing is this other woman was my friend since high school and her daughter has been friends with my daughter for years.

Apparently they hooked up a couple years back or maybe even earlier. He's been out of the house for almost two years and we're still in throes of divorce.

This does fuel my fire to want to get back everything he robbed me of. He spent thousands of dollars on restaurants and hotels so they could have their little trysts while we were separated. He's taking her on a cruise this summer.

I'm not pissed that he's with her anymore, I'm just ticked that he lied through his teeth as to why he left me in the first place. She was acting a bit distant when we did see each other and guess I got my answers.

What amazes me most is the trouble these ex-spouses go through to cover up. He told my daughters that they just started dating. Lies, lies... more lies.

The silver lining in all this is I'm happier in my life and I've met an amazing guy whose soon-to-be-ex cheated on him too. There are nice, honest guys out there. There really are.

Anybody else ever run into their ex and the other woman during divorce or before? I have been imagining when this is all over, what it will be like.

I don't intend to make small talk with her. In fact, I'd like to give her the thumbs up with a smile and say, "Way to go!

You got him!" I'd walk away and that would be close to the last thing I'd ever say to her.

♦♦♦♦

I saw my husband and the other woman on my neighbor's deck, laughing and talking. I wish I could have been calm and collected but it's too soon for me.

So glad you're happy. It gives me hope!

♦♦♦♦

I also saw them hand-in-hand, laughing happily, and taking a stroll near a market where we both live. I turned and chose another way before actually having to "greet" them.

It upset my whole evening; but I also hope one day will come when I will not care anymore about anything related to him.

♦♦♦♦

No, I would have been too angry to wait this long. He's out of your home for two years and you haven't gotten a divorce yet? What amazes me is how long you've let him get away with this without shutting him down.

Yet he's spending marital money that he's supposed to use to support the family with on the other woman trysting around — thousands of dollars of YOUR money. You need to recoup that money.

I'm surprised you've waited this long. Get to a lawyer, one with fangs. I hope you have good paperwork to back this up or the lawyer can depose him and get a child support and alimony agreement going during this separation until the divorce.

Wouldn't it be better the next time you or someone "bumps into them" that you've gotten your settlement, recouped their "play money," and you can look them in the eye with dignity knowing that you did what you were supposed to do two years ago?

If he hasn't come back by now he never will. It's past due for you to take the next step to protect yourself and your children financially.

◆◆◆◆

I'm just waiting on the discovery. I am on attorney number two and he's good but I'm the one who knows how the business runs, what money goes where, etc.

The bad news is besides dissipation, I have to prove that he makes much more than he states on our income taxes. I refused to sign and he's pissed, but tough luck. I will get my day and I can hardly wait!

◆◆◆◆

I too have the daunting task of proving my husband earns way more than what he admitted in his taxes and we've agreed to have a "special master" do an evaluation of his "true income" by the next court date.

My lawyer said "they are not nice" about it, as they are investigators of corporate fraud, auditing everything, and all his "not work related" business expenses will be "added back to his true income."

He may have gotten away with cheating Uncle Sam, but if he thinks he can continue to live like a bachelor king, and pay next to nothing to support his wife and three kids, he has a huge serving of humble pie waiting to be forced down his throat!

I'm also excited about how we agreed to become "legally divorced" after the six month mark before a property settlement, because I don't want to end up in limbo for two years without any closure on our marital status. I just want to move forward and wash that man right out of my hair.

When I was doing all kinds of investigating when he moved out, I saw that he put on an online site that he was "divorced" as his status the day after he moved.

I love to read updates on your situation, because we have so many similarities. I even asked him why he didn't let me know sooner that he was planning this, since I, too, am a stay at home mom, and told him I could have at least had a few months to find a job to provide for our kids. His answer was, "I didn't plan this."

BULL! The credit card statements showed him "looking online" for other married women to hook up with for sex. I even learned that he was trying to hook up with women online years ago. I never heard of it until news of the divorce came out in the family.

The devious snakes deserve all the bad karma that will certainly catch up with them. I no longer care or have sympathy for what awaits him, as he made the choices that hurt so many people.

◆◆◆◆

We do have a lot of similarities. Doesn't their level of deception just amaze you?

What do you mean by legally divorce within six months? I filed and we are legally separated and have come up with a joint custody agreement, however, with all this discovery crap, we can't finalize a divorce until we get this other stuff cleared up. Does your state have different law about that?

I have a pre-trial coming up in a couple months so it would indeed be nice if we could settle matters. I can't see it happening right now though because he has fought me on just about everything — taxes, college savings plan for our daughter, life insurance. It's so annoying.

All I know is I'd rather break the toy than let him play with it, and I intend to try and get back every penny I can of dissipation.

♦♦♦♦

In my state you have to have filed for divorce for at least six months to have one granted, so our lawyers both wrote into our agreement to have the legal divorce by that time, and the property settlement/custody will continue. I just want closure on the whole thing, and finally being able to say "I'm divorced" would really put my soul at ease.

I'd like to start dating again, and I can't lie, so when I say to people that "I'm separated," it sounds like there's still a chance that I'm cheating on my husband or might reconcile... NOT!

My husband has caused enough damage in my life, and I just want to move forward without any negative after-effects of his wrath. I feel like a butterfly in my divorce, like coming out of a cocoon as a thing of beauty, unlike anything I was before I entered it.

I will peel away all the negatives that came from his existence in my life, and add to it all the hopes and dreams I lost when I met him. It's wonderful to see a divorce as your biggest tragedy in life, but also the biggest blessing that ever was.

♦♦♦♦

I'm just so sick of the lies and deception. It amazes me how many he's told, and with a straight face or, "How dare you accuse me of being with her." My gut was right!

It's times like this when you really do have to look at the positives. Cross your fingers for me when I meet with the accountants. Hope they help me come up with a game plan that proves he has a lot more shares in the company than he says.

♦♦♦♦

Yes, the burn of knowing how long they've been deceiving you seems to linger the longest. My husband was trying to hook up with women on MySpace years ago (and he denied "meeting up with them" but never felt he did anything wrong by instigating it!). They can live their own sinful lives on their own.

It's cleansing to get them out of our "hair" and out of our lives for good! I'm so glad my conscience is clean. No ghosts, no cheats, no lies.

♦♦♦♦

Right now the other woman lives across the country but I am terrified of her moving here and having to deal with her on a regular basis. It just seems too cruel!

♦♦♦♦

The answer is you don't DEAL with her. You live your life and let HER deal with his baggage about YOU.

The best revenge is living well and not giving a shit about the gnats of the world who buzz around trying to be important. Time will show you this and you will reach a stage of calm indifference to their drama.

♦♦♦♦

Why get angry at a situation that might never happen? How likely is that your cheating spouse wants her in the life in your children? How old are your children? Can they decide for themselves whether they want to meet her or not?

I think that it's better to not worry so much about the future. We all know that the future is full of strange surprises and it's not worth it to consume so much energy and so many tears for hypothetical situations.

What about imagining a better outcome for you? Like wayward spouse moving away with her and leaving you and the kids in blissful peace?

♦♦♦♦

You're borrowing trouble! I know... I do it, too. Stop... until you know for sure what is going to happen. (Now, I will try to take that advice too!)

♦♦♦♦

Should I tell if I knew someone was being betrayed?

There have been several mentions, as if being betrayed was not bruising enough, of the absolute humiliation that other people knew and the wife was the last to know.

So, if you knew that someone in your circle was betraying their spouse, what would you do?

♦♦♦♦

I have to say that I'd stay out of it. Somebody else's marriage isn't my business. I remember that Ann Landers got asked this question several times over the years. She always said to keep quiet. Because the spouse often knows and it further humiliates them to know that you do, too.

♦♦♦♦

That really is a tough one. They always say to "take the high road," but all I ever felt like (when I found out) is that I wish someone would have given me an anonymous tip so that I could start my own digging to see his cheating ways.

I never suspected anything, even when he said he just wanted to move out. Nothing made sense.

If I had wind of his infidelity, I could have at least had some major proof with his phone bill or charges and kept an eye on how much money he was withdrawing.

Too late for that now. I'd probably do something to give her a heads up, but only if I was SURE of cheating. Otherwise, you're just meddling in other people's personal business.

♦♦♦♦

Ann landers had some good answers. I never thought this was one of them. I think the spouse knows a whole lot less

486 | Adultery At Midlife

frequently than some believe, especially in days long gone by.

I've heard many betrayed spouses say they would have preferred someone at least drop a hint, as so many are just blindsided after it's been an established fact for a while.

And even if it is just smoke, it is a legitimate opening for a serious relationship overview and discussion.

◆◆◆◆

I tried to drop a hint to my older sister. Her husband would stay out all night and give her some phony story (out with the boys drinking and didn't want to drive but also didn't call to let her know he wouldn't be home).

I asked her one day didn't she think there might be a problem in her marriage? She informed me the next day that she asked her husband that question and he said there wasn't any problem. I never brought it up again

◆◆◆◆

If directly asked what I knew, or my opinion, I'd share it with the possibly-betrayed spouse but nobody else! Otherwise, I'd stay out of it as I would want others to do for me.

Since we don't know what somebody would want, MY values are that it's rude to foist OUR need to share/tell/protect onto somebody else without being invited. We do it so WE can feel better about the situation; because WE decided it's the right thing to do; because WE would want to be told.

But, it's not OUR place to decide for somebody else.

◆◆◆◆

In my case, my sister-in-law had big suspicions, and her kids KNEW. I wish like hell they would have told me. Things might be different. Maybe not, but the way it played out was horrendous to the family, etc. Our teen son saw them at a birthday party for a mutual friend.

I think I would say something.

♦♦♦♦

I would bring up the question and say what I observed along with the advice to the faithful spouse what I "thought was happening" and let it go at that.

To me, if others knew about him fooling around and I didn't, then I would feel betrayed not only by him but also by my friends.

I say put the information out there and what gets done about the information is the other person's decision.

It is like knowing if your teenagers are doing drugs. I would want to know so I could work from an "informed" position.

♦♦♦♦

If the betrayed wife were a close friend of mine and if I were sure of my suspicions, I would tell her. In my case, a close friend chose not to tell.

I am not sure if things had been different if she would have told me in time, but probably I could have been spared the humiliation of finding out about his affair in public, in front of many of my friends.

♦♦♦♦

This happened to me. My husband began his midlife crisis five years ago by having an emotional affair with one of my very good friends.

We were a close knit group of friends. She lived with my other friend who suspected something was going on but didn't tell. When another friend found out, I found out the next evening because that's what friends do.

This had gone on under my nose for months and I never suspected. So don't always assume the wife knows. I didn't in this case; I was the last to know.

What was funny is that in hindsight my "so called" friend would question me about my husband all the time. Looking back now, it all made total sense.

♦♦♦♦

I think I would maybe bring it up indirectly. In my case I wish someone would have even said something like, "Looks like your husband is really settling into his new job, have you met any of his new work friends? He's spending so much time with "X" I figured you all must be getting together."

Other cases would be, "Did you enjoy your dinner at ___? I saw your husband the other night but didn't have time to stop and say hi."

It's not that you are accusing the person of an affair but it would have given me a head's up that he's not telling me everything. That he's spending a lot of time with someone and I haven't heard anything about them.

If the spouse knows about the friendship and is also friends with the person, you haven't accused anyone. If they don't know, they can choose to trust, get info whatever.

If I knew about it, I would try to find some nonjudgmental or non-accusing way of giving the spouse an indicator so they could look into things.

♦♦♦♦

How many of us knew, weren't blindsided, and chose to look the other way? I used to long for a phone call, "Do you know what your husband is doing?" My first answer would have been "what's her name?" followed by "tell me everything you know."

It's funny. I didn't know and I knew. I was being gas lighted horribly and cruelly, and I thought I was going mad. Knowing is much better.

♦♦♦♦

People told me when I was married the first time. I didn't believe them. Can we say "denial"?

♦♦♦♦

As a wife who was completely and totally clueless, oblivious, in denial, whatever, I would have appreciated a head's up from someone, anyone!

I finally did get one, in the form of an anonymous letter. Which, in my opinion, was a brilliant move! Whoever sent it, just wanted to give me the information, but they did not want to be involved in the drama or have any other part in it.

No one to blame. No "shoot the messenger." No one to pester for answers to all my questions. Just a kind person who saw that I was being duped and wanted me to know. Who gave me information and then left it in my hands.

I am eternally grateful to whoever did that for me. I believe I would do the same for someone else if I were absolutely sure they were being deceived.

♦♦♦♦

This is a very difficult question for me to consider because I was in a position where many people knew before I did. I was very, very angry at everyone who knew for quite some time. Not so much now. I think that putting people in this position is just another despicable thing cheaters do.

People don't want to have to make these decisions nor know these about these private matters. It's very unfair to them. My ex and the other woman apparently did/do not agree. A few people I do believe betrayed their friendship with me by not telling me.

We all have people in our lives that we feel are loyal friends to US. Those people should have told me. Now that some time has passed, I think that if I was a casual friend, I wouldn't tell because I wouldn't know enough about the situation. However, I have a few very close friends who I would definitely tell.

◆◆◆◆

A business acquaintance of my husband's, someone I hardly knew, called to tell me that she'd just seen my husband's car and the other woman's car at a motel. I'm sure she expected me to be outraged and do something right then but I thanked her and hung up. I didn't quit shaking for hours.

I kept quiet. I knew about the affair. I wasn't looking for evidence; I had plenty. I wasn't ready to confront him.

Sometimes the betrayed spouse knows but isn't ready to take action. Being told may make them feel they now have to confront just to save face with people who do know.

◆◆◆◆

If I am certain, then I tell. I do it kindly as possible to people I know, and I have sent anonymous letters, with photographic proof, to the wives of co-workers.

MY conscience would not let me rest if I thought another woman was at risk and I didn't speak up. She can choose to do something with it or hate me, but that's not the point. The point is at least she knows reality.

When I was in college, my best friend's mother caught a friend's husband having an affair. She wrestled with it and said nothing. Her friend got AIDS from the cheater and died a couple of years later. Her kids were teenagers. That made a lasting impression on me.

This could easily be life or death. Don't people deserve to know if their lives are in danger? Don't people deserve to know that their children could be left without a parent?

♦♦♦♦

Yes. In a word, Yes, I would tell. As difficult as it might be, I would definitely share what I KNEW, beyond a shadow of a doubt, to be true.

After living this experience and being made the fool for being the last to know, you bet I'd want to spare someone else all the disillusionment and have enough respect for them to share what I know as FACT.

I've thought about this a bit. Depending on the friendship, I "might" be inclined to confront the cheater first and give him/her an opportunity to fess up to their spouse. Not sure about this but, I'd definitely tell the person being cheated on. And, if that means losing a friendship, so be it.

♦♦♦♦

I would want to be told. I would thank the anonymous person on the phone, whether she was the other woman or not, and extract the most amount of information (I am good at that) from her as possible.

Gas lighting — I truly wondered if I was insane — is terrible. Anything – the truth – is better.

♦♦♦♦

Didn't need to even think about this.

I would tell and I would make it anonymous. I actually did this a few weeks ago when my sister-in-law's sister told my grown son SHE was having an affair. I sent an anonymous email to her husband.

He must have confronted her because she sent me an email saying how she was upset because she would "never" do this. I told my son and he said, "She told me and I asked her why she told me that! Do they all just keep lying?"

I am going to send an anonymous email every month for the next six months. He will know it isn't a prank. This news, finding out after years, is devastating. Nobody, not my worst enemy, deserves that pain.

♦♦♦♦

Of course I'd tell. My daughter kept it a secret from me for three months. When I found out I felt awful. I would tell even through a note. If you care about the person please tell.

♦♦♦♦

Seriously, if one of my friends was cheating on their spouse, I would have it out with them first. Let them know that they needed to get their shit together or I would get it together for them.

♦♦♦♦

I sure wished at least one of the many people who knew would have at least given me a hint.

♦♦♦♦

If I truly loved the one being betrayed I'd sing like a canary! If I didn't love them I'd keep my mouth shut.

Used to be that I would tell, regardless. Then I had to tell my niece that her boyfriend was trying to hook up with someone I knew. She was angry at me for a while but has since dumped him and is no longer angry with me.

Because of that experience, and a few other less dramatic experiences, I'd have to say that I might tell or I might not depending on the situation. I realize that just because I'd want to know doesn't mean that everyone would want to know.

♦♦♦♦

I also think gas lighting has the malevolent intent to weaken and confuse the spouse, not just mislead them. It's one thing to lie to somebody, but when your purpose is to make them doubt themselves, that's one step beyond.

A lot of people believe their own lies, need to, and need others to believe them. Bullshitters may do it for pure entertainment value.

Gas lighters know they're lying, and are conspiring to give their lies the best chance of manipulating and undermining someone else.

◆◆◆◆

I just can't answer this with any certainty. Lots of factors would need to be thought out. Perhaps I would send her a book about it.

◆◆◆◆

People can lie and distort the truth. But not if you look at the way things are, not what others tell you they are, unless you know it in your heart to be true.

◆◆◆◆

Should I believe him if he says he has broken up with the other woman?

Proceed with caution.

My ex told me for months he had broken up with the other woman. He kept coming back to the house saying he wanted our marriage to work and was 100% committed to us (his words, not mine). The whole time the other woman was already in his apartment in the city. It was just BS.

While he kept saying this, I had mutual friends calling me to say he was introducing her as his new partner to them, that we had amicably separated. Nothing was further from the truth.

I hired a private detective, told him I knew she was living with him, told him we were done, and filed for divorce.

You want actions, not words. Keep protecting yourself and assets and see what happens.

♦♦♦

Your ex can talk all the talk he wants. What is he actually DOING??

♦♦♦

My soon-to-be-ex actually came home and told me all of these things, verbatim. He had moved out of the other woman's house. She wanted things he could not give her. He made a mistake. He wanted to work it out. He was confused. He loved me, he loved me, he loved me.

Six days later he left me… again. Ran back to her with his tail between his legs. They're still together. I think their nine month adulterous anniversary is approaching. It makes me ill.

Proceed with caution and don't let your guard down.

◆◆◆◆

Like everybody says, if it turns out he works out his stuff and really wants you back, he'll figure out a way to do it. In the meantime, you'll be in a better position to decide if you really want that.

I understand how hearing him talking like this is making your mind whirl. Maybe it is true, maybe it isn't. But his actions will show loud and clear what's going on.

I think sometimes we stop ourselves from truly moving on because, "what if he wants to come back?" We don't want to make it TOO hard.

What we should be thinking is: if making an effort to get us back is too much work, so much that they won't do it, then they don't really want us back enough, they don't deserve us, and we don't really want to be back with them.

◆◆◆◆

Thankfully, I'm not worried about making it too hard for several reasons:

1. I can see that the other woman is suffocating him. He needs time to think on his own. He's appreciating his alone time. I want to be able to give him that. Not just for him, but for me too.

2. We BOTH need to be sure that being together is what we want. Not just sure, really, REALLY sure because we are already facing some pretty big obstacles and it will take real determination and a united front to stand up to the challenge. We'll both need to be as strong emotionally and psychologically as possible.

3. Unless we do the work, neither of us will be as strong as we could be, and I want us both to be stronger for this

than we ever have been. Stronger individually and stronger as a couple IF that's where we end up.

4. I DON'T want to undo the progress I've made so far! It has been hard won and we probably will go our separate ways anyhow.

I don't think I have my hopes up. I think mostly I'm in a bit of a different place than I was. A couple of days ago, I felt we weren't going to be together by choice (he doesn't want me, I don't want him, or neither of us wants the other).

Today I feel like we aren't going to be together by circumstance (we want each other but he wants his own children and we can't make that happen together, so it's time for each of us to let the other fly). Does that make sense?

◆◆◆◆

He's still playing the Blame Game, and not taking responsibility for establishing his own boundaries, making his own choices, and accepting the consequences.

Put him back in the oven, he's not done cooking yet.

Seriously, he needs to END IT with the other woman, and spend several months on his own and preferably in counseling. Then, when he's completely over (and has no contact with) the other woman "and" the repercussions of that relationship, AND taken control of and responsibility for his behavior, AND established personal boundaries, AND stopped blaming external elements for everything that doesn't suit him about his life, you can begin to take him seriously.

I'm not saying that to be harsh on him OR you. Just, having experienced, and watched so many other left behind spouses' experience, this same scenario, it gets pretty easy to see another one getting ahead of herself (not to mention the wayward spouse) when things just barely start to show some potential changes.

♦♦♦♦

He is now back in my house. He asked to come back after a week. I told him he could come back only if he stopped all contact with her.

I know, go ahead and ask, how do you know he did stop all contact? I have asked myself that same question every day.

We are still going to marriage counseling. I do not think we are making any progress with counseling. I still feel like I am an emotional mess. I have seen a lawyer.

I am angry and jealous. Right now there are very few things that he has done or can do that do not piss me off. I do not like being this person. I do not know how to get past this point.

I really think that I was not ready for him to be back in the house. I do not feel like I have had time to process my emotions. But I thought him sleeping on my couch was better than him sleeping on her couch.

♦♦♦♦

Set rules, boundaries, and limitations. Ask for "transparency." If he's not in contact with the other woman, or planning to, then he has no reason not to give you all passwords and access to any and all accounts, including phone records. Observe spending patterns, etc.

If you hate to look at him, don't look at him until you feel more "even" emotionally, and continue to get your ducks in a row.

♦♦♦♦

He has been home for a month. Things have not really changed. Yes, he stopped talking to the other women, but did he really?

We are still doing marriage counseling, but have not really hit on HIS issues. I am still doing everything around the house and with the kids with no help from him. I am starting to see double standards in the relationship.

His life is all about him. He has a ton of free time, but where is my free time? I have been very angry. I do not want the anger to consume my life. On one hand I feel very strong and on the other hand I am mess.

There are moments when I feel like I do not want him there and then there are moments when I just him to hold me tight.

I have not asked for very many things from my husband and I think I have asked him for he cannot or will not provide. Damn it, he should be bending over backwards!

◆◆◆◆

The reason he won't bend over backwards is because he doesn't value what you do, or you, or his family, or his home.

Unfortunately, he is caught up in a self-defeating midlife crisis and using you as the punching bag. It is all about his needs and your flaws. You can't win this game — you are being set up for failure.

The reason you are doing all the housework and all the kid stuff is because you value those things. The reason you have him in your home right now is you value the marriage — you think things can get better — you believe with love patience and kindness he will see how much he will lose.

But, if he is in midlife crisis la-la land he doesn't value any of it — not with much depth. Doesn't matter if you kick his butt to kingdom come, serve him French cuisine by candlelight dressed only in a French maid apron, are super smart, swear at him, smack him, kiss him, provoke him, massage him, do all the yard work, win the lottery.

What you can do... is detach. Look after you. If he has to live there, treat him like a paid live-in boarder. Be polite, keep your distance, and demand respect. You need to make space for you. This will not be easy.

Get your finances in order. I wish I had taken half of the savings, I may have had some left. He used it all. See a lawyer.

Please try and hold on to your values and make life as easy as you can for you and your kids. Try to detach from him. If he is in your home, try not to let him upset you.

Just so you know, I was in a similar situation about a year before you. I told him to leave, in front of almost-adult kids, and it was a big nasty soap opera drama. I have no regrets about that. It is one thing wanting to protect children from bad stuff, but it is another to mask the truth.

♦♦♦♦

What these people in midlife crisis fail to realize is this is life, not some fantasy la-la land. I think the big difference between me and my ex was that these so-called "mundane" or "boring" aspects of ordinary life were something I actually valued and found comfort and security in, and he didn't.

He used to, but then he wanted to get on a thrill ride with his hookers. He is now distracting himself with a "new and improved" girlfriend that he will have the very same issues with when the infatuation ends and they are living ordinary life just as we were.

The thing that gets me is, if you need change, or excitement, or passion, or whatever, there are myriad ways to do this that don't involve affairs, deceit, and busting up the marriage.

And how sad about a messy house. I worked a full time job just as my ex did. He had higher standards for orderliness and cleanliness than I did.

I did my best to meet him in the middle. Cleaned with him on the weekends, and would not leave things laying around the common areas of the house for him to pick up. But, my areas of the house (that no one really saw) were often in disarray.

I wouldn't leave the marriage because he was anal and had OCD tendencies. So what if my office space was a mess, suck it up and deal with it.

Oh, and newsflash: Kids misbehave, are loud, messy, and require a huge amount of attention and time.

♦♦♦♦

He said he knew lots of people that lived in a messy house and therefore he felt something was wrong with me because we did not.

I tried to tell him we certainly would, it was just that I picked up after everyone and did the cleaning, and I didn't mind it. We led a very busy life and it was easier to stay on top of things than to let things slide, then everyone could find their stuff etc.

Now he lives without me, and has our two boys living with him. He has his wish. The three slobs live together, and he is forever screaming at the boys because of the mess, the damage to his new house, and their attitude. But, he is ineffectual, because he is screaming at them while doing the work himself.

Bet he misses our family clean ups now! He found out Tinkerbell does not flash through the house in the dead of night when he is sleeping and clean up for him. That was actually ME.

◆◆◆◆

So many things have changed. Here is the update: I found him at the other woman's house, he moved out to be with her, I filed for divorce, I have the kids, he is getting transferred or losing his job in the next month or so.

It has been nine weeks since he moved out to be with her and I still think of him all the time. Why? When will it stop? I need help moving on. The whole affair started two years ago. Why am I still holding on?

◆◆◆◆

It may have started two years ago but for YOU, it's been nine hellish weeks of finally knowing the full extent of his betrayal. Way too soon to be trying to "move on."

Be kind to yourself. Your head is taking the right steps. It's going to take time for your heart to catch up.

◆◆◆◆

The worst part is waiting and believing that he will change. My husband came back home after three months with the other woman and presumed that I would be so thrilled that life would resume as before, no questions asked.

When he realized that was not going to be the case, he left after three days and is back with the other woman.

We are now filing for divorce and I actually feel better, even though very sad. I am actually doing something, and going somewhere now, and not sitting in limbo.

◆◆◆◆

Their relationship is 'official' on Facebook!

All along he didn't want to hurt my feelings. As of yesterday his Facebook status has changed to "in a relationship with (slut's name)" with a big heart next to it.

He's a friend of a friend so it popped up on my news feed. Now I have to block him.

He's always hated Facebook and I'm surprised he's back on. I truly think it's just to hurt me and to let the kids know it's official. What a dirt bag.

I will not write anything negative on my wall that can be used to fuel the flames. I'll just sit quietly and wait for one of them to drive the other crazy, which everyone tells me is bound to happen.

◆◆◆◆

What is it about damn Facebook that people take as a sign of approval? Really? There's nothing state-sanctioned about a freakin' Facebook status!

◆◆◆◆

I find it extremely distasteful and immature that two almost 50-year-old people, one of whom is still married, choose to profess their love to the world through Facebook.

It is cold and callous. Absolutely no feelings (except hormonal) for anyone but themselves.

◆◆◆◆

Your husband was tacky and lacked empathy as well. Sometimes you just have to shake your head and wonder.

◆◆◆◆

Midlife crisis is a revisiting of adolescence, so the Facebook fits in nicely. A month after we separated, my husband posted photos of the other woman on his Facebook page. It was awful. I had to force myself to stay away from Facebook, it was too painful.

◆◆◆◆

Methinks the other woman had something to do with it. She wants to shove it in everyone's face, especially mine. No tact, no class, no morals, no scruples, no dignity, and no respect.

Soon-to-be-ex was never a fan of Facebook. Said that people should find better things to do than to look at what other people are doing in their lives. She controls everything he does anyway so it wouldn't surprise me in the least.

I have not yet changed my relationship status because I set up my account ages ago. It just irks me that he would put his status as, "In a relationship with x," especially when he is still married to me.

It was just her way of slapping me in the face. Wait until I slap him with divorce papers.

◆◆◆◆

Facebook -- the new brown paper book cover.

◆◆◆◆

My ex, pre-midlife crisis, was very private and would never have entertained the thought of going on Facebook.

When he started his second adolescence, he joined up, and started flaunting his new lifestyle.

On top of that, he put pictures in his bedroom of him and the other woman (we were still living together but not sharing a bedroom).

His Blackberry and iPod touch were loaded with pictures of the other woman. He never carried photos of me around with him.

Everything about this man changed, like somehow he thinks if he just does the opposite of what he would normally do, or what I would do, he would find what he was looking for.

◆◆◆◆

I have not put anything negative about my soon-to-be-ex or his whore girlfriend on my Facebook page out of respect in the off chance either one of them sees it. Of course, once again, the high road is a lonely place. I think the two of them enjoy the low road.

I learned through counseling last evening that it's his Id talking, not his ego or his super-ego. The Id is that portion of your psyche (I believe) that allows you to throw caution to the wind with no remorse or guilt. If there are any psychiatrists out there, please, correct me if I'm mistaken.

No matter. He's an ass and I have to learn to live with it.

◆◆◆◆

There's less traffic on the high road and the view is better. Be strong. There's a lot less regret as well.

One day soon you'll realize how wonderful your life is, especially if you've taken the road less travelled. It does make a difference.

◆◆◆◆

Like everything on the net, Facebook is great if used wisely.

It's a great tool to keep in touch with family and friends especially those who live far away but it can be abused as possibly in this case. It may have been the girlfriend's idea BUT your ex took the initiative to change his status.

I have myself "In a Relationship" as does my boyfriend but we're not on each other's Facebook pages so no one knows who either of us is "In a Relationship" with! I don't think the "In a Relationship" status on Facebook is "tacky" as such but it's certainly "tactless."

Blocking them is a good idea. De-friend them if necessary for your emotional well-being. Facebook will have its time then there will be another "fad." It's not really "all that and a bag of chips" anyway.

♦♦♦♦

What a night. I found a Facebook message to the other woman. It stated how much he loved her and how much he could not wait to see her again. I kicked him out. I am going to file for divorce tomorrow.

The only thing I wish I could change is that the blow-up did not happen in front of the kids. I wish I could change that part.

♦♦♦♦

He took the other woman on vacation!

My husband moved out two and a half months ago. He was cheating with a 20-year-old two months prior to that. This week they are vacationing on a tropical island.

I knew this was coming but I wake up every day angry, vengeful, and sad, as I picture them lying on the beach. I am recovering from surgery, have our two young children to take care of, and he left us practically bankrupt. Not sure how he can even pay for this trip.

To top it off, he never told me or the kids that he will be away. He doesn't know that I know and the kids think they are going to be spending the night with him on Wednesday. What a prick.

♦♦♦♦

Do you have a lawyer yet? If he's running off while you're mired in debt, it will give you peace of mind to have your finances in order.

Take good notes. Start a journal of dates and times when he's been off misspending marital funds.

If you've got access to any of his accounts online, download statements, print them out, and also back them up to a flash drive.

Note that he's not reliable regarding his visitation with the kids. Keeping focused on the details of what you can prove will help you later if it comes down to divorce.

Try and keep yourself focused on recovering so you're healthy and strong for your kids. You all deserve so much better than he's giving. Hug those babies!

♦♦♦♦

He may not be paying for the vacation. Sometimes in an attempt to "keep" the wayward spouse, the other woman will foot the bill for things.

I know my soon-to-be-ex's whore pays for everything for him -- new clothes, new shoes, dinners, whatever -- just so he'll stay with her. She paid the deposit on his new apartment and helped him buy furniture.

Getting an attorney, or at least speaking with one (some will give a free consultation), is probably a good idea. I went through the Women's Center at our local college and got a one hour consult with an attorney free of charge. I ended up hiring her.

Look around and see what you can find. Money is a huge issue for me as well. I live paycheck to paycheck and had to take out a loan to pay her.

♦♦♦♦

The mental images are killing me. And also the harsh reality that the marriage is really over. I don't understand how he became this person but I can't stop him.

I tried to work on the marriage after I got the speech but he had already moved on. I looked into online marriage programs, read books, and tried marriage counseling. There was no effort from him; he only cares about himself.

I seem to have one productive day where I look towards a bright future, and then I have one, or several, down in the dumps days. This happens to be one of those.

This has all happened so fast. I still can't believe this is really my situation. The person that I thought was my best friend abandoned me and our children and is currently vacationing with his stripper. And no, she isn't paying.

♦♦♦♦

I remember how horrified I was when I was still living at home, and my ex was seeing an escort that he was "in love with," and passing off as his girlfriend.

He took her to work functions, social events, and then planned a week-long trip to Europe, to a place we had been early in our relationship, where I always wanted to return with him someday. He took a whore there in my place, like it was nothing.

I used to try to detach and not interfere with whatever craziness he was up to while he was deep in the heart of midlife crisis "la-la land."

The night he was packing for that trip, I lost it. I gave him the necklace he had given me just a few months prior for our tenth anniversary and told him to give it to her.

I asked him over and over why he was doing this, and told him he could make a last-minute decision not to go. It was horrible.

Finally, I thought, screw it, he's going to go, and maybe it will get him to realize what this woman is really all about. I knew she was extremely unstable and a week with her would bring out her true colors.

It did, but he continued to see her. But, it was on this vacation that he realized she was crazy. (So was he and he had a harder time recognizing that, though he did later admit to me that while he was with her, he was off the wall.)

I'll never forget the note he left me when he left for that trip. He said he was sorry for all the pain he caused me. He did not feel good about himself because of that, and he needed to get his head straightened out. He said he still cared for me very much.

To this day, I don't understand how these guys can be so split. If he was so sorry, and not feeling good about himself, and still cared for me, why go on that trip? What was so out of his control that he couldn't call a whore and say, "Sorry, this trip is off and we are done"?

If he wasn't really sorry, why bother leaving me that note? Was it to make him feel less guilty? Who knows?

All I know is when things settled down and his hooker broke things off with him, he didn't come back to me. He put an ad on eHarmony and started seeing someone else, who is now his girlfriend.

They go on all sorts of trips together, too, and I have such a hard time when I think about him taking her to places we visited that were so special to us (or so I thought).

That they can so easily replace us and not be bothered by the memories is appalling. I wish at least my ex would travel to different places with his "new and improved" girlfriend. Like another planet. Permanently.

♦♦♦♦

My ex did this and I couldn't understand how he paid for it, and he pays for everything, big showoff. Found out months later he had a separate bank account.

You need a lawyer and fast. Leaving you in this state is because he is an asshole who thinks he can do what he wants with no responsibilities. They do and can if you let them.

You need a lawyer to file for discovery, three years of tax returns, his employment contract, all bank accounts, and credit cards.

And get your name off any and all bank accounts and credit cards now, get your own.

And where is the child support he should be paying and temporary spousal support for you?

Get together copies and a list of all bills pertaining to your household, go through everything and see what you can find. Who normally pays the bills?

Gather up bank and credit card statements, check stubs, receipts, etc. Mark off items that are his on credit cards, add it up. Do the same with bank statements. Keep track as much as you can with what he is spending.

If there is money in the joint account, take it out in cash, you can argue over it later. You need that to feed your kids and pay bills.

My lawyer said if he takes $500 out then you do the same and put into your own account even if you don't need it, but match him.

Get a lawyer now. You need advice fast as to what you can and cannot do.

♦ ♦ ♦ ♦

Why does the other woman try to contact me?

My 46-year old husband had an affair with a 30-year old bar maid. She made a fake Facebook page and emailed me some insulting emails. I emailed her back asking her who she was, etc. And I kept calm.

It went on like that for a bit. I eventually found out her real name and she called my house to talk to me. There is a lot more to it of course but what I wonder is WHY they call the wife? In my case my husband did not respond well to it and it ended things between them.

♦♦♦♦

They are so insecure and know they are an outsider/intruder, even if your husband is in love with them, they want to get the "down low" on the "competition." They do this in a sick way to see if you're a lion or a lamb.

Immaturity is another one or just plain stupidity. Curiosity is a big one also.

But as you can see, wayward spouses don't like when the other woman contacts their wife behind their back. No, no!

♦♦♦♦

I think that sometimes the other woman feels it will speed up the process if they call the wife, wife confronts husband and throws him out, and their married boyfriend runs to THEM.

♦♦♦♦

I think they believe that by speaking to the wife they can make her understand that what they have with her husband is true love and somehow the wife will see that and give them her blessing!

♦♦♦♦

Who knows why anyone does anything? Since you can't read her mind, and you don't know what was said between them, you will never know. I wouldn't dwell on it.

◆◆◆◆

I know I shouldn't waste my time worrying about it. I just find it odd that she called, made a Facebook account, emailed me, and verbally attacked me. What did she think would happen? Idiotic.

◆◆◆◆

One thing many other women seem to share with many wayward spouses is a craving for DRAMA. The betrayed spouse is frequently a rich source of that drama, if she plays along.

◆◆◆◆

I think any or all of the above is true, but in the case of my husband's other woman, she wanted me to bow out gracefully. And she played the kid card, that her 4-year-old needed a daddy (he has one, but daddy never married the other woman).

She said that my husband had run home to me over Christmas because they didn't exchange gifts in her family, because they believed in the Bible and it was Jesus' birthday, not anybody else's. And I said, oh, you read the Bible? So you missed the part about thou shalt not commit adultery.

◆◆◆◆

What do I do when he moves in with the other woman?

Well, so far I was only playing the guessing game. He'd admitted to an emotion affair with another woman but nothing else. Eight weeks past the speech I found out that she left her boyfriend and they've signed up for a condo together.

She's 20 years my junior (10 years his) and they want kids together (which he never had). He is in heaven, actually used the same words he used 10 years ago when he met me.

On the one hand I'm glad I found out so no more hoping for reconciliation. On the other hand I would like to know if that knowledge will get me even more depressed than I already am? Really go back to square one, relapse?

I really need help here. I'm actually devastated and sweating and shaking.

Shall I file for divorce or wait till he does?

♦♦♦♦

If you have to ask about filing for divorce, then you are not ready yet. You will know when it is time. Besides, you are too emotional right now. Allow yourself to get over this period, in a day, a week, a month.

The nicest thing my ex ever did for me was to stop coming home one day. It took me two weeks to track him down and find out if it was true since he couldn't be bothered to mention it to me, much less drop me an email.

I could finally quit walking on eggshells; I could do what I wanted, when I wanted. I could breathe.

So be kind to yourself. Get your ducks in a row so if something happens and you have to "jump" quickly, you are ready to (like out of control spending).

Do some preliminary meetings with attorneys, (I talked to four before picking one several months prior to me filing).

Then sit back, and allow yourself time to absorb this latest setback. Hang in there.

♦♦♦♦

I found all kinds of evidence of the other woman before my husband moved out, but he denied everything (made up all kinds of excuses for all of them in fact).

He did eventually move in with her and calls her his "roommate" to our kids. They saw pictures of him hugging her in his apartment, but he'd never admit to anything. I found a charge for a diamond jeweler on his discovery documents just a few months after he left.

He recently texted me that "he's trying to get rid of his roommate so the kids can have overnight visits."

It doesn't really matter who the other woman is, because she is only a fantasy that builds their ego (low self-esteem). The adrenaline rush from the affair is mistaken as "love," and they lose their heads for what they think is the right choice (by dumping their wife).

Try to calm yourself, and detach. I definitely advise seeking a lawyer, and start stashing cash for an emergency. Drink lots of water, and snack often if you can't eat much. See a therapist and tell them everything you feel.

Contact family and friends for support. You need all the help you can get now.

Hang in there, and with some time, you will hear your head above your heart and know what you have to do.

♦♦♦♦

What should I do if he brings the other woman to family events?

You WILL end up facing him bringing her to events sooner or later, so preparing yourself and your children for that eventuality is the best approach.

And asking him NOT to do something is very often treated like a dare. He may do that just to defy authority and prove "you're not the boss of me!"

I endorse the non-entity approach. Pretend that she is invisible and inaudible. Look right past her without any facial expression at all, and don't respond to anything she might say or do. That speaks louder and makes a bigger (and better) impression than anything you might actually say or do.

It would be nice to walk right through her, too, but unfortunately, bowling her over would probably create an unwanted scene.

♦♦♦♦

My brother's kids are just shy of being teenagers. I don't believe anybody notified them, but they're not dumb and they don't fall for the "justafriend" line.

So it doesn't serve them to sugar-coat information. That just makes you look as evasive as the cheating spouse.

On the other hand, I'm not sure I'd volunteer information ahead of time, but I'd be ready to answer direct questions as age- and situation-appropriately as necessary. But you can also tell them that they should ask their Dad, too.

♦♦♦♦

I wouldn't volunteer information ahead of time. I think it will add stress to the kids. I would be prepared to answer any questions that come up honestly. If you knew she was coming, I would tell them, probably the night before, so you would have time to talk if they wanted to.

◆◆◆◆

I'm sure that bringing the other person is meant to make me feel uncomfortable and has nothing to do with my son. I will take your example to heart and use it to help me get through if, and most likely, when, she shows up at something. Turn the tables on them. I love it! Thanks!!

◆◆◆◆

I love your chutzpah to sit at the same table and stare them down. I will have that opportunity in the future and intend to follow your very strong lead.

◆◆◆◆

Just learned that the other woman will be joining the family get-together. I was doing well until I heard that.

◆◆◆◆

I wonder if he will be happy with the other woman.

I was just wondering, from your experience, have the cheater husbands been happy with the other woman? Remarried? Long term relationship?

Mine has not yet moved with her; their emotional affair has lasted for the past nine months and their physical affair began five months ago. They plan to move in this year. So far, they look very satisfied together.

My guess is that once they move in, they might discover that they are not "soul mates" after all, but I might be wrong.

I am curious to find out what you think or what your experience was.

♦♦♦♦

It's always possible that an extramarital affair can lead to a long-term marriage. As far as how "happy" the couple is, how could anybody know? Most of us LOOKED like we were in happy marriages, right up until they imploded.

It's difficult to get reliable facts about the origins of second marriages. How many people will admit that their relationship with New Spouse started out as an affair?

Statistically, second marriages don't last as long, or happen as often, as first marriages. So whether they were begun innocently or not, they're not as likely to be as successful as first marriages.

Whether or not a couple is physically involved, the initial infatuation hormones that bring them together naturally fade within three years. Our bodies simply cannot keep producing them. At that point, we either bond and decide to remain together or drift apart. During that time, most couples have spent a lot of time together but haven't really seen each other clearly because of the hormones distracting them.

Once they start to really see and know each other, there's no telling what they might decide to do.

Some affair partners stay together out of pride — if they ditched the previous mate for this one, how embarrassing to admit this one wasn't The One, either!

All of this to say, there's really no answer to your question, and no matter how important it might seem to you, it really isn't relevant.

IF they can be happy together, then he isn't a good partner for YOU anymore. What you lost was the man he WAS, not the one he IS now, with her.

But, and here's the critical thing: Just because he decides he isn't happy with her, it does NOT mean he's going to come back to, or be happy with, YOU.

Too many left behind wives make that assumption and end up hurting even worse!

◆◆◆◆

There was not another woman as far as I know just the desire for one which he got busy on immediately after dropping the divorce bomb.

Since everything in the marriage was my fault, he did no work on himself. I know this for sure. Our daughter was living with him and she tells me what's going on.

He dated another woman hot and heavy for about eight months until she dumped him. My guess is he let his true (narcissist) colors show and she isn't as tolerant as I am. THEN he went to counseling, at least for a while. He's alone now.

◆◆◆◆

Haven't a clue. He married his other woman as soon as legally possible. They have lived together almost three years now, married two plus.

But the most important thing, is that "I" am happy.

♦♦♦♦

I really do hope to find a way to regain my inner equilibrium and trust in a good future. I am still far from acceptance of the situation, though the depressing thoughts are less often now than they used to be.

Logically, I also tell myself that if he is fitting well with the other woman, then he is no match for me anymore. But it's painful when I think about what I thought to be a very good, above-the-average, marriage that we had.

And I really hate the idea that our daughter will be raised partly by the other woman. So far he wants to remain very involved in our daughter's upbringing, even more than when he was with me, which really pisses me off. Our daughter is only five years old, and we split the time with her every week.

♦♦♦♦

I'm having difficulty accepting the situation and I hate the thought of my two kids being partially raised by the woman he had an emotional affair with.

I think I could handle it better if they broke up and he found someone else. I have the hardest time with this.

I also thought we had a good marriage. It certainly appeared that way to friends and family who are shocked by our breakup.

He was well into the emotional affair a year ago, asked for a divorce within a month, moved in with her two months later, and three months later they bought a house together.

He's moved fast. I don't know what that means for the future for them. I don't know what will happen with them and I am working on not caring which hard when kids are involved.

He is acting like a teenager. They go on trips, wine tasting weekends, buying sprees. Even his family doesn't recognize him anymore.

Work on the steps for letting go, it's helping me.

♦♦♦♦

Yes, it does happen. I think that all we read and absorb about how the odds are so against it etc. etc. etc. but it doesn't prepare us for it when it does happen. I also think it happens a lot more than those "statistics" say.

I think if the true statistics were out there, those of us who are in this situation wouldn't feel so alone. Yes, he's still with the other woman. Yes, he's happy. I know him and so I do know when he's happy.

♦♦♦♦

My ex just divorced his other woman after being married three months, and they were together three years previous to that. My ex said that he was happy at times, but he knew things didn't fit right.

He was embarrassed because the other woman looked even younger than she was, and people kept making reference to her being his daughter.

He also said that when he would discuss things with friends concerning his era, she simply did not get it, or could not carry on a conversation because she had nothing in common to relate too.

He is still very prideful and has trouble admitting that it was a mistake. But he has told me on a couple of occasions that he made a big mistake and really can't stand to even think about her. He is also angry right now that his world fell apart after he retired, and his soul mate didn't work out for him.

But being alone now is helping him to do a lot of soul searching, and he is starting to think a lot clearer.

Hopefully, the longer he is away from the other woman, the less clouded his thinking will be, and he can really work on finding himself.

♦♦♦♦

Sounds very similar to my case. They also moved very fast, though they still don't live together because of her kids, who are not happy with the situation. Am I the only one when the other woman is older?

Anyway, this shouldn't matter, as well as it shouldn't matter for me if they are happy or not. But as you said, it's hard when there are children involved.

The scenario that frightens me most is, what if I am unable to overcome my bitterness? And, while he is happily involved with the other woman and her children, our daughter starts to prefer to spend time with them instead of spending time with me? She will see them as happy couple and will have their older children to play with, assuming they all accept the situation.

I have no idea how to start to overcome my bitterness.

♦♦♦♦

I don't know if my ex is happy with the other woman or not and I don't really care. He has no one but himself to blame if this one doesn't work out.

After 23 years, he got caught and kicked out after having an affair with a woman 21 years younger than him. He tried to come back for the first four to six months and when I said no, he got nasty and has stayed that way to this day.

We were separated two years and finally divorced earlier this year. He married her one month after divorce.

He says he is still not happy, he says he doesn't know what he wants, but he married her.

I would like to think that with the devastation he has caused in our family, to me and our three kids, that he will find happiness. The trouble is, he thinks it is up to everyone else to make him happy. He hasn't learned he is responsible for his own happiness.

He now leads a very superficial life and our kids rarely see him or speak to him. His choice not theirs. He makes contact every now and then, but no real effort. It blows me away that the man I once knew and loved is now someone I don't know or like.

◆◆◆◆

You are not the only one with another woman who is older. She is three years older than my husband and six years older than me. It's not about age with him. Or looks, because many people who have seen her say that she looks like a boy and that she isn't attractive at all.

After one year of driving myself crazy trying to figure out why, I'm done. I no longer care what it was. It just was, and that's his mess to deal with now.

◆◆◆◆

I find it hard not to be bitter as well. I feel like the other woman's trying to take my place. I don't know how old she is, close to my age, maybe older.

◆◆◆◆

This is one of those questions where it is interesting to read statistics about their chances. The wondering and thinking of any particular midlife crisis man/other woman combo, is totally unhealthy for the left behind spouse who needs to work at detaching from that situation.

♦♦♦♦

Well, it's all very fresh for me, husband filed for divorce and moved in with the other woman at the same time, but here's my update.

I found out (from seeing all the adulterous credit card charges he spent with the other woman) that he was seeing her possibly as long as eight months.

Within three months (right after our 15th wedding anniversary) he gave me speech #1, but the next day said he would "give it another chance."

I became super-duper wife! After another three months, he said although I've changed a lot, he still feels the same way. He is no longer in love with me, and just wants out of the marriage.

Two months after moving in with the other woman, he purchased a diamond ring (a month after contracting an STD). The next month he tells me and our kids that he's on an online dating site, and he met a woman who looks like me and even has three kids, like we do.

A couple months later I hear he's complaining at work about how he's having problems with his "girlfriend" (whom he's been calling his "roommate" until now).

Yesterday, he invited me to be with him and the kids during his visit, since it was my birthday and he wanted to surprise me with dinner at a restaurant. It was awkward at first, but we were both very civil, and the kids were so happy to be with all of us "like old times." This time, I didn't once see him texting even though the kids always complained how he was always doing so during his visits.

I guess the three month "honeymoon" phase is over for them, and he's tired of her. At least he put up with me for fifteen years... kind of makes me proud of myself.

We'll see what he's up to, but I now see I can be strong and not feel anything for him, even if he's being nice to me.

◆◆◆◆

He started his affair a couple of months after the birth of our third son. It lasted for about six months. I found out about three months after the affair ended.

There was a halfhearted effort to make our marriage work, but three months later I found new evidence of phone calls to the other woman. I asked him to leave, which he did.

He continued seeing the other woman at work every day, and decided about two months ago he wanted to be with her which I was informed of two weeks ago.

Even though it should not matter to me whether or not this relationship will be successful, it does. For myself, I sure hope it fails. I do wish this on her. Probably in due time, I will have detached myself enough to not care. But for now, let it fail!

◆◆◆◆

Make yourself too busy to think about him or the other woman or both or either. The more you allow yourself to dwell on him, or them, the more you create a state of being "stuck" within yourself. Work at it, as if it's a bad habit you are determined to break.

◆◆◆◆

Could the other woman turn into a friend?

I know it's rare... but I was thinking recently about a friend of mine whose husband went off with another woman a few years ago.

At the time, my friend wept and told me her husband said the marriage was "no fun" any more and it was all her fault. I didn't know a thing about midlife crisis back then.

They had two small girls and my friend had recently miscarried. He said there was no other woman. Lo and behold, another woman was produced; he met her "a few weeks after" leaving his wife and kids.

After the divorce, he married the other woman and of course the other woman got to know the two little girls. They liked her, which caused my friend agony.

Over time, my friend went to family occasions which her ex and the other woman attended. And bit by bit they got to know and then like each other.

The other woman would ask things about the husband and my friend ended up gossiping with her about the husband's character.

There would be times when the other woman would call my friend about the girls if they were staying with her and their dad. And sometimes the three adults would all attend school plays and other events.

My friend told me that eventually her ex sometimes felt a bit "left out" because, with the other woman/now wife, the ex-wife, and the two daughters, there'd be "too many females" around. And they'd often be chatting away together and sometimes criticizing him.

Just made me laugh that in a strange way the four women in his life seem to have ended up on one "side" and he's on the other.

♦♦♦♦

How is your friend doing now? It's five years later and if she is able to attend functions with her ex and the other woman and chat and be friendly with her, she must be doing great, but I still have to ask. Is she happy alone or is she in a relationship with someone else?

She sounds incredibly brave and like she has a tremendously big heart. I admire that.

♦♦♦♦

I don't want the married other woman anywhere near my adult children or my grandchildren. Our children are adults and neither require a stepmother nor need any new friends of her moral fiber.

I consider the woman to be a predator and would deal with her as one would deal with a chicken killing bobcat if she ever made a move to establish a relationship with any of my grandchildren.

My ex knows that he would have to kill me to prevent mayhem. I don't think he is going to push that issue. Like the woman? Make friends? NO!

And, you who have to put up with having insult added to injury have my sympathies. I just don't think I could endure what I see some of you enduring.

♦♦♦♦

Anything is possible, but it may be easier when the other woman is a complete stranger. In my case she was a friend of mine before ex cheated with her, so I got the double betrayal.

I wouldn't bother to be friends again with someone that can so disrespect me and disregard my feelings.

However, I do think that situations such as the one your friend is in are pretty rare.

♦♦♦♦

I could never be friends, though don't think I could if she'd been a stranger, either. I am lucky enough to have some very caring, loyal friends. Why would I want to be friends with a selfish, cheating, bitch like her?

When I first found out I referred to her as "Judas" to my ex and he nearly exploded with rage! At least Judas showed remorse and did the decent thing and hung himself!

Unfortunately for me, my adult kids do see her, I think more for their father's sake. I loathed it in the beginning but, now I feel more secure in their love and I don't care too much. She will never replace me in their eyes.

♦♦♦♦

It can be amazing the things you discover you can tolerate. The other woman in my ex's case was his colleague and she used to give my younger daughter birthday presents because they shared a birthday. In 15 years I never once met her which gives you a clue as to her wiliness.

As I said to my ex when he revealed his "friend," it is odious to meet the wife of the man you are in a emotional affair with, because that might just be awkward, no? She kept it completely under wraps for several years, as did my ex.

To be fair, I believe he was like that frog who was put into the cold water and did not realize how much trouble he was in until the pot was too hot. I'll never know because we have really had an honest conversation about it and never will.

Since he married her, she interacts with my daughters and grandkids. And that, my friends, is the hardest part of all at this point.

But it is what it is, and it's certainly easier now than it was five years ago. She is not so keen on having the youngest kids visit her anymore. They are a rambunctious group.

And, to make matters worse, I can never say a snarky thing in front of them. It's just not my nature in front of children. Snarky is as snarky does.

I'm trying to teach them kindness, but I sometimes wonder if you can bleed to death from biting your tongue. I may find out.

◆◆◆◆

My ex's sister had an affair with her husband's friend and they eventually divorced. All three remained good friends which I found really odd even then. They even lived in the same house for a while.

I think my ex thought the same would happen to us although his other woman just-a-friend didn't last long.

◆◆◆◆

I can't imagine ever finding enough common ground with someone who was an other woman to become "friends" with her, or remain friends, if I discovered she was an other woman, even if her affair wasn't with my husband.

I just can't accept that sort of lack of integrity in a person and trust them with my friendship. Of course, a "recovered" other woman might be a different story. But marrying the wayward spouse does NOT equal "recovery" from being another woman in my book. The ends do not justify the means!

And if her affair was with my husband, I can't imagine "bonding" with another woman over his foibles no matter how "over" him I might become.

And IF there were co-parenting involved, I can see where you'd have to behave cooperatively as much as possible, so over time that could evolve into friendly behavior. That's not the same as friendship, though.

But just because I can't imagine something doesn't mean it couldn't happen, I suppose. My life has certainly taught me that lesson! Luckily this isn't a scenario I will have to experience, at least not with ex's other woman.

♦♦♦♦

I totally agree! Our secretary had an affair with her best friend's husband and he left his wife for her. Being a bit outspoken, I made it very clear what I thought of her.

She's left her job now but avoids me like the plague. Loyalty is very high on my agenda with family and friends as well as in a marriage, and I can't tolerate betrayal in any form.

♦♦♦♦

Just as I can't, and really don't want to, be friends with him... I don't like untrustworthy people... so hell will freeze over before I would ever consider being friends with the other woman.

♦♦♦♦

My very true and honest Dad said, "If your own family can't trust you who can?" This is the creed I was raised with, thank God for Dad!

I too don't want my girls or grandkids anywhere near her. Good part is they hated her before the affair/marriage and this didn't help!!

♦♦♦♦

He can't tell me what is missing in our marriage that caused him to cheat.

Went to a marriage counseling session today. We had a 30 minute conversation afterwards. I am so confused. We have had the same conversation over and over and over.

He continues to say that I did nothing wrong, that I am a good person and that the problem is that he just feels he is missing something.

He has no idea what that is, but seems to think that if I was gone the right thing would fill that whole. I know the other woman is part of this, but even outside of this he says he has felt this for years.

I just so desperately want him to be able to articulate what it is that he feels he is missing. Has anyone ever had any luck getting this out of their wayward spouse? Or, can they not put it into words? Or is it not really even the truth to begin with?

It just doesn't make sense to me. I know I shouldn't try to think about this in a rationale manner, but I am so frustrated that my life is falling apart and I have no say in it.

♦♦♦♦

No, because he had already found it in someone else's panties. Actually I heard many different variations of the typical excuses that cheaters use to justify their infidelity. If these lame excuses were met with logical and irrefutable rebuttal... the story changed.

His story changed so many times, he would have been right at home in the fitting room at a Macy's 90% off retail basement sale closeout.

He feels he is missing something? I'd bet money he did not have that feeling until somebody gave him the "I worship you" treatment and/or vigorously applied some strange nookie.

Lust crazed dementia is a form of addiction as potent as alcoholism. You cannot do anything about this. Save yourself because you will get NO help from his direction, although he might, metaphorically speaking, "repeatedly hold your head under the water until you start to suffocate."

When you accept that you have been de-humanized and objectified, then you will get an inkling of what you are up against.

Take care of you. He does not want your help and isn't going to let you help him. He does not trust you... because he cannot trust himself.

◆◆◆◆

He is telling you what he feels. It doesn't have to make sense, be logical, consider anyone else's needs or feelings, or defer to prior obligations.

No, he probably can't explain it to you; he probably doesn't understand it himself. It's not a matter of "getting it out of him." You've gotten all there is to get out of him!

And, unfortunately, nobody, not you, not a counselor, not a parent or trusted friend can give him, or you, the answer, something that will either make his compelling feelings go away, or make them make sense.

That's why we so often recommend individual counseling rather than marriage counseling. We all rushed to marriage counseling (or wished we could) as the way to find common ground, or, perhaps, to reach them, but they simply aren't in the mental or emotional place to benefit from what you can learn in marriage counseling.

As far as your life falling apart, we've all been there, too. And, no, it's NOT fair and there isn't anything you can do to stop it. You built that life with another person, and that other person is currently bowing out. The thing is, we always ran that risk; we just didn't know it!

Going forward, we will still run the risk of things beyond our control messing up our carefully constructed plans. That is the life lesson "we" all need to learn; to find a way to cope with all the uncertainty we'd fooled ourselves into thinking did not exist in Life.

And the odd thing is, once you've learned to do that, it actually feels better than the false security we used to enjoy. You're no longer dependent on life going according to plan in order to be happy; you can be happy anyway.

But it takes a while to get there, and a lot of work... and letting go of your previous assumptions. A good individual counselor can help you with that. You might want to consider that instead of marriage counseling for a while.

◆◆◆◆

I am seeing a counselor and she has been a great help. I am not overly optimistic about the marriage counseling, but our communication has been so bad lately that I wanted to at least say we tried it.

I actually liked the guy we saw today quite a bit. I am not optimistic for the outcome but appreciate another point of view.

I saw a glimmer of hope today but it was crushed later.

Thank you for your words. I know I will need to hear things over and over again to really get it through my skull.

My life is based so much on rationale behavior. Things have an answer and you can analyze them and think through them. It's just going to take more time to get there.

♦♦♦♦

One interesting part of our most recent conversations has revolved around our kids. I think the main reason he hasn't done anything is for the kids.

During the session today the counselor said something that I understand but I think my husband took the wrong way. He said that you shouldn't stay in a relationship just for the kids (which I completely agree with), but I think for the first time my husband somehow saw this as an out.

He has been so incredibly grumpy with them for well over a year and has no patience with them. He said today that he doesn't think being with them 100% of the time, being so grumpy, is good (which I agree with) and implied being not grumpy and seeing them less would be better.

While I can agree with some pieces of this, the piece I don't get is how he thinks he's going to be any better or happier moving out. Everything he is unhappy with in life has very little to do with me but the answer to his problems is ridding himself of me.

My husband is my son's every breath of life. I know he will make it through, but I'm so concerned with the scars that will occur. (I already have him in counseling for anxiety). Why can't you at least try?? This whole thing sucks.

♦♦♦♦

I know in the case of my ex he believed that being married to me was the source of his unhappiness. He felt that once he got out of the house and away from me he would be happy. I have no idea if that is true, but I believe he still has himself convinced that is the case. Now he can do whatever he wants.

They really look at us as the thing that is tying them to the life they don't want. So if they get rid of us, they can start the shiny new life.

This does suck and it sucks most for the kids involved. I have seen mine suffer, yet he thinks they are just faring so well and are so happy. His mind is on himself and justifying what he's done.

Your husband probably has no clue what he is thinking or what he really wants other than out. That's the frustrating part.

♦♦♦♦

Google and read Jed Diamond's article entitled, "Why Midlife Men Leave Perfectly Good Marriages." You will find a starting point there.

You were a constant in his life when he became unhappy. According to *The Law of Association*, he has paired you with unpleasant things long enough for him to perceive you as the cause. (Operant Conditioning at its most potent... whether you agree with Behaviorist theories or not.)

This craziness happens to women who were virtual saints in the marriage. That is why his behavior is NOT about you. It is also why you need to protect yourself from him.

When these men say, "It is me and not you," there is truth in that. They are not saying it as truth. They do believe it is you and are just trying to continue being, "Mr. Nice Guy." But the ironic thing is: They ARE telling the truth... all the while believing they are manipulating the situation again.

♦♦♦♦

I have heard that so many times on these and other midlife crisis boards. I thought I was the only one. My ex was always needing that "one more" thing. Another project, hobby, child, dog, car, something to fill the hole in his heart.

Dr. William Sears, in his attachment theory, very much adheres to a simple belief: a need met in childhood is a need met; a need not met is a need forever. And that's what I think most people in midlife crisis are trying to do: meet an unknown childhood need that will never be met.

We all have them, unconditional love and acceptance of our parents, because none of us are perfect people with perfect parents. But people in midlife crisis can't face their dark side, so they keep looking outside for that one more thing to make them whole.

I always characterized ex, even to him, as having a hole that could never be filled and it was tiring to me, not to mention expensive to keep trying.

♦♦♦♦

I think my husband (I guess he's now my soon-to-be-ex-husband) suffers from the same issue, and yet he has no clue. He is in complete denial that he has pain from a very unloving, absent, and often verbally abusive, father.

His mother taught him denial from a young age, and with that, combined with her smothering love and perfect affection, he was able to get through childhood feeling decent.

The only problem is he has now convinced himself that he's perfectly fine, that he bears no scars or unmet needs from childhood. But he doesn't connect that with the fact that he told me he felt "abandoned" when I would go to bed early. I work full-time and we have little kids, so I'm tired at night!

He has said so many times these last nine months that I didn't meet his needs and that he wants to be loved the way his mom loved him.

Maybe someone is up to that task, but I clearly have not fit the bill. I just wish he were more self-aware and/or more willing to learn more about himself and deal with some of that pain in his past.

I know, it's just easier to start over with a "shiny new life." Reality can be tougher than denial, for sure, and the light of day can hurt your eyes. But I'd rather live in truth and light than the darkness of denial.

♦♦♦♦

Yes, it does suck! And yes, my husband made very explicit lists of all the things that were wrong with me, the things "I" needed to work on, to be a whole, healthy person in our marriage.

So, he left, I did the work, am still doing it, and voila! Husband came back, said he'd done the work, hasn't done the work (now admits it's "too painful"), and he's a similar mess to what he was.

I am sorry we stopped marriage counseling after four months as husband bitched about the out-of-pocket cost and he frankly wasn't willing to do any of the work out of the therapist's office.

It is up and down, a long and winding, bumpy road. I am getting there, still filled with grief much of the time that husband is killing a 25-year marriage and a family with four amazing kids.

♦♦♦♦

I heard almost that same thing. I sometimes tell people that my ex left me for other woman, but he really left me for his mother. I am pretty sure neither of them is very good in bed.

I hope he finds that ONE THING that will make him happy. I hope all your husbands do too, but I promise, even if they find it, it will be fleeting.

And that thing about being abandoned, I heard that all the time. I do get tired, and I like to sleep. I tried to get my husband to understand that if he actually slept a little more he might be less depressed, Not to mention if he came to bed with me, we could have sex, which might make him tired and then he could sleep. But he wasn't interested.

◆◆◆◆

We used to have long conversations after leaving the few marriage counseling sessions we had. I probably learned more in the car in the parking lot than in front of the counselor because he used to clam up.

I asked him what he wanted once, and his answer was that he wanted to "just live an honest life." We didn't discuss it further because I lashed into him about how "honest" being a serial cheater was.

In hindsight, I believe what he meant was honest in the sense that his image of himself matched the image of him the other woman had, carefully constructed with the parts he didn't want her to know well hidden. He's a master at manipulation but I knew too much so he wanted to start over.

I also believe that quest for image control is behind his delaying the divorce. So long as I'm to blame for his not being able to commit to her, he can continue his free and easy partying lifestyle. Once he's free to settle down, he'll probably then say it's too late for kids (again, my fault!).

He's worked very hard to keep us separated. I'm sure she'd love to know his true feelings on having more kids (he didn't, and it was one of our biggest conflicts) as she's a very doting aunt. It's really not necessary. No way I'd ever tell and spoil her surprise.

◆◆◆◆

My ex was awful to our youngest daughter, angry and irritated, and eventually he began to turn on me and elder daughter. I now think he was feeling guilty but rather than face his feelings he was taking them out on those closest to him and easiest to blame.

Elder daughter did pick him up on his behavior and say how nasty he had been and he replied, "if I was that bad to you then it was better I left." This was one of the few things I have bothered to pick him up on as I was not going to have him putting the blame for his actions anywhere near the kids.

I told him to look to himself and not to try and blame the children. He moaned to eldest daughter that I'd tried to say he was blaming the children.

Saying this has just helped reinforce for me how bad his behavior was towards the end. I know I tried everything and would have supported him forever but now, with a bit more distance, I'm still sad he destroyed our family and our relationship, but glad not to have the man he became in my life anymore.

As to the original question, my ex doesn't believe he's looking for anything, it was all about our relationship and being away from me (even though he didn't dislike me, hate me, say he didn't love me anymore), will apparently make him happy. He never made sense and changed his story so often I became confused.

I wish you luck but sadly, in my opinion, they don't know what they're looking for, they just think it isn't us.

♦♦♦♦

A wayward spouse may offer explanations that spin their actions in a positive light or allow them to avoid having to offer more truthful explanations that may be messy, require too much self-revelation, or may make you mad which is a hassle to them.

So, yes, "Something is missing in my life. It's not you, you are great!" might translate to "I want to be free to run wild on match.com while my insurance still picks up Viagra!"

♦♦♦♦

I try not to listen anymore. It makes no sense to me, it hurts, and there's nothing we can do to change it. He tells me all different things. And I think it has to do with the mood he's in, how I make him feel at that moment, or what he's been talking about with the other woman.

In the beginning it was his entire fault, he didn't know why. He told me he probably felt like this (not IN love) for the last few years. It had nothing to do with the other woman. This is the answer I got when I asked him in a friendly way without crying, drama, etc.

Every time the other woman came up in a "conversation," he told me that she had all the qualities I lacked. And that's why he doesn't want to be with me anymore.

And when I start crying, or I confront him with something, he has a long list of things that are wrong with me.

Sure, he's right about a few of them. But no reason to leave me. And when he starts saying things like "I hate it that you don't like tuna as much as I do and other woman does," I know it's him and not me!

♦♦♦♦

It is ridiculously crazy how exactly similar all our stories are! My husband, too, left me really for his mother not the other woman.

Also had an absent, clueless, unempathetic, and selfish dad who left the family when my husband was the same age as our youngest. Do you see history repeating itself?

He had many unmet needs from both parents as a child, I thought he had worked through many of them; guess not.

Now I'm getting blamed for the pain when he felt rejected by me and the boys. What!? Ten years of serial cheating because you felt rejected? The boys weren't even born yet! Want to take any responsibility here? Nope, he does not.

♦♦♦♦

I try to tell myself over and over to not listen, but some days are just harder than others. Last night was especially bad. He told me that, outside of the kids, we have no connection. This after hearing that he doesn't remember being friends.

I told my sister-in-law and she said "I can't believe he can't remember you being friends. You always had a great friendship."

There are days I just can't take the pain. Today is one of them. Hope others are having a better day than me.

♦♦♦♦

Outside of the kids you have no connection because he cut you off. That is what you have to see. He is in denial and has turned away from what is to justify his running off.

Please walk away when he begins deluding himself like that, or at least learn to tell him that he's free to believe such fantasy, but you know better and walk away.

He's rewriting history to suit his current path. It is not truth but it is his reality right now because perception is reality. Reality is not always truth.

♦♦♦♦

Funny, a few years ago we went for marriage counseling and the therapist said that she rarely saw a couple of our generation who were friends to the same level we were. We also had friends who, when they heard we had split, told me they figured we'd be the last ones to part ways.

My therapist told me to think of my marriage as a house. That the foundation was solid, that the whole house was intact, but I needed a bathroom to be renovated. She figured he'd be back in a few months. After all, who throws 25 years of hard work away?

But to hear him tell it, I'm a plague and I deserve to go to hell. Guess I won the lottery, huh?

♦♦♦♦

It's all Kool-Aid, don't drink it. My ex honestly told me that our brother-in-law told him that it is so great that he dumped me since he is now back to being "himself."

Well I know he did not say that, I am not sure what he said that sounded like that to ex... BUT even if he did say that it could not even be possible since we were a couple long before brother-in-law ever came into the picture.

Their minds are so addled, they won't even remember what they said when they finally "wake up." Do not drink the Kool-Aid!!

♦♦♦♦

Just to chime in here... they will tell you one thing and the other woman another. He says to me, he doesn't know what is missing in his life. He says to her, it is she that is missing in his life.

A person in midlife crisis will say whatever they can to protect themselves.

All you can do is stop asking and don't listen. I asked and listened until the cows came home. In the end, all I got was cowshite.

◆◆◆◆

I know what you mean about rewriting our histories. My husband started off saying that the last year of our marriage was bad and he was unhappy, then the last two, then the last five, then the last ten.

When he finally reaches the whole 20 years of our marriage as being bad, I'm going to jump up and shout BINGO!

◆◆◆◆

When I was new to this and trying to find the answer, ex replied that he already told me, that we have exhausted the topic, that I do not listen, and he will not repeat it. He told me yesterday, we already had this conversation.

I started walking around with a piece of paper and told him to tell me once more, I will write it down, and I will not bother him again, I will read the paper since I forget. He refused because he said I already know, he told me. That was two years ago.

The guy proved to be one big loser in everyone's eyes. I do vent to him on occasion, and ask him if he found what he was looking for. Because everyone else thinks he is an idiot.

◆◆◆◆

He can't allow himself to remember being friends, because it doesn't "fit" with the picture HE needs to paint for himself.

That's why it's so pointless to try to question or reason with these guys. They not only are not open to your point of view, they are actively defending themselves against it.

Even if something you say does penetrate their defenses and get them thinking/doubting, it will likely result in him reinforcing his position, not changing it!

About the best answer you can expect to "What do you want?" is "NOT THIS!"

And don't ask "why." That's just handing them an opportunity to tear you down or tear you apart, if they even bother to answer.

♦ ♦ ♦ ♦

I kept trying to talk to my soon-to-be-ex about why and what he was doing to us and our family. What I got was "I have to be true to myself." "I finally feel comfortable in my own skin." "I have never been more sane or real in my entire life."

Says the grandfather of five as he rides off into the sunset on his new Harley with one of his women. What he wants isn't us.

♦ ♦ ♦ ♦

I know that my husband believes that he HAS to do this. He's come too far now (almost three years) to say sorry, I made a mistake. That's how he thinks.

I sat thinking yesterday about the idiocy of my situation. He lives less than a mile away, in a four bedroom home, alone, and makes no effort to work on US or work on his poor relationship with his children.

That's when another light bulb moment hit: if he wanted us, all of us, he would be here!

♦ ♦ ♦ ♦

They don't even know what they are looking for. They use us to JUSTIFY their behavior even though they and their whores have to know it AIN'T working.

After over 40+ years of him calling me "the best thing that ever happened to him," I look at him like the alien he is.

The fact that he has married a whore who has never slept with an unmarried man in her life says it all.

He left a paid off home, retirement in the near future, pretty much not owing anything. After we split everything neither of us will have a comfortable retirement. Mine will be better with the house paid for. She put him in debt for the house they bought.

I remember saying, "Trying to talk to him is like throwing dirt at Plexiglas; you can literally see it just slide off." They are the "out-to-lunch bunch." Don't drink the Kool-Aid!!

♦♦♦♦

Mine did the whole "I've been unhappy with you for the last year... really it's been more like the last two... actually, it's been more like the last five..." etc., etc.

Meanwhile, I have cards, notes, emails; all saying how much he loves me, and remember so many times he said he was happy to be with me.

♦♦♦♦

My ex and I used to have the exact same conversation over and over again, too. I know now it's because he had no idea what was really going on in his head and the subject he kept wanting to discuss was the one thing he had memorized, so he could discuss it.

No wonder it never went anywhere, I think my ex's midlife crisis turned his brains to cottage cheese.

And yes, he did tell me, in his own disjointed way, what he (thought) he wanted. Some were realistic goals, some were so far out there I had a hard time keeping a straight face.

Fast forward five years and 99% of them never came to pass. It's just too bad that so many people in midlife crisis completely rearrange their lives for NOTHING and end up destroying something very concrete (a wonderful family, a good career, etc., etc.) for a mirage.

◆◆◆◆

Am I now the other woman?

My husband left almost three months ago and moved in with the other woman. He continues to e-mail and text me, although it was less frequent since I asked repeatedly to be no contact except for business/finance issues.

When we meet, I am friendly and welcoming but I have been very straightforward that I will not seriously discuss reconciliation until he moves out of her home.

He has been repeatedly bringing up the subject of reconciliation for over a month now. He tells me that he has found a place to live (with friends that I know) and will be moving there the middle of this month.

The past few weeks, his "friendly" e-mails and texts have increased. He even texted me last week that he has been thinking about me and, "I just wanted to tell you I love you."

He also has been commenting or liking my Facebook posts just about every day. She took down her Facebook page, so she isn't seeing this.

I believe that he truly does not know what he wants right now, and I am trying to face the fact that none of this indicates in any way that he will actually follow through on his promises.

But there is something that is bothering me. I think that I am picking up on a pattern that he is texting and e-mailing me when she is not around.

He has even started scheduling our periodic meetings to discuss finances as we go through mediation, at a time when he could be telling her that he is working. Since his affair is secret, she won't contact him at work any way but by text.

I have serious doubts that she has any idea that he is intending to leave, or considering leaving, or even has any idea that he is keeping in touch with me so much.

Am I now in the role of the other woman? Is he getting his kicks via the thrill of the taboo contact? If so, is there some further boundary that I need to set to remove myself from this role?

We are finalizing our mediation agreement and I hope to have it in place by month's end, so I am being fairly friendly back, but I do not (usually) respond to the frivolous texts.

My intention is to truly go no contact once the mediation agreement is signed, because we don't have kids and once we iron out the finances, there will be very infrequent need to discuss anything.

I don't like this feeling that he is beginning to give me that he is now having an emotional affair with ME. No matter how much of a skank this bitch is for what she did, no one deserves to be abandoned without at least the common courtesy of an honest conversation.

I think that he is planning to repeat his behavior and "sneak" out of her home the way he "snuck" out of ours without even telling me he was leaving.

Have any of you experienced this type of behavior and if so, how did you handle it? Should I just ride it out until I get the mediation agreement I want, or should I try to put an end to it now, and risk making him angry or resentful?

♦♦♦♦

Are you sure he isn't playing you to get favorable mediation?

♦♦♦♦

I was never aware of a "significant other" in ex's life, but I have noticed that most of his calls and emails come when he is out of town (which is most of the time, to be honest).

Maybe he is just lonely away from his new friends/life, or maybe he is hiding his contact with me from them (or whatever "her" there might be).

I do know that, while we were separated, people questioned him about how much contact he had with me, and it worried him. I have no way of knowing what's going on now.

Frankly, I don't worry about it too much. His behavior is on him, not me. I'm not responsible for figuring out what his situation is, and then making sure he is behaving appropriately, whether I am in the role of wife, or friend, or "other."

I'm not pursuing him or seducing him; I am just allowing the platonic/affectionate conversation that we'd always shared. If he has given someone in his life a different impression of things, again, that's on HIM and between THEM. I've been in his life for more than 30 years, after all.

I wouldn't be surprised if any wandering spouse, including mine, needed and relied on triangulation to keep up the drama, or to protect themselves from too much intimacy in any one relationship. I won't knowingly feed into that, but I'm also not going to tiptoe around it or try to compensate for that.

So I'd think about how you're interacting with him, and why, and whether it violates any of your own values or hurts you in any way. Then make whatever changes you feel necessary to maintain your values and protect yourself. Then let the rest of it go; let him shoulder the responsibility for his actions.

♦♦♦♦

No, you're not the other woman. You're still THE WIFE, and if he decides to tell you he loves you that's between the two of you.

Take it however you want it: the sign of a confused wandering spouse, a butter-you-up tactic going into mediation, or perhaps a glimpse of the old pre-midlife crisis husband.

As for him telling you he wants to move out of the other woman's place, and that relationship is fizzling, wait and see. You're only getting one side of the story. It may be he's transferred the role of other woman to you to keep up that adrenaline rush.

Take care of you.

♦♦♦♦

I admit that I don't always have the self-discipline to not reply to him, but I try very hard not to reply to anything that is just frivolous. That delicate balance between being detached and being cold is so hard to maintain.

I think I will spend the next few weeks paying close attention to how we BOTH communicate with each other, and hold off making any changes that might make him less cooperative in the mediation until after the agreement is signed.

I really want to go no contact totally after the agreement to protect my own sanity. I still have anxiety attacks every time I am going to see him, or if I expect to hear from him and he doesn't contact me right away.

I need to go no contact to remove myself from his craziness so that he can't drag me down with him.

♦♦♦♦

What would worry me is his pattern of not discussing things, keeping secrets, bailing out when he is unhappy, and seeking happiness through relationships with others.

He has some "me" work to do in my opinion.

♦♦♦♦

The other woman? Not quite, but he's being an ass.

Really, it's about how YOU feel about this situation. For myself, I'm very careful these days to try to respect the boundaries with my ex-husband and his new fiancée. Simply because it's the kind of respect I expect so I extend it. "Do unto others as you'd have done unto you."

Others might say, "Well, she is a skank," etc., but that doesn't mean WE lower OUR standards of behavior!

Your husband left you, now he's being "nice." The time for being nice isn't now when he's living with another woman and planning divorce. Polite is sufficient for that.

Don't drink his frigging Kool-Aid. It really boosts their ego to have their "new" woman and their "old" woman hanging on their every word and move. Don't be sucked into his "Fan Club."

♦♦♦♦

He could be just buttering you up to try and "win" the mediation, or, yes, he could be trying to prolong his emotional connection with you.

There can be (and is discussed in the literature) a sort of role reversal where the wife becomes the "dangerous other woman," and the other woman gets cast in the betrayed wife's role. Says a lot for his view of how to treat a "wife."

Just do not let this affect the set of your "business hat." In and of itself this should give strong indicators of just how inconsistent and sneaky he is still being.

♦♦♦♦

I kind of went through the same thing. He was out of the house, openly in a relationship with her, and still calling, texting, and coming to the house. She'd call me, bitching. He started to leave his cellphone in the truck because she'd be blowing it up.

I don't know, the way I saw it then, and see it now, is that I wanted him in my life. If he wanted to be in my life he had to show me that through actions, not just words. She had no concern for me or my feelings, so I had no concern for hers. He's a big boy, and he's make his choices.

The difference in this is that he never lived with her (she's a bum with no house and many burnt bridges… so that wasn't even a concern).

I doubt I could have interacted with him as I did if he was actually living with another woman.

To be honest, I don't really know what I'd do in your situation. Probably just continue to do my own thing, limiting contact until such a time as he changed his living arrangements. I'd be brutally honest with him on this point.

◆◆◆◆

I totally relate to your current situation. I am in exactly the same position. At the moment, he texts me every day but only day time when she is not about.

He talks about leaving and has looked at some property on the internet but, to date, no positive action.

I think the only way forward for me is to go no contact and set a date when he needs to do something positive!!!

I wish you well and hope we both get what we need in the end. I'm sorry I have no words of advice. I can only empathize with your current situation. I keep telling myself things will and can only get better.

◆◆◆◆

This is exactly what happened to me about a year ago! Nothing came of it, although I did think at the time we might be reconciling, and started having intercourse with him again.

Thanks to the women here, I came to my senses, worked out what I wanted (divorce, stop the emotional abuse I had been a victim of for years, start a new life journey without him because I know I deserve better) and gave him my bottom line: give up the other woman, start counseling, or stop communicating with me.

He didn't give up the other woman, but moved in instead. He has only just stopped contacting me.

♦♦♦♦

Why is he so angry and resentful when he's the one who cheated?

My husband and I get on the phone and our conversations are strained. But we are talking. I get a sense that he is resentful. I feel like I messed up his perfect plan of messing around until it was time to come home.

I do believe that was his plan but I could be kidding myself. I have a tendency to second guess myself a lot lately. Anyone else feel this way too?

When I go against my instincts I most always get burned. My instincts are telling me that he is resentful.

♦♦♦♦

I got that vibe from my wayward husband at first, but I think now he sees that he was being totally childish, and my reactions were appropriate. Comments like, "I screwed up so I guess I'm gonna pay for it the rest of my life!" come to mind.

We have a different relationship now than before I discovered his affair. I used to have him on a pedestal. I thought he was perfect. Now I am learning to love a flawed man.

I may forgive but I'll never forget. That may seem like it's a lifetime of punishment to some but I will carry the scars for the rest of my life, too. Even if we split up.

♦♦♦♦

You did mess up his plan. He didn't come out and confess to you. You caught him, and damn, that pisses him off. Everything would have been fine if you just hadn't found out, don't you know that?

I know a serial cheater. One of his justifications for cheating is that his wife caught him cheating, and didn't divorce him, so he has no respect for her anymore and thus it's ok to cheat on someone he doesn't respect. How's that for some self-centered, circular logic?

Don't ever ignore your gut. It may get the details wrong, but it almost always gets the main gist of the situation right.

♦♦♦♦

Hell, yes, he IS resentful. He wants his way and he wants you to condone it. Your instincts are correct.

Stop second guessing yourself and make a plan of action to protect yourself financially and emotionally.

♦♦♦♦

He says he just started dating the other woman.

I read my soon-to-be-ex's pre-trial memorandum in detail the other day, and one sentence that appalled me more than anything (besides the fact that he wants me to take on the mortgage completely even though I've been a stay at home mom for 17 years), is "Respondent admits dating paramour **** but denies ever having an affair during marriage."

What a joke! The memo further challenges me to prove it. That's really easy because I have receipts when he went to restaurants near her house, and even buying a book about how to divorce that he put on his corporate credit card. Of course, he'll deny those charges were for her.

♦♦♦♦

Can you get copies of phone records? They seem to tell a story all by themselves.

♦♦♦♦

Phone records tell a major story. And have the computer checked, if it matters in the settlement. Experts can find all the deleted stuff too.

So common to for them to try to minimize.

♦♦♦♦

It hurts to hear and read their feeble attempts to remain "the good guy," and you may be tempted to throw it in his face. Don't. Hold it until you need it. Gather all the info you can and share it with your lawyer. It's a huge bargaining chip.

Depending upon where you live, if he's been dissipating marital assets to wine and dine this chick, you're probably entitled to half of it back. Keep digging, and hang in there.

♦♦♦♦

If you have proof the relationship started/existed before he left, and if it matters in your state, she can be subpoenaed to court. I settled in mediation but that was an option my lawyer brought up if he was not willing to negotiate fairly. My attorney said the other woman usually does not want this to happen and gives the left behind spouse leverage.

◆◆◆◆

I live in a fault state. Actually, the private investigator proof I had was immediately after he left, but that did not matter. He was still married to me and there was no agreement for us to see other people. I know each state is different. Good luck.

◆◆◆◆

I live in a no-fault state but great suggestions about playing my cards right in the end to subpoena the other woman or getting phone records.

He actually slept with his phone and keys once so I wouldn't know that he was sleeping with her (that was right after he left).

Today, I saw that in one year alone, he took out almost $22,000 from paychecks. Where did that money go?

◆◆◆◆

I'm filing for divorce.

Made an appointment with a lawyer for next week. I still feel like I am on an emotional roller coaster, I really want to get off this ride.

I am so thankful that I have a wonderful family and friends for support. I have to keep telling myself there are better days ahead.

♦♦♦♦

In your toughest moments think to yourself, "High road, high road," and work to make decisions from your head.

Please get to a therapist to deal with the emotional issues and work with your attorney to deal with practicalities. We have all faced this fire. You are not alone

♦♦♦♦

There "are" better days. There'll be more crappy ones, too, but the longer you distance yourself from his insanity, the more likely the better days will outnumber the crappy ones.

♦♦♦♦

Yes, welcome to the roller coaster ride. Come on in, sit down, and hold on tight. When you can, take your hands off of the handle bar, and enjoy the feeling of the wind in your hair. When you need to hang on, hang on tight, but relax. It's going to be a while before you are stepping off. Don't fight it.

♦♦♦♦

Several months ago I answered my husband's cell phone. A former co-worker was on the line and she called me "babes." I asked him if that was her new name for him and he grabbed the phone. I left the room.

He came into the bedroom where I was and told me that he had feelings for her. I wanted to know how long and he said three months. That they had just started talking and the relationship wasn't physical.

I believed him until an imp told me to check his cell phone. There I got the shock of my life when I saw texts back and forth from them.

She was saying that she could not wait for his divorce so that they could get married. Him saying that she needed to be patient because he had to work out things between me and our son, but make no mistake he was 100% committed to their relationship! I could not believe it!

I later found out that the relationship was over a year old, and that he had taken her on two overseas trips with him as well as bought jewelry, furniture and appliances.

Paid credit card bills, hospital and doctor bills, as well as supplementing the food and household expenses.

I also found boxes of condoms and sexual enhancers hidden in another room so I knew then that it was also a physical relationship.

Since this, he has moved downstairs. He has still been paying the household bills, etc., but hasn't given up the other woman.

Last weekend he told me that he is planning to move out soon, and wants to discuss how we split our assets.

He has spoken to his lawyer, and he wants to be fair, and after all is said and done, be my friend. I can't wait for him to leave!

My son and I have begun counseling. After 30 years together and married almost 23 this is really the end of an era.

What I have learned from this is that sometimes you have to let them go. Concentrate on you and trust in God to get you through the rough times.

It may be a shock to you, but these men have been plotting and planning their escape for months. When the opportunity arises for them to bail they are ready to go.

Make no mistake, your husband didn't just up and decide to leave. He planned this for a while.

♦♦♦♦

Is he threatened by me being nice to him?

I have been nicer to my husband lately, meaning I've been able to actually look at him and talk to him. The roof leaked and he came over to the house and chopped a lot of ice off the roof last night.

I was making sandwiches, made him one, and invited him to sit and eat with us, as I really appreciated him taking care of it. It was strange. I actually felt comfortable with him there (maybe because now it's MY turf at the house?) and enjoyed him there with our son and me.

I noticed that when I went to dinner at the in-laws the other day and he was sitting across from me, he would talk with me, but didn't look AT me. Same thing last night.

Think maybe he's avoiding eye contact because of guilt? Could he be scared from my niceness to him?

I'm not looking for anything from this, but with all the anger, tension, betrayal, etc., it's strange to suddenly look at him and not feel that. Yes, those come and go, but this has been within the past few days.

He invited me to go on a trip with our daughter, but I declined as I knew he had serious stuff to discuss with her. I'd really love to invite him to go biking, just the two of us, but is that passing a line right now?

As far as I know the married other woman is still in the picture, so I wouldn't consider any "dating" or anything like that as long as there's a third person in this marriage.

I'd love to talk with him about doing stuff like that again but I don't know right now if that's a good idea. I kind of feel like I'm starting to cave.

♦♦♦♦

I think they're confused by their own reactions to things, especially when we aren't behaving as they expect.

I know that when we'd have a really "good" visit together, more often than not, my ex would distance immediately afterwards.

He didn't WANT to feel "good" about me or us, it just muddied his waters. How was he supposed to convince himself, let alone anyone else, that he "needed" to be free of "us," when it was so good?

That's frequently when the left behind spouse gets the "no false hope" speech, too. It's still not about US.

◆◆◆◆

I don't think it is "threatened" so much as it is a statement of distance.

◆◆◆◆

Their anger is a self-preservation/self-defense mechanism that protects them from having "positive feelings" toward or about us. They are, in my opinion, scared to death of getting "sucked back in" again!!

◆◆◆◆

You're right! I guess the same way that we have our "self-preservation" defenses. Although ours are justified and necessary to prevent further hurt and destruction from them. I never actually thought about them needing to do that.

Ours is for good, theirs is for evil (themselves). So, killing them with kindness is like kryptonite, huh?

◆◆◆◆

Do you really want to be part of their drama?

Let him pay a therapist if he needs one. All that will come out of you listening to him is that YOU lose even more respect for him and he feels like you're ok with his cheating.

◆◆◆◆

Sorry, what I wrote was confusing. He had invited me to go with him and our daughter when they went biking the other day. I didn't go, as he needed to talk with her one on one.

And he did, admitted to her that he's just realized through counseling that he's disrespectful, especially to me, and actually told her that it's his entire fault, which is also what he told his mom and me.

What I had meant to ask opinions on was whether or not it was a good idea if I asked him over to dinner while my son was still home, or even to go biking together.

◆◆◆◆

I would personally never consider inviting my husband to anything if I knew he was involved with another woman. I find the idea of competing with another woman for his attention to be not healthy for me. I would not be his friend.

◆◆◆◆

If there is a little voice somewhere inside you suggesting that you need to do these things to "stay connected" or to "remind him what a wonderful family you have/wonderful woman you are" I would urge you not to give in to that voice.

Seriously, I'd really encourage you to ask yourself how on earth this might be a "good idea"? The answer might be most revealing and illuminating for you.

◆◆◆◆

I think I was having a weak moment. Thanks for the head slaps, friends. Much needed.

◆◆◆◆

I totally agree that this is unhealthy for me, too. I have tried to do family things with my husband and it backfires on my emotional health.

He lives full time with his girlfriend in another state and he drops in occasionally for birthdays, etc. He acts as if nothing has changed.

It can almost be hard to remember that he will be going right back to her. It's hard to realize that we mean very little to him other than being a trophy family. My husband would balance between both of us if he could, getting his needs met while giving nothing back. It's sad but true.

I have been fooled, willingly, over and over again. Being nice and being his friend has led to only pain for me. I need to detach myself over and over again and it gets harder if I let myself hope.

◆◆◆◆

I recently found out that my being nice to my husband makes him feel guilty, and because he's done such a bad thing (and these are his words, not mine), he doesn't deserve my caring or my compassion.

He also cannot look at me. Doesn't when he is talking to me, or when I am talking to him. He chooses to text or email me over telephone calls, and, in fact, once texted me while we were in the same room about four feet from each other!! He did it under the pretense of a joke, but I don't know.

In any case I am not being nice to him to make him feel bad about what he did, though that is an added bonus that is his cross to bear.

I am being nice to him because that is the kind of person that I am. I will not allow my morals and values, and the very essence of who I am as a person, be compromised because of him.

I do not like to see people I care about being hurt. It doesn't make me happy to know that he did all of this in the name of greater happiness for himself only to end up more miserable than he claimed to be before.

I don't enjoy knowing that he is now where I was in the summer when this was all new, not eating, not sleeping, crying all the time. I wouldn't wish that on anyone, let alone someone I love.

For me, the bottom line is this: do what you would do if it were anyone else. If you would be nice to them, then be nice. If you wouldn't, then don't. Just don't change who you are because of what he has done.

◆◆◆◆

My wandering spouse and I agreed to spend the holidays together for the kids and that's what we did. And on the days that he is nice and actually looks at me, he becomes tearful. And then I know that I will pay later. He will become distant and/or mean and hateful. So, I no longer invite him to do things with us.

I've let down my defenses too many times to be hit between the eyes again. When I used to track married other woman's comings and goings, his behaviors directly correlated with when she was in town or out of town. If she was out of town, he was sweet as pie. If she was in town, he was monster deluxe.

◆◆◆◆

Of course he can't look at you; you are the one he cheated on. I am amazed you both go to a relative's house and eat across the table from each other. I find it amazing the relative would have the nerve to invite you both with what you are dealing with.

Glad he is coming over and fixing things for you.

Only thing I want to add is this, I think complete no contact with him would be best so he misses you. You are sending a message that you are fine with him doing this. Is that the message you want to send?

I think letting him wonder is best, and not seeing you, it will make him think about coming back more.

◆◆◆◆

My in-laws had invited me to dinner with my daughter before she went back to college. It wasn't uncomfortable at all. It was like a "pre-midlife crisis" Sunday dinner, actually.

I am lucky to have a very good relationship with the in-laws and I always banter back and forth in fun. We all play games on the Wii, etc. I had a good time there.

If anything was said about me after I left, it would have been my father-in-law asking my husband, "What the hell's the matter with you?" as I hear he does all the time.

◆◆◆◆

Would he have cheated if he wasn't in the military?

I found out my husband cheated when he was deployed. Did he cheat because he was in the military and away from home? Did being in combat turn him into a cheater or would he have cheated anyway?

◆◆◆◆

Military marriages have much more stress and strain than the plain old average marriage. I'm sure you have heard that. Deployments are hell on a family.

Certain jobs have a "culture" of infidelity. Sorry to say, the military is one. Especially when deployed to high risk areas. It is only the strongest who can resist this.

My son explained to me the pressures they face beyond the obvious. Compartmentalization is rampant. It is how most are able to cope.

In high stress areas you have many times of extreme adrenaline followed by long periods of boredom. That in itself is pressure that results in people looking for relief.

Many become addicted to online games. Some turn to other things. You have a situation where a lot of people are with loose ends and away from the stabilizing comfort of being with their families for long extended periods.

When you really think of all they are dealing with and going through, you have to totally recognize how strong and positive those who do remain faithful are. It's not surprising so many fail.

They have counselors on base that can help you. If he's put in his 20, leaving service may be the only option to making a reconciliation work. If he hasn't, the counseling will help you in dealing with the odds of his backsliding when faced with those former coping methods.

♦♦♦♦

I agree that deployments are hell on a family and that only the strongest can resist temptation. Totally true. However, there is a double standard that exists.

While these men are deployed, the women back home are expected to keep the home fires burning and remain faithful loving spouses (which I did).

So when a man cheats due to his deployment, hey... it can be understood why that could happen. If the woman back home cheats... what a total bitch! How could she! So there you go, the ole double standard!

If only people could understand that cheating is cheating no matter who does it, and no matter the reason or circumstances.

I remained faithful because that is who I am. He cheated because he has a character flaw. That's how I see it. I'm also a U.S. Army veteran. I've seen it all!

♦♦♦♦

When will I stop hurting so much?

When will I have a day when I don't hurt so bad I feel like I'm dying? The "I'm doing okay" never lasts more than a few hours.

It's only been three and a half months but if sorrow could kill, I'd have died a thousand deaths already.

♦♦♦♦

About a month for every year of marriage was what I read and my timetable was amazingly close to that.

Thirty-three years of marriage and about three years of serious healing for me.

That fourth year things picked up at warp speed but that first year was pure, ungodly living torturous hell.

The thing that gave me the most closure was finally getting all the tiny details of the property settlement made a done deal, and all money changed hands that needed to change hands.

The longer they are away from you the more they turn into a hideous and cruel Scrooge. Get the most advantageous property settlement you can get and get it IMMEDIATELY, even before the divorce, if possible.

♦♦♦♦

I don't think there is a formula that applies to everybody. Each of us, and each of our situations, are unique. Some people are more resilient, while some have deeper scars from other life situations that cause them to take longer to recover.

Some of us have other things happen while we're trying to recover from this, and it just piles on. Some people weren't as attached, or codependent, or entangled, or "in love with" their spouses (or their marriages, at least) as others. Some wayward spouses are just easier to get over!

So, it takes as long as it takes. All you can do is keep striving, keep taking care of yourself, protecting yourself, avoiding things that hurt you, or set you back.

Work on finding meaningful things to fill the gap in your life, and your heart, that he has created, and focus on the good things that remain, despite what he's done.

The best advice I got was "put away the watch and even the calendar." Stop focusing on "how long" and instead focus on NOW. Eventually you'll be able to look back and see just how many "now's" you've lived through, and healed during.

◆◆◆◆

It all comes on its on timeline. One day you will notice that your entire day was not consumed with thoughts of the status of your relationship.

One day you will remember you laughed a little more. One day you will notice the pain recedes a little easier.

Don't rush it, because each one of those moments that you break down teaches you something about yourself, and what you are going through. You may even cycle through a few times before it sticks.

This is normal; you are not alone in this. I know it seems like it is not possible, but it is.

When I first got here, some wise people told me it takes T-I-M-E. That is the only answer, give yourself time.

◆◆◆◆

Those early days/weeks/months are the absolute worst. I think I was more in shock than anything. And I think I was in some ways in denial, thinking that my ex would "come to his senses," and "wake up," from the outrageous acting out he was doing.

My timetable seems to be much longer, because after I caught him cheating, we had a false reconciliation which lasted for six months, until he went on eHarmony and met his "new and improved" girlfriend.

After two months he was completely enmeshed with her and wanted me out for good.

It took me a year to find a place and move out. That added a whole other dimension to my grieving, not only leaving him for good, but leaving my home of ten years.

I have ok days, some good days, and still many difficult or bad days. It's been almost two years since the bomb drop, and I still don't feel anywhere near healed, but definitely not as horrible as it was in the beginning stages of all this mess.

◆◆◆◆

Is your marriage imploding at midlife?
Visit The Midlife Club: MidlifeClub.com

About the Author

PAT GAUDETTE is an author, publisher, and website developer. Her books include:

How to Survive Your Husband's Midlife Crisis: Strategies and Stories From the Midlife Wives Club

Journaling through His Midlife Crisis: Redefining Your Life As He Reinvents His

Have I Finally Found Out How To Just "Be"? One Man's Journey From Marital Crisis To Self-Discovery

Madonna/Whore Complex: Love without Sex; Sex without Love

Teen Mom: A Journal

Advice for an Imperfect Single World

Advice for an Imperfect Married World

Midnight Confessions: True Stories of Adultery

How to Be a Self-Published Author: A Step-by-Step Guide

Sparky the AIBO: Robot Dogs & Other Robotic Pets

UGLY DOLLS the Naber Kids Story

She is the founder/webmaster of popular relationship-oriented websites *The Midlife Club,* (MidlifeClub.com), and *Friends and Lovers,* (FriendsandLovers.com). She and her husband live in Florida.

Email her at: pat@patg.com

Visit her website: patg.com

Search for her books and ebooks on Amazon.com, BarnesandNoble.com, and elsewhere.

How to Survive Your Husband's Midlife Crisis: Strategies and Stories from The Midlife Wives Club

Authors: Pat Gaudette & Gay Courter
Home & Leisure Publishing, Inc.
ISBN 978-0-9825617-5-1
Available in Paperback, Kindle
& eBook Versions

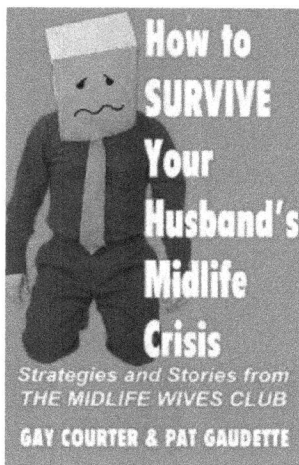

You've heard all the jokes about men's midlife crises – the new sports car, the new exercise regimen... and the new girlfriend. But when you're the wife trying to cope, it's no laughing matter.

A midlife crisis can devour a relationship. It may be devouring yours. The Midlife Wives Club is a supportive sisterhood for midlife mates – a chance to vent some steam, share advice, or just get a reminder that you're not alone. In this guide, you'll find wisdom from both midlife wives and experts on:

•Recognizing *the symptoms*
•Coping *with the threat (or reality) of infidelity*
•Identifying *underlying problems like depression and anger*
•Deciding *when to stick it out – and when to pack it in*
•Protecting *your kids from the fallout*
•Making it through the crisis... *and coming out stronger, saner, and more self-reliant*

With personal stories from real women (and men) and a comprehensive list of resources, **How to Survive Your Husband's Midlife Crisis** *can help you get past the rough spots – and turn this tumultuous time into a change for the better.*

Available in paperback as well as eBook and Kindle versions through Amazon.com and other retailers.

For immediate support for midlife issues visit www.MidlifeClub.com.

Teen Mom: A Journal

Edited by: Pat Gaudette
Home & Leisure Publishing, Inc.
ISBN 978-0976121084
Available in Paperback, Kindle
& eBook Versions

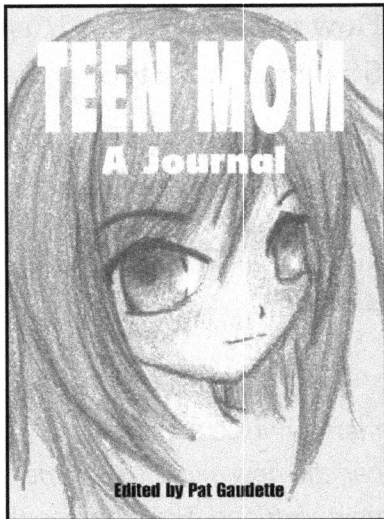

Sixteen-year-old "Katie" was half way through her junior year of high school when she became pregnant. Throughout her pregnancy and for several months afterward, she kept a journal. This is her story as told in that journal.

Katie is not one teenager dealing with unplanned pregnancy, she is one of many. She may be the girl next door or the girl in the next block. She may be your daughter. She may be you.

Teens are more openly sexually active than in past generations and unplanned pregnancy is not the social stigma of years ago. The pregnancy of pop idol Britney Spears' 16-year-old sister, actress Jamie Lynn Spears, was good fodder for the media but it didn't cause her to lose a starring role in Zoey 101, *a television show drawing a large viewership aged 9-14. When vice-presidential candidate Sarah Palin announced her 17-year-old daughter, Bristol, was five months pregnant, it gave teen pregnancy even more of a stamp of "normalcy."*

What is it like to be a pregnant teen? Let teen mom Katie tell you about it. She is one of more than half a million teens facing unplanned pregnancies each year according to data from The National Campaign to Prevent Teen and Unplanned Pregnancy.

Available in bookstores and online through Amazon.com and other retailers.

Midnight Confessions: True Stories of Adultery

Author: Pat Gaudette
Home & Leisure Publishing, Inc.
ISBN 978-0976121046
Available in Paperback, Kindle
& eBook Versions

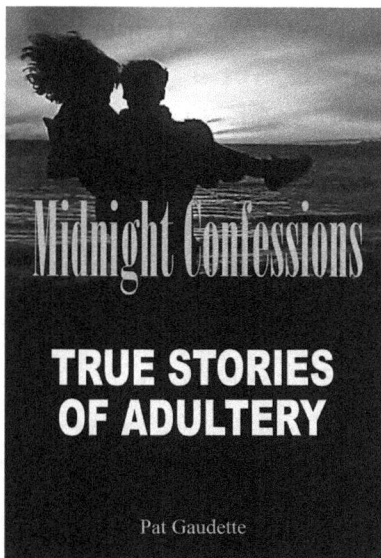

Why does a person cheat? What type of person cheats? What type of person loves a cheat? Can adultery be forgiven? Can a marriage survive the adultery of one or both partners? Can a cheater be trusted not to cheat again?

Love and lust are powerful forces but with enough time and tears each of us comes to a point of decision making when faced with betrayal.

If you are the betrayed spouse, do you confront? Do you leave? Do you get revenge by cheating? If you are the betrayer, do you lie or tell the truth? Do you keep the affair going or end it to save your marriage? If you are the other person, do you accept what you can get or do you force confrontation to "get it all"?

Midnight Confessions: True Stories of Adultery *examines adultery from the adulterer's point of view, as well as that of the betrayed spouse and the other person. These are their stories in their words. Perhaps after reading their stories and the thought-provoking discussions in this book you will have a better understanding of the decision you need to make to fit your situation.*

Available in bookstores and online through Amazon.com and other retailers.

Advice for an Imperfect Single World
ISBN 978-0976121008

Advice for an Imperfect Married World
ISBN 978-0976121022

Available in Paperback, Kindle & eBook Versions

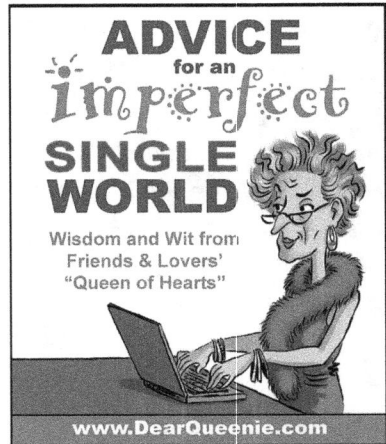

ADVICE for an *imperfect* SINGLE WORLD
Wisdom and Wit from Friends & Lovers' "Queen of Hearts"
www.DearQueenie.com

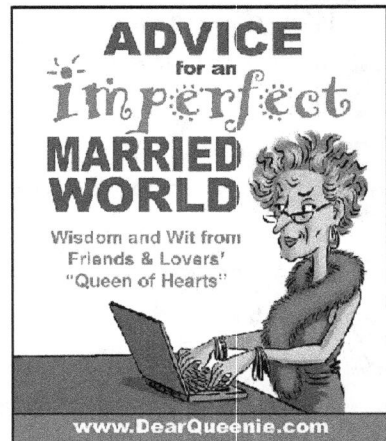

ADVICE for an *imperfect* MARRIED WORLD
Wisdom and Wit from Friends & Lovers' "Queen of Hearts"
www.DearQueenie.com

The outspoken "Queen of Hearts" is rarely without an opinion and since 1996 she has been sharing her thoughts about relationships in her advice column for the Friends and Lovers *Web site.* Advice for an Imperfect Married World *focuses on situations facing married couples and couples involved in long term relationships.* Advice for an Imperfect Single World, *focuses on dating issues.*

"Dear Queenie, me and my wife have split up and now we're trying to get back but she wants to be friends and take it slow. I'm afraid that we will just be friends and that's all. I want to know if we can be good friends and still be husband and wife and how can I show her that I want both?" - *Peter.*

"Peter, what you're really asking is how do you fast forward through all the friendship stuff and get right down to having sex again. While sex may be your top priority, developing a strong friendship is hers. If you are serious about wanting to repair your marriage you'll put your sex drive on hold and work on the friendship for now." - *Queenie*

www.ingramcontent.com/pod-product-compliance
Lightning Source LLC
Chambersburg PA
CBHW071947270326
41928CB00009B/1375